BSS5
SMARTBOOK

Fifth Edition

the
BATTLE STAFF

Leading, Planning & Conducting Military Operations

The Lightning Press
Norman M Wade

The Lightning Press

2227 Arrowhead Blvd.
Lakeland, FL 33813
24-hour Voicemail/Fax/Order: 1-800-997-8827
E-mail: SMARTbooks@TheLightningPress.com
www.TheLightningPress.com

Fifth Edition
(BSS5) The Battle Staff SMARTbook
Leading, Planning & Conducting Military Operations

This is the fifth revised edition of The Battle Staff SMARTbook, incorporating the full scope of new material from FM 6-0 (w/change 1), Commander and Staff Organization and Operations (May '15); ATP 2-01.3/MCRP 2-3A, Intelligence Preparation of the Battlefield/Battlespace (Nov '14); ADRP 1-02, Operational Terms and Military Symbols (Feb '15); FM 3-09, Field Artillery Operations and Fire Support (Apr '14); ATP 3-60, Targeting (May '15); and ATP 5-19 (w/change 1), Risk Management (Apr '14).

Printed and bound in the United States of America.

[BSS5]
Notes to Reader

Leading, Planning & Conducting Military Operations

Commanders, supported by their staffs, use the operations process to drive the conceptual and detailed planning necessary to understand, visualize, and describe their operational environment; make and articulate decisions; and direct, lead, and assess military operations. The Army's framework for exercising mission command is the operations process: planning, preparing, executing, and continuously assessing the operation.

Planning is the art and science of understanding a situation, envisioning a desired future, and laying out effective ways of bringing that future about. **Design** is a methodology for applying critical and creative thinking to understand, visualize, and describe complex, ill-structured problems and develop approaches to solve them. **Preparation** is activities that units perform to improve their ability to execute an operation. **Execution** puts a plan into action by applying combat power to accomplish the mission and using situational understanding to assess progress and make execution and adjustment decisions. **Assessment** is continuously monitoring and evaluating the current situation and the progress of an operation.

The Battle Staff SMARTbook covers the operations process (ADRP 5-0); commander's activities (Understand, Visualize, Describe, Direct, Lead, Assess); the military decisionmaking process and troop leading procedures (FM 6-0: MDMP & TLP); integrating processes and continuing activities (IPB, targeting, risk management); plans and orders (WARNOs/FRAGOs/OPORDs); mission command, command posts, liaison (ADRP 6-0); rehearsals & after action reviews; and operational terms and military symbols (ADRP 1-02).

This is the fifth revised edition of The Battle Staff SMARTbook, incorporating the full scope of new material from FM 6-0 (w/change 1), Commander and Staff Organization and Operations (May '15); ATP 2-01.3/MCRP 2-3A, Intelligence Preparation of the Battlefield/Battlespace (Nov '14); ADRP 1-02, Operational Terms and Military Symbols (Feb '15); FM 3-09, Field Artillery Operations and Fire Support (Apr '14); ATP 3-60, Targeting (May '15); and ATP 5-19 (w/change 1), Risk Management (Apr '14).

SMARTbooks - DIME is our DOMAIN!

SMARTbooks: Reference Essentials for the Instruments of National Power (D-I-M-E: Diplomatic, Informational, Military, Economic)! Recognized as a "whole of government" doctrinal reference standard by military, national security and government professionals around the world, SMARTbooks comprise a comprehensive professional library designed with all levels of Soldiers, Sailors, Airmen, Marines and Civilians in mind.

SMARTbooks can be used as quick reference guides during actual operations, as study guides at education and professional development courses, and as lesson plans and checklists in support of training. Visit **www.TheLightningPress.com**!

[BSS5]
References

The following references were used to compile The Battle Staff SMARTbook. All references are considered public domain, available to the general public, and designated as "approved for public release; distribution is unlimited." The Battle Staff SMARTbook does not contain classified or sensitive material restricted from public release.

Army Doctrinal Publications (ADPs) and Army Doctrinal Reference Publications (ADRPs)

ADRP 1-02	Feb 2015	Operational Terms and Military Symbols
ADP/ADRP 2-0	Aug 2012	Intelligence
ADP/ADRP 3-0	May 2012	Unified Land Operations
ADP/ADRP 3-09	Aug 2012	Fires
ADP/ADRP 3-90	Aug 2012	Offense and Defense
ADP/ADRP 5-0	May 2012	The Operations Process
ADP/ADRP 6-0	May 2012	Mission Command (w/change 1)

Army Techniques Publications (ATPs) and Army Tactics, Techniques and Procedures (ATTPs)

ATP 2-01.3/ MCRP 2-3A	Nov 2014	Intelligence Preparation of the Battlefield/*Battlespace* (w/change 1, Mar 2015, unlimited distribution)
ATP 3-60	May 2015	Targeting
ATP 5-19	Apr 2014	Risk Management (w/change 1)

Field Manuals (FMs)

FM 3-09	Apr 2014	Field Artillery Operations and Fire Support
FM 3-90-1	Mar 2013	Offense and Defense (Volume I)
FM 3-90-2	Mar 2013	Reconnaissance, Security, And Tactical Enabling Tasks (Volume 2)
FM 6-0	May 2015	Commander and Staff Organization and Operations (w/change 1)
FM 6-01.1	Jul 2012	Knowledge Management Operations

Joint Publications (JPs)

JP 3-0	Aug 2011	Joint Operations
JP 5-0	Aug 2011	Joint Operation Planning

(BSS5)
Table of Contents

Chap 1
The Operations Process

Military Decision Making (MDMP &TLP)

Chap 4

Plans & Orders

Chap 5

Mission Command

Chap 6 — Rehearsals & After Action Reviews (AARs)

Operational Terms, Acronyms & Graphics

I. Fundamentals of the Operations Process

Ref: ADP 5-0, The Operations Process (Mar '12) and ADRP 5-0, The Operations Process (Mar '12), chap. I.

The Army's framework for exercising mission command is the operations process—the major mission command activities performed during operations: planning, preparing, executing, and continuously assessing the operation (ADP 5-0). Commanders, supported by their staffs, use the operations process to drive the conceptual and detailed planning necessary to understand, visualize, and describe their operational environment; make and articulate decisions; and direct, lead, and assess military operations.

The Operations Process

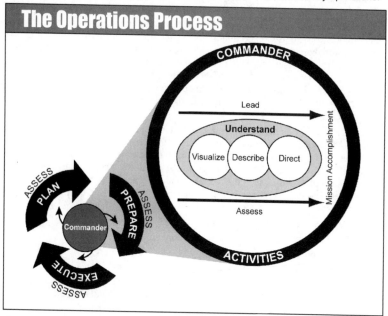

Ref: ADRP 5-0, The Operations Process, fig. 1-1, p. 1-2.

The activities of the operations process are not discrete; they overlap and recur as circumstances demand. Planning starts an iteration of the operations process. Upon completion of the initial order, planning continues as leaders revise the plan based on changing circumstances. Preparing begins during planning and continues through execution. Execution puts a plan into action by applying combat power to seize, retain, and exploit the initiative to gain a position of relative advantage. Assessing is continuous and influences the other three activities.

Both the commander and staff have important roles within the operations process. The commander's role is to drive the operations process through the activities of understanding, visualizing, describing, directing, leading, and assessing operations as depicted earlier. The staff's role is to assist commanders with understanding situations, making and implementing decisions, controlling operations, and assessing progress. In addition, the staff assists subordinate units (commanders and staffs), and keeps units and organizations outside the headquarters informed throughout the conduct of operations.

ADRP 5-0: Major Changes (from FM 5-0)

Ref: ADP 5-0, The Operations Process (Mar '12), introduction.

ADRP 5-0 is a new publication that expands on the principles of the operations process found in ADP 5-0. **Overall, the doctrine in ADRP 5-0 remains consistent with Field Manual (FM) 5-0, The Operations Process. The most significant change from FM 5-0 is the restructuring of doctrinal information.** The principles of the operations process are now found in ADP 5-0 and ADRP 5-0. A new field manual (currently under development) will address the specific tactics and procedures associated with planning, preparing, executing, and assessing operations. In the interim, ATTP 5-0.1, Commander and Staff Officers Guide, contains these details.

ADRP 5-0 updates doctrine on the operations process to include incorporating the Army's operational concept of unified land operations found in ADP 3-0 and the principles of mission command found in ADP 6-0. While the major activities of the operations process have not changed, the following is a summary of changes by chapter.

ADRP 5-0 provides a starting point for conducting the operations process. It establishes a common frame of reference and offers intellectual tools Army leaders use to plan, prepare for, execute, and assess operations. By establishing a common approach and language for exercising mission command, doctrine promotes mutual understanding and enhances effectiveness during operations. The doctrine in this publication is a guide for action rather than a set of fixed rules. In operations, effective leaders recognize when and where doctrine, training, or even their experience no longer fits the situation, and adapt accordingly.

Chapter 1 describes the nature of operations in which commanders, supported by their staffs, exercise mission command. Next, this chapter defines and describes the operations process. A discussion of the principles commanders and staffs consider for the effective execution of the operations process follows. The chapter concludes with discussions of the integrating processes, continuing activities, battle rhythm, and running estimates. The following are significant changes from FM 5-0 in chapter 1. The principles of the operations process now include—

- Commanders drive the operations process
- Build and maintain situational understanding
- Apply critical and creative thinking
- Encourage collaboration and dialogue

ADRP 5-0 adopts the joint definitions of operational approach, commander's intent, and risk management. ADRP 5-0 replaces the continuing activity of intelligence, surveillance, and reconnaissance with information collection.

Chapter 2 defines planning and plans and lists the values of effective planning. Next, this chapter describes integrated planning and operational art. The chapter next describes the Army's planning methodologies: Army design methodology, the military decisionmaking process, and troop leading procedures. This chapter then describes key components of a plan or order. This chapter concludes by offering guidelines for effective planning and describes planning pitfalls that commanders and staffs guard against. The following are significant changes from FM 5-0. ADRP 5-0—

- Retitles design to Army design methodology and modifies the definition
- Associates the Army design methodology with conceptual planning and operational art
- Modifies the definition of the military decisionmaking process
- Modifies step 7 of the military decisionmaking process from "orders production" to "orders production, dissemination, and transition"
- Reintroduces "key tasks" as a component of commander's intent
- Modifies guidelines to effective planning

Chapter 3 defines preparation and lists the preparation activities commonly performed within the headquarters and across the force to improve the unit's ability to execute operations. The chapter concludes by providing guidelines for effective preparation. The following are significant changes from FM 5-0. ADRP 5-0—

- Adds the preparation activity "initiate network preparations"
- Modifies the preparation activity "initiate reconnaissance and surveillance" to "initiate information collection"
- Modifies the guidelines to effective preparation

Chapter 4 provides guidelines for effective execution. It describes the role of the commander and staff in directing and controlling current operations. Next, this chapter describes decisionmaking in execution. The chapter concludes with a discussion of the rapid decisionmaking and synchronization process. ADRP 5-0 modifies guidelines to effective execution to seize the initiative through action and accept prudent risk to exploit opportunities.

Chapter 5 defines assessment as a continuous activity of the operations process and describes its purpose. Next, it describes an assessment process and offers guidelines commanders and staffs consider for effective assessment. This chapter concludes with a discussion of assessment working groups and assessment support from operations research and systems analysis.

The following are significant changes from FM 5-0. ADRP 5-0—

- Adopts the joint definition of assessment
- Modifies guidelines to effective assessment

FM 6-0, Commander and Staff Organization and Operations (May '14)
The following appendixes formally found in FM 5-0 are now found in FM 6-0:

- Command post organization and operations
- Military decisionmaking process
- Troop leading procedures
- Army operation plan and order format
- Task organization formats
- Running estimates
- Formal assessment plans
- Rehearsals
- Military briefings

ADP 5-0 and ADRP 5-0 (New & Modified Terms)
Introductory Table-1. New Army terms

Term	Remarks
Army design methodology	Replaces design.

Introductory Table-2. Modified Army terms

Term	Remarks
assessment	Adopts the joint definition.
design	Formal definition replaced by Army design methodology.
direct support	Modifies the definition.
general support-reinforcing	Modifies the definition.
military decisionmaking process	Modifies the definition.
operational approach	Adopts the joint definition.
planning	Modifies the definition modified.

I. Activities of the Operations Process

Ref: ADP 5-0, The Operations Process (Mar '12), pp. 2 to 6 (and fig. 1, p. iv).

The Army's framework for exercising mission command is the operations process—the major mission command activities performed during operations: planning, preparing, executing, and continuously assessing the operation. Commanders, supported by their staffs, use the operations process to drive the conceptual and detailed planning necessary to understand, visualize, and describe their operational environment; make and articulate decisions; and direct, lead, and assess military operations.

The Operations Process

The Army's framework for exercising mission command is the **operations process**—the major mission command activities performed during operations: planning, preparing, executing, and continuously assessing the operation.

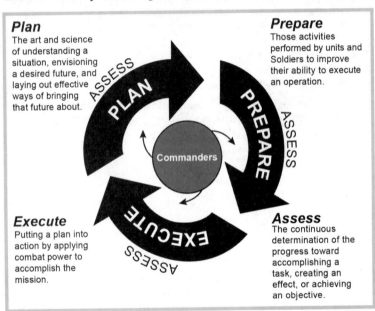

Plan
The art and science of understanding a situation, envisioning a desired future, and laying out effective ways of bringing that future about.

Prepare
Those activities performed by units and Soldiers to improve their ability to execute an operation.

Execute
Putting a plan into action by applying combat power to accomplish the mission.

Assess
The continuous determination of the progress toward accomplishing a task, creating an effect, or achieving an objective.

Central idea...
Commanders, supported by their staffs, use the **operations process** to drive the conceptual and detailed planning necessary to understand, visualize, and describe their operational environment; make and articulate decisions; and direct, lead, and assess military operations.

Principles

guided by...

- Commanders drive the operations process
- Apply critical and creative thinking
- Build and maintain situational understanding
- Encourage collaboration and dialogue

The activities of the operations process are not discrete; they overlap and recur as circumstances demand. Planning starts an iteration of the operations process. Upon completion of the initial order, planning continues as leaders revise the plan based on changing circumstances. Preparing begins during planning and continues through execution. Execution puts a plan into action by applying combat power to seize, retain, and exploit the initiative to gain a position of relative advantage. Assessing is continuous and influences the other three activities.

Commanders Drive the Operations Process

Commanders are the most important participants in the operations process. While staffs perform essential functions that amplify the effectiveness of operations, commanders drive the operations process through understanding, visualizing, describing, directing, leading, and assessing operations. *See pp. 1-15 to 1-28 for further discussion.*

Understand

To understand something is to grasp its nature and significance. Understanding includes establishing context—the set of circumstances that surround a particular event or situation. Throughout the operations process, commanders develop and improve their understanding of their operational environment and the problem. An operational environment is a composite of the conditions, circumstances, and influences that affect the employment of capabilities and bear on the decisions of the commander (JP 3-0).

Visualize

As commanders begin to understand their operational environment and the problem, they start visualizing a desired end state and potential solutions to solve the problem. Collectively, this is known as commander's visualization—the mental process of developing situational understanding, determining a desired end state, and envisioning an operational approach by which the force will achieve that end state. Commander's visualization begins in planning and continues throughout the operations process until the force accomplishes the mission.

Describe

After commanders visualize an operation, they describe it to their staffs and subordinates to facilitate shared understanding and purpose. During planning, commanders ensure subordinates understand their visualization well enough to begin course of action development. During execution, commanders describe modifications to their visualization resulting in fragmentary orders that adjust the original order. Commanders describe their visualization in doctrinal terms, refining and clarifying it as circumstances require. Commanders express their visualization in terms of commander's intent; planning guidance, including an operational approach; commander's critical information requirements (CCIRs); and essential elements of friendly information (EEFI).

Direct

Commanders direct all aspects of operations by establishing their commander's intent, setting achievable objectives, and issuing clear tasks to subordinate units.

Lead

Through leadership, commanders provide purpose, direction, and motivation to subordinate commanders, their staff, and Soldiers. In many instances, a commander's physical presence is necessary to lead effectively. Where the commander locates within the area of operations is an important leadership consideration. Commanders balance their time between leading the staff through the operations process and providing purpose, direction, and motivation to subordinate commanders and Soldiers away from the command post.

Assess

Commanders continuously assess the situation to better understand current conditions and determine how the operation is progressing. Continuous assessment helps commanders anticipate and adapt the force to changing circumstances. Commanders incorporate the assessments of the staff, subordinate commanders, and unified action partners into their personal assessment of the situation. Based on their assessment, commanders modify plans and orders to adapt the force to changing circumstances.

See pp. 1-67 to 1-74 for further discussion

II. The Nature of Operations

To understand doctrine on mission command and the operations process, Soldiers must have an appreciation for the general nature of operations. Military operations are human endeavors, contests of wills characterized by continuous and mutual adaptation among all participants. In operations, Army forces face thinking and adaptive enemies, differing agendas of various actors (organizations and individuals), and changing perceptions of civilians in an operational area. As all sides take actions, each side reacts, learns, and adapts. Appreciating these relationships among human wills is essential to understanding the fundamental nature of operations. In operations, friendly forces fiercely engage a multifaceted enemy force. Each side consists of numerous diverse and connected parts, each interdependent and adapting to changes within and between each other. In addition, an operational environment is not static. It continually evolves. This evolution results, in part, from humans interacting within an operational environment as well as from their ability to learn and adapt. The dynamic nature of an operational environment makes determining the relationship between cause and effect difficult and contributes to the uncertainty of military operations.

Uncertainty pervades operations in the form of unknowns about the enemy, the people, and the surroundings. Even the behavior of friendly forces is often uncertain because of human mistakes and the effects of stress on Soldiers. Chance and friction contribute to the uncertain nature of operations. The sudden death of a local leader that causes an eruption of violence illustrates chance. The combinations of countless factors that impinge on the conduct of operations, from broken equipment that slows movement to complicated plans that confuse subordinates, are examples of friction. During operations leaders make decisions, develop plans, and direct actions under varying degrees of uncertainty. Commanders seek to counter the uncertainty of operations by empowering subordinates at the scene to make decisions, act, and quickly adapt to changing circumstances. As such, the philosophy of mission command guides commanders, staffs, and subordinates throughout the conduct of operations.

III. Mission Command

Mission command is the exercise of authority and direction by the commander using mission orders to enable disciplined initiative within the commander's intent to empower agile and adaptive leaders in the conduct of unified land operations (ADP 6-0). Mission command is also a warfighting function. The mission command warfighting function is the related tasks and systems that develop and integrate those activities enabling a commander to balance the art of command and the science of control in order to integrate the other warfighting functions (ADRP 3-0). Through the mission command warfighting function, commanders and staffs integrate the other war fighting functions into a coherent whole to mass the effects of combat power at the decisive place and time.

Principles of Mission Command

- Build cohesive teams through mutual trust
- Create shared understanding
- Provide a clear commander's intent
- Exercise disciplined initiative
- Use mission orders
- Accept prudent risk

See chap. 5 for a detailed discussion of the mission command and the mission command warfighting function.

Unified Land Operations (Army)

Ref: ADP 3-0, Unified Land Operations (Oct '11).

Unified land operations describes how the Army seizes, retains, and exploits the initiative to gain and maintain a position of relative advantage in sustained land operations through simultaneous offensive, defensive, and stability operations in order to prevent or deter conflict, prevail in war, and create the conditions for favorable conflict resolution. ADP 3-0, Unified Land Operations, is the Army's basic warfighting doctrine and is the Army's contribution to unified action.

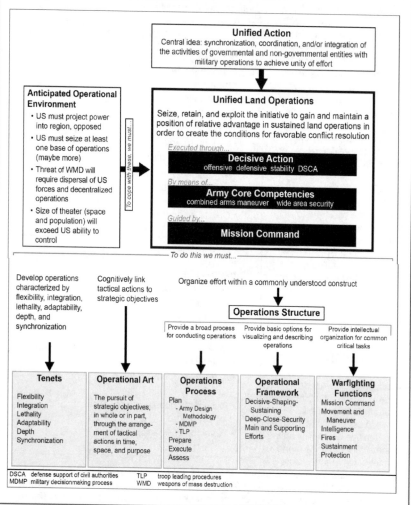

Unified Action

Central idea: synchronization, coordination, and/or integration of the activities of governmental and non-governmental entities with military operations to achieve unity of effort

Anticipated Operational Environment

- US must project power into region, opposed
- US must seize at least one base of operations (maybe more)
- Threat of WMD will require dispersal of US forces and decentralized operations
- Size of theater (space and population) will exceed US ability to control

To cope with these, we must...

Unified Land Operations

Seize, retain, and exploit the initiative to gain and maintain a position of relative advantage in sustained land operations in order to create the conditions for favorable conflict resolution

Executed through...

Decisive Action
offensive defensive stability DSCA

By means of...

Army Core Competencies
combined arms maneuver   wide area security

Guided by...

Mission Command

―――――――― *To do this we must...* ――――――――

Develop operations characterized by flexibility, integration, lethality, adaptability, depth, and synchronization

Cognitively link tactical actions to strategic objectives

Organize effort within a commonly understood construct

Operations Structure

Provide a broad process for conducting operations

Provide basic options for visualizing and describing operations

Provide intellectual organization for common critical tasks

Tenets	Operational Art	Operations Process	Operational Framework	Warfighting Functions
Flexibility	The pursuit of strategic objectives, in whole or in part, through the arrangement of tactical actions in time, space, and purpose	Plan	Decisive-Shaping-Sustaining	Mission Command
Integration		- Army Design Methodology	Deep-Close-Security	Movement and Maneuver
Lethality		- MDMP	Main and Supporting Efforts	Intelligence
Adaptability		- TLP		Fires
Depth		Prepare		Sustainment
Synchronization		Execute		Protection
		Assess		

DSCA defense support of civil authorities   TLP   troop leading procedures
MDMP military decisionmaking process   WMD   weapons of mass destruction

Refer to The Army Operations & Doctrine SMARTbook (Guide to Unified Land Operations and the Six Warfighting Functions) for discussion of the fundamentals, principles and tenets of Army operations, plus chapters on each of the six warfighting functions: mission command, movement and maneuver, intelligence, fires, sustainment, and protection.

Decisive Action (Unified Land Operations)

Ref: ADRP 3-0, Operations (Mar '12), pp. 2-4 to 2-8 (and table 2-1, p. 2-5).

Decisive action requires simultaneous combinations of offense, defense, and stability or defense support of civil authorities tasks.

A. Offensive Tasks

An offensive task is a task conducted to defeat and destroy enemy forces and seize terrain, resources, and population centers. Offensive tasks impose the commander's will on the enemy. In combined arms maneuver, the offense is a task of decisive action. Against

a capable, adaptive enemy, the offense is the most direct and a sure means of seizing, retaining, and exploiting the initiative to gain physical and psychological advantages and achieve definitive results. In the offense, the decisive operation is a sudden, shattering action against an enemy weakness that capitalizes on speed, surprise, and shock. If that operation does not destroy the enemy, operations continue until enemy forces disintegrate or retreat to where they no longer pose a threat. Executing offensive tasks compels the enemy to react, creating or revealing additional weaknesses that the attacking force can exploit.

Refer to The Army Operations & Doctrine SMARTbook and ADRP 3-90.

B. Defensive Tasks

A defensive task is a task conducted to defeat an enemy attack, gain time, economize forces, and develop conditions favorable for offensive or stability tasks. Normally the defense alone cannot achieve a decision.

Offensive Tasks

Primary Tasks
- Movement to contact
- Attack
- Exploitation
- Pursuit

Purposes
- Dislocate, isolate, disrupt and destroy enemy forces
- Seize key terrain
- Deprive the enemy of resources
- Develop intelligence
- Deceive and divert the enemy
- Create a secure environment for stability operations

Defensive Tasks

Primary Tasks
- Mobile defense
- Area defense
- Retrograde

Purposes
- Deter or defeat enemy offensive operations
- Gain time
- Achieve economy of force
- Retain key terrain
- Protect the populace, critical assets and infrastructure
- Develop intelligence

However, it can set conditions for a counteroffensive or counterattack that enables Army forces to regain the initiative. Defensive tasks can also establish a shield behind which wide area security can progress. Defensive tasks are a counter to the enemy offense. They defeat attacks, destroying as much of the attacking enemy as possible. They also preserve and maintain control over land, resources, and populations. The purpose of defensive tasks is to retain terrain, guard populations, and protect critical capabilities against enemy attacks. Commanders can conduct defensive tasks to gain time and economize forces so offensive tasks can be executed elsewhere.

Refer to The Army Operations & Doctrine SMARTbook and ADRP 3-90 for further discussion.

C. Stability Tasks

Stability is an overarching term encompassing various military missions, tasks, and activities conducted outside the United States in coordination with other instruments of national power to maintain or reestablish a safe and secure environment, provide essential governmental services, emergency infrastructure reconstruction, and humanitarian relief. (See JP 3-0.) Army forces conduct stability tasks during both combined arms maneuver and wide area security. These tasks support a host-nation or an interim government or part of a transitional military authority when no government exists. Stability tasks involve both coercive and constructive actions. They help to establish or maintain a safe and

Stability Tasks

Primary Tasks

- Establish civil security (including security force asst)
- Establish civil control
- Restore essential services
- Support to governance
- Support to economic and infrastructure development

Purposes

- Provide a secure environment
- Secure land areas
- Meet the critical needs of the populace
- Gain support for host-nation government
- Shape the environment for interagency and host-nation success

secure environment and facilitate reconciliation among local or regional adversaries. Stability tasks can also help establish political, legal, social, and economic institutions while supporting the transition to legitimate host-nation governance. Stability tasks cannot succeed if they only react to enemy initiatives. Stability tasks must maintain the initiative by pursuing objectives that resolve the causes of instability.

Refer to The Stability, Peace, & Counterinsurgency SMARTbook and ADRP 3-07 for further discussion.

Defense Support of Civil Authorities Tasks

Primary Tasks

- Provide support for domestic disasters
- Provide support for domestic CBRN incidents
- Provide support for domestic civilian law enforcement agencies
- Provide other designated support

Purposes

- Save lives
- Restore essential services
- Maintain or restore law and order
- Protect infrastructure and property
- Maintain or restore local government
- Shape the environment for interagency success

D. Defense Support of Civil Authority Tasks

DSCA is support provided by U.S. Federal military forces, Department of Defense civilians, Department of Defense contract personnel, Department of Defense component assets, and National Guard forces (when the Secretary of Defense,

in coordination with the Governors of the affected States, elects and requests to use those forces in Title 32, U.S. Code, status). This support is in response to requests for assistance from civil authorities for domestic emergencies, law enforcement support, and other domestic activities, or from qualifying entities for special events. Defense support of civil authorities is a task that takes place only in the homeland, although some of its tasks are similar to stability tasks. Defense support of civil authorities is always conducted in support of another primary or lead federal agency.

Refer to The Army Operations & Doctrine SMARTbook and JP 2-28 for further discussion.

IV. Principles of the Operations Process

The operations process, while simple in concept (plan, prepare, execute, and assess), is dynamic in execution. Commanders and staffs use the operations process to integrate numerous tasks executed throughout the headquarters and with subordinate units. Commanders must organize and train their staffs and subordinates as an integrated team to simultaneously plan, prepare, execute, and assess operations. In addition to the principles of mission command, commanders and staffs consider the following principles for the effective use of the operations process:

Principles of the Operations Process

- **Commanders drive the operations process**

- **Build and maintain situational understanding**

- **Apply critical and creative thinking**

- **Encourage collaboration and dialogue**

A. Commanders Drive the Operations Process

Commanders are the most important participants in the operations process. While staffs perform essential functions that amply the effectiveness of operations, commanders drive the operations process through understanding, visualizing, describing, directing, leading, and assessing operations. Accurate and timely running estimates are key knowledge management tools that assist commanders in driving the operations process.

See pp. 1-13 to 1-26 for further discussion of commander's activities in terms of "Understand, Visualize, Describe, Direct, Lead and Assess."

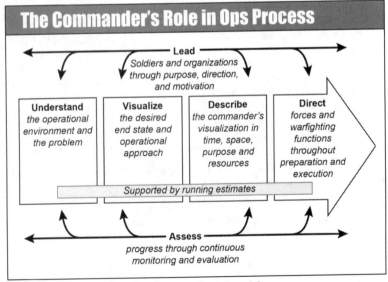

The Commander's Role in Ops Process

Lead
Soldiers and organizations through purpose, direction, and motivation

Understand	**Visualize**	**Describe**	**Direct**
the operational environment and the problem	the desired end state and operational approach	the commander's visualization in time, space, purpose and resources	forces and warfighting functions throughout preparation and execution

Supported by running estimates

Assess
progress through continuous monitoring and evaluation

Ref: ADRP 5-0, The Operations Process, fig. 1-2, p. 1-3.

B. Build and Maintain Situational Understanding

Success in operations demands timely and effective decisions based on applying judgment to available information and knowledge. As such, commanders and staffs seek to build and maintain situational understanding throughout the operations process. Situational understanding is the product of applying analysis and judgment to relevant information to determine the relationships among the operational and mission variables to facilitate decision-making (ADP 5-0). Building and maintaining situational understanding is essential to establishing the situation's context, developing effective plans, assessing operations, and making quality decisions throughout the operations process. Commanders continually strive to maintain their situational understanding and work through periods of reduced understanding as the situation evolves.

1. Operational and Mission Variables

Commanders and staffs use the operational and mission variables to help build their situational understanding. They analyze and describe an operational environment in terms of eight interrelated operational variables: political, military, economic, social, information, infrastructure, physical environment, and time (PMESII-PT). Upon receipt of a mission, commanders filter information categorized by the operational variables into relevant information with respect to the mission. They use the mission variables, in combination with the operational variables, to refine their understanding of the situation and to visualize, describe, and direct operations. The mission variables are mission, enemy, terrain and weather, troops and support available, time available, and civil considerations (METT-TC).

See pp. 1-16 to 1-17 for further discussion of operational and mission variables.

2. Cultural Understanding

As part of building their situational understanding, commanders consider how culture (both their own and others within an operational area) affects operations. Culture is the shared beliefs, values, norms, customs, behaviors, and artifacts members of a society use to cope with the world and each other. Culture influences how people make judgments about what is right and wrong and how they assess what is important and unimportant. Culture provides a framework for thought and decisions. What one culture considers rational, another culture may consider irrational. Understanding the culture of a particular society or group within a society can significantly improve the force's ability to accomplish the mission.

Understanding other cultures applies to all operations, not just operations dominated by stability. Leaders are mindful of cultural factors in four contexts:

• Awareness of how one's own culture affects how one perceives a situation

• Awareness of the cultures within a region where the unit operates

• Awareness of how history has shaped the culture of a region where the unit operates

• Sensitivity to the different backgrounds, traditions, and operational methods of the various unified action partners

Understanding the culture of unified action partners is crucial to building mutual trust and shared understanding. Leaders consider how culture influences the situational understanding and decision-making of their military and civilian partners. This mutual understanding between leaders and their counterparts helps build unity of effort.

C. Apply Critical and Creative Thinking

Commanders and staffs apply critical and creative thinking throughout the operations process to assist them with understanding situations, making decisions, and directing action. Critical thinking is purposeful and reflective judgment about what to believe or what to do in response to observations, experience, verbal or written expressions, or arguments. Creative thinking involves creating something new or original. Creative thinking leads to new insights, novel approaches, fresh perspectives, and new ways of understanding and conceiving things.

Red teams assist commanders and staffs with critical and creative thinking and help them avoid groupthink, mirror imaging, cultural missteps, and tunnel vision throughout the conduct of operations. Red teaming enables commanders to explore alternative plans and operations in the context of their operational environment, and from the perspective of unified action partners, adversaries, and others. Throughout the operations process, red team members help identify relevant actors, clarify the problem, and explain how others (unified action partners, the population, and the enemy) may view the problem from their perspectives. They challenge assumptions and the analysis used to build the plan. In essence, red teams provide commanders and staffs with an independent capability to challenge the organization's thinking.

D. Encourage Collaboration and Dialogue

Throughout the operations process, commanders encourage continuous collaboration and dialogue among the staff and with unified action partners. Collaboration and dialogue aids in developing shared understanding throughout the force and with unified action partners. Collaboration is two or more people or organizations working together toward common goals by sharing knowledge and building consensus. Dialogue is a way to collaborate that involves the candid exchange of ideas or opinions among participants and that encourages frank discussions in areas of disagreement. Throughout the operations process, commanders, subordinate commanders, staffs, and unified action partners actively collaborate and dialogue, sharing and questioning information, perceptions, and ideas to better understand situations and make decisions.

Through collaboration and dialogue, the commander creates a learning environment by allowing participants to think critically and creatively and share their ideas, opinions, and recommendations without fear of retribution. Effective dialogue requires candor and a free, yet mutually respectful, competition of ideas. Participants must feel free to make viewpoints based on their expertise, experience, and insight; this includes sharing ideas that contradict the opinions held by those of higher rank. Successful commanders willingly listen to novel ideas and counterarguments concerning any problem.

V. Battle Rhythm

Within the operations process, commanders and staffs must integrate and synchronize numerous activities, meetings, and reports within their headquarters, with their higher headquarters, and with subordinate units. They do this by establishing the unit's battle rhythm. Battle rhythm is a deliberate daily cycle of command, staff, and unit activities intended to synchronize current and future operations (JP 3-33).

See chap. 5, Mission Command, for a discussion of command post operations to include establishing working groups and boards and battle rhythm (pp. 5-26 to 5-27).

VI. Running Estimates

Effective plans and successful execution hinge on accurate and current running estimates. A running estimate is the continuous assessment of the current situation used to determine if the current operation is proceeding according to the commander's intent and if planned future operations are supportable (ADP 5-0). Failure to maintain accurate running estimates may lead to errors or omissions that result in flawed plans or bad decisions during execution.

See pp. 2-4 to 2-5 for further discussion of running estimates.

II. Understand, Visualize Describe, Direct, Lead, Assess

Ref: ADRP 5-0, The Operations Process (Mar '12), chap. I.

Commander's Activities

Commanders are the most important participants in the operations process. While staffs perform essential functions that amply the effectiveness of operations, **commanders drive the operations process** through understanding, visualizing, describing, directing, leading, and assessing operations.

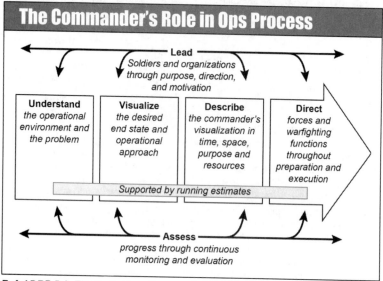

The Commander's Role in Ops Process

Lead — Soldiers and organizations through purpose, direction, and motivation

Understand	Visualize	Describe	Direct
the operational environment and the problem	the desired end state and operational approach	the commander's visualization in time, space, purpose and resources	forces and warfighting functions throughout preparation and execution

Supported by running estimates

Assess — progress through continuous monitoring and evaluation

Ref: ADRP 5-0, The Operations Process, fig. 1-2, p. 1-3.

I. Understand

Understanding is fundamental to the commander's ability to establish a situation's context. It is essential to effective decision making during planning and execution. Analysis of the operational and mission variable provides the information used to develop understanding and frame the problem. In addition, conceptual and detailed planning assist commanders in developing their initial understanding of the operational environment and the problem. To develop a better understanding of an operational environment, commanders circulate within the area of operations as often as possible, collaborating with subordinate commanders and with Soldiers. Using personal observations and inputs from others (to include running estimates from the staff), commanders improve their understanding of their operational environment throughout the operations process.

Information collection (to include reconnaissance and surveillance) is indispensable to building and improving the commander's understanding. Formulating CCIRs, keeping them current, determining where to place key personnel, and arranging for liaison also contribute to improving the commander's understanding. Greater understanding enables commanders to make better decisions throughout the conduct of operations.

See pp. 1-16 to 1-17 (operational and mission variables) and p. 1-26 (principles of war and joint operations).

II. Visualize

As commanders begin to understand their operational environment and the problem, they start visualizing a desired end state and potential solutions to solve the problem. Collectively, this is known as commander's visualization—the mental process of developing situational understanding, determining a desired end state, and envisioning an operational approach by which the force will achieve that end state (ADP 5-0). Assignment of a mission provides the focus for developing the commander's visualization that, in turn, provides the basis for developing plans and orders. During preparation and execution, the commander's visualization helps commanders determine if, when, and what to decide, as they adapt to changing conditions.

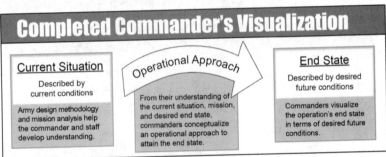

Completed Commander's Visualization

Current Situation

Described by current conditions

Army design methodology and mission analysis help the commander and staff develop understanding.

Operational Approach

From their understanding of the current situation, mission, and desired end state, commanders conceptualize an operational approach to attain the end state.

End State

Described by desired future conditions

Commanders visualize the operation's end state in terms of desired future conditions.

Ref: ADRP 5-0, The Operations Process, fig. 1-3, p. 1-4.

In building their visualization, commanders first seek to understand those conditions that represent the current situation. Next, commanders envision a set of desired future conditions that represents the operation's end state. Commanders complete their visualization by conceptualizing an operational approach—a description of the broad actions the force must take to transform current conditions into those desired at end state (JP 5-0).

Commanders apply the Army design methodology and use the elements of operational art when developing and describing their commander's visualization. They also actively collaborate with higher, subordinate and adjacent commanders, the staff, and unified action partners to assist them in building their visualization. Unified action partners are those military forces, governmental and nongovernmental organizations, and elements of the private sector that Army forces plan, coordinate, synchronize, and integrate with during the conduct of operations (ADRP 3-0). Because of the dynamic nature of military operations, commanders must continuously validate their visualization throughout the operations process.

See p. 1-35 for discussion of the elements of operational design and art.

III. Describe

After commanders visualize an operation, they describe it to their staffs and subordinates to facilitate shared understanding and purpose. During planning, commanders ensure subordinates understand their visualization well enough to begin course of action development. During execution, commanders describe modifications to their visualization in updated planning guidance and directives resulting in fragmentary orders that adjust the original order. Commanders describe their visualization in doctrinal terms, refining and clarifying it, as circumstances require. Commanders express their visualization in terms of:

- Commander's intent
- Planning guidance, including an operational approach
- Commander's critical information requirements
- Essential elements of friendly information

See pp. 1-18 to 1-19 for further discussion of the above elements.

IV. Direct

Commanders direct all aspects of operations by establishing their commander's intent, setting achievable objectives, and issuing clear tasks to subordinate units. Throughout the operations process, commanders direct forces by—

- Preparing and approving plans and orders
- Establishing command and support relationships
- Assigning and adjusting tasks, control measures, and task organization
- Positioning units to maximize combat power
- Positioning key leaders at critical places and times to ensure supervision
- Allocating resources to exploit opportunities and counter threats
- Committing the reserve as required

See pp. 1-20 to 1-21 for discussion of the operational framework, elements of combat power, and the six warfighting functions.

V. Lead

Through leadership, commanders provide purpose, direction, and motivation to subordinate commanders, their staff, and Soldiers. In many instances, a commander's physical presence is necessary to lead effectively. Where the commander locates within the area of operations is an important leadership consideration. Commanders balance their time between leading the staff through the operations process and providing purpose, direction, and motivation to subordinate commanders and Soldiers away from the command post.

Refer to The Leader's SMARTbook for complete discussion of the basis of leadership; the Army leader; leading, developing, achieving; counseling, coaching, mentoring; training for full spectrum operations and METL development; training plans, meetings and schedules; training execution and training exercises; and training assessments and AARs!

VI. Assess

Commanders continuously assess the situation to better understand current conditions and determine how the operation is progressing. Continuous assessment helps commanders anticipate and adapt the force to changing circumstances. Commanders incorporate the assessments of the staff, subordinate commanders, and unified action partners into their personal assessment of the situation. Based on their assessment, commanders modify plans and orders to adapt the force to changing circumstances.

See pp. 1-65 to 1-72 for further discussion of "assessment" to include the assessment process activities, evaluation criteria (MOEs, MOPs, and indicators), and formal assessment plans.

Operational & Mission Variables (Understand)

Ref: ADRP 5-0, The Operations Process (Mar '12), pp. 1-7 to 1-9.

Operational Variables (PMESII-PT)

The operational variables are fundamental to developing a comprehensive understanding of an operational environment.

Variable	Description
P - Political	Describes the distribution of responsibility and power at all levels of governance— formally constituted authorities, as well as informal or covert political powers
M - Military	Explores the military and paramilitary capabilities of all relevant actors (enemy, friendly, and neutral) in a given operational environment
E - Economic	Encompasses individual and group behaviors related to producing, distributing, and consuming resources
S - Social	Describes the cultural, religious, and ethnic makeup within an operational environment and the beliefs, values, customs, and behaviors of society members
I - Information	Describes the nature, scope, characteristics, and effects of individuals, organizations, and systems that collect, process, disseminate, or act on information
I - Infrastructure	Is composed of the basic facilities, services, and installations needed for the functioning of a community or society
P - Physical environment	Includes the geography and manmade structures, as well as the climate and weather in the area of operations
T - Time	Describes the timing and duration of activities, events, or conditions within an operational environment, as well as how the timing and duration are perceived by various actors in the operational environment

Ref: ADRP 5-0, The Operations Process, table 1-1, p. 1-7.

Operational Subvariables

Each of the eight operational variables also has associated subvariables.

Political variable	Social variable	Physical Environment	Economic variable
Attitude toward the United States	Demographic mix	Terrain	Economic diversity
Centers of political power	Social volatility	▪ Observation and fields of fire	Employment status
Type of government	Education level	▪ Avenues of approach	Economic activity
Government effectiveness and legitimacy	Ethnic diversity	▪ Key terrain	Illegal economic activity
Influential political groups	Religious diversity	▪ Obstacles	Banking and finance
International relationships	Population movement	▪ Cover and concealment	
	Common languages	▪ Landforms	**Infrastructure variable**
	Criminal activity	▪ Vegetation	Construction pattern
	Human rights	▪ Terrain complexity	Urban zones
	Centers of social power	▪ Mobility classification	Urbanized building density
	Basic cultural norms and values	Natural Hazards	Utilities present
		Climate	Utility level
Military variable	**Information variable**	Weather	Transportation architecture
Military forces	Public communications media	▪ Precipitation	**Time variable**
Government paramilitary forces	Information warfare	▪ High temperature-heat index	Cultural perception of time
Nonstate paramilitary forces	▪ Electronic warfare	▪ Low temperature-wind chill index	Information offset
Unarmed combatants	▪ Computer warfare	▪ Wind	Tactical exploitation of time
Nonmilitary armed combatants	▪ Information attack	▪ Visibility	Key dates, time periods, or events
Military functions	▪ Deception	▪ Cloud cover	
▪ Command and control (mission command)	▪ Physical destruction	▪ Relative humidity	
▪ Maneuver	▪ Protection and security measures		
▪ Information warfare	▪ Perception management		
▪ Reconnaissance, intelligence, surveillance, and target acquisition	Intelligence		
▪ Fire support	Information management		
▪ Protection			
▪ Logistics			

Ref: ADRP 5-0, The Operations Process, table 1-2, p. 1-8.

Mission Variables (METT-TC)

Mission variables describe characteristics of the area of operations, focusing on how they might affect a mission. Incorporating the analysis of the operational variables into METT–TC ensures Army leaders consider the best available relevant information about conditions that pertain to the mission. Using the operational variables as a source of relevant information for the mission variables allows commanders to refine their situational understanding of their operational environment and to visualize, describe, direct, lead and assess operations.

Variable		Description
Mission	**M**	Commanders and staffs view all of the mission variables in terms of their impact on mission accomplishment. The mission is the task, together with the purpose, that clearly indicates the action to be taken and the reason therefore. It is always the first variable commanders consider during decisionmaking. A mission statement contains the "who, what, when, where, and why" of the operation.
Enemy	**E**	The second variable to consider is the enemy—dispositions (including organization, strength, location, and tactical mobility), doctrine, equipment, capabilities, vulnerabilities, and probable courses of action.
Terrain and weather	**T**	Terrain and weather analysis are inseparable and directly influence each other's impact on military operations. Terrain includes natural features (such as rivers and mountains) and manmade features (such as cities, airfields, and bridges). Commanders analyze terrain using the five military aspects of terrain expressed in the memory aid **OAKOC**: observation and fields of fire, avenues of approach, key and decisive terrain, obstacles, cover and concealment. The military aspects of weather include visibility, wind, precipitation, cloud cover, temperature, humidity.
Troops and support available	**T**	This variable includes the number, type, capabilities, and condition of available friendly troops and support. These include supplies, services and support available from joint, host nation and unified action partners. They also include support from Civilians and contractors employed by military organizations, such as the Defense Logistics Agency and the Army Materiel Command.
Time available	**T**	Commanders assess the time available for planning, preparing, and executing tasks and operations. This includes the time required to assemble, deploy, and maneuver units in relationship to the enemy and conditions.
Civil considerations	**C**	Civil considerations are the influence of manmade infrastructure, civilian institutions, and cultures and activities of the civilian leaders, populations, and organizations within an area of operations on the conduct of military operations. Civil considerations comprise six characteristics, expressed in the memory aid **ASCOPE**: areas, structures, capabilities, organizations, people, and events.

Ref: ADRP 5-0, The Operations Process, table 1-3, p. 1-9.

METT-TC is a memory aid that identifies the mission variables: Mission, Enemy, Terrain and weather, Troops and support available, Time available, and Civil considerations.

OAKOC - The Military Aspects of Terrain
For tactical operations, terrain is analyzed using the five military aspects of terrain, expressed in the memory aid, OAKOC: Observation and fields of fire, Avenues of approach, Key and decisive terrain, Obstacles, Cover and concealment.

See pp. 3-14 to 3-15 for further discussion of the military aspects of terrain (OAKOC).

ASCOPE - Civil Considerations
Commanders and staffs analyze civil considerations in terms of the categories expressed in the memory aid ASCOPE: Areas, Structures, Capabilities, Organizations, People, Events.

See pp. 3-14 to 3-15 for further discussion of civil considerations (ASCOPE).

Refer to FM 6-0 (C1), Commander and Staff Organization and Operations (May '15), for further discussion of operational and mission variables.

3. Describe

Ref: ADRP 5-0, The Operations Process (Mar '12), pp. 1-4 to 1-6.

After commanders visualize an operation, they describe it to their staffs and subordinates to facilitate shared understanding and purpose. During planning, commanders ensure subordinates understand their visualization well enough to begin course of action development. During execution, commanders describe modifications to their visualization in updated planning guidance and directives resulting in fragmentary orders that adjust the original order. Commanders describe their visualization in doctrinal terms, refining and clarifying it, as circumstances require. Commanders express their visualization in terms of:

- Commander's intent
- Planning guidance, including an operational approach
- Commander's critical information requirements
- Essential elements of friendly information

A. Commander's Intent

The commander's intent is a clear and concise expression of the purpose of the operation and the desired military end state that supports mission command, provides focus to the staff, and helps subordinate and supporting commanders act to achieve the commander's desired results without further orders, even when the operation does not unfold as planned (JP 3-0). During planning, the initial commander's intent drives course of action development. In execution, the commander's intent guides disciplined initiative as subordinates make decisions when facing unforeseen opportunities or countering threats. Commanders develop their intent statement personally. It must be easy to remember and clearly understood by commanders and staffs two echelons lower in the chain of command. The more concise the commander's intent, the easier it is to recall and understand.

B. Planning Guidance

Commanders provide planning guidance to the staff based upon their visualization. Planning guidance must convey the essence of the commander's visualization, including a description of the operational approach. Effective planning guidance reflects how the commander sees the operation unfolding. It broadly describes when, where, and how the commander intends to employ combat power to accomplish the mission, within the higher commander's intent. Broad and general guidance gives the staff and subordinate leaders' maximum latitude; it lets proficient staffs develop flexible and effective options.

Commanders use their experience and judgment to add depth and clarity to their planning guidance. They ensure staffs understand the broad outline of their visualization while allowing them the latitude necessary to explore different options. This guidance provides the basis for the concept of operations without dictating the specifics of the final plan. As with their intent, commanders may modify planning guidance based on staff and subordinate input and changing conditions. (See ATTP 5-0.1 for a detailed discussion of developing and issue planning guidance).

C. Commander's Critical Information Requirements (CCIR)

A commander's critical information requirement is an information requirement identified by the commander as being critical to facilitating timely decision-making. The two key elements are friendly force information requirements and priority intelligence requirements (JP 3-0). A commander's critical information requirement (CCIR) directly influences decision making and facilitates the successful execution of military operations. Commanders decide to designate an information requirement as a CCIR based on likely decisions and their visualization of the course of the operation. A CCIR may support one or more decisions. During planning, staffs recommend information requirements for commanders to designate as CCIRs. During preparation and execution, they recommend changes to CCIRs based on assessment. A CCIR is:

- Specified by a commander for a specific operation
- Applicable only to the commander who specifies it
- Situation dependent—directly linked to a current or future mission
- Time-sensitive

Always promulgated by a plan or order, commanders limit the number of CCIRs to focus the efforts of limited collection assets. The fewer the CCIRs, the easier it is for staffs to remember, recognize, and act on each one. This helps staffs and subordinates identify information the commander needs immediately. While most staffs provide relevant information, a good staff expertly distills that information. It identifies answers to CCIRs and gets them to the commander immediately. It also identifies vital information that does not answer a CCIR but that the commander nonetheless needs to know. A good staff develops this ability through training and experience. Designating too many CCIRs limits the staff's ability to immediately recognize and react to them. Excessive critical items reduce the focus of collection efforts.

The list of CCIRs constantly changes. Commanders add and delete them throughout an operation based on the information needed for specific decisions. Commanders determine their own CCIRs, but they may select some from staff nominations. Once approved, a CCIR falls into one of two categories: priority intelligence requirements (PIRs) and friendly force information requirements (FFIRs).

Priority Intelligence Requirement (PIR)

A priority intelligence requirement is an intelligence requirement, stated as a priority for intelligence support, which the commander and staff need to understand the adversary or the operational environment (JP 2-0). PIRs identify the information about the enemy and other aspects of the operational environment that the commander considers most important. Lessons from recent operations show that intelligence about civil considerations may be as critical as intelligence about the enemy. Thus, all staff sections may recommend information about civil considerations as PIRs. The intelligence officer manages PIRs for the commander through planning requirements and assessing collection.

Friendly Force Information Requirement (FFIR)

A friendly force information requirement is information the commander and staff need to understand the status of friendly force and supporting capabilities (JP 3-0). FFIRs identify the information about the mission, troops and support available, and time available for friendly forces that the commander considers most important. In coordination with the staff, the operations officer manages FFIRs for the commander.

D. Essential Elements of Friendly Information (EEFI)

Commanders also describe information they want protected as essential elements of friendly information. An essential element of friendly information is a critical aspect of a friendly operation that, if known by the enemy, would subsequently compromise, lead to failure, or limit success of the operation and therefore should be protected from enemy detection. Although EEFIs are not CCIRs, they have the same priority. EEFIs establish elements of information to protect rather than one to collect. Their identification is the first step in the operations security process and central to the protection of information.

4. Direct

Ref: ADRP 5-0, The Operations Process (Mar '12), p. 1-5.

Commanders direct all aspects of operations by establishing their commander's intent, setting achievable objectives, and issuing clear tasks to subordinate units. Throughout the operations process, commanders direct forces by—

- Preparing and approving plans and orders
- Establishing command and support relationships
- Assigning and adjusting tasks, control measures, and task organization
- Positioning units to maximize combat power
- Positioning key leaders at critical places and times to ensure supervision
- Allocating resources to exploit opportunities and counter threats
- Committing the reserve as required

Operational Framework

ADRP 3-0, Unified Land Operations (Mar '12), pp. 1-9 to 1-13 (and fig. 1-1, p. 1-10).

Area of Operations

When establishing the operational framework, commanders use control measures to assign responsibilities, coordinate fires and maneuver, and control combat operations. One of the most important control measures is the area of operations. An area of operations is an operational area defined by the joint force commander for land and maritime forces that should be large enough to accomplish their missions and protect their forces (JP 3-0). For land operations, an area of operations includes subordinate areas of operations as well. The Army command or joint force land component commander is the supported commander within an area of operations designated by the joint force commander for land operations. Within their areas of operations, commanders integrate and synchronize combat power. To facilitate this integration and synchronization, commanders have the authority to designate targeting priority, effects, timing, and effects of fires within their areas of operations.

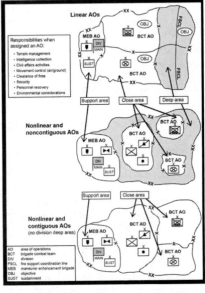

Area of Influence

Commanders consider a unit's area of influence when assigning it an area of operations. An area of influence is a geographical area wherein a commander is directly capable of influencing operations by maneuver or fire support systems normally under the commander's command or control (JP 3-0). The area of influence normally surrounds and includes the area of operations. Understanding the area of influence helps the commander and staff plan branches to the current operation in which the force uses capabilities outside the area of operations. An area of operations should not be substantially larger than the unit's area of influence. Ideally, the area of influence would encompass the entire area of operations.

Area of Interest

An area of interest is that area of concern to the commander, including the area of influence, areas adjacent thereto, and extending into enemy territory. This area also includes areas occupied by enemy forces who could jeopardize the accomplishment of the mission (JP 3-0). An area of interest for stability or defense support of civil authorities tasks may be much larger than that area associated with the offense and defense.

Deep–Close–Security

The deep-close-security operational framework has historically been associated with terrain orientation but can be applied to temporal and organizational orientations as well.

- **Deep operations** involve efforts to prevent uncommitted enemy forces from being committed in a coherent manner. The purpose of deep operations is frequently tied to other events distant in time, space or both. Deep operations might aim to disrupt the movement of operational reserves, for example, or prevent the enemy from employing long-range cannon, rocket, or missile fires.
- **Close operations** are operations that are within a subordinate commander's area of operations. Operations projected in close areas are usually against hostile forces in immediate contact and are often the decisive operation. A close operation requires speed and mobility to rapidly concentrate overwhelming combat power at the critical time and place and to exploit success.
- **Security operations** involve efforts to provide an early and accurate warning of enemy operations and to provide time and maneuver space within which to react to the enemy. These operations protect the force from surprise and develop the situation to allow the commander to use the force effectively. Security operations include necessary actions to retain freedom of action and ensure uninterrupted support or sustainment of all other operations.
- In deep, close, and security operations, a commander may refer to a **support area**.

Decisive–Shaping–Sustaining

The decisive-shaping-sustaining framework lends itself to a broad conceptual orientation.

- **The decisive operation** is the operation that directly accomplishes the mission. It determines the outcome of a major operation, battle, or engagement. The decisive operation is the focal point around which commanders design an entire operation. Decisive operations lead directly to the accomplishment of a commander's intent. Commanders typically identify a single decisive operation, but more than one subordinate unit may play a role in a decisive operation.
- **A shaping operation** is an operation that establishes conditions for the decisive operation through effects on the enemy, other actors, and the terrain. Inform and influence activities, for example, may integrate Soldier and leader engagement tasks into the operation to reduce tensions between Army units and different ethnic groups through direct contact between Army leaders and local leaders. Shaping operations preserve conditions for the success of the decisive operation. Commanders may designate more than one shaping operation.
- **A sustaining operation** is an operation at any echelon that enables the decisive operation or shaping operation by generating and maintaining combat power. Sustaining operations differ from decisive and shaping operations in that they focus internally (on friendly forces) rather than externally (on the enemy or environment). Sustaining operations include personnel and logistics support, rear area security, movement control, terrain management, and infrastructure development.

Main and Supporting Efforts

The main and supporting efforts operational framework—simpler than other organizing frameworks—focuses on prioritizing effort among subordinate units. Therefore, leaders can use the main and supporting efforts with either the deep-close-security framework or the decisive-shaping-sustaining framework.

- **The main effort** is a designated subordinate unit whose mission at a given point in time is most critical to overall mission success. It is usually weighted with the preponderance of combat power. Typically, commanders shift the main effort one or more times during execution. Designating a main effort temporarily prioritizes resource allocation. When commanders designate a unit as the main effort, it receives priority of support and resources.
- **A supporting effort** is a designated subordinate unit with a mission that supports the success of the main effort. Commanders may provide augmentation to the main effort or develop a supporting plan synchronized with the higher plan. They resource supporting efforts with the minimum assets necessary to accomplish the mission. Forces often realize success of the main effort through success of supporting efforts.

Elements of Combat Power (Direct)

Ref: ADRP 3-0, Unified Land Operations (Mar '12), pp. 3-1 to 3-2 (and fig. 3-1).

Combined arms maneuver and wide area security, executed through simultaneous offensive, defensive, stability, or defense support of civil authorities tasks, require continuously generating and applying combat power, often for extended periods. Combat power is the total means of destructive, constructive, and information capabilities that a military unit or formation can apply at a given time. Army forces generate combat power by converting potential into effective action.

To execute combined arms operations, commanders conceptualize capabilities in terms of combat power. Combat power has eight elements: leadership, information, mission command, movement and maneuver, intelligence, fires, sustainment, and protection. The Army collectively describes the last six elements as the **warfighting functions**. Commanders apply combat power through the warfighting functions using leadership and information.

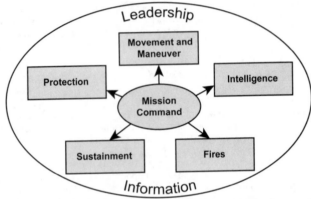

Generating and maintaining combat power throughout an operation is essential to success. Factors contributing to generating combat power include employing reserves, rotating committed forces, and focusing joint support. Commanders balance the ability to mass lethal and nonlethal effects with the need to deploy and sustain the units that produce those effects. They balance the ability of accomplishing the mission with the ability to project and sustain the force. Commanders apply **leadership** through mission command. Leadership is the multiplying and unifying element of combat power. **Information** enables commanders at all levels to make informed decisions on how best to apply combat power. Ultimately, this creates opportunities to achieve definitive results. Knowledge management enables commanders to make informed, timely decisions despite the uncertainty of operations.

Organizing Combat Power

Ref: ADRP 3-0, Unified Land Operations (Mar '12), pp. 3-6 to 3-7.

Commanders employ three means to organize combat power: force tailoring, task-organizing, and mutual support.

- **Force tailoring** is the process of determining the right mix of forces and the sequence of their deployment in support of a joint force commander.
- **Task-organizing** is the act of designing an operating force, support staff, or sustainment package of specific size and composition to meet a unique task or mission.
- **Mutual support.** Commanders consider mutual support when task-organizing forces, assigning areas of operations, and positioning units. Mutual support is that support which units render each other against an enemy, because of their assigned tasks, their position relative to each other and to the enemy, and their inherent capabilities (JP 3-31).

The Six Warfighting Functions

ADRP 3-0, Unified Land Operations (Mar '12), pp. 3-2 to 3-8.

1. Mission Command

The mission command warfighting function is the related tasks and systems that develop and integrate those activities enabling a commander to balance the art of command and the science of control in order to integrate the other warfighting functions. Commanders, assisted by their staffs, integrate numerous processes and activities within the headquarters and across the force as they exercise mission command.

2. Movement and Maneuver

The movement and maneuver warfighting function is the related tasks and systems that move and employ forces to achieve a position of relative advantage over the enemy and other threats. Direct fire and close combat are inherent in maneuver. The movement and maneuver warfighting function includes tasks associated with force projection related to gaining a position of advantage over the enemy. Movement is necessary to disperse and displace the force as a whole or in part when maneuvering. Maneuver is the employment of forces in the operational area.

3. Intelligence

The intelligence warfighting function is the related tasks and systems that facilitate understanding the enemy, terrain, and civil considerations. This warfighting function includes understanding threats, adversaries, and weather. It synchronizes information collection with the primary tactical tasks of reconnaissance, surveillance, security, and intelligence operations. Intelligence is driven by commanders and is more than just collection. Developing intelligence is a continuous process that involves analyzing information from all sources and conducting operations to develop the situation.

4. Fires

The fires warfighting function is the related tasks and systems that provide collective and coordinated use of Army indirect fires, air and missile defense, and joint fires through the targeting process. Army fires systems deliver fires in support of offensive and defensive tasks to create specific lethal and nonlethal effects on a target.

5. Sustainment

The sustainment warfighting function is the related tasks and systems that provide support and services to ensure freedom of action, extend operational reach, and prolong endurance. The endurance of Army forces is primarily a function of their sustainment. Sustainment determines the depth and duration of Army operations. It is essential to retaining and exploiting the initiative. Sustainment provides the support necessary to maintain operations until mission accomplishment.

6. Protection

The protection warfighting function is the related tasks and systems that preserve the force so the commander can apply maximum combat power to accomplish the mission. Preserving the force includes protecting personnel (combatants and noncombatants) and physical assets of the United States and multinational military and civilian partners, to include the host nation. The protection warfighting function enables the commander to maintain the force's integrity and combat power. Protection determines the degree to which potential threats can disrupt operations and then counters or mitigates those threats.

Refer to The Army Operations & Doctrine SMARTbook (Guide to Unified Land Operations and the Six Warfighting Functions) for discussion of the fundamentals, principles and tenets of Army operations, plus chapters on each of the six warfighting functions: mission command, movement and maneuver, intelligence, fires, sustainment, and protection.

Integrating Processes & Continuing Activities (Direct)

Ref: ADRP 5-0, The Operations Process (Mar '12), pp. 1-11 to 1-12.

Throughout the operations process, commanders and staffs integrate the warfighting functions to synchronize the force in accordance with the commander's intent and concept of operations. Commanders and staffs use several integrating processes and continuing activities to do this.

A. Integrating Processes (See p. 3-1)

In addition to the major activities of the operations process, commanders and staffs use several integrating processes to synchronize specific functions throughout the operations process. The integrating processes are—

1. Intelligence Preparation of the Battlefield (IPB)

Intelligence preparation of the battlefield (IPB) is a systematic, continuous process of analyzing the threat and other aspects of an operational environment within a specific geographic area. Led by the intelligence officer, the entire staff participates in IPB to develop and sustain an understanding of the enemy, terrain and weather, and civil considerations. IPB helps identify options available to friendly and threat forces. IPB consists of four steps. Each step is performed or assessed and refined to ensure that IPB products remain complete and relevant. The four IPB steps are—

- Define the Operational Environment
- Describe Environmental Effects On Operations/*Describe The Effects On Operations*
- Evaluate the Threat/*Adversary*
- Determine Threat/*Adversary* Courses Of Action

2. Targeting

Targeting is the process of selecting and prioritizing targets and matching the appropriate response to them, considering operational requirements and capabilities (JP 3-0). The purpose of targeting is to integrate and synchronize fires into operations. Targeting begins in planning, and it is an iterative process that continues through preparation and execution. The steps of the Army's targeting process are—

- Decide
- Detect
- Deliver
- Assess

3. Risk Management

Risk management is the process of identifying, assessing, and controlling risks arising from operational factors and making decisions that balance risk cost with mission benefits (JP 3-0). Identifying and accepting prudent risk is a principle of mission command. Throughout the operations process, commanders and staffs use risk management to identify and mitigate risks associated with all hazards that have the potential to injure or kill friendly and civilian personnel, damage or destroy equipment, or otherwise impact mission effectiveness. Like targeting, risk management begins in planning and continues through preparation and execution. Risk management consists of the following steps:

- Identify hazards
- Assess hazards to determine risks
- Develop controls and make risk decisions
- Implement controls
- Supervise and evaluate

B. Continuing Activities *(See p. 3-2)*

While units execute numerous tasks throughout the operations process, commanders and staffs always plan for and coordinate the following continuing activities:

1. Liaison

Liaison is that contact or intercommunication maintained between elements of military forces or other agencies to ensure mutual understanding and unity of purpose and action (JP 3-08). Most commonly used for establishing and maintaining close communications, liaison continuously enables direct, physical communications between commands. Commanders use liaison during operations and normal daily activities to help facilitate communications between organizations, preserve freedom of action, and maintain flexibility. Effective liaison ensures commanders that subordinates understand implicit coordination. Liaison provides commanders with relevant information and answers to operational questions, thus enhancing the commander's situational understanding.

2. Information Collection

Information collection is an activity that synchronizes and integrates the planning and employment of sensors, assets, and processing, exploitation, and dissemination systems in direct support of current and future operations. Information collection integrates the intelligence and operations staffs' functions that are focused on answering the commander's critical information requirements. For joint operations, this is referred to as intelligence, surveillance, and reconnaissance (ISR). The Army expands the joint ISR doctrine contained in JP 2-01 by defining information collection as an activity that focuses on answering the CCIRs. This highlights aspects that influence how the Army operates as a ground force in close and continuous contact with the threat and local populace. At the tactical level, reconnaissance, surveillance, security, and intelligence operations are the primary means by which a commander plans, organizes and executes tasks to answer the CCIR. Refer to FM 3-55 for a detailed discussion of information collection.

3. Security Operations

Commanders and staffs continuously plan for and coordinate security operations throughout the conduct of operations. Security operations are those operations undertaken by a commander to provide early and accurate warning of enemy operations, to provide the force being protected with time and maneuver space within which to react to the enemy, and to develop the situation to allow the commander to effectively use the protected force (FM 3-90). The five forms of security operations are screen, guard, cover, area security, and local security. *Refer to FM 3-90 for a detailed discussion of security operations.*

4. Terrain Management

Terrain management is the process of allocating terrain by establishing areas of operation, designating assembly areas, and specifying locations for units and activities to deconflict activities that might interfere with each other. Throughout the operations process, commanders assigned an area of operations manage terrain within their boundaries. Through terrain management, commanders identify and locate units in the area. The operations officer, with support from others in the staff, can then deconflict operations, control movements, and deter fratricide as units get in position to execute planned missions. Commanders also consider unified action partners located in their area of operations and coordinate with them for the use of terrain.

5. Airspace Control

Airspace control is the process used to increase operational effectiveness by promoting the safe, efficient, and flexible use of airspace (JP 3-52).Throughout the operations process, commanders and staffs must integrate and synchronize forces and war fighting functions within an area of operations (ground and air). Through airspace control, commanders and staffs establish both positive and procedural controls to maximize the use of air space to facilitate air-ground operations. Airspace is inherently joint, and the Army processes and systems used to control and manage airspace are joint compliant.

Principles of War and Joint Operations (Understand)

Ref: JP 3-0, Joint Operations (Aug '11), app. A.

The nine principles of war represent the most important nonphysical factors that affect the conduct of operations at the strategic, operational, and tactical levels. The Army published its original principles of war after World War I. In the following years, the Army adjusted the original principles modestly as they stood the tests of analysis, experimentation, and practice. The principles of war are not a checklist. While they are considered in all operations, they do not apply in the same way to every situation. Rather, they summarize characteristics of successful operations. Applied to the study of past campaigns, major operations, battles, and engagements, the principles of war are powerful analysis tools. Joint doctrine adds three principles of operations.

- **Objective.** Direct every military operation toward a clearly defined, decisive, and attainable objective.
- **Offensive.** Seize, retain, and exploit the initiative.
- **Mass.** Concentrate the effects of combat power at the decisive place and time.
- **Economy of Force.** Allocate minimum essential combat power to secondary efforts.
- **Maneuver.** Place the enemy in a disadvantageous position through the flexible application of combat power.
- **Unity of Command.** For every objective, ensure unity of effort under one responsible commander.
- **Security.** Never permit the enemy to acquire an unexpected advantage.
- **Surprise.** Strike the enemy at a time, place or in a manner for which he is unprepared.
- **Simplicity.** Prepare clear, uncomplicated plans and clear, concise orders to ensure thorough understanding.

Additional Principles of Joint Operations

In addition to these nine principles, JP 3-0 adds three principles of operations—perseverance, legitimacy, and restraint. Together with the principles of war, these twelve make up the principles of joint operations.

- **Perseverance.** Ensure the commitment necessary to attain the national strategic end state. Commanders prepare for measured, protracted military operations in pursuit of the desired national strategic end state. Some joint operations may require years to reach the desired end state. Resolving the underlying causes of the crisis may be elusive, making it difficult to achieve conditions supporting the end state.
- **Legitimacy.** Develop and maintain the will necessary to attain the national strategic end state. For Army forces, legitimacy comes from three important factors. First, the operation or campaign must be conducted under U.S. law. Second, the operation must be conducted according to international laws and treaties recognized by the United States, particularly the law of war. Third, the campaign or operation should develop or reinforce the authority and acceptance for the host-nation government by both the governed and the international community.
- **Restraint.** Limit collateral damage and prevent the unnecessary use of force. Restraint requires careful and disciplined balancing of security, the conduct of military operations, and the desired strategic end state. Excessive force antagonizes those friendly and neutral parties involved. Hence, it damages the legitimacy of the organization that uses it while potentially enhancing the legitimacy of any opposing party.

Chap 1

(The Operations Process)
A. Planning

Ref: ADRP 5-0, The Operations Process (Mar '12), chap. 2.

Planning is the art and science of understanding a situation, envisioning a desired future, and laying out effective ways of bringing that future about (ADP 5-0). Planning helps commanders create and communicate a common vision between commanders, their staffs, subordinate commanders, and unified action partners. Planning results in a plan and orders that synchronize the action of forces in time, space, and purpose to achieve objectives and accomplish missions.

Army Planning Methodologies

Successful planning requires the integration of both conceptual and detailed thinking. Army leaders employ three methodologies for planning, determining the appropriate mix based on the scope of the problem, their familiarity with it, the time available, and the availability of a staff. Methodologies that assist commanders and staffs with planning include:

Army Planning Methodologies

Army Design Methodology
See pp. 1-34 to 1-41.

The Military Decisionmaking Process (MDMP) *See pp. 2-1 to 2-56.*

Troop Leading Procedures (TLP)
See pp. 2-57 to 2-60.

Ref: ADRP 5-0, The Operations Process.

Planning is both a continuous and a cyclical activity of the operations process. While planning may start an iteration of the operations process, planning does not stop with the production of an order. During preparation and execution, the plan is continuously refined as the situation changes. Through assessment, subordinates and others provide feedback as to what is working, what is not working, and how the force can do things better. In some circumstances, commanders may determine that the current order (to include associated branches and sequels) is no longer relevant to the situation. In these instances, instead of modifying the current plan, commanders reframe the problem and develop an entirely new plan.

Planning may be highly structured, involving the commander, staff, subordinate commanders, and others to develop a fully synchronized plan or order. Planning may also be less structured, involving a platoon leader and squad leaders rapidly determining a scheme of maneuver for a hasty attack. Planning is conducted for different planning horizons, from long-range to short-range. Depending on the echelon and circumstances, units may plan in years, months, or weeks, or in days, hours, and minutes.

Plans and Orders

A product of planning is a plan or order—a directive for future action. Commanders issue plans and orders to subordinates to communicate their understanding of the situation and their visualization of an operation. A plan is a continuous, evolving framework of anticipated actions that maximizes opportunities. It guides subordinates as they progress through each phase of the operation. Any plan or order is a framework from which to adapt, not a script to be followed to the letter. The measure of a good plan is not whether execution transpires as planned, but whether the plan facilitates effective action in the face of unforeseen events. Good plans and orders foster initiative.

Plans and orders come in many forms and vary in the scope, complexity, and length of time they address. Generally, commanders and staffs develop a plan well in advance of execution, and the plan is not executed until directed. A plan becomes an order when directed for execution based on a specific time or event. Some planning results in written orders complete with attachments. Other planning produces brief fragmentary orders first issued verbally and then followed in writing.

See chap. 4, Plans and Orders, for further discussion.

Integrating Planning

Planning activities occupy a continuum ranging from conceptual to detail. On one end of the continuum is conceptual planning. Understanding the operational environment and the problem, determining the operation's end state, establishing objectives, and sequencing the operation in broad terms all illustrate conceptual planning. Conceptual planning generally corresponds to the art of operations and is the focus of the commander with staff support. The commander's activities of understanding and visualization are key aspects of conceptual planning.

At the other end of the continuum is detailed planning. Detailed planning translates the broad operational approach into a complete and practical plan. Generally, detailed planning is associated with the science of control, including movement rates, fuel consumption, weapon effects, and time-distance factors. Detailed planning falls under the purview of the staff, focusing on specifics of execution. Detailed planning works out the scheduling, coordination, or technical problems involved with moving, sustaining, synchronizing, and directing the force.

The commander personally leads the conceptual component of planning. While commanders are engaged in parts of detailed planning, they often leave the specifics to the staff. Conceptual planning provides the basis for all subsequent planning. For example, the commander's intent and operational approach provide the framework for the entire plan. This framework leads a concept of operations and associated schemes of support, such as schemes of intelligence, maneuver, fires, protection, and sustainment. In turn, the schemes of support lead to the specifics of execution, including tasks to subordinate units and detailed annexes to the operations plan or order. However, the dynamic does not operate in only one direction. Conceptual planning must respond to detailed constraints. For example, the realities of a deployment schedule (a detailed concern) influence the operational approach (a conceptual concern).

The Value Of Planning

Ref: ADRP 5-0, The Operations Process (Mar '12), pp. 2-1 to 2-3.

All planning is based on imperfect knowledge and assumptions about the future. Planning cannot predict exactly what the effects of the operation will be, how enemies will behave with precision, or how civilians will respond to the friendly force or the enemy. Nonetheless, the understanding and learning that occurs during planning have great value. Even if units do not execute the plan precisely as envisioned—and few ever do—the process of planning results in improved situational understanding that facilitates future decision-making. All military activities benefit from some kind of planning.

A. Understand and Develop Solutions to Problems

A problem is an issue or obstacle that makes it difficult to achieve a desired goal or objective. In a broad sense, a problem exists when an individual becomes aware of a significant difference between what actually is and what is desired. In the context of operations, an operational problem is the issue or set of issues that impede commanders from achieving their desired end state.

Throughout operations, leaders face various problems, often requiring unique and creative solutions. Planning helps commanders and staffs understand problems and develop solutions. Not all problems require the same level of planning.

Just as planning is only part of the operations process, planning is only part of problem solving. In addition to planning, problem solving includes implementing the planned solution (execution), learning from the implementation of the solution (assessment), and modifying or developing a new solution as required. The object of problem solving is not just to solve near-term problems, but to do so in a way that forms the basis for long-term success.

B. Anticipate Events & Adapt to Changing Circumstances

The defining challenges to effective planning are uncertainty and time. Uncertainty increases with the length of the planning horizon and the rate of change in an operational environment. A tension exists between the desire to plan far into the future to facilitate preparation and the fact that the farther into the future the commander plans, the less certain the plan will remain relevant. Given the uncertain nature of operations, the object of planning is not to eliminate uncertainty, but to develop a framework for action in the midst of such uncertainty.

Planning provides an informed forecast of how future events may unfold. It entails identifying and evaluating potential decisions and actions in advance to include thinking through consequences of certain actions. Planning involves thinking about ways to influence the future as well as how to respond to potential events. Put simply, planning is thinking critically and creatively about what to do and how to do it, while anticipating changes along the way.

C. Task-Organize the Force and Prioritize Efforts

A key aspect of planning is organizing the force for operations. Task-organizing is the act of configuring an operating force, support staff, or sustainment package of specific size and composition to meet a unique task or mission (ADRP 3-0). Through task organization, commanders establish command or support relationships and allocate resources to weight the **decisive operation** or **main effort**. Command and support relationships provide the basis for unity of command and unity of effort in operations.

In addition to task-organizing, commanders establish priorities of support. A priority of support is a priority set by the commander to ensure a subordinate unit has support in accordance with its relative importance to accomplish the mission. Priorities of movement, fires, sustainment, protection, and information all illustrate priorities of support that commanders use to weight the decisive operation, or the main effort in phased operations.

Problem Solving Steps

Ref: FM 6-0 (C1), Commander and Staff Organization and Operations (May '15), chap. 4.

Problem solving is a daily activity for leaders. Problem solving is a systematic way to arrive at the best solution to a problem. It applies at all echelons and includes the steps needed to develop well-reasoned, supportable solutions.

Note: These problem solving steps are not addressed in ADRP 5-0 (May '12).

1. Identify the Problem

The first step in problem solving is recognizing and defining the problem. A problem exists when there is a difference between the current state or condition and a desired state or condition. When identifying the problem, leaders actively seek to identify its root cause, not merely the symptoms on the surface. Using a systematic approach to identifying problems helps avoid the "solving symptoms" pitfall.

After identifying the root causes, leaders develop a problem statement. A problem statement is written as an infinitive phrase: such as, "To determine the best location for constructing a multipurpose vehicle wash rack facility during this fiscal year." When the problem under consideration is based upon a directive from a higher authority, it is best to submit the problem statement to the decision maker for approval.

Once they have developed the problem statement, leaders make a plan to solve the problem using the reverse-planning technique. Leaders make the best possible use of available time and allocate time for each problem-solving step.

2. Gather Information

After completing the problem statement, leaders continue to gather information relevant to the problem. Gathering information begins with problem definition and continues throughout the problem solving process. Leaders never stop acquiring and assessing the impact of new or additional information.

Leaders gather information from primary sources whenever possible.

Two types of information are required to solve problems: facts and assumptions.

Fully understanding these types of information is critical to understanding problem solving. In addition, leaders need to know how to handle opinions and how to manage information when working in a group.

- **Facts**. Facts are verifiable pieces of information or information presented that has objective reality.
- **Assumptions**. An assumption is information accepted as true in the absence of facts.

When gathering information, leaders evaluate opinions carefully. Opinions cannot be totally discounted. They are often the result of years of experience.

Organizing information includes coordination with units and agencies that may be affected by the problem or its solution.

3. Develop Criteria

The next step in the problem solving process is developing criteria. A criterion is a standard, rule, or test by which something can be judged-a measure of value. Problem solvers develop criteria to assist them in formulating and evaluating possible solutions to a problem. Criteria are based on facts or assumptions. Problem solvers develop two types of criteria: screening and evaluation criteria.

- **Screening Criteria**. Screening criteria defines the limits of an acceptable solution. As such, they are tools to establish the baseline products for analysis.
- **Evaluation Criteria**. After developing screening criteria, the problem solver develops the evaluation criteria in order to differentiate among possible solutions. Well-defined evaluation criteria have five elements: short title, definition, unit of measure, benchmark, and a formula.

Pair wise comparison is an analytical tool that brings objectivity to the process of assigning criteria weights. In performing a pair wise comparison, the decision maker or expert methodically assesses each evaluation criterion against each of the others and judges its relative importance.

4. Generate Possible Solutions

After gathering information relevant to the problem and developing criteria, leaders formulate possible solutions. They carefully consider the guidance provided by the commander or their superiors, and develop several alternatives to solve the problem. Several alternatives should be considered, however too many possible solutions may result in wasted time. Experience and time available determine how many solutions to consider. Leaders should consider at least two solutions. Doing this enables the problem solver to use both analysis and comparison as problem solving tools. Developing only one solution to "save time" may produce a faster solution, but risks creating more problems from factors not considered. Generating solutions has two steps:

- Generate Options. The basic technique for developing new ideas in a group setting is brainstorming.

- Summarize the Solution in Writing and Sketches

5. Analyze Possible Solutions

Having identified possible solutions, leaders analyze each one to determine its merits and drawbacks. If criteria are well defined, to include careful selection of benchmarks, analysis is greatly simplified.

Leaders use screening criteria and benchmarks to analyze possible solutions. They apply screening criteria to judge whether a solution meets minimum requirements. For quantitative criteria, they measure, compute, or estimate the raw data values for each solution and each criterion. In analyzing solutions, which involve predicting future events, it is useful to have a process for visualizing those events. Wargaming, models, and simulations are examples of tools that can help problem solvers visualize events and estimate raw data values for use in analysis. Once raw data values have been determined, the leader judges them against applicable screening criteria to determine if a possible solution merits further consideration. A solution that fails to meet or exceed the set threshold of one or more screening criteria is screened out.

6. Compare Possible Solutions

During this step, leaders compare each solution against the others to determine the optimum solution. Solution comparison identifies which solution best solves the problem based on the evaluation criteria. Leaders use any comparison technique that helps reach the best recommendation. Quantitative techniques (such as decision matrices, select weights, and sensitivity analyses) may be used to support comparisons. However, they are tools to support the analysis and comparison. They are not the analysis and comparison themselves. *The most common technique is a decision matrix (see p. 2-49).*

7. Make and Implement the Decision

After completing their analysis and comparison, leaders identify the preferred solution. For simple problems, leaders may proceed straight to executing the solution. For more complex problems, a leader plan of action or formal plan may be necessary (see FM 22-100). If a superior assigned the problem, leaders prepare the necessary products (verbal, written, or both) needed to present the recommendation to the decision maker. Before presenting findings and a recommendation, leaders coordinate their recommendation with those affected by the problem or the solutions. In formal situations, leaders present their findings and recommendations as staff studies, decision papers, or decision briefings

Once leaders have given instructions, leaders monitor their implementation and compare results to the criteria of success and the desired end state established in the approved solution. A feedback system that provides timely and accurate information, periodic review, and the flexibility to adjust must also be built into the implementation plan.

Problem solving does not end with identifying the best solution or obtaining approval of a recommendation. It ends when the problem is solved.

Joint Operation Planning

Ref: JP 5-0, Joint Operation Planning (Aug '11).

Joint operation planning consists of planning activities associated with joint military operations by combatant commanders (CCDRs) and their subordinate joint force commanders (JFCs) in response to contingencies and crises. It **transforms national strategic objectives into activities** by development of operational products that include planning for the mobilization, deployment, employment, sustainment, redeployment, and demobilization of joint forces. It ties the **military instrument of national power** to the achievement of **national security goals and objectives** and is essential to securing strategic end states across the range of military operations.

Joint Operation Planning Activities

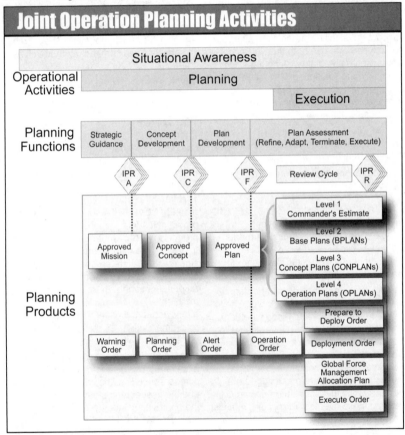

Ref: JP 5-0, Joint Operation Planning, fig. II-5, p II-14.

Joint operation planning provides a common basis for discussion, understanding, and change for the joint force, its subordinate and higher headquarters, the joint planning and execution community (JPEC), and the national leadership. The **Adaptive Planning and Execution (APEX)** system facilitates iterative dialogue and collaborative planning between the multiple echelons of command to ensure that the military instrument of national power is employed in accordance with national priorities, and that the plan is continuously reviewed and updated as required and adapted according to changes in strategic guidance, resources, or the operational environment.

(Joint) Deliberate and Crisis Action Planning

Planning translates strategic guidance and direction into campaign plans, contingency plans, and operation orders (OPORDs). Joint operation planning may be based on defined tasks identified in the GEF and the JSCP. Alternatively, joint operation planning may be based on the need for a military response to an unforeseen current event, emergency, or time-sensitive crisis.

Deliberate and Crisis Action Planning

I Deliberate Planning

(Campaign and Contingency Planning)

II Crisis Action Planning (CAP)

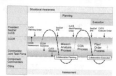

(Current Event, Emergency or Time-Sensitive Crisis)

Joint operation planning encompasses the preparation of a number of planning and execution-related products produced during deliberate planning or CAP.

Deliberate Planning

Deliberate planning encompasses the preparation of plans that occur in non-crisis situations. It is used to develop campaign and contingency plans for a broad range of activities based on requirements identified in the GEF, JSCP, or other planning directives. Theater and global campaign plans are the centerpiece of DOD's planning construct. They provide the means to translate CCMD theater or functional strategies into executable plans.

Crisis Action Planning (CAP)

Planning for crises is initiated to respond to an unforeseen current event, emergency, or time-sensitive crisis. It is based on planning guidance, actual circumstances, and usually limits force planning considerations to apportioned forces.

Crisis Action Planning (CAP) provides the CJCS and CCDRs a process for getting vital decision-making information up the chain of command to the President and SecDef. It also outlines the mechanisms for monitoring the execution of the operation. CAP encompasses the activities associated with the time-sensitive development of OPORDs for the deployment, employment, and sustainment of assigned, attached, and allocated forces and capabilities in response to a situation that may result in actual military operations. CAP procedures provide for the rapid and effective exchange of information and analysis, the timely preparation of military COAs for consideration by the President or SecDef, and the prompt transmission of their decisions to the JPEC.

Refer to The Joint Forces Operations & Doctrine SMARTbook (Guide to Joint, Multinational & Interagency Operations) for complete discussion of joint strategic planning -- to include strategic direction, deliberate and crisis action planning, operational art and design, the Joint Operation Planning Process (JOPP), joint operation plan (OPLAN) format, assessment, and the fundamentals of joint targeting.

I. Army Design Methodology

Army design methodology is an approach for applying critical and creative thinking to understand, visualize, and describe problems and approaches to solving them (ADP 5-0). Army design methodology is particularly useful as an aid to conceptual planning, but must be integrated with the detailed planning typically associated with the MDMP to produce executable plans. Key concepts that underline the Army design methodology include:

- Critical and creative thinking *(see p. 1-11)*
- Collaboration and dialogue *(see p. 1-12)*
- Framing
- Narrative construction
- Visual modeling

Framing

Framing is the act of building mental models to help individuals understand situations and respond to events. Framing involves selecting, organizing, interpreting, and making sense of an operational environment and a problem by establishing context. How individuals or groups frame a problem will influence potential solutions. For example, an organization that frames an insurgent group as "freedom fighters" probably will approach solving a conflict differently from an organization that frames the insurgent group as "terrorists."

The Army design methodology involves deliberately framing an operational environment and problem through dialogue and critical and creative thinking by a group. The group considers the perspective and world views of others to understand the situation fully. This contextual understanding of an operational environment serves as a frame of reference for developing solutions to solve problems. Framing facilitates constructing hypotheses, or modeling, that focuses on the part of an operational environment or problem under consideration. Framing provides a perspective from which commanders and staffs can understand and act on a problem. Narrative construction and visual modeling facilitate framing.

Narrative Construction

In a broad sense, a narrative is a story constructed to give meaning to things and events. Individuals, groups, organizations, and countries all have narratives with many components that reflect and reveal how they define themselves. Political parties, social organizations, and government institutions, for example, all have stories bound chronologically and spatially. They incorporate symbols, historical events, and artifacts tied together with a logic that explains their reason for being. To narrate is to engage in the production of a story—an explanation of an event or phenomenon by proposing a question or questions in relation to the artifacts themselves. These questions may include:

- What is the meaning of what I see?
- Where does the story begin and end?
- What happened, is happening, and why?

Narrative construction—the conscious bounding of events and artifacts in time and space—is central to framing. Commanders, staffs, and unified action partners construct a narrative to help understand and explain the operational environment, the problem, and the solutions. Not only is the narrative useful in communicating to others, the act of constructing the narrative itself is a key learning event for the command.

Operational Art and Planning

Ref: ADRP 5-0, The Operations Process (Mar '12), p. 2-4 and ADRP 3-0, Unified Land Operations (Mar '12), pp. 4-2 to 4-9.

Conceptual planning is directly associated to operational art—the cognitive approach by commanders and staffs—supported by their skill, knowledge, experience, creativity, and judgment—to develop strategies, campaigns, and operations to organize and employ military forces by integrating ends, ways, and means (JP 3-0). Operational art is a thought process that guides conceptual and detailed planning to produce executable plans and orders.

In applying operational art, commanders and their staffs use a set of intellectual tools to help them communicate a common vision of the operational environment as well as visualizing and describing the operational approach. Collectively, this set of tools is known as the elements of operational art. These tools help commanders understand, visualize, and describe combinations of combat power and help them formulate their intent and guidance. Commanders selectively use these tools in any operation. However, their application is broadest in the context of long-term operations. These tools are useful when using Army design methodology and the military decision-making process and may frequently be used in both, simultaneously.

The elements of operational art support the commander in identifying objectives that link tactical missions to the desired end state. They help refine and focus the operational approach that forms the basis for developing a detailed plan or order. During execution, commanders and staffs consider the elements of operational art as they assess the situation. They adjust current and future operations and plans as the operation unfolds.

Elements of *Operational Design*

Within operational art, joint force commanders and staffs consider elements of operational design. Elements of operational design are individual tools that help the joint force commander and staff visualize and describe the broad operational approach.

- Termination
- Military end state
- Objective
- Effects
- Center of gravity
- Decisive point
- Lines of operations and lines of effort
- Direct and indirect approach
- Anticipation
- Operational reach
- Culmination
- Arranging operations
- Force and functions

Refer to The Joint Forces Operations & Doctrine SMARTbook and JP 3-0 for further discussion (operational design).

Elements of *Operational Art*

As some elements of operational design apply only to joint force commanders, the Army modifies the elements of operational design into elements of operational art, adding Army specific elements. During the planning and execution of Army operations, Army commanders and staffs consider the elements of operational art as they assess the situation.

- End state and conditions
- Center of gravity
- Decisive points
- Lines of operations and lines of effort
- Operational reach
- Basing
- Tempo
- Phasing and transitions
- Culmination
- Risk

Refer to The Army Operations & Doctrine SMARTbook and ADRP 3-0 for further discussion (elements of operational art).

Visual Modeling

Army design methodology relies heavily on forming and presenting ideas in both narrative and visual (graphic) form. Visual information tends to be stimulating and therefore, creativity can be enhanced by using visual models and constructs. The complexity of some problems requires creating a model of the problem. A visual model, based on logical inference from evidence, helps creative thought to develop into understanding. A graphic can often point to hidden relationships that were not considered through conversation alone. In addition, visually displaying periodic summaries of work helps individuals see the results of what is being thought. This, in turn, points to new ways of thinking and possible areas for further examination. In other words, seeing something drawn graphically helps individuals think through challenging problems, especially when examining abstract concepts.

Activities of the Army Design Methodology

Army design methodology entails framing an operational environment, framing a problem, and developing an operational approach to solve the problem. Army design methodology results in an improved understanding of the operational environment, a problem statement, initial commander's intent, and an operational approach that serves as the link between conceptual and detailed planning. Based on their understanding and learning gained during Army design methodology, commanders issue planning guidance, to include an operational approach, to guide more detailed planning using the MDMP.

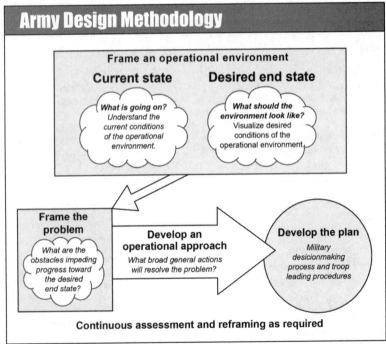

Ref: ADRP 5-0, The Operations Process, fig. 2-2, p. 2-6.

The understanding developed through Army design methodology continues through preparation and execution in the form of continuous assessment. Assessment, to include updated running estimates, helps commanders measure the overall effectiveness of employing forces and capabilities to ensure that the operational approach remains feasible and acceptable within the context of the higher commander's intent and concept of operations. If the current operational approach fails to meet these criteria, or if aspects of the operational environment or problem change significantly, the commander may decide to reframe. Reframing involves revisiting earlier hypotheses, conclusions, and decisions that underpin the current operational approach. Reframing can lead to a new problem statement and operational approach, resulting in an entirely new plan. While planners complete some activities before others, the learning generated in one activity may require revisiting the learning derived in another activity. The movement between the activities is not entirely unidirectional, because what the commander, staff, and partners learn later will affect previous conclusions and decisions.

A. Frame an Operational Environment

The commander, members of the staff, subordinate commanders, and unified action partners act as a planning team to establish context for describing the problem and developing an operational approach by framing an operational environment. This framing facilitates hypothesizing, or modeling, that focuses on the part of the operational environment under consideration. Framing provides a perspective from which commanders can understand and act on a complex problem.

In framing an operational environment, the planning team focuses on defining, analyzing, and synthesizing the characteristics of the operational and mission variables. Members of the planning team capture their work in an operational environmental frame (using narrative and visual models) that describes and depicts the history, culture, current state, relationships, and future goals of relevant actors in an operational environment. An operational environmental frame consists of two parts—the current state of the operational environment and the desired end state of the operational environment.

See pp. 1-16 to 1-17 for discussion of operational and mission variables.

1. Current State of an Operational Environment

The commander and staff develop a contextual understanding of the situation by framing the current conditions of an operational environment. In doing so, the planning team considers the characteristics of all the operation and mission variables relevant to a particular operational environment. This includes identifying and explaining behaviors of relevant actors in the operational environment. An actor is an individual or group within a social network who acts to advance personal interests. Relevant actors may include individuals, states and governments, coalitions, terrorist networks, and criminal organizations. They may also include multinational corporations, nongovernmental organizations, and others able to influence the situation.

A diagram illustrating relevant actor relationships enables understanding and visualizing the operational environment. Often relationships among actors have many facets, and these relationships differ depending on the scale of interaction and temporal aspects (history, duration, type, and frequency). Clarifying the relationships among actors requires intense effort since these relationships must be examined from multiple perspectives. Commanders can also depict relationships by identifying and categorizing their unique characteristics.

See following page (p. 1-39) for a sample presentation diagram.

2. Desired End State of an Operational Environment

The second part of an operational environmental frame involves envisioning desired conditions of an operational environment (a desired end state). A desired end state consists of those desired conditions that, if achieved, meet the objectives of policy, orders, guidance, and directives issued by higher authorities. A condition is a reflection of the existing state of the operational environment. Thus, a desired condition is a sought-after future state of the operational environment.

Conditions may be tangible or intangible, military or nonmilitary. They may focus on physical or psychological factors. When describing conditions that constitute a desired end state, the commander considers their relevance to higher policy, orders, guidance, or directives. Since every operation focuses on a clearly defined, decisive, and attainable end state, success hinges on accurately describing those conditions. These conditions form the basis for decisions that ensure operations progress consistently toward a desired end state.

A method for envisioning a desired end state is to consider the natural tendencies and potential of relevant actors. Tendencies reflect the inclination to think or behave in a certain manner. Tendencies identify the likely pattern of relationships between the actors without external influence. Once identified, commanders and staffs evaluate the potential of these tendencies to manifest within the operational environment. Potential is the inherent ability or capacity for the growth or development of a specific interaction or relationship. Not all interactions and relationships support achieving a desired end state. A desired end state accounts for tendencies and potentials that exist among the relevant actors or other aspects of the operational variables in an operational environment frame.

See facing page (p. 1-39) for a sample presentation diagram.

B. Frame the Problem

A problem is an issue or obstacle that makes it difficult to achieve a desired goal or objective. In a broad sense, a problem exists when an individual becomes aware of a significant difference between what actually is and what is desired. In the context of operations, an operational problem is the issue or set of issues that impede commanders from achieving their desired end state. Problem framing involves identifying and understanding those issues that impede progress toward the desired end state.

The planning team frames the problem to ensure that they are solving the right problem, instead of solving the symptoms of the problem. Framing the problem involves understanding and isolating the root causes of conflict. The planning team closely examines the symptoms, the underlying tensions, and the root causes of conflict. Tension is the resistance or friction among and between actors. From this perspective, the planning team can identify the fundamental problem with greater clarity and consider more accurately how to solve it. A technique for framing the problem begins with two basic questions:

- What is the difference between the current state and the desired state of the operational environment?
- What is preventing US forces from reaching the desired end state?

Answers to these questions help identify the problem. For example, based on the operational environment frame of Newland, the planning team may start to ask:

- Is the problem General E?
- Is the problem the drug cartels?
- Is the problem the Newland defense force?

Based on the problem frame, the planning team develops a problem statement—a concise statement of the issue or issues requiring resolution. A potential problem statement based on the sample operational environment frame and problem frame of Newland follows:

The Newland defense force is the primary impediment to establishing a democratic government in Newland and the primary factor of instability in the region. For over forty years, the Newland defense force has maintained power for itself and the regime by oppressing all opposition within society. In addition, the Newland defense force has a history of intimidating Country Z through force (both overtly and covertly). Corruption in the Newland defense force is rampant within the leadership, and it has close ties to several drug cartels. General E is the latest of two dictators emerging

Frame an Operational Environment (Example)

Ref: ADRP 5-0, The Operations Process (Mar '12), pp. 2-6 to 2-9.

A diagram illustrating relevant actor relationships enables understanding and visualizing the operational environment. Often relationships among actors have many facets, and these relationships differ depending on the scale of interaction and temporal aspects (history, duration, type, and frequency). Clarifying the relationships among actors requires intense effort since these relationships must be examined from multiple perspectives. Commanders can also depict relationships by identifying and categorizing their unique characteristics.

Current State of an Operational Environment

Ref: ADRP 5-0, The Operations Process, fig. 2-3, p. 2-8.

The Newland defense force controls the population and provides General E his power. The president, in turn, provides direction and power to the Newland defense force to control the society. The people are expected to comply with the direction provided by the president and the Newland defense forces. Those who do not comply are oppressed. In exchange for sanctuary, the drug cartels provide funding to the regime. They also harass and terrorize the section of the society that opposes the regime. Countries X and Y provide material capabilities to the Newland defense force and international legitimacy to the regime. In turn, the regime maintains an anti-U.S. policy stance. Over the last six months, over 100,000 persons have fled Newland to Country Z. It is temporarily providing Newland refugees humanitarian assistance and protection. Several border clashes have erupted between Newland defense forces and Country Z

in the last three weeks. The antidemocratic dictatorship of Newland that oppresses its people encourages instability in the region, and supports criminal and terrorist activities is unacceptable to U.S. interests.

Desired End State of an Operational Environment

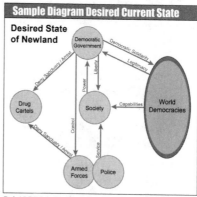

Ref: ADRP 5-0, The Operations Process, fig. 2-4, p. 2-9.

The country of Newland is a friendly democracy that no longer oppresses its people, threatens its neighbors, or provides sanctuary for criminal and terrorist organizations. The society has replaced the Newland defense force as the source of power for the democratic government. The Newland defense force is replaced with an army and navy that serves the society and protects the country from external aggression. Local and national police forces serve the population by providing law and order for society. World democracies support the new government by providing legitimacy and capabilities to the government of Newland and the society. In turn, the new government of Newland supports the rule of law among nations and human rights.

from the Newland defense force. Even if General E is removed from power, the potential of a new dictator emerging from the Newland defense force is likely. There is no indication that the leadership of the Newland defense force is willing to relinquish their power within Newland.

C. Develop an Operational Approach

Based on their understanding of the operational environment and the problem, the planning team considers operational approaches—the broad general actions—to solve the problem. The operational approach serves as the main idea that informs detailed planning and guides the force through preparation and execution.

The planning team uses the elements of operational art (see ADRP 3-0) to help think through the operational environment and visualize and describe the operational approach. As the planning team considers various approaches, it evaluates the types of defeat or stability mechanisms that may lead to conditions that define the desired end state. Thus, the operational approach enables commanders to begin visualizing and describing possible combinations of actions to reach the desired end state, given the tensions identified in the operational environment and problem frames. The staff uses operational approaches to develop courses of action during detailed planning.

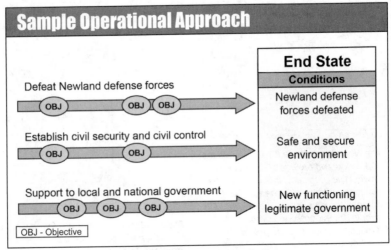

Ref: ADRP 5-0, The Operations Process, fig. 2-5, p. 2-10.

Planners can depict the operational approach by using lines of effort that graphically articulate the links among tasks, objectives, conditions, and the desired end state. Army design methodology offers the latitude to portray the operational approach in a manner that best communicates its vision and structure. Ultimately, the commander determines the optimal method to articulate the operational approach. However, it is important that narratives accompany lines of effort to ensure subordinate commanders and Soldiers understand the operational approach.

Document Results

Commanders and staffs document the results of Army design methodology to inform more detailed planning. Key outputs of Army design methodology conveyed in text and graphics include:

- Problem statement
- Initial commander's intent
- Planning guidance, to include an operational approach

The problem statement generated during problem framing communicates the commander's understanding of the problem or problem set upon which the organization will act. The initial commander's intent describes the purpose of the operation and the desired end state. The operational approach organizes combinations of potential actions in time, space, and purpose that will guide the force to the desired end state. Planning guidance orients the focus of operations, linking desired conditions to potential combinations of actions the force may employ to achieve the desired end state.

Reframing

Through continuous assessment, the commander and staff monitor the operational environment and progress toward setting conditions and achieving objectives. Assessment helps commanders measure the overall effectiveness of employing forces and capabilities to ensure that the operational approach remains feasible and acceptable in the context of the higher commander's intent and concept of operations. If the current operational approach is failing to meet these criteria, or if aspects of the operational environment or problem change significantly, the commander may decide to begin reframing efforts.

Reframing is the activity of revisiting earlier design hypotheses, conclusions, and decisions that underpin the current operational approach. In essence, reframing reviews what the commander and staff believe they understand about the operational environment, the problem, and the desired end state. At any time during the operations process, the decision to reframe may be triggered by factors such as—

- Assessment reveals a lack of progress
- Key assumptions prove invalid
- Unanticipated success or failure
- A major event that causes "catastrophic change" in the operational environment
- A scheduled periodic review that shows a problem
- A change in mission or end state issued by higher authority

During operations, commanders decide to reframe after realizing the desired conditions have changed, are not achievable, cannot be attained through the current operational approach, or because of change of mission or end state. Reframing provides the freedom to operate beyond the limits of any single perspective. Conditions will change during execution, and such change is expected because forces interact within the operational environment. Recognizing and anticipating these changes is fundamental to Army design methodology and essential to an organization's ability to learn.

II. The Military Decisionmaking Process (MDMP)

The military decisionmaking process is an iterative planning methodology to understand the situation and mission develop a course of action, and produce an operation plan or order (ADP 5-0). The military decisionmaking process (MDMP) integrates the activities of the commander, staff, subordinate headquarters, and unified action partners to understand the situation and mission; develop and compare courses of action; decide on a course of action that best accomplishes the mission; and produce an operation plan or order for execution. The MDMP helps leaders apply thoroughness, clarity, sound judgment, logic, and professional knowledge to understand situations, develop options to solve problems, and reach decisions. The MDMP results in an improved understanding of the situation and a plan or order that guides the force through preparation and execution.

The MDMP consists of seven steps. Each step of the MDMP has various inputs, a method (step) to conduct, and outputs. The outputs lead to an increased understanding of the situation and to facilitating the next step of the MDMP. Commanders and staffs generally perform these steps sequentially; however, they may revisit several steps in an iterative fashion, as they learn more about the situation before.

See chap. 2, Military Decisionmaking Process (MDMP), for complete discussion.

Key Components of a Plan

Ref: ADRP 5-0, The Operations Process (Mar '12), pp. 2-14 to 2-22.

The unit's task organization, mission statement, commander's intent, concept of operations, tasks to subordinate units, coordinating instructions, and control measures are key components of a plan. Commanders ensure their mission and end state nest with those of their higher headquarters. While the commander's intent focuses on the end state, the concept of operations focuses on the way or sequence of actions by which the force will achieve the end state. The concept of operations expands on the mission statement and commander's intent. Within the concept of operations, commanders may establish objectives as intermediate goals toward achieving the operation's end state. When developing tasks for subordinate units, commanders ensure that the purpose of each task nests with the accomplishment of another task, with the achievement of an objective, or directly to the attainment of an end state condition.

Task Organization

Task organization is a temporary grouping of forces designed to accomplish a particular mission. Commanders task organize the force by establishing command and support relationships. **Command relationships** define command responsibility and authority. Support relationships define the purpose, scope, and effect desired when one capability supports another. The unit's task organization is in the base plan or order or in Annex A (Task Organization). Army **support relationships** are similar but not identical to joint support relationships. See JP 3-0 for a discussion of joint command and support relationships.

See pp. 4-7 to 4-14 for further discussion of task organization. Command relationships are discussed on p. 4-10 and support relationships are discussed on p. 4-11.

Mission Statement

The mission is the task, together with the purpose, that clearly indicates the action to be taken and the reason therefore (JP 3-0). Commanders analyze a mission as the commander's intent two echelons above them, specified tasks, and implied tasks. They also consider the mission of adjacent units to understand how they contribute to the decisive operation of their higher headquarters. Results of that analysis yield the essential tasks that—with the purpose of the operation—clearly specify the action required. This analysis produces the unit's mission statement—a clear statement of the action to be taken and the reason for taking it. The mission statement contains the elements of who, what, when, where, and why, but seldom specifies how. The format for writing a task to subordinate units also follows this format.

Commander's Intent

The commander's intent succinctly describes what constitutes success for the operation. It includes the operation's purpose, key tasks, and the conditions that define the end state. It links the mission, concept of operations, and tasks to subordinate units. A clear commander's intent facilitates a shared understanding and focuses on the overall conditions that represent mission accomplishment. During execution, the commander's intent spurs disciplined initiative.

The commander's intent must be easy to remember and clearly understood by leaders and Soldiers two echelons lower in the chain of command. The shorter the commander's intent, the better it serves these purposes. Commanders develop their intent statement personally using the following components:

- Expanded purpose
- Key tasks
- End state

When describing the **expanded purpose** of the operations, the commander's intent does not restate the "why" of the mission statement. Rather, it addresses the broader purpose of the operations and its relationship to the force as a whole. **Key tasks** are those activities the force most perform as a whole to achieve the desired end state. Key tasks are not specified tasks for any subordinate unit; however, they may be sources of implied tasks. Acceptable courses of action accomplish all key tasks. During execution—when significant opportunities present themselves or the concept of operations no longer fits the situation—subordinates use key tasks to keep their efforts focused on achieving the desired end state. The **end state** is a set of desired future conditions the commander wants to exist when an operation is concluded. Commanders describe the operation's end state by stating the desired conditions of the friendly force in relationship to desired conditions of the enemy, terrain, and civil considerations. A clearly defined end state promotes unity of effort among the force and with unified action partners.

Concept of Operations

The concept of operations is a statement that directs the manner in which subordinate units cooperate to accomplish the mission and establishes the sequence of actions the force will use to achieve the end state. The concept of operations expands on the commander's intent by describing how the commander wants the force to accomplish the mission. It states the principal tasks required, the responsible subordinate units, and how the principal tasks complement one another. Commanders and staff use the following operational frameworks to help conceptualize and describe their concept of operation:

- Deep-close-security
- Decisive-shaping-sustaining
- Main and supporting effort

See pp. 1-20 to 1-21 for further discussion of this operational framework from ADRP 3-0.

In addition to the operational frameworks, commanders and staffs consider nested concepts, the sequence of actions and phasing, decisive points and objectives, and lines of operations and lines of effort when conceptualizing and describing the concept of operations.

Tasks to Subordinate Units

Tasks to subordinate units direct individual units to perform a specific action. Tasks are specific activities that contribute to accomplishing missions or other requirements. Tasks direct friendly action. The purpose of each task should nest with completing another task, achieving an objective, or attaining an end state condition. When developing tasks for subordinate units, commanders and staffs use the same who, what (task), when, where, and why (purpose) construct that they did to develop the unit's mission statement. Sometimes commanders may want to specify the type or form of operation to use to accomplish a task.

Coordinating Instructions

Coordinating instructions apply to two or more units. They are located in the coordinating instructions subparagraph of paragraph 3 (execution) of plans or orders. Examples include CCIRs, fire support coordination and airspace coordinating measures, rules of engagement, risk mitigation measures, and the time or condition when the operation order becomes effective.

Control Measures

Commanders exercise control through control measures established throughout an OPLAN or OPORD. A control measure is a means of regulating forces or warfighting functions (ADP 6-0). Control measures are established under a commander's authority; however, commanders may authorize staff officers and subordinate leaders to establish them. Commanders may use control measures for several purposes: for example, to assign responsibilities, require synchronization between forces, impose restrictions, or establish guidelines to regulate freedom of action. Control measures are essential to coordinating subordinates' actions. They can be permissive or restrictive. Permissive control measures allow specific actions to occur; restrictive control measures limit the conduct of certain actions.

Guides to Effective Planning

Ref: ADRP 5-0, The Operations Process (Mar '12), pp. 2-22 to 2-24.

Planning helps commanders understand and develop solutions to problems, anticipate events, adapt to changing circumstances, task-organize the force, and prioritize efforts. Effective planning requires dedication, study, and practice. Planners must be technically and tactically competent within their areas of expertise and disciplined in the use of doctrinally correct terms and symbols. The following guides aid in effective planning:

Commanders Focus Planning

Commanders are the most important participants in effective planning. They focus the planning effort by providing their commander's intent, issuing planning guidance, and making decisions throughout the planning process. Commanders apply discipline to the planning process to meet the requirements of time, planning horizons, simplicity, level of detail, and desired outcomes. Commanders ensure that all operation plans and orders comply with domestic and international laws. They also confirm that the plan or order is relevant and suitable for subordinates. Generally, the more involved commanders are in planning, the faster staffs can plan. Through personal involvement, commanders ensure the plan reflects their commander's intent.

Develop Simple, Flexible Plans Through Mission Orders

Effective plans and orders are simple and direct. Staffs prepare clear, concise orders that communicate a clear understanding of the operation through the use of doctrinally correct operational terms and symbols. Doing this minimizes chances of misunderstanding. Clarity and brevity are key components of effective plans. Developing shorter, rather than longer, plans aids in maintaining simplicity. Shorter plans are easier to disseminate, read, and remember.

Flexible plans help units adapt quickly to changing circumstances. Commanders and planners build opportunities for initiative into plans by anticipating events. This allows them to operate inside of the enemy's decision cycle or to react promptly to deteriorating situations. Identifying decision points and designing branches ahead of time—combined with a clear commander's intent—help create flexible plans.

Commanders stress the importance of using mission orders as a way of building simple, flexible plans. Mission orders are directives that emphasize to subordinates the results to be attained, not how they are to achieve them (ADP 6-0). Mission orders clearly convey the unit's mission and the commander's intent. Mission orders focus subordinates on what to do and the purpose of doing it, without prescribing exactly how to do it. Commanders establish control measures to aid cooperation among forces without imposing needless restriction on freedom of action.

Optimize Available Planning Time

Time is a critical variable in operations. Therefore, time management is important in planning. Whether done deliberately or rapidly, all planning requires the skillful use of available time to optimize planning and preparation throughout the unit. Taking more time to plan often results in greater synchronization; however, any delay in execution risks yielding the initiative—with more time to prepare and act—to the enemy. When allocating planning time to staffs, commanders must ensure subordinates have enough time to plan and prepare their own actions prior to execution. Commanders follow the **"one-third—two-thirds rule"** as a guide to allocate time available. They use one-third of the time available before execution for their planning and allocate the remaining two-thirds of the time available before execution to their subordinates for planning and preparation.

Both collaborative and parallel planning help optimize available planning time. **Collaborative planning** is several echelons developing plans and orders together. Commanders, subordinate commanders, and staffs share their understanding of the situation and participate in course of action development and decisionmaking for development of the higher headquarters plan or order.

Parallel planning is two or more echelons planning for the same operation through the sequential sharing of information through warning orders from the higher headquarters prior to the higher headquarters publishing their operation plan or operation order. Since several echelons develop their plans simultaneously, parallel planning can significantly shorten planning time. The higher headquarters continuously shares information concerning future operations with subordinate units through warning orders and other means. Frequent communication between commanders and staffs and sharing of information (such as intelligence preparation of the battlefield products) help subordinate headquarters plan. Parallel planning requires significant interaction among echelons. During parallel planning, subordinate units do not wait for their higher headquarters to publish an order to begin developing their own plans and orders.

Higher commanders are sensitive not to overload subordinates with planning requirements. Generally, the higher the headquarters, the more time and staff resources are available to plan and explore options. Higher headquarters involve subordinates with developing those plans and concepts that have the highest likelihood of being adopted or fully developed.

Planning Pitfalls

Commanders and staffs recognize the value of planning and avoid common planning pitfalls. These pitfalls generally stem from a common cause: the failure to appreciate the unpredictability and uncertainty of military operations. Pointing these out is not a criticism of planning, but of planning improperly. The four pitfalls consist of—

Attempting to forecast and dictate events too far into the future

The first pitfall, attempting to forecast and dictate events too far into the future, may result from believing a plan can control the future. Planners tend to plan based on assumptions that the future will be a linear continuation of the present. These plans often underestimate the scope of changes in directions that may occur and the results of second- and third-order effects. Even the most effective plans cannot anticipate all the unexpected events. Often, events overcome plans much sooner than anticipated. Effective plans include sufficient branches and sequels to account for the nonlinear nature of events.

Trying to plan in too much detail

The second pitfall consists of trying to plan in too much detail. Sound plans include necessary details; however, planning in unnecessary detail consumes limited time and resources that subordinates need. This pitfall often stems from the desire to leave as little as possible to chance. In general, the less certain the situation, the fewer details a plan should include. However, planners often respond to uncertainty by planning in more detail to try to account for every possibility. Preparing detailed plans under uncertain conditions generates even more anxiety, which leads to even more detailed planning. Often this over planning results in an extremely detailed plan that does not survive the friction of the situation and constricts effective action.

Using the plan as a script for execution

The third pitfall, using the plan as a script for execution, tries to prescribe the course of events with precision. When planners fail to recognize the limits of foresight and control, the plan can become a coercive and overly regulatory mechanism. Commanders, staffs, and subordinates mistakenly focus on meeting the requirements of the plan rather than deciding and acting effectively.

Institutionalizing rigid planning methods

The fourth pitfall is the danger of institutionalizing rigid planning methods that leads to inflexible or overly structured thinking. This tends to make planning rigidly focused on the process and produces plans that overly emphasize detailed procedures. Effective planning provides a disciplined framework for approaching and solving complex problems. The danger is in taking that discipline to the extreme.

Army Design Methodology and the Military Decision-making Process (MDMP)

Depending on the situation—to include the familiarity of the problem—commanders conduct Army design methodology before, in parallel with, or after the MDMP. When faced with an unfamiliar problem or when developing initial plans for extended operations, commanders often initiate the Army design methodology before the MDMP. This sequence helps them better understand the operational environment, frame the problem, and develop an operational approach to guide more detailed planning.

Commanders may also elect to conduct the Army design methodology in parallel with the MDMP. In this instance, members of the staff conduct mission analysis as the commander and other staff members engage in framing the operational environment and the problem. Knowledge products—such as results from intelligence preparation of the battlefield and running estimates—help inform the Army design methodology team about the operational environment. Commanders may direct some staff members to focus their mission analysis on certain areas. This focus helps commanders better understand aspects of the operational environment. The results of mission analysis (to include intelligence preparation of the battlefield and running estimates) inform commanders as they develop their operational approach that, in turn, facilitates course of action development during the MDMP.

In time-constrained conditions requiring immediate action, or if the problem is familiar, commanders may conduct the MDMP and publish an operation order without formally conducting Army design methodology. As time becomes available during execution, commanders may then initiate Army design methodology to help refine their commander's visualization and the initial plan developed using the MDMP.

III. Troop Leading Procedures (TLP)

Troop leading procedures extend the MDMP to the small-unit level. The MDMP and troop leading procedures (TLP) are similar but not identical. Commanders with a coordinating staff use the MDMP as their primary planning process. Company-level and smaller units lack formal staffs and use TLP to plan and prepare for operations. This places the responsibility for planning primarily on the commander or small-unit leader.

Troop leading procedures are a dynamic process used by small-unit leaders to analyze a mission, develop a plan, and prepare for an operation (ADP 5-0). These procedures enable leaders to maximize available planning time while developing effective plans and preparing their units for an operation. TLP consist of eight steps. The sequence of the steps of TLP is not rigid. Leaders modify the sequence to meet the mission, situation, and available time. Leaders perform some steps concurrently, while other steps may be performed continuously throughout the operation.

Leaders use TLP when working alone or with a small group to solve tactical problems. For example, a company commander may use the executive officer, first sergeant, fire support officer, supply sergeant, and communications sergeant to assist during TLP.

Parallel planning hinges on distributing information as it is received or developed. Leaders cannot complete their plans until they receive their unit mission. If each successive WARNO contains enough information, the higher headquarters' final order will confirm what subordinate leaders have already analyzed and put into their tentative plans. In other cases, the higher headquarters' order may change or modify the subordinate's tasks enough that additional planning and reconnaissance are required.

See pp. 2-59 to 2-62 for complete discussion of the troop leading procedures (eight steps).

(The Operations Process)
B. Preparation

Ref: ADRP 5-0, The Operations Process (Mar '12), chap. 3.

I. Preparation Activities

Preparation consists of those activities performed by units and Soldiers to improve their ability to execute an operation (ADP 5-0). Preparation creates conditions that improve friendly forces' opportunities for success. It requires commander, staff, unit, and Soldier actions to ensure the force is trained, equipped, and ready to execute operations. Preparation activities help commanders, staffs, and Soldiers understand a situation and their roles in upcoming operations.

Preparation Activities

Continue to coordinate and conduct liaison	Conduct rehearsals
Initiate information collection	Conduct plans-to-operations transitions
Initiate security operations	Refine the plan
Initiate troop movement	Integrate new Soldiers and units
Initiate sustainment preparations	Complete task organization
Initiate network preparations	Train
Manage terrain	Perform pre-operations checks and inspections
Prepare terrain	Continue to build partnerships and teams
Conduct confirmation briefs	

Ref: ADRP 5-0, The Operations Process, table 3-1, p. 3-1.

Mission success depends as much on preparation as on planning. Higher headquarters may develop the best of plans; however, plans serve little purpose if subordinates do not receive them in time. Subordinates need enough time to understand plans well enough to execute them. Subordinates develop their own plans and preparations for an operation. After they fully comprehend the plan, subordinate leaders rehearse key portions of it and ensure Soldiers and equipment are positioned and ready to execute the operation.

See following pages (pp. 1-48 to 1-51) for further discussion of activities Commanders, units, and Soldiers conduct to ensure the force is protected and prepared for execution.

Refer to The Small Unit Tactics SMARTbook for further discussion of preparation (and pre-combat inspections) from a small unit perspective. Chapters include tactical mission fundamentals, offensive operations, defensive operations, stability and counterinsurgency operations, tactical enabling operations, special purpose attacks, urban operations and fortifications, and patrols and patrolling.

Preparation Activities

Ref: ADRP 5-0, The Operations Process (Mar '12), pp. 3-1 to 3-5.

Commanders, units, and Soldiers conduct the following activities to ensure the force is protected and prepared for execution.

Continue To Coordinate and Conduct Liaison

Coordinating and conducting liaison helps ensure that leaders internal and external to the headquarters understand their unit's role in upcoming operations, and that they are prepared to perform that role. In addition to military forces, many civilian organizations may operate in the operational area. Their presence can both affect and be affected by the commander's operations. Continuous coordination and liaison between the command and unified action partners helps to build unity of effort.

During preparation, commanders continue to coordinate with higher, lower, adjacent, supporting, and supported units and civilian organizations.

Establishing and maintaining liaison is vital to external coordination. Liaison enables direct communications between the sending and receiving headquarters. It may begin with planning and continue through preparing and executing, or it may start as late as execution. Available resources and the need for direct contact between sending and receiving headquarters determine when to establish liaison. Establishing liaisons with civilian organizations is especially important in stability operations because of the variety of external organizations and the inherent coordination challenges.

See pp. 5-29 to 5-34 for further discussion.

Initiate Information Collection

During preparation, commanders take every opportunity to improve their situational understanding prior to execution. This requires aggressive and continuous information collection. Commanders often direct information collection (to include reconnaissance operations) early in planning that continues in preparation and execution. Through information collection, commanders and staffs continuously plan, task, and employ collection assets and forces to collect timely and accurate information to help satisfy CCIRs and other information requirements (see FM 3-55).

Initiate Security Operations

The force as a whole is often most vulnerable to surprise and enemy attack during preparation, when forces are often concentrated in assembly areas. Leaders are away from their units and concentrated together during rehearsals. Parts of the force could be moving to task-organize. Required supplies may be unavailable or being repositioned. Security operations—screen, guard, cover, area security, and local security—are essential during preparation. Units assigned security missions execute these missions while the rest of the force prepares for the overall operation.

Refer to The Small Unit Tactics SMARTbook for further discussion.

Initiate Troop Movements

The repositioning of forces prior to execution is a significant activity of preparation. Commanders position or reposition units to the right starting places before execution. Commanders integrate operations security measures with troop movements to ensure these movements do not reveal any intentions to the enemy. Troop movements include assembly area reconnaissance by advance parties and route reconnaissance. They also include movements required by changes to the task organization. Commanders can use warning orders to direct troop movements before they issue the operation order.

Refer to The Sustainment & Multifunctional Logistician's SMARTbook for further discussion.

Initiate Sustainment Preparation

Re-supplying, maintaining, and issuing supplies or equipment occurs during preparation. Any repositioning of sustainment assets can also occur. In addition, sustainment elements need to accomplish many other activities.

During preparation, sustainment planners at all levels take action to optimize means (force structure and resources) for supporting the commander's plan. These actions include, but are not limited to, identifying and preparing bases, host-nation infrastructure and capabilities, contract support requirements, and lines of communications. They also include forecasting and building operational stocks as well as identifying endemic health and environmental factors. Integrating environmental considerations will sustain vital resources and help reduce the logistics footprint.

Planners focus on identifying the resources currently available and ensuring access to them. During preparation, sustainment planning continues to support operational planning (branch and sequel development) and the targeting process.

Refer to The Sustainment & Multifunctional Logistician's SMARTbook for further discussion.

Initiate Network Preparation

During preparation, the information network must be tailored and engineered to meet the specific needs of each operation. This includes not only the communications, but also how the commander expects information to move between and be available for leaders and units within an area of operations.

Manage Terrain

Terrain management is the process of allocating terrain by establishing areas of operation, designating assembly areas, and specifying locations for units and activities to deconflict other activities that might interfere with each other. Terrain management is an important activity during preparation as units reposition and stage prior to execution. Commanders assigned an area of operations manage terrain within their boundaries. Through terrain management, commanders identify and locate units in the area. The operations officer, with support from others in the staff, can then deconflict operations, control movements, and deter fratricide as units get in position to execute planned missions. Commanders also consider unified action partners located in their area of operations and coordinate with them for the use of terrain.

Prepare Terrain

Terrain preparation starts with the situational understanding of terrain through proper terrain analysis. It involves shaping the terrain to gain an advantage, such as improving cover, concealment and observation, fields of fire, new obstacle effects through reinforcing obstacles, or mobility operations for initial positioning of forces. It can make the difference between the operation's success and failure. Commanders must understand the terrain and the infrastructure of their area of operations as early as possible to identify potential for improvement, establish priorities of work, and begin preparing the area.

Conduct Confirmation Briefs

The confirmation brief is a key part of preparation. Subordinate leaders give a confirmation brief to the commander immediately after receiving the operation order. Ideally, the commander conducts confirmation briefs in person with selected staff members of the higher headquarters present.

Conduct Rehearsals

A rehearsal is a session in which the commander and staff or unit practices expected actions to improve performance during execution. Commanders use this tool to ensure staffs and subordinates understand the concept of operations and commander's intent. Rehearsals also allow leaders to practice synchronizing operations at times and places

Continued on next page

Continued from previous page

Preparation Activities (Cont.)

Ref: ADRP 5-0, The Operations Process (Mar '12), pp. 3-1 to 3-5.

critical to mission accomplishment. Effective rehearsals imprint a mental picture of the sequence of the operation's key actions and improve mutual understanding and coordination of subordinate and supporting leaders and units. The extent of rehearsals depends on available time. In cases of short-notice requirements, detailed rehearsals may not be possible.

See pp. 6-1 to 6-12 for further discussion.

Conduct Plans-To-Operations Transition

The plans-to-operations transition is a preparation activity that occurs within the headquarters. It ensures members of the current operations cell fully understand the plan before execution. During preparation, the responsibility for developing and maintaining the plan shifts from the plans (or future operations) cell to the current operations cell. This transition is the point at which the current operations cell becomes responsible for controlling execution of the operation order. This responsibility includes answering requests for information concerning the order and maintaining the order through fragmentary orders. This transition enables the plans cell to focus its planning efforts on sequels, branches, and other planning requirements directed by the commander.

The timing of the plans-to-operations transition requires careful consideration. It must allow enough time for members of the current operations cell to understand the plan well enough to coordinate and synchronize its execution. Ideally, the plans cell briefs the members of the current operations cell on the plans-to-operations transition before the combined arms rehearsal. This briefing enables members of the current operations cell to understand the upcoming operation as well as identify friction points and issues to solve prior to its execution. The transition briefing is a mission briefing that generally follows the five-paragraph operation order format. Specific areas addressed include, but are not limited to:

- Task organization
- Situation
- Higher headquarters' mission (one and two echelons up in the chain of command)
- Mission
- Commander's intent (one and two echelons up in the chain of command)
- Concept of operations
- Commander's critical information requirements
- Decision support template and matrix.
- Branches and sequels
- Sustainment
- Command and signal
- Outstanding requests for information and outstanding issues

Continued from previous page

Following the combined arms rehearsal, planners and members of the current operations cell review additional planning guidance issued by the commander and modify the plan as necessary. Significant changes may require assistance from the plans cell to include moving a lead planner to the current operations cell. The plans cell continues planning for branches and sequels.

See pp. 2-53 to 2-54 for further discussion.

Revise and Refine the Plan

Revising and refining the plan is a key activity of preparation. The commander's situational understanding may change over the course of operations, enemy actions may require revision of the plan, or unforeseen opportunities may arise. During preparation, assumptions made during planning may be proven true or false. Intelligence analysis may confirm or deny enemy actions or show changed conditions in the area of operations because of shaping operations. The status of friendly forces may change as the situation changes. In any of these cases, commanders identify the changed conditions and assess how the changes might affect the upcoming operation.

Complete Task Organization

During preparation, commanders complete task-organizing their force to obtain the right mix of capabilities and expertise to accomplish a specific mission. The receiving commander integrates units that are attached, placed under operational control, or placed in direct support. The commander directing the task organization also makes provisions for sustainment. The commander may direct task organization to occur immediately before the operation order is issued. This task-organizing is done with a warning order. Doing this gives units more time to execute the tasks needed to affect the new task organization. Task-organizing early allows affected units to become better integrated and more familiar with all elements involved. This is especially important with inherently time-consuming tasks, such as planning technical network support for the organization.

See pp. 4-7 to 4-14 for further discussion.

Integrate New Soldiers and Units

Commanders, command sergeants major, and staffs help assimilate new Soldiers into their units and new units into the force. They also prepare Soldiers and new units in performing their duties properly and integrating into an upcoming operation smoothly. Integration for new Soldiers includes training on unit SOPs and mission-essential tasks for the operation. It also means orienting new Soldiers on their places and roles in the force and during the operation. This integration for units includes, but is not limited to:

- Receiving and introducing new units to the force and the area of operations
- Exchanging SOPs.
- Conducting briefings and rehearsals
- Establishing communications links.
- Exchanging liaison teams (if required)

Refer to The Leader's SMARTbook for further discussion.

Train

Training prepares forces and Soldiers to conduct operations according to doctrine, SOPs, and the unit's mission. Training develops the teamwork, trust, and mutual understanding that commanders need to exercise mission command and that forces need to achieve unity of effort. Training does not stop when a unit deploys. If the unit is not conducting operations or recovering from operations, it is training. While deployed, unit training focuses on fundamental skills, current SOPs, and skills for a specific mission.

Refer to The Leader's SMARTbook for further discussion.

Conduct Pre-Operations Checks and Inspections

Unit preparation includes completing pre-operations checks and inspections. These checks ensure Soldiers, units, and systems are as fully capable and ready to execute the mission as time and resources permit. The inspections ensure the force has the resources necessary to accomplish the mission. During pre-operations checks and inspections, leaders also check Soldiers' ability to perform crew drills that may not be directly related to the mission. Some examples of these include drills that respond to a vehicle rollover or an onboard fire.

Refer to The Small Unit Tactics SMARTbook for further discussion.

Guides to Effective Preparation

Ref: ADRP 5-0, The Operations Process (Mar '12), pp. 3-5 to 3-6.

The following guidelines aid in effective preparation:

A. Secure and Protect the Force

The force as a whole is often most vulnerable to surprise and enemy attack during preparation. As such, security operations—screen, guard, cover, area security, and local security—are essential during preparation. In addition, commanders ensure integration of the various tasks of the protection war fighting function to safeguard bases, secure routes, and protect the force, while it prepares for operations.

B. Improve Situational Understanding

During preparation, commanders may realize that the initial understanding they developed during planning may be neither accurate nor complete. As such, commanders strive to validate assumptions and improve their situational understanding, as they prepare for operations. Information collection (to include reconnaissance, surveillance, and intelligence operations) helps improve understanding of the enemy, terrain, and civil considerations. Inspections, rehearsals, liaison, and coordination help leaders improve their understanding of the friendly force.

C. Understand, Refine, and Rehearse the Plan

A successful transition from planning to execution requires those charged with executing the order to understand the plan fully. The transition between planning and execution takes place both internally in the headquarters and externally between the commander and subordinate commanders. Rehearsals, including confirmation briefings and the plans-to-operations transition briefing, help improve understanding of the concept of operations, control measures, decision points, and command and support relationships. Rehearsals are key events during preparation that assist the force with understanding the plan and practicing expected actions to improve performance during execution.

D. Integrate, Organize, and Configure the Force

During preparation, commanders allocate time to put the new task organization into effect. This includes detaching units, moving forces, and receiving and integrating new units and Soldiers into the force. When units change task organization, they need preparation time to learn the gaining unit's standard operating procedures and the plan the gaining unit will execute. The gaining unit needs preparation time to assess the new unit's capabilities and limitations and to integrate new capabilities.

E. Ensure Forces and Resources Are Ready and Positioned

Effective preparation ensures the right forces are in the right place, at the right time, with the right equipment and other resources ready to execute the operation. Concurrent with task organization, commanders use troop movement to position or reposition forces to the correct locations prior to execution. This includes positioning sustainment units and supplies.

Ref: ADRP 5-0, The Operations Process (Mar '12), chap. 4.

Execution is putting a plan into action by applying combat power to accomplish the mission (ADP 5-0). In execution, commanders, staffs, and subordinate commanders focus their efforts on translating decisions into actions. They apply combat power to seize, retain, and exploit the initiative to gain and maintain a position of relative advantage. This is the essence of unified land operations.

Army forces seize, retain, and exploit the initiative through combined arms maneuver and wide area security. Through combined arms maneuver, commanders seize and exploit the initiative by forcing the enemy to respond to friendly action. Combined arms maneuver forces the enemy to react continuously until the enemy is finally driven into untenable positions. Seizing the initiative pressures enemy commanders into abandoning their preferred options and making costly mistakes. As enemy mistakes occur, friendly forces seize opportunities and create new avenues for exploitation. While combined arms maneuver is about seizing and exploiting the initiative, wide area security is about retaining the initiative. In wide area security, commanders focus combat power to protect populations, friendly forces, and infrastructure; to deny the enemy positions of advantage; and to consolidate gains to retain the initiative.

See pp. 1-54 to 1-55 for discussion of the fundamentals of execution.

I. Responsibilities during Execution

During execution, commanders focus their activities on directing, assessing, and leading while improving their understanding and modifying their visualization. Initially, commanders direct the transition from planning to execution as the order is issued and the responsibility for integration passes from the plans cell to the current operations integration cell. During execution, the staff directs units, within delegated authority, to keep the operation progressing successfully. Assessing allows the commander and staff to determine the existence and significance of variances from the operations as envisioned in the initial plan. The staff makes recommendations to the commander about what action to take concerning identified variances in the plan. During execution, leading is as important as decision-making, as commanders influence subordinates by providing purpose, direction, and motivation.

A. Commanders, Deputies, and Command Sergeants Major

During execution, commanders at all levels locate themselves where they can exercise command and sense the operation. Sometimes this is at the command post. At other times, commanders may use the command group or mobile command post to command from a forward location. Commanders balance the need to make personal observations, provide command presence, and sense the mood of subordinates from a forward location with the ability to maintain communication and control with the entire force from a command post. No matter where they are located, commanders are always looking beyond the current operation to anticipate future actions. They must periodically step back from the current situation and look at how the force is positioning itself for future operations.

Deputy commanders provide a command resource during execution. First, they can serve as senior advisors to their commander. Second, deputy commanders may

II. Fundamentals of Execution

Ref: ADRP 5-0, The Operations Process (Mar '12), pp. 4-1 to 4-3.

Army forces seize, retain, and exploit the initiative through combined arms maneuver and wide area security. Through combined arms maneuver, commanders seize and exploit the initiative by forcing the enemy to respond to friendly action. Combined arms maneuver forces the enemy to react continuously until the enemy is finally driven into untenable positions. Seizing the initiative pressures enemy commanders into abandoning their preferred options and making costly mistakes. As enemy mistakes occur, friendly forces seize opportunities and create new avenues for exploitation. While combined arms maneuver is about seizing and exploiting the initiative, wide area security is about retaining the initiative. In wide area security, commanders focus combat power to protect populations, friendly forces, and infrastructure; to deny the enemy positions of advantage; and to consolidate gains to retain the initiative.

During execution, the situation may change rapidly. Operations the commander envisioned in the plan may bear little resemblance to actual events in execution. Subordinate commanders need maximum latitude to take advantage of situations and meet the higher commander's intent when the original order no longer applies. Effective execution requires leaders trained in independent decision-making, aggressiveness, and risk taking in an environment of mission command. During execution, leaders must be able and willing to solve problems within the commander's intent without constantly referring to higher headquarters. Subordinates need not wait for top-down synchronization to act.

The following guides aid in effective execution:

Execution Fundamentals

 A   Seize the Initiative Through Action

 B   Accept Prudent Risk to Exploit Opportunities

A. Seize the Initiative through Action

Commanders create conditions for seizing the initiative by acting. Without action, seizing the initiative is impossible. Faced with an uncertain situation, people naturally tend to hesitate and gather more information to reduce their uncertainty. However, waiting and gathering information might reduce uncertainty, but they will not eliminate it. Waiting may even increase uncertainty by providing the enemy with time to seize the initiative. It is far better to manage uncertainty by acting and developing the situation.

In operations dominated by stability tasks, commanders act quickly to improve the civil situation while preventing conditions from deteriorating further. Immediate action to stabilize the situation and provide for the immediate humanitarian needs of the people begins the process toward stability. Friendly forces dictate the terms of action and drive positive change to stabilize the situation rapidly. In turn, this improves the security environment, creating earlier opportunities for civilian agencies and organizations to contribute. By acting proactively to influence events, Army forces exploit the initiative to ensure steady progress toward conditions that support stability. Failing to act quickly may create a breeding ground for dissent and possible recruiting opportunities for enemies or adversaries.

B. Accept Prudent Risk to Exploit Opportunities

Uncertainty and risk are inherent in all military operations. Successful commanders are comfortable operating under conditions of uncertainty, as they balance various risks and take advantage of opportunities. Opportunities are events that offer better ways to succeed. Commanders recognize opportunities by continuously monitoring and evaluating the situation. Failure to understand the opportunities inherent in an enemy's action surrenders the initiative. Most opportunities are fleeting. When they present themselves, commanders usually have only a short window of time in which to act. In operations, it is better to err on the side of speed, audacity, and momentum than on the side of caution, all else being equal. Bold decisions give the best promise of success; however, when acting on an opportunity, commanders must consider the difference between a prudent risk and a gamble.

Prudent risk is a deliberate exposure to potential injury or loss when the commander judges the outcome in terms of mission accomplishment as worth the cost (ADP 6-0). Reasonably estimating and intentionally accepting risk is not gambling. Gambling, in contrast to prudent risk taking, is staking the success of an entire action on a single event without considering the hazard to the force should the event not unfold as envisioned. Therefore, commanders avoid taking gambles. Commanders carefully determine risks, analyze and minimize as many hazards as possible, and then take prudent risks to exploit opportunities.

Because uncertainty exists in all military operations, every military decision contains risk. Commanders exercise the art of command when deciding how much risk to accept. The commander has several techniques available to reduce the risk associated in a specific operation. Some of these techniques for reducing risk take resources from the decisive operation, which reduces the concentration of effects at the decisive point.

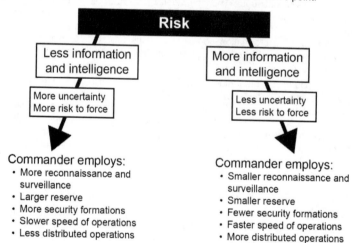

Ref: ADRP 5-0, The Operations Process, fig. 4-1, p. 4-2.

The commander has the option to redirect the efforts of forces previously used to reduce risk toward strengthening the force's decisive operation as more information becomes available. In any operation, the relationship between information, uncertainty, risk, size of reserves and security forces, and the disposition of the main body may change frequently. The commander must continually weigh this balance and make adjustments as needed. These adjustments can create problems. Too many changes or changes made too rapidly in task organization, mission, and priorities can have negative effects on the operations process.

See also p. 2-19 to 2-20. Refer to The Small Unit Tactics SMARTbook and ADRP 3-90 for a detailed discussion of the art of tactics and risk reduction.

directly supervise a specific war fighting function (for example, sustainment). Finally, deputy commanders can command a specific operation (such as a gap crossing), area, or part of the unit (such as the covering force) for the commander.

The command sergeant major provides another set of senior eyes to assist the commander. The command sergeant major assists the commander with assessing operations as well as assessing the condition and morale of forces. In addition, the command sergeant major provides leadership and expertise to units and Soldiers at critical locations and times during execution.

B. Staff

The chief of staff (COS) or executive officer (XO) integrates the efforts of the whole staff during execution. These efforts include the assignment of responsibilities among staff sections and command post cells for conducting analysis and decision-making. While the unit standard operating procedures might specify a division of responsibilities among integrating cells for these matters, often the COS (XO) makes specific decisions allocating responsibilities among cells.

In execution, the staff—primarily through the current operations integration cell—integrates forces and war fighting functions to accomplish the mission. The staff assesses short-term actions and activities as part of this integration. While the COS (XO) integrates staff activities among all functional and integrating cells and separate sections, the operations officer integrates the operation through the current operations integration cell. Other staff principals integrate within their areas of expertise.

Formal and informal integration of the war fighting functions by functional and integrating cells is continuous. The integration occurs both within and among command post cells and staff sections and between headquarters. When staffs need a more structured integration, they establish meetings (to include working groups and boards) to share information, coordinate actions, and solve problems. The COS (XO) also identifies staff members to participate in the higher commander's working groups and boards.

The current operations integration cell is the integrating cell in the command post with primary responsibility for execution. Staff members in the current operations integration cell actively assist the commander and subordinate units in controlling the current operation. They provide information, synchronize staff and subordinate unit or echelon activities, and coordinate support requests from subordinates. The current operations integration cell solves problems and acts within the authority delegated by the commander. It also performs some short-range planning using the rapid decision-making and synchronization process.

III. Decisionmaking during Execution

Decisionmaking is tied to disciplined initiative and is inherent in executing operations. Commanders observe the progress of operations and intervene when necessary to ensure success. Because operations never unfold exactly as envisioned and because understanding of the situation changes, a commander's decisions made during execution are critical to an operation's success. During execution, commanders direct their units forcefully and promptly to overcome the difficulties of enemy action, friendly failures, errors, and other changes in their operational environment.

Commanders make execution and adjustment decisions throughout execution. Execution decisions implement a planned action under circumstances anticipated in the order. An execution decision is normally tied to a decision point—a point in space or time the commander or staff anticipate making a key decision concerning a specific course of action (JP 5-0). An adjustment decision is the selection of a course of action that modifies the order to respond to unanticipated opportunities or threats. An adjustment decision may include a decision to reframe the problem and develop an entirely new plan.

Executing, adjusting, or abandoning the original operation is part of decision-making in execution. By fighting the enemy and not the plan, successful commanders balance the tendency to abandon a well-conceived plan too soon against persisting in a failing effort too long. Effective decision-making during execution:

- Relates all actions to the commander's intent and concept of operations to ensure they support the decisive operation
- Is comprehensive, maintaining integration of combined arms rather than dealing with separate functions
- Relies heavily on intuitive decision-making by commanders and staffs to make rapid adjustments
- Is continuous and responds effectively to any opportunity or threat

A. Assessment and Decisionmaking

As commanders assess an operation, they determine when decisions are required. Plans usually identify some decision points; however, unexpected enemy actions or other changes often present situations that require unanticipated decisions. Commanders act when these decisions are required; they do not wait for a set time in the battle rhythm. As commanders assess the operation, they describe their impressions to the staff and subordinates and discuss the desirability of choices available. Once commanders make decisions, their staffs transmit the necessary directives.

Assessment in execution identifies variances, their magnitude and significance, and the need for and types of decisions—whether execution or adjustment—to be made. The commander and staff assess the probable outcome of the operation to determine whether changes are necessary to accomplish the mission, take advantage of opportunities, or react to unexpected threats. The following figure depicts a basic model of assessing and decision-making during execution.

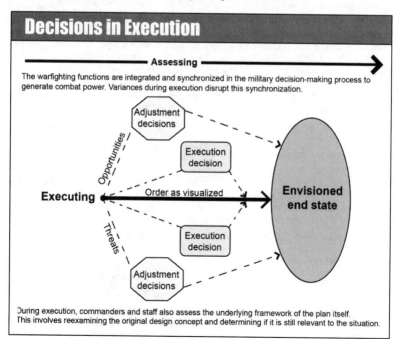

Decisions in Execution

Assessing

The warfighting functions are integrated and synchronized in the military decision-making process to generate combat power. Variances during execution disrupt this synchronization.

Adjustment decisions

Execution decision

Opportunities

Executing — Order as visualized — Envisioned end state

Threats

Execution decision

Adjustment decisions

During execution, commanders and staff also assess the underlying framework of the plan itself. This involves reexamining the original design concept and determining if it is still relevant to the situation.

Ref: ADRP 5-0, The Operations Process, fig. 4-2, p. 4-5.

Activities Of Execution

Ref: FM 6-0 (C1), Commander and Staff Organization and Operations (May '15), pp. 14-1 to 14-2.

Planning and preparation accomplish nothing if the command does not execute effectively. Execution is putting a plan into action by applying combat power to accomplish the mission (ADRP 5-0). In execution, commanders, supported by their staffs, focus their efforts on translating decisions into actions. Inherent in execution is deciding whether to execute planned actions, such as changing phases or executing a branch plan. Execution also includes adjusting the plan based on changes in the situation and an assessment of the operation's progress. (See ADRP 5-0 for fundamentals of execution).

Throughout execution, commanders, supported by their staffs, assess the operation's progress, make decisions, and direct the application of combat power to seize, retain, and exploit the initiative. Major activities of execution include—

- **Assessment**: Monitoring current operations and evaluating progress.
- **Decisionmaking**: Making decisions to exploit opportunities or counter treats.
- **Directing actio**n: Apply combat power at decisive points and times.

Assessment During Execution

During execution, continuous assessment is essential. Assessment involves a deliberate comparison of forecasted outcomes to actual events, using criteria to judge operational progress towards success. The commander and staff assess the probable outcome of the operation to determine whether changes are necessary to accomplish the mission, take advantage of opportunities, or react to unexpected threats. Commanders also assess the probable outcome of current operations in terms of their impact on potential future operations in order to develop concepts for these operations early.

Assessment includes both monitoring the situation and evaluating progress. During monitoring, commanders and staffs collect and use relevant information to develop a clear understanding of the command's current situation. Commanders and staffs also evaluate the operation's progress in terms of measures of performance (MOPs) and measures of effectiveness (MOEs). This evaluation helps commanders assess progress and identify variances—the difference between the actual situation and what the plan forecasted the situation would be at that time or event. Identifying variances and their significance leads to determining if a decision is required during execution.

Refer to ADRP 5-0 for fundamentals of assessment.

Decisionmaking During Execution

When operations are progressing satisfactorily, variances are minor and within acceptable levels. Commanders who make this evaluation—explicitly or implicitly—allow operations to continue according to plan. This situation leads to execution decisions included in the plan. Execution decisions implement a planned action under circumstances anticipated in the order. An execution decision is normally tied to a decision point.

An assessment may determine that the operation as a whole, or one or more of its major actions, is not progressing according to expectations. Variances of this magnitude present one of two situations:

- Significant, unforeseen opportunities to achieve the commander's intent.
- Significant threats to the operation's success.

In either case, the commander makes an adjustment decision. An adjustment decision is the selection of a course of action that modifies the order to respond to unanticipated opportunities or threats. An adjustment decision may include a decision to reframe the problem and develop an entirely new plan.

Executing, adjusting, or abandoning the original operation is part of decisionmaking in execution. By fighting the enemy and not the plan, successful commanders balance the tendency to abandon a well-conceived plan too soon against persisting in a failing effort too long. Effective decisionmaking during execution—

- Relates all actions to the commander's intent and concept of operations.
- Is comprehensive, maintaining integration of combined arms rather than dealing with separate functions.
- Relies heavily on intuitive decisionmaking by commanders and staffs to make rapid adjustments.

Directing Action

To implement execution or adjustment decisions, commanders direct actions that apply combat power. Based on the commander's decision and guidance, the staff resynchronizes the operation to mass the maximum effects of combat power to seize, retain, and exploit the initiative. This involves synchronizing the operations in time, space, and purpose and issuing directives to subordinates.

Table 14-1, below, provides for a summary of a range of possible actions with respect to decisions made during execution.

Decision types		Actions
Execution decisions	Minor variances from the plan Operation proceeding according to plan. Variances are within acceptable limits.	**Execute planned actions** • Commander or designee decides which planned actions best meet the situation and directs their execution. • Staff issues fragmentary order. • Staff completes follow-up actions.
	Anticipated situation Operation encountering variances within the limits for one or more branches or sequels anticipated in the plan.	**Execute a branch or sequel** • Commander or staff review branch or sequel plan. • Commander receives assessments and recommendations for modifications to the plan, determines the time available to refine it, and either issues guidance for further actions or directs execution of a branch or sequel. • Staff issues fragmentary order. • Staff completes follow-up actions.
Adjustment decisions	Unanticipated situation— friendly success Significant, unanticipated positive variances result in opportunities to achieve the end state in ways that differ significantly from the plan.	**Make an adjustment decision** • Commander recognizes the opportunity or threat and determines time available for decisionmaking. • Based on available planning time, commanders determine if they want to reframe the problem and develop a new plan. In these instances, the decision initiates planning. Otherwise, the commander directs the staff to refine a single course of action or directs actions by subordinates to exploit the opportunity or counter the threat and exercise initiative within the higher commander's intent.
	Unanticipated situation— enemy threat Significant, unanticipated negative variances impede mission accomplishment.	• Commander normally does not attempt to restore the plan. • Commander issues a verbal warning or fragmentary order to subordinate commanders. • Staff resynchronizes operation, modifies measures of effectiveness, and begins assessing the operation for progress using new measures of effectiveness.

Ref: FM 6-0 (C1), Commander & Staff Organization & Operations, table 14-1, p. 14-2.

B. Variances

A variance is a difference between the actual situation during an operation and what the plan forecasted the situation would be at that time or event. Staffs ensure information systems display relevant information that allows them to identify variances. The commander and staff evaluate emerging variances. If necessary, staffs update the conclusions and recommendations of their running estimates for the commander, who directs the necessary action. Two forms of variances exist: opportunities and threats.

1. Opportunity to Accomplish

The first form of variance is an opportunity to accomplish the mission more effectively. Opportunity results from forecasted or unexpected success. When commanders recognize an opportunity, they alter the order to exploit it if the change achieves the end state without incurring unacceptable risk. When exploiting an opportunity, the concept of operations may change, but the commander's intent usually remains the same.

2. Threat to Mission Accomplishment

The second form of variance is a threat to mission accomplishment or survival of the force. When recognizing a threat, the commander adjusts the order to eliminate the enemy advantage, restore the friendly advantage, and regain the initiative. Not all threats to the force or mission involve hostile or neutral persons. Disease, toxic hazards, and natural disasters are examples of other threats.

In some instances, the variance is so extreme that no branch or sequel is available or the current plan lacks enough flexibility to respond to the variance. In this situation, the commander and staff may have to reframe the operational environment and the problem resulting in a new plan.

C. Types of Decisions

Decisions made during execution are either execution decisions or adjustment decisions. Execution decisions involve options anticipated in the order. Adjustment decisions involve options that commanders did not anticipate. These decisions may include a decision to reframe the problem and develop an entirely new plan. Commanders may delegate authority for some execution decisions to the staff; however, commanders are always responsible for and involved in decisions during execution.

1. Execution Decisions

Execution decisions implement a planned action under circumstances anticipated in the order. In their most basic form, execution decisions are decisions the commander foresees and identifies for execution during the operation. They apply resources at times or situations already established in the order. For example, changing a boundary, altering the task organization, transitioning between phases, and executing a branch are execution decisions. Commanders are responsible for those decisions but may direct the COS (XO) or staff officer to supervise implementation. The current operations integration cell oversees the synchronization of integrating processes needed to implement execution decisions.

2. Adjustment Decisions

Adjustment decisions modify the operation to respond to unanticipated opportunities and threats. They often require implementing unanticipated operations and re-synchronizing the war fighting functions. Commanders make these decisions, delegating implementing authority only after directing the major change themselves.

See following pages (pp. 1-62 to 1-63) for sample "change indicators."

Decision Support Tools

Ref: ADRP 5-0, The Operations Process (Mar '12), p. 4-4.

Several decision support tools assist the commander and staff during execution. Among the most important are the decision support template, decision support matrix, and execution matrix. The current operations integration cell uses these tools, among others, to help control operations and to determine when anticipated decisions are coming up for execution.

Decision Support Template (DST)

A decision support template is a combined intelligence and operations graphic based on the results of war gaming. The decision support template depicts decision points, timelines associated with movement of forces and the flow of the operation, and other key items of information required to execute a specific friendly course of action (JP 2-01.3). Part of the decision support template is the decision support matrix. A decision support matrix is a written record of a war-gamed course of action that describes decision points and associated actions at those decision points. The decision support matrix lists decision points, locations of decision points, criteria to be evaluated at decision points, actions that occur at decision points, and the units responsible to act on the decision points. It also lists the units responsible for observing and reporting information affecting the criteria for decisions.

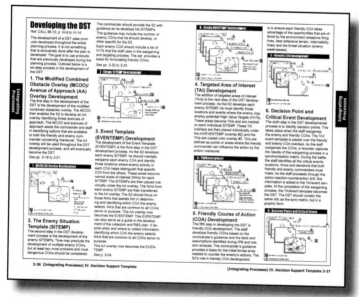

Execution Matrix

An execution matrix is a visual and sequential representation of the critical tasks and responsible organizations by time. An execution matrix could be for the entire force, such as an air assault execution matrix, or it may be specific to a war fighting function, such as a fire support execution matrix. The current operations integration cell uses the execution matrix to determine which friendly actions to expect forces to execute in the near term or, in conjunction with the decision support matrix, which execution decisions to make.

Change Indicators

Ref: FM 6-0 (C1), Commander and Staff Organization and Operations (May '15), table 14-2.

Types	Indicators	
General	• Answer to a commander's critical information requirement. • Identification of an information requirement. • Change in mission. • Change in organization of unit. • Change in leadership of unit. • Signing or implementation of peace treaty or other key political arrangement.	• Change in capabilities of subordinate unit. • Change in role of host-nation military force. • Climate changes or natural disasters impacting on the population, agriculture, industry. • Upcoming local election. • Changes in key civilian leadership.
Intelligence	• Identification of enemy main effort. • Identification of enemy reserves or counterattack. • Indications of unexpected enemy action or preparation. • Increase in enemy solicitation of civilians for intelligence operations. • Identification of an information requirement. • Insertion of manned surveillance teams. • Disruption of primary and secondary education system. • Unexplained disappearance of key members of intelligence community.	• Enemy electronic attack use. • Indicators of illicit economic activity. • Identification of threats from within the population. • Increased unemployment within the population. • Interference with freedom of religious worship. • Identification of high-value targets. • Unmanned aircraft system launch. • Answer to a priority intelligence requirement. • Enemy rotary-wing or unmanned aircraft system use.
Movement and Maneuver	• Success or failure in breaching or gap crossing operations. • Capture of significant numbers of enemy prisoners of war, enemy command posts, supply points, or artillery units. • Establishment of road blocks along major traffic routes. • Unexplained displacement of neighborhoods within a given sector.	• Success or failure of a subordinate unit task. • Modification of an airs pace control measure. • Numbers of dislocated civilians sufficient to affect friendly operations. • Damages to civilian infrastructure affecting friendly mobility. • Loss of one or more critical transportation systems.
Fires	• Receipt of an air tasking order. • Battle damage assessment results. • Unplanned repositioning of firing units. • Identification of high-payoff targets. • Identification of an information requirement.	• Execution of planned fires. • Modification of a fi re support coordination measure. • Effective enemy counterfire. • Negative effects of fires on civilians. • Destruction of any place of worship by friendly fire.
Protection	• Chemical, biological, radiological, nuclear report or other indicators of enemy chemical, biological, radiological, nuclear use. • Report or other indicators of enemy improvised explosive device use. • Indicators of coordinated enemy actions against civilians or friendly forces. • Increased criminal activity in a given sector. • Increase in organized protests or riots.	• Identification of threats to communications or computer systems. • Reports of enemy targeting critical host-nation infrastructure. • Identification of threat to base or sustainment facilities. • Escalation of force incidents. • Loss of border security.
Sustainment	• Significant loss of capability in any class of supply. • Opening or closing of civilian businesses within a given area. • Identification of sign ificant incidences of disease and nonbattle injury casualties. • Closing of major financial institutions. • Mass casualties. • Receipt of significant resupply. • Disruption of one or more essential civil services (such as water or electricity). • Contact on a supply route. • Answer to a friendly force information requirement. • Mass detainees.	• Degradations to essential civilian infrastructure by threat actions. • Civilian mass casualty event beyond capability of host-nation resources. • Identification of sign ificant shortage in any class of supply. • Outbreak of epidemic or famine within the civilian population. • Medical evacuation launch. • Dislocated civilian event beyond capability of host-nation resources. • Disruption of key logistics lines of communication. • Changes in availability of host-nation support.
Mission Command	• Impending changes in key military leadership. • Interference with freedom of the press or news media. • Receipt of a fragmentary order or warning order from higher headquarters.	• Effective adversary information efforts on civilians. • Loss of civilian communications nodes. • Loss of contact with a command post or commander. • Jamming or interference.

Editor's note: These questions for assessment are not provided in ADRP 5-0 (Mar '12) and were adapted from previous references.

Questions for Assessment (Execution/Adjustment Decisions)

Important questions when assessing execution are "Has something changed?" and if so, "Does it affect my area and does this change require action?" If the answers to both are yes, the commander or designated representative determines which options to exercise as choices arise. Commanders and staffs use variances identified by such changes to alert themselves and the command to opportunities that modify the operation to make it more effective or to guard against a developing vulnerability. Commanders or staff officers make execution decisions if the plan is still valid and the variances from expectations are acceptable. They make adjustment decisions if the variances from expectations require altering the operation from the plan.

One aid to assessment in execution is the following list of questions:

- Can the force achieve its objectives in the time required by continuing its current operation?
- What options are available during the conduct of the operation? Which will accomplish the mission most effectively?
- Will changes in light or weather influence the operations?
- Where are enemy forces? Doing what? How?
- What is the tempo of the operation? Is this satisfactory?
- What are the enemy force's weaknesses, vulnerabilities, and seams? How can friendly forces exploit them?
- What are the friendly force's problems? How can friendly forces correct them?
- What are the enemy force's opportunities? How can friendly forces deny them?
- What are the friendly force's opportunities? How can friendly forces exploit them?
- Are any changes needed to the friendly force's concept of operations, task organization, or mission?
- What changes need to be made to the ISR plan?
- What changes need to be made to the current list of CCIRs?
- How are civil considerations affecting the operation? How will available options affect civil conditions?
- What are the perceived causes for instability?
- What changes in civil considerations have occurred in the area of operations within the past twelve months?
- What is the greatest civil problem currently facing the area of operations?
- What actions can the friendly force take to mitigate it?
- Whom does the population trust to solve the problems?
- Which civil problem should be solved first?
- What essential services must the friendly force provide to enhance local political stability?
- Which groups are using violence to control and coerce the population?
- What are the local and regional political (or governance) processes and structures? Are they based on tribe, clan, ethnicity, religion, or ideology?
- Is there an illicit or shadow economy? If so, who controls it and why are the people using it?

IV. Rapid Decisionmaking and Synchronization Process (RDSP)

Ref: ADRP 5-0, The Operations Process (Mar '12), pp. 4-6 to 4-9

The rapid decision-making and synchronization process (RDSP) is a decision-making and synchronization technique that commanders and staffs commonly use during execution. While identified here with a specific name and method, the approach is not new; its use in the Army is well established. Commanders and staffs develop this capability through training and practice. The RDSP includes five steps. The first two may be performed in any order, including concurrently. The last three are performed interactively until commanders identify an acceptable course of action.

While the military decision-making process (MDMP) seeks the optimal solution, the RDSP seeks a timely and effective solution within the commander's intent, mission, and concept of operations. Using the RDSP lets leaders avoid the time-consuming requirements of developing decision criteria and comparing courses of action (COAs). Operational and mission variables continually change during execution. This often invalidates or weakens COAs and decision criteria before leaders can make a decision. Under the RDSP, leaders combine their experience and intuition with situational awareness to quickly reach situational understanding. Based on this, they develop and refine workable COAs.

Rapid Decisionmaking & Sync Process

- Compare the current situation to the order
- Determine that a decision, and what type, is required

Performed concurrently or sequentially.

- Develop a course of action
- Refine and validate the course of action
- Implement

If the action is unacceptable, develop a new course of action.

Ref: ADRP 5-0, The Operations Process, fig. 4-3, p. 4-6.

A. Compare the Current Situation to the Order

During execution, commanders and staffs monitor the situation to identify changes in conditions. Then they ask if these changes affect the overall conduct of operations or their part of it and if the changes are significant. Finally, they identify if the changed conditions represent variances from the order—especially opportunities and risks. Staff members use running estimates to look for indicators of variances that affect their areas of expertise. The commander, COS (XO), and command post cell chiefs look for indicators of variances that affect the overall operation.

Staff members are particularly alert for answers to CCIRs that support anticipated decisions. They also watch for exceptional information. Exceptional information is information that would have answered one of the commander's critical information requirements if the requirement for it had been foreseen and stated as one of the commander's critical information requirements.

B. Determine the Type of Decision Required

When a variance is identified, the commander directs action while the chief of operations leads chiefs of the current operations integration cell and selected functional cells in quickly comparing the current situation to the expected situation. This assessment accomplishes the following:

- Describes the variance
- Determines if the variance provides a significant opportunity or threat and examines the potential of either
- Determines if a decision is needed by identifying if the variance:

- Indicates an opportunity that can be exploited to accomplish the mission faster or with fewer resources Directly threatens the decisive operation's success

- Threatens a shaping operation such that it may threaten the decisive operation directly or in the near future

- Can be addressed within the commander's intent and concept of operations. (If so, determine what execution decision is needed.)

- Requires changing the concept of operations substantially (If so, determine what adjustment decision or new approach will best suit the circumstances.)

For minor variances, the chief of operations works with other cell chiefs to determine whether changes to control measures are needed. If so, they determine how those changes affect other war fighting functions. They direct changes within their authority (execution decisions) and notify the COS (XO) and the affected command post cells and staff elements.

Commanders intervene directly in cases that affect the overall direction of the unit. They describe the situation, direct their subordinates to provide any additional information they need, and order either implementation of planned responses or development of an order to redirect the force.

C. Develop a Course of Action

If the variance requires an adjustment decision, the designated integrating cell and affected command post cell chiefs recommend implementation of a COA or obtain the commander's guidance for developing one. They use the following conditions to screen possible COAs:

- Mission
- Commander's intent
- Current dispositions and freedom of action
- CCIRs
- Limiting factors, such as supply constraints, boundaries, and combat strength

The new options must conform to the commander's intent. Possible COAs may alter the concept of operations and CCIRs, if they remain within the commander's intent. However, the commander approves changes to the CCIRs. Functional cell chiefs and other staff section leaders identify areas that may be affected within their areas of expertise by proposed changes to the order or mission. The commander is as likely as anyone else to detect the need for change and to sketch out the options. Whether the commander, COS (XO), or chief of operations does this, the future operations cell is often directed to further develop the concept and draft the order. The chief of operations and the current operations integration cell normally lead this effort, especially if the response is needed promptly or the situation is not complex. The commander or COS (XO) is usually the decision-making authority, depending on the commander's delegation of authority.

Continued on next page —

Continued from previous page

D. Refine and Validate the Course of Action

Once commanders describe the new COA, the current operations integration cell conducts an analysis to validate its feasibility, suitability, and acceptability. If acceptable, the COA is refined to resynchronize the war fighting functions enough to generate and apply the needed combat power. Staffs with a future operations cell may assign that cell responsibility for developing the details of the new COA and drafting a fragmentary order to implement it. The commander or COS (XO) may direct an "on-call" operations synchronization meeting to perform this task and ensure rapid resynchronization.

Validation and refinement are done quickly. Normally, the commander and staff officers conduct a mental war game of the new COA. They consider potential enemy reactions, the unit's counteractions, and secondary effects that might affect the force's synchronization:

- Is the new COA feasible in terms of my area of expertise?
- How will this action affect my area of expertise?
- Does it require changing my information requirements?
  - Should any of the information requirements be nominated as a CCIR?
  - What actions within my area of expertise does this change require?
  - Will this COA require changing objectives or targets nominated by the staff section?
- What other command post cells and elements does this action affect?
- What are potential enemy reactions?
- What are the possible friendly counteractions?
  - Does this counteraction affect my area of expertise?
  - Will it require changing my information requirements?
  - Are any of my information requirements potential CCIRs?
  - What actions within my area of expertise does this counteraction require?
  - Will it require changing objectives or targets nominated by the staff section?
  - What other command post cells and elements does this counteraction affect?

The validation and refinement will show if the COA will acceptably solve the problem. If it does not, the COS or chief of operations modifies it through additional analysis or develops a new COA. The COS (XO) informs the commander of any changes made to the COA.

E. Implement

When a COA is acceptable, the COS (XO) recommends implementation to the commander or implements it directly, if the commander has delegated that authority. Implementation normally requires a fragmentary order; in exceptional circumstances, it may require a new operation order. That order changes the concept of operations (in adjustment decisions), resynchronizes the war fighting functions, and disseminates changes to control measures. The staff uses warning orders to alert subordinates to a pending change. The staff also establishes sufficient time for the unit to implement the change without losing integration or being exposed to unnecessary tactical risk.

Commanders often issue orders to subordinates verbally in situations requiring quick reactions. At battalion and higher levels, written fragmentary orders confirm verbal orders to ensure synchronization, integration, and notification of all parts of the force. If time permits, leaders verify that subordinates understand critical tasks. Methods for doing this include the confirmation brief and back brief. These are conducted both between commanders and within staff elements to ensure mutual understanding.

After the analysis is complete, the current operations integration cell and command post cell chiefs update decision support templates and synchronization matrixes. When time is available, the operations officer or chief of operations continues this analysis to the operation's end to complete combat power integration. Staff members begin the synchronization needed to implement the decision. This synchronization involves collaboration with other command post cells and subordinate staffs.

(The Operations Process)
D. Assessment

Ref: ADRP 5-0, The Operations Process (Mar '12), chap. 5.

Assessment is the determination of the progress toward accomplishing a task, creating an effect, or achieving an objective (JP 3-0). Assessment precedes and guides the other activities of the operations process. Assessment involves deliberately comparing forecasted outcomes with actual events to determine the overall effectiveness of force employment. More specifically, assessment helps the commander determine progress toward attaining the desired end state, achieving objectives, and performing tasks. It also involves continuously monitoring and evaluating the operational environment to determine what changes might affect the conduct of operations.

I. The Assessment Process

Assessment is continuous; it precedes and guides every operations process activity and concludes each operation or phase of an operation.

Assessment Process Activities

 Monitoring

 Evaluating

 Recommending or Directing Action

Broadly, assessment consists of, but is not limited to, the following activities:

- **Monitoring** the current situation to collect relevant information
- **Evaluating** progress toward attaining end state conditions, achieving objectives, and performing tasks
- **Recommending or directing action** for improvement

Throughout the operations process, commanders integrate their own assessments with those of the staff, subordinate commanders, and other unified action partners. Primary tools for assessing progress of the operation include the operation order, the common operational picture, personal observations, running estimates, and the assessment plan. The latter includes measures of effectiveness, measures of performance, and reframing criteria. The commander's visualization forms the basis for the commander's personal assessment of progress. Running estimates provide information, conclusions, and recommendations from the perspective of each staff section.

See following page for further discussion of the assessment process. See pp. 6-13 to 6-22 for discussion of after action reviews (AARs).

The Assessment Process

Ref: ADRP 5-0, The Operations Process (Mar '12), pp. 5-1 to 5-4.

A. Monitoring

Monitoring is continuous observation of those conditions relevant to the current operation. Monitoring within the assessment process allows staffs to collect relevant information, specifically that information about the current situation that can be compared to the forecasted situation described in the commander's intent and concept of operations. Progress cannot be judged, nor execution or adjustment decisions made, without an accurate understanding of the current situation.

During planning, commanders monitor the situation to develop facts and assumptions that underlie the plan. During preparation and execution, commanders and staffs monitor the situation to determine if the facts are still relevant, if their assumptions remain valid, and if new conditions emerged that affect their operations.

Commander's critical information requirements and decision points focus the staff's monitoring activities and prioritize the unit's collection efforts. Information requirements concerning the enemy, terrain and weather, and civil considerations are identified and assigned priorities through intelligence, surveillance, and reconnaissance (ISR) synchronization. The operations officers use friendly reports to coordinate.

Staffs monitor and collect information from the common operational picture and friendly reports. This information includes operational and intelligence summaries from subordinate, higher, and adjacent headquarters and communications and reports from liaison teams. Staffs apply information management and knowledge management principles to facilitate getting this information to the right people at the right time. Staff sections record relevant information in running estimates. Each staff section maintains a continuous assessment of current operations as a basis to determine if they are proceeding according to the commander's intent.

B. Evaluating

The staff analyzes relevant information collected through monitoring to evaluate the operation's progress. Evaluating is using criteria to judge progress toward desired conditions and determining why the current degree of progress exists. Evaluation is the heart of the assessment process where most of the analysis occurs. Evaluation helps commanders determine what is working, determine what is not working, and gain insights into how to better accomplish the mission.

See following pages (pp. 1-70 to 1-71) for discussion of evaluation criteria (measures of effectiveness, measures of performance, and indicators).

C. Recommending or Directing Action

Monitoring and evaluating are critical activities; however, assessment is incomplete without recommending or directing action. Assessment may diagnose problems, but unless it results in recommended adjustments, its use to the commander is limited.

Based on the evaluation of progress, the staff brainstorms possible improvements to the plan and makes preliminary judgments about the relative merit of those changes. Staff members identify those changes possessing sufficient merit and provide them as recommendations to the commander or make adjustments within their delegated authority. Recommendations to the commander range from continuing the operation as planned, executing a branch, or making adjustments not anticipated. Making adjustments includes assigning new tasks to subordinates, reprioritizing support, adjusting the ISR synchronization plan, and significantly modifying the course of action. Commanders integrate recommendations from the staff, subordinate commanders, and other partners with their personal assessment. From those recommendations, they decide if and how to modify the operation to better accomplish the mission.

II. Assessment Working Groups

Assessing progress is the responsibility of all staff sections and not the purview of any one staff section or command post cell. Each staff section assesses the operation from its specific area of expertise. However, these staff sections must coordinate and integrate their individual assessments and associated recommendations across the warfighting functions to produce comprehensive assessments for the commander, particularly in protracted operations. They do this in the assessment working group.

Assessment working groups are more common at higher echelons (division and above) and are more likely to be required in protracted operations. Normally, the frequency of meetings is part of a unit's battle rhythm. The staff, however, does not wait for a scheduled working group to inform the commander on issues that require immediate attention. Nor do they wait to take action in those areas within their delegated authority.

The assessment working group is cross-functional by design and includes membership from across the staff, liaison personnel, and other unified action partners outside the headquarters. Commanders direct the chief of staff, executive officer, or a staff section leader to run the assessment working group. Typically, the operations officer, plans officer, or senior operations research/systems analysis (ORSA) staff section serves as the staff lead for the assessment working group.

Minority views are heard and dissenters speak up in the assessment working group. Commanders encourage all subject matter experts and relevant staff sections to debate vigorously on the proper understanding of observed trends and their associated causes. Minority views often create critical insights; they are also presented to the commander at the assessment board.

The frequency with which the assessment working group meets depends on the situation. Additionally, the assessment working group may present its findings and recommendations to the commander for decision. Subordinate commanders may participate and provide their assessments of the operations and recommendations along with the staff. Commanders combine these assessments with their personal assessment, consider recommendations, and then direct changes to improve performance and better accomplish the mission.

Assessment Support

The ORSA staff section supports assessment on many levels. Staff analytical resources and expertise increase at each echelon. Division and corps headquarters, for example, have an assigned ORSA staff section. In addition to managing a formal assessment framework, these staff sections can provide other capabilities to assist the commander. These capabilities include trend analysis, hypothesis testing, and forecasting.

ORSA staff sections use various mathematical techniques to identify and analyze trends in data. They confirm or rule out suspected trends in a statistically rigorous manner. They can also determine how much a given trend depends on other variables within the information. For example, given sufficient information, the ORSA staff section can determine which essential services trends correlate most to the trend in the number of attacks.

The ORSA staff section confirms or rules out many theories about given information. For example, the commander may propose a hypothesis that enemy surface-to-air attacks increased because helicopter flight patterns became too predictable. The ORSA cell can analyze the flight patterns and determine a correlation to attacks to confirm or rule out the hypothesis.

The ORSA staff section can use statistical techniques to predict the next information point in a series. Margins of error for this activity can be significant, but it is one more tool the commander can use to develop estimates in an unknown situation.

III. Evaluation Criteria (MOEs, MOPs, Indicators)

Ref: ADRP 5-0, The Operations Process (Mar '12), pp. 5-2 to 5-3.

The staff analyzes relevant information collected through monitoring to evaluate the operation's progress. Evaluating is using criteria to judge progress toward desired conditions and determining why the current degree of progress exists.

Criteria in the forms of measures of effectiveness (MOE's) and measures of performance (MOP's) aid in determining progress toward performing tasks, achieving objectives, and attaining end state conditions. MOE's help determine if a task is achieving its intended results. MOP's help determine if a task is completed properly. MOE's and MOP's are simply criteria—they do not represent the assessment itself. MOE's and MOP's require relevant information in the form of indicators for evaluation.

MOE	MOP	Indicator
Answers the question: Are we doing the right things?	Answers the question: Are we doing things right?	Answers the question: What is the status of this MOE or MOP?
Measures purpose accomplishment.	Measures task completion.	Measures raw data inputs to inform MOEs and MOPs.
Measures why in the mission statement.	Measures what in the mission statement.	Information used to make measuring what or why possible.
No hierarchical relationship to MOPs.	No hierarchical relationship to MOEs.	Subordinate to MOEs and MOPs.
Often formally tracked in formal assessment plans.	Often formally tracked in execution matrixes.	Often formally tracked in formal assessment plans.
Typically challenging to choose the correct ones.	Typically simple to choose the correct ones.	Typically as challenging to select correctly as the supported MOE or MOP.

Ref: ADRP 5-0, The Operations Process, table 5-1, p. 5-3.

A. Measures of Effectiveness (MOEs)

A measure of effectiveness is a criterion used to assess changes in system behavior, capability, or operational environment that is tied to measuring the attainment of an end state, achievement of an objective, or creation of an effect. MOE's help measure changes in conditions, both positive and negative. MOE's help to answer the question "Are we doing the right things?" MOE's are commonly found and tracked in formal assessment plans. Examples of MOE's for "Provide a safe and secure environment" may include:

• Decrease in insurgent activity
• Increase in population trust of host-nation security forces

B. Measures of Performance (MOPs)

A measure of performance is a criterion used to assess friendly actions that is tied to measuring task accomplishment (JP 3-0). MOP's help answer questions such as, "Was the action taken?" or "Were the tasks completed to standard?" A MOP confirms or denies that a task has been properly performed. MOP's are commonly found and tracked at all levels in execution matrixes. MOP's are also heavily used to evaluate training. MOP's help to answer the question "Are we doing things right?"

At the most basic level, every Soldier assigned a task maintains a formal or informal checklist to track task completion. The items on that checklist are MOP's. Similarly, operations consist of a series of collective tasks sequenced in time, space, and purpose to accomplish missions. The current operations cells use MOP's in execution matrixes and running estimates to track completed tasks. The uses of MOP's are a primary element of battle tracking. MOP's focus on the friendly force. Evaluating task accomplishment using MOP's is relatively straightforward and often results in a yes or no answer.

Examples of MOPs include:

- Route X cleared
- Generators delivered, are operational, and secured at villages A, B, and C
- Hill 785 secured
- Aerial dissemination of 10,000 leaflets over village D

C. Indicators

In the context of assessment, an indicator is an item of information that provides insight into a measure of effectiveness or measure of performance. Staffs use indicators to shape their collection effort as part of ISR synchronization. Indicators take the form of reports from subordinates, surveys and polls, and information requirements. Indicators help to answer the question "What is the current status of this MOE or MOP?" A single indicator can inform multiple MOP's and MOE's. Examples of indicators for the MOE "Decrease in insurgent activity" are:

- Number of hostile actions per area each week
- Number of munitions caches found per area each week

Evaluation includes analysis of why progress is or is not being made according to the plan. Commanders and staffs propose and consider possible causes. In particular, the question of whether changes in the situation can be attributed to friendly actions is addressed. Subject matter experts, both internal and external to the staff, are consulted on whether the correct underlying causes for specific changes in the situation have been identified. Assumptions identified in the planning process are challenged to determine if they are still valid.

A key aspect of evaluation is determining variances—the difference between the actual situation and what the plan forecasted the situation would be at the time or event. Based on the significance of the variances, the staff makes recommendations to the commander on how to adjust operations to accomplish the mission more effectively. Evaluating includes considering whether the desired conditions have changed, are no longer achievable, or are not achievable through the current operational approach.

Quantitative and Qualitative Indicators (not in ADRP 5-0)

Effective assessment incorporates both quantitative (observation based) and qualitative (opinion based) indicators. Human judgment is integral to assessment. A key aspect of any assessment is the degree to which it relies upon human judgment and the degree to which it relies upon direct observation and mathematical rigor.

- **Quantitative**. In the context of assessment, a quantitative indicator is an observation-based (objective) item of information that provides insight into a measure of effectiveness or measure of performance. Little human judgment is involved in collecting a quantitative indicator. Someone observes an event and counts it. For example, they tally the monthly gallons of diesel provided to host-nation security forces by a unit or the monthly number of tips provided to a particular tips hotline. Quantitative indicators prove less biased than qualitative indicators. In general, numbers based on observations are impartial.

- **Qualitative**. In the context of assessment, a qualitative indicator is an opinion-based (subjective) item of information that provides insight into a measure of effectiveness or measure of performance. A high degree of human judgment is involved when collecting qualitative indicators. Qualitative indicators are themselves opinions, not just observed opinions of others such as polls. For example, the division commander estimates the effectiveness of the host-nation forces on a scale of 1 to 5. Sources of qualitative indicators include subject matter experts' opinions and judgments as well as subordinate commanders' summaries of the situation. Qualitative indicators can account for real-world complexities that cannot be feasibly measured using quantitative indicators.

See following pages (pp. 1-72 to 1-73) for further discussion of developing formal assessment plans from FM 6-0.

IV. Assessment Plan Development

Ref: FM 6-0 (C1), Commander and Staff Organization and Operations (May '15), pp. 15-4 to 15-9.

Critical to the assessment process is developing an assessment plan. Units use assessment working groups to develop assessment plans when appropriate. A critical element of the commander's planning guidance is determining which assessment plans to develop. An assessment plan focused on attainment of end state conditions often works well. It is also possible, and may be desirable, to develop an entire formal assessment plan for an intermediate objective, a named operation subordinate to the base operation plan, or a named operation focused solely on a single line of operations or geographic area. The time, resources, and added complexity involved in generating an assessment plan strictly limit the number of such efforts.

Commanders and staffs integrate and develop an assessment plan within the military decisionmaking process (MDMP). As the commander and staff begin mission analysis, they also need to determine how to measure progress towards the operation's end state.

Effective assessment incorporates both quantitative (observation-based) and qualitative (judgment-based) indicators. Human judgment is integral to assessment. A key aspect of any assessment is the degree to which it relies upon human judgment and the degree to which it relies upon direct observation and mathematical rigor. Rigor offsets the inevitable bias, while human judgment focuses rigor and processes on intangibles that are often key to success. The appropriate balance depends on the situation—particularly the nature of the operation and available resources for assessment—but rarely lies at the ends of the scale.

1. Gather Tools and Assessment Data

Planning begins with receipt of mission. The receipt of mission alerts the staffs who begin updating their running estimates and gather the tools necessary for mission analysis and continued planning. Specific tools and information gathered regarding assessment include, but are not limited to—

- The higher headquarters' plan or order, including the assessment annex if available
- If replacing a unit, any current assessments and assessment products
- Relevant assessment products (classified or open-source) produced by civilian and military organizations
- The identification of potential data sources, including academic institutions and civilian subject matter experts

2. Understand Current and Desired Conditions

Fundamentally, assessment is about measuring progress toward the desired end state. To do this, commanders and staffs compare current conditions in the area of operations against desired conditions. Army design methodology and the MDMP help commanders and staffs develop an understanding of the current situation. As planning continues, the commander identifies desired conditions that represent the operation's end state.

Early in planning, commanders issue their initial commander's intent, planning guidance, and commander's critical information requirements (CCIRs). The end state in the initial commander's intent describes the desired conditions the commander wants to achieve. The staff element responsible for the assessment plan identifies each specific desired condition mentioned in the commander's intent. These specific desired conditions focus the overall assessment of the operation. Understanding current conditions and desired conditions forms the basis for building the assessment framework.

3. Develop an Assessment Framework

All plans and orders have a general logic. This logic links tasks to subordinate units to the achievement of objectives, and the achievement of objectives to attainment of the operation's end state. An assessment framework incorporates the logic of the plan and uses measures (MOEs, MOPs, and indicators).

Developing assessment measures and potential indicators involves—

- Selecting and writing MOEs
- Organizing the measures into an assessment framework.

Based on their understanding of the plan, members of the staff develop specific MOEs and MOPs (with associated indicators) to evaluate the operations process. Measures of effectiveness are tools used to help measure the attainment of end state conditions, achievement of objectives, or creation of effects. Measures of performance are criteria used to assess friendly actions that are tied to measuring task accomplishment.

Commanders select only MOEs that measure the degree to which the desired outcome is achieved. There must be an expectation that a given MOE will change as the conditions being measured change. Commanders choose MOEs for each condition as distinct from each other as possible. Using similar MOEs can skew the assessment by containing virtually the same MOE twice. Commanders include MOEs from differing relevant causal chains for each condition whenever possible. When MOEs have a cause and effect relationship with each other, either directly or indirectly, it decreases their value in measuring a particular condition. Measuring progress towards a desired condition by multiple means adds rigor to the assessment.

MOPs are criteria used to assess friendly actions that are tied to measuring task accomplishment. MOPs help to answer questions such as "Was the action taken?" or "Were the tasks completed to standard?" A MOP confirms or denies that a task has been properly performed. MOPs are commonly found and tracked at all levels in execution matrixes.

Staffs develop indicators that provide insights into MOEs and MOPs. Staffs can gauge a measurable indicator either quantitatively or qualitatively.

4. Develop the Collection Plan

Each indicator represents an information requirement. In some situations, staffs feed these information requirements into the information collection synchronization process. Then, staffs task information collection assets to collect on these information requirements. In other situations, reports in the unit standard operating procedures (SOPs) may suffice. If not, the unit may develop a new report. Staffs may collect the information requirement from organizations external to the unit. For example, a host nation's central bank may publish a consumer price index for that nation. The assessment plan identifies the source for each indicator as well as the staff member who collects that information. Assessment information requirements compete with other information requirements for resources. When an information requirement is not resourced, staffs cannot collect the associated indicator and must remove it from the plan. Staffs then adjust the assessment framework to ensure that the MOE or MOP is properly worded.

5. Assign Responsibilities and Generate Recommendations

In addition to assigning responsibility for collection, commanders assign staff members to analyze assessment data and develop recommendations. For example, the intelligence officer leads the assessment of enemy forces. The engineer officer leads the effort on assessing infrastructure development. The civil affairs operations officer leads assessment concerning the progress of local and provincial governments. The chief of staff aggressively requires staff principals and subject matter experts to participate in processing the formal assessment and in generating smart, actionable recommendations. The operations research and analysis officer assists the commander and staff with developing both assessment frameworks and the command's assessment process.

6. Identify Feedback Mechanisms

A formal assessment with meaningful recommendations never heard by the appropriate decisionmaker wastes time and energy. The assessment plan identifies the who, what, when, where, and why of that presentation. Feedback leading up to and following that presentation is discussed as well. Feedback might include which assessment working groups are required and how to act and follow up on recommendations.

V. Guides to Effective Assessment
Ref: ADRP 5-0, The Operations Process (Mar '12), pp. 5-4 to 5-5.

Throughout the conduct of operations, commanders integrate their own assessments with those of the staff, subordinate commanders, and other partners in the area of operations. The following guides aid in effective assessment:

Guides to Effective Assessment

- **Commanders Prioritize the Assessment Effort**
- **Incorporate the Logic of the Plan**
- **Use Caution When Establishing Cause and Effect**
- **Combine Quantitative and Qualitative Indicators**

Commanders Prioritize the Assessment Effort
Commanders establish priorities for assessment in their planning guidance, CCIRs, and decision points. By prioritizing the effort, commanders avoid excessive analyses when assessing operations. Committing valuable time and energy to developing excessive and time-consuming assessment schemes squanders resources better devoted to other operations process activities. Commanders reject the tendency to measure something just because it is measurable. Effective commanders avoid burdening subordinates and staffs with overly detailed assessments and collection tasks. Generally, the echelon at which a specific operation, task, or action is conducted should be the echelon at which it is assessed.

Incorporate the Logic of the Plan
Effective assessment relies on an accurate understanding of the logic (reasoning) used to build the plan. Each plan is built on assumptions and an operational approach. The reasons or logic as to why the commander believes the plan will produce the desired results are important considerations when staffs determine how to assess operations. Recording and understanding this logic helps the staffs recommend the appropriate measures of effectiveness, measures of performance, and indicators for assessing the operation.

Use Caution When Establishing Cause and Effect
Although establishing cause and effect is sometimes difficult, it is crucial to effective assessment. Sometimes, establishing causality between actions and their effects can be relatively straightforward, such as in observing a bomb destroy a bridge. In other instances, especially regarding changes in human behavior, attitudes, and perception, establishing links between cause and effect proves difficult. Commanders and staffs must guard against drawing erroneous conclusions in these instances.

Combine Quantitative and Qualitative Indicators
Effective assessment incorporates both quantitative (observation-based) and qualitative (opinion-based) indicators. Human judgment is integral to assessment. A key aspect of any assessment is the degree to which it relies upon human judgment and the degree to which it relies upon direct observation and mathematical rigor. Rigor offsets the inevitable bias, while human judgment focuses rigor and processes on intangibles that are often key to success. The appropriate balance depends on the situation—particularly the nature of the operation and available resources for assessment—but rarely lies at the ends of the scale.

See p. 1-71 for discussion of quantitative and qualitative indicators.

The Military Decision-making Process (MDMP)

Ref: FM 6-0 (C1), Commander and Staff Organization and Operations (May '15), chap. 9.

The military decisionmaking process is an iterative planning methodology to understand the situation and mission develop a course of action, and produce an operation plan or order (ADP 5-0).

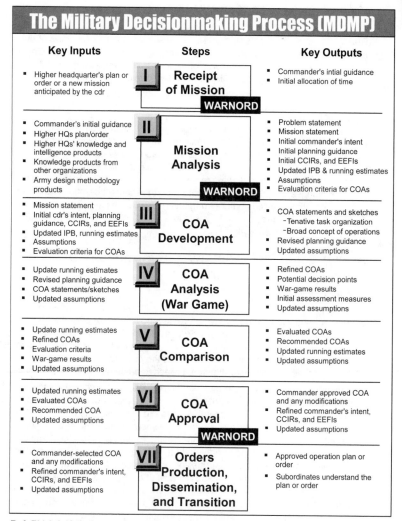

The Military Decisionmaking Process (MDMP)

Key Inputs	Steps	Key Outputs
• Higher headquarter's plan or order or a new mission anticipated by the cdr	**I Receipt of Mission** *WARNORD*	• Commander's initial guidance • Initial allocation of time
• Commander's initial guidance • Higher HQs plan/order • Higher HQs' knowledge and intelligence products • Knowledge products from other organizations • Army design methodology products	**II Mission Analysis** *WARNORD*	• Problem statement • Mission statement • Initial commander's intent • Initial planning guidance • Initial CCIRs, and EEFIs • Updated IPB & running estimates • Assumptions • Evaluation criteria for COAs

• Mission statement
• Initial cdr's intent, planning guidance, CCIRs, and EEFIs
• Updated IPB, running estimates
• Assumptions
• Evaluation criteria for COAs
	III COA Development	• COA statements and sketches
		  - Tenative task organization
		  - Broad concept of operations
		• Revised planning guidance
		• Updated assumptions

• Update running estimates • Revised planning guidance • COA statements/sketches • Updated assumptions	**IV COA Analysis (War Game)**	• Refined COAs • Potential decision points • War-game results • Initial assessment measures • Updated assumptions
• Update running estimates • Refined COAs • Evaluation criteria • War-game results • Updated assumptions	**V COA Comparison**	• Evaluated COAs • Recommended COAs • Updated running estimates • Updated assumptions
• Updated running estimates • Evaluated COAs • Recommended COA • Updated assumptions	**VI COA Approval** *WARNORD*	• Commander approved COA and any modifications • Refined commander's intent, CCIRs, and EEFIs • Updated assumptions
• Commander-selected COA and any modifications • Refined commander's intent, CCIRs, and EEFIs • Updated assumptions	**VII Orders Production, Dissemination, and Transition**	• Approved operation plan or order • Subordinates understand the plan or order

Ref: FM 6-0 (C1), Commander and Staff Organization and Operations, fig. 9-1, p. 4-3.

The military decision making process (MDMP) helps leaders apply thoroughness, clarity, sound judgment, logic, and professional knowledge to understand situations, develop options to solve problems, and reach decisions. This process helps commanders, staffs, and others think critically and creatively while planning.

Collaborative Planning

The MDMP facilitates collaborative planning. The higher headquarters solicits input and continuously shares information concerning future operations through planning meetings, warning orders, and other means. It shares information with subordinate and adjacent units, supporting and supported units, and other military and civilian partners. Commanders encourage active collaboration among all organizations affected by the pending operations to build a shared understanding of the situation, participate in course of action development and decision making, and resolve conflicts before publishing the plan or order.

Assessment

During planning, assessment focuses on developing an understanding of the current situation and determining what to assess and how to assess progress using measures of effectiveness and measures of performance. Developing the unit's assessment plan occurs during the MDMP—not after developing the plan or order.

See pp. 1-67 to 1-74 for further discussion of assessment.

Preparation

The MDMP also drives preparation. Since time is a factor in all operations, commanders and staffs conduct a time analysis early in the planning process. This analysis helps them determine what actions they need and when to begin those actions to ensure forces are ready and in position before execution. This may require the commander to direct subordinates to start necessary movements, conduct task organization changes, begin surveillance and reconnaissance operations, and execute other preparation activities before completing the plan. As the commander and staff conduct the MDMP, they direct the tasks in a series of warning orders (WARNOs).

See pp. 1-47 to 1-52 for further discussion of preparation.

Army Design Methodology and the Military Decision-making Process (MDMP)

See pp. 1-34 to 1-41 for further discussion of the Army design methodology.

Depending on the situation—to include the familiarity of the problem—commanders conduct Army design methodology before, in parallel with, or after the MDMP. When faced with an unfamiliar problem or when developing initial plans for extended operations, commanders often initiate the Army design methodology before the MDMP. This sequence helps them better understand the operational environment, frame the problem, and develop an operational approach to guide more detailed planning.

Commanders may also elect to conduct the Army design methodology in parallel with the MDMP. In this instance, members of the staff conduct mission analysis as the commander and other staff members engage in framing the operational environment and the problem. Knowledge products—such as results from intelligence preparation of the battlefield and running estimates—help inform the Army design methodology team about the operational environment. Commanders may direct some staff members to focus their mission analysis on certain areas. This focus helps commanders better understand aspects of the operational environment. The results of mission analysis (to include intelligence preparation of the battlefield and running estimates) inform commanders as they develop their operational approach that, in turn, facilitates course of action development during the MDMP.

In time-constrained conditions requiring immediate action, or if the problem is familiar, commanders may conduct the MDMP and publish an operation order without formally conducting Army design methodology. As time becomes available during execution, commanders may then initiate Army design methodology to help refine their commander's visualization and the initial plan developed using the MDMP.

Steps of the Military Decisionmaking Process

The MDMP consists of seven steps. Each step of the MDMP has various inputs, a method (step) to conduct, and outputs. The outputs lead to an increased understanding of the situation facilitating the next step of the MDMP. Commanders and staffs generally perform these steps sequentially; however, they may revisit several steps in an iterative fashion as they learn more about the situation before producing the plan or order.

Commanders initiate the MDMP upon receipt of or in anticipation of a mission. Commanders and staffs often begin planning in the absence of a complete and approved higher headquarters' operation plan (OPLAN) or operation order (OPORD). In these instances, the headquarters begins a new planning effort based on a WARNO and other directives, such as a planning order or an alert order from their higher headquarters. This requires active collaboration with the higher headquarters and parallel planning among echelons as the plan or order is developed.

This chapter describes the methods and provides techniques for conducting each step of the MDMP. This section also describes how the following processes are integrated throughout the MDMP:

- Intelligence preparation of the battlefield *(see pp. 3-3 to 3-46)*
- Targeting *(see pp. 3-47 to 3-58)*
- Risk management *(see pp. 3-59 to 3-62)*

Modifying the MDMP

The MDMP can be as detailed as time, resources, experience, and the situation permit. Conducting all steps of the MDMP is detailed, deliberate, and time-consuming. Commanders use the full MDMP when they have enough planning time and staff support to thoroughly examine two or more COAs and develop a fully synchronized plan or order. This typically occurs when planning for an entirely new mission.

Commanders may alter the steps of the MDMP to fit time-constrained circumstances and produce a satisfactory plan. In time-constrained conditions, commanders assess the situation, update the commander's visualization, and direct the staff to perform the MDMP activities that support the required decisions. In extremely compressed situations, commanders rely on more intuitive decision making techniques, such as the rapid decision making and synchronization process.

See pp. 2-57 to 2-58 for discussion of planning in a time-constrained environment.

An Army headquarters (battalion through Army Service component command) uses the MDMP and publishes plans and orders in accordance with the Army plans and orders format. An Army headquarters that forms the base of a joint task force uses the joint operation planning process (JOPP) and publishes plans and orders in accordance with the joint format (see JP 5-0 and CJCSM 3122.03C).

An Army headquarters (such as Army Corps) that provides the base of a joint force or coalition forces land component command headquarters will participate in joint planning and receive a joint formatted plan or order. This headquarters then has the option to use the MDMP or JOPP to develop its own supporting plan or order written in the proper Army or joint format to distribute to subordinate commands.

Refer to The Joint Forces Operations & Doctrine SMARTbook.

II. Running Estimates

Ref: FM 6-0 (C1), Commander and Staff Organization and Operations (May '15), chap. 8.

A running estimate is the continuous assessment of the current situation and future operations used to determine if the current operation is proceeding according to the commander's intent and if future operations are supportable. The commander and each staff section maintain a running estimate. In their running estimates, the commander and each staff section continuously consider the effects of new information and update the following:

- Facts
- Assumptions
- Friendly force status
- Enemy activities and capabilities
- Civil considerations
- Conclusions and recommendations

Commanders maintain their running estimates to consolidate their understanding and visualization of an operation. The commander's running estimate includes a summary of the problem and integrates information and knowledge of the staff's and subordinate commanders' running estimates.

Each staff element builds and maintains running estimates. The running estimate helps the staff to track and record pertinent information and provide recommendations to commanders. Running estimates represent the analysis and expert opinion of each staff element by functional area. Staffs maintain running estimates throughout the operations process to assist commanders in the exercise of mission command.

Each staff element and command post functional cell maintains a running estimate focused on how its specific areas of expertise are postured to support future operations. Because an estimate may be needed at any time, running estimates must be developed, revised, updated, and maintained continuously while in garrison and during operations. While in garrison, staffs must maintain a running estimate on friendly capabilities. Running estimates can be presented verbally or in writing.

A comprehensive running estimate addresses all aspects of operations and contains both facts and assumptions based on the staff's experience within a specific area of expertise. Each staff element modifies it to account for its specific functional areas. All running estimates cover essential facts and assumptions, including a summary of the current situation by the mission variables, conclusions, and recommendations. Once they complete the plan, commanders and staff elements continuously update their estimates.

See pp. 2-14 to 2-17 for sample staff guidelines for mission analysis.

The base running estimate addresses information unique to each functional area. It serves as the staff's initial assessment of the current readiness of equipment and personnel and how the factors considered in the running estimate affect their ability to accomplish the mission. The staff identifies functional area friendly and enemy strengths, systems, training, morale, leadership, weather and terrain effects, and how all these factors define both the operational environment and area of operations. Because the running estimate is a picture relative to time, facts, and assumptions, it is constantly updated as new information arises, as assumptions become facts or are invalidated, when the mission changes, or when the cdr requires additional input.

Running Estimates In The Operations Process

Commanders and staff elements immediately begin updating their running estimates upon receipt of a mission. They continue to build and maintain their running estimates throughout the operations process in planning, preparation, execution, and assessment. Running estimates can be presented verbally or in writing.

Generic Base Running Estimate Format

1. SITUATION AND CONSIDERATIONS.

a. Area of Interest. Identify and describe the area of interest that impact or affect functional area considerations.

b. Characteristics of the Area of Operations.

(1) Terrain. State how terrain affects staff functional area's capabilities.

(2) Weather. State how weather affects staff functional area's capabilities.

(3) Enemy Forces. Describe enemy disposition, composition, strength, capabilities, systems, and possible courses of action (COAs) with respect to their effect on functional area.

(4) Friendly Forces. List current functional area resources in terms of equipment, personnel, and systems. Identify additional resources available for functional area located at higher, adjacent, or other units. Compare requirements to current capabilities and suggest solutions for satisfying discrepancies.

(5) Civilian Considerations. Describe additional personnel, groups, or associations that cannot be categorized as friendly or enemy. Discuss possible impact these entities may have on functional area.

c. Assumptions. List all assumptions that affect the functional area.

2. MISSION. Show the restated mission resulting from mission analysis.

3. COURSES OF ACTION.

a. List friendly COAs that were war-gamed.

b. List enemy actions or COAs that were templated that impact functional area.

c. List the evaluation criteria identified during COA analysis. All staff use the same criteria.

4. ANALYSIS. Analyze each COA using the evaluation criteria from COA analysis. Review enemy actions that impact functional area as they relate to COAs. Identify issues, risks, and deficiencies these enemy actions may create with respect to functional area.

5. COMPARISON. Compare COAs. Rank order COAs for each key consideration. Use a decision matrix to aid the comparison process.

6. RECOMMENDATION AND CONCLUSIONS.

a. Recommend the most supportable COAs from the perspective of the functional area.

b. Prioritize and list issues, deficiencies, and risks and make recommendations on how to mitigate them.

Each staff element continuously analyzes new information during operations to create knowledge and to understand if operations are progressing according to plan. During planning, staffs develop measures of effectiveness and measures of performance to support assessment, including analysis of anticipated decisions during preparation and execution. The assessment of current operations also supports validation or rejection of additional information that will help update the estimates and support further planning. At a minimum, a staff element's running estimate assesses the following::

- Friendly force capabilities with respect to ongoing and planned operations.
- Enemy capabilities as they affect the staff element's area of expertise for current operations and plans for future operations.
- Civil considerations as they affect the staff element's area of expertise for current operations and plans for future operations.

III. The Role of Commanders and Staff

Ref: FM 6-0 (C1), Commander and Staff Organization and Operations (May '15), p. 9-2.

The **commander** is the most important participant in the MDMP. More than simply the decision makers in this process, commanders use their experience, knowledge, and judgment to guide staff planning efforts. While unable to devote all their time to the MDMP, commanders remain aware of the current status of the planning effort, participate during critical periods of the process, and make sound decisions based upon the detailed work of the staff. During the MDMP, commanders focus their battle command activities on understanding, visualizing, and describing.

The **chief of staff (COS)** or **executive officer (XO)** is a key participant in the MDMP. The COS or XO manages and coordinates the staff's work and provides quality control during the MDMP. The COS or XO must clearly understand the commander's intent and guidance because COS's or Sox supervise the entire process. They provide timelines to the staff, establish briefing times and locations, and provide any instructions necessary to complete the plan.

The **staff's** effort during the MDMP focuses on helping the commander understand the situation, making decisions, and synchronizing those decisions into a fully developed plan or order. Staff activities during planning initially focus on mission analysis. The products developed during mission analysis help commanders understand the situation and develop the commander's visualization. During course of action (COA) development and COA comparison, the staff provides recommendations to support the commander in selecting a COA. After the commander makes a decision, the staff prepares the plan or order that reflects the commander's intent, coordinating all necessary details.

	Cdr	Staff Officers	Staff NCOs	RTOs	Clerks/ Typists
Mission Analysis					
Prepare charts for msn analysis				x	x
Prepare terrain sketches				x	x
Update/post unit reports/status			x	x	
Prepare TOC for planning			x	x	x
Conduct mission analysis		x	x		
Serve as recorder			x	x	x
Brief commander and staff	x	x	x		
Commander's Guidance					
Assist cdr in developing guidance		x	x		
Issue guidance	x				
Record/post cdr's guidance		x	x	x	x
COA Development					
Prepare charts				x	x
Sketch COAs				x	x
Develop COAs	x	x	x		
COA Analysis					
Collect and prepare tools/charts				x	x
Serve as war-game recorders			x	x	x
Conduct war-game session	x	x	x		
COA Approval					
Make recommendation to cdr		x	x		
Decide	x				
Record/post cdr's guidance		x	x	x	x
Orders Preparation					
Write annexes		x	x		
Consolidate annexes			x	x	
Type order			x	x	x
Reproduce order/graphics				x	x
Review order	x	x	x		
Approve order	x				

Ref: Adapted from FM 101-5, fig. K-1 (not found in FM 6-0).

MDMP Step I.
Receipt of Mission

Ref: FM 6-0 (C1), Commander and Staff Organization and Operations (May '15), pp. 9-4 to 9-6.

Commanders initiate the MDMP upon receipt or in anticipation of a mission. This step alerts all participants of the pending planning requirements, enabling them to determine the amount of time available for planning and preparation and decide on a planning approach, including guidance on design and how to abbreviate the MDMP, if required. When commanders identify a new mission, commanders and staffs perform the actions and produce the expected key outputs.

I. Receipt of Mission

Key Inputs	Key Outputs
• Higher headquarters plan or order or a new mission anticipated by the commander	• Commander's initial guidance • Initial allocation of time **WARNORD**

1 Alert the Staff and Other Key Participants

2 Gather the Tools

3 Update Running Estimates

4 Conduct Initial Assessment

5 Issue the Commander's Initial Guidance

6 Issue the Initial Warning Order

Ref: FM 6-0 (C1), Commander and Staff Organization and Operations, fig. 9-2, p. 9-4.

1. Alert the Staff and Other Key Participants

As soon as a unit receives a new mission (or when the commander directs), the current operations integration cell alerts the staff of the pending planning requirement. Unit standard operating procedures (SOPs) should identify members of the planning staff who participate in mission analysis. In addition, the current operations integration cell also notifies other military, civilian, and host-nation organizations of pending planning events as required.

2. Gather the Tools

Once notified of the new planning requirement, the staff prepares for mission analysis by gathering the needed tools. These tools include, but are not limited to:

- Appropriate publications, including ADRP 1-02
- All documents related to the mission and area of operations, including the higher headquarters' OPLAN and OPORD, maps and terrain products, and operational graphics
- Higher headquarters' and other organizations' intelligence and assessment products
- Estimates and products of other military and civilian agencies and organizations
- Both their own and the higher headquarters' SOPs
- Current running estimates
- Any Army design methodology products

The gathering of knowledge products continues throughout the MDMP. Staff officers carefully review the reference sections (located before paragraph 1. Situation) of the higher headquarters' OPLANs and OPORDs to identify documents (such as theater policies and memoranda) related to the upcoming operation. If the MDMP occurs while in the process of replacing another unit, the staff begins collecting relevant documents—such as the current OPORD, branch plans, current assessments, operations and intelligence summaries, and SOPs—from that unit.

3. Update Running Estimates

While gathering the necessary tools for planning, each staff section begins updating its running estimate—especially the status of friendly units and resources and key civil considerations that affect each functional area. Running estimates compile critical facts and assumptions not only from the perspective of each staff section, but also include information from other staff sections and other military and civilian organizations. While this task is listed at the beginning of the MDMP, developing and updating running estimates is continuous throughout the MDMP and the operations process.

See pp. 2-4 to 2-5 for further discussion of running estimates.

4. Conduct Initial Assessment

During receipt of mission, the commander and staff conduct an initial assessment of time and resources available to plan, prepare, and begin execution of an operation. This initial assessment helps commanders determine:

- The time needed to plan and prepare for the mission for both headquarters and subordinate units
- Guidance on conducting the Army design methodology and abbreviating the MDMP, if required
- Which outside agencies and organizations to contact and incorporate into the planning process
- The staff's experience, cohesiveness, and level of rest or stress

This assessment primarily identifies an initial allocation of available time. The commander and staff balance the desire for detailed planning against the need for immediate action. The commander provides guidance to subordinate units as early as possible to allow subordinates the maximum time for their own planning and preparation of operations. As a rule, commanders allocate a minimum of two-thirds of available time for subordinate units to conduct their planning and preparation. This leaves one-third of the time for commanders and their staff to do their planning. They use the other two-thirds for their own preparation. Time, more than any other factor, determines the detail to which the commander and staff can plan.

Initial Allocation of Available Time

Ref: Adapted from FM 5-0, The Operations Process (Mar '10), pp. B-5 (not found in FM 6-0).

A key product of this assessment is an initial allocation of available time. The commander and staff balance the desire for detailed planning against the need for immediate action. The commander provides guidance to subordinate units as early as possible to allow subordinates the maximum time for their own planning and preparation of operations. As a rule, the commander allocates a minimum of two-thirds of available time for subordinate units to conduct their planning and preparation. This leaves one-third of the time for commanders and their staff to do their planning. They use the other two-thirds for their own preparation. Time, more than any other factor, determines the detail in which the commander and staff can plan.

Based on the commander's initial allocation of time, the COS or XO develops a staff planning timeline that outlines how long the headquarters can spend on each step of the MDMP. The staff planning timeline indicates what products are due, who is responsible for them, and who receives them. It includes times and locations for meetings and briefings. It serves as a benchmark for the commander and staff throughout the MDMP.

A generic time line could be based on the one-third/two-thirds rule:

• Mission analysis	30%
• COA development	20%
• COA analysis/comparison/decision	30%
• Orders production	20%

One-Third, Two-Thirds Rule

Effective execution requires issuing timely plans and orders to subordinates. Timely plans are those issued soon enough to allow subordinates enough time to plan, issue their orders, and prepare for operations. At a minimum, commanders follow the "one-third–two-thirds rule" to allocate time available. They use one-third of the time available before execution for their planning and allocate the remaining two-thirds to their subordinates for planning and preparation.

Parallel and Collaborative Planning

Commanders ensure that plans are sent to subordinates in enough time to allow them to adequately plan and prepare their own operations. To accomplish this, echelons plan in parallel as much as possible. Additionally, new information systems (INFOSYS) enable echelons to plan collaboratively without being co-located.

Parallel planning is two or more echelons planning for the same operation nearly simultaneously. Since several echelons develop their plans simultaneously, parallel planning can significantly shorten planning time. The higher headquarters continuously shares information concerning future operations with subordinate units through warning orders and other means. Frequent communication between commanders and staff and sharing of information, such as intelligence preparation of the battlefield products, helps subordinate headquarters plan. Parallel planning requires significant interaction among echelons.

Collaborative planning is when commanders, subordinate commanders, staffs and other partners share information, knowledge, perceptions, ideas, and concepts regardless of physical location throughout the planning process. Collaboration occurs during all operations process activities, not just planning. During planning, commanders, subordinate commanders, and others in the area of operations share assessments, statuses, and ideas.

See pp. 2-57 to 2-58 for discussion of planning in a time-constrained environment.

Based on the commander's initial allocation of time, the COS (XO) develops a staff planning timeline that outlines how long the headquarters can spend on each step of the MDMP. The staff planning timeline indicates what products are due, who is responsible for them, and who receives them. It includes times and locations for meetings and briefings. It serves as a benchmark for the commander and staff throughout the MDMP.

5. Issue the Commander's Initial Guidance

Once time is allocated, the commander determines whether to initiate Army design methodology, perform Army design methodology in parallel with the MDMP, or proceed directly into the MDMP without the benefits of formal Army design methodology activities. In time-sensitive situations where commanders decide to proceed directly into the MDMP, they may also issue guidance on how to abbreviate the process. Having determined the time available together with the scope and scale of the planning effort, commanders issue initial planning guidance. Although brief, the initial guidance includes, but is not limited to:

- Initial time allocations
- A decision to initiate Army design methodology or go straight into the MDMP
- How to abbreviate the MDMP, if required
- Necessary coordination to exchange liaison officers
- Authorized movements and initiation of information collection
- Collaborative planning times and locations
- Initial information requirements
- Additional staff tasks

6. Issue the Initial Warning Order

The last task in receipt of mission is to issue a WARNORD to subordinate and supporting units. This order includes at a minimum the type of operation, the general location of the operation, the initial timeline, and any movement or reconnaissance to initiate.

See p. 4-21 for a sample warning order format.

MDMP Step II. Mission Analysis

Ref: FM 6-0 (C1), Commander and Staff Organization and Operations (May '15), pp. 9-6 to 9-16.

The MDMP continues with an assessment of the situation called mission analysis. Commanders (supported by their staffs and informed by subordinate and adjacent commanders and by other partners) gather, analyze, and synthesize information to orient themselves on the current conditions of the operational environment. The commander and staff conduct mission analysis to better understand the situation and problem, and identify *what* the command must accomplish, *when* and *where* it must be done, and most importantly *why*—the purpose of the operation.

II. Mission Analysis

Key Inputs	Key Outputs
▪ Commander's initial guidance ▪ Higher headquarters plan or order ▪ Higher headquarters knowledge and intelligence products ▪ Knowledge products from other organizations ▪ Updated running estimates ▪ Army design methodology products	▪ Problem statement ▪ Mission statement ▪ Initial commander's intent ▪ Initial planning guidance ▪ Initial CCIRs, and EEFIs ▪ Updated IPB products and running estimates ▪ Assumptions ▪ Evaluation criteria for COAs **WARNORD**

1 Analyze the Higher HQ Plan or Order	**10** Update Plan for Use of Available Time
2 Perform Initial IPB	**11** Develop Initial Themes and Messages
3 Determine Specified, Implied and Essential Tasks	**12** Develop a Proposed Problem Statement
4 Review Available Assets and Identify Resource Shortfalls	**13** Develop a Proposed Mission Statement
5 Determine Constraints	**14** Present the Mission Analysis Briefing
6 Identify Critical Facts and Develop Assumptions	**15** Develop and Issue Initial Commander's Intent
7 Begin Risk Management	**16** Develop and Issue Initial Planning Guidance
8 Develop Initial CCIR and EEFI	**17** Develop COA Evaluation Criteria
9 Develop the Initial Information Collection Plan	**18** Issue a Warning Order

Ref: FM 6-0 (C1), Commander and Staff Organization and Operations, fig. 9-3, p. 9-7.

Since no amount of subsequent planning can solve an insufficiently understood problem, mission analysis is the most important step in the MDMP. This understanding of the situation and the problem allows commanders to visualize and describe how the operation may unfold in their initial commander's intent and planning guidance. During mission analysis, the commander and staff perform the process actions and produce the outputs.

Commanders and staffs may also begin the development of evaluation criteria during this step. These evaluation criteria are continually developed and refined throughout the MDMP and become a key input during Step 5—Course of Action Comparison.

MDMP
& TLP

1. Analyze the Higher Headquarters Plan or Order

Commanders and staffs thoroughly analyze the higher headquarters' plan or order. They determine how their unit—by task and purpose—contributes to the mission, commander's intent, and concept of operations of the higher headquarters. The commander and staff seek to completely understand:

- The higher headquarters'
  - Commander's intent
  - Mission
  - Concept of operations
  - Available assets
  - Timeline
- The missions of adjacent, supporting, and supported units and their relationships to the higher headquarters' plan
- The missions or goals of unified action partners that work in the operational areas
- Their assigned area of operations

If the commander misinterprets the higher headquarters' plan, time is wasted. Additionally, when analyzing the higher order, the commander and staff may identify difficulties and contradictions in the higher order. Therefore, if confused by the higher headquarters' order or guidance, commanders must seek immediate clarification. Liaison officers familiar with the higher headquarters' plan can help clarify issues. Collaborative planning with the higher headquarters also facilitates this task. Staffs use requests for information to clarify or obtain additional information from the higher headquarters.

2. Perform Initial Intelligence Preparation of the Battlefield (IPB)

IPB is the systematic process of analyzing the mission variables of enemy, terrain, weather, and civil considerations in an area of interest to determine their effect on operations. The IPB process identifies critical gaps in the commander's knowledge of an operational environment. As a part of the initial planning guidance, commanders use these gaps as a guide to establish their initial intelligence requirements. IPB products enable the commander to assess facts about the operational environment and make assumptions about how friendly and threat forces will interact in the operational environment. The description of the operational environment's effects identifies constraints on potential friendly COAs. It also identifies key aspects of the operational environment, such as avenues of approach, engagement areas, and landing zones, which the staff integrates into potential friendly COAs and their running estimates. For mission analysis, the intelligence staff, along with the other staff elements, will use IPB to develop detailed threat COA models, which depict a COA available to the threat. The threat COA models provide a basis for formulating friendly COAs and completing the intelligence estimate.

See facing page for an overview, and pp. 3-3 to 3-46 for a discussion of the IPB process.

IPB during MDMP Overview

Ref: ATP 2-01.3/MCRP 2-3A, Intelligence Preparation of the Battlefield/Battlespace (Nov '14), fig. 2-1, p. 2-2.

The intelligence staff, in collaboration with other staffs, develops other IPB products during mission analysis. That collaboration should result in the drafting of initial priority intelligence requirements (PIRs), the production of a complete modified combined obstacles overlay, a list of high value targets, and unrefined event templates and matrices. IPB should provide an understanding of the threat's center of gravity, which then can be exploited by friendly forces.

Figure 2-1 shows the relationship between IPB and the steps of MDMP/MCPP.

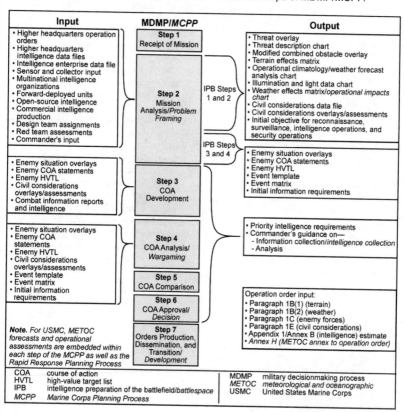

Input	MDMP/MCPP	Output
• Higher headquarters operation orders • Higher headquarters intelligence data files • Intelligence enterprise data file • Sensor and collector input • Multinational intelligence organizations • Forward-deployed units • Open-source intelligence • Commercial intelligence production • Design team assignments • Red team assessments • Commander's input	**Step 1** Receipt of Mission **Step 2** Mission Analysis/Problem Framing *IPB Steps 1 and 2*	• Threat overlay • Threat description chart • Modified combined obstacle overlay • Terrain effects matrix • Operational climatology/weather forecast analysis chart • Illumination and light data chart • Weather effects matrix/operational impacts chart • Civil considerations data file • Civil considerations overlays/assessments • Initial objective for reconnaissance, surveillance, intelligence operations, and security operations
• Enemy situation overlays • Enemy COA statements • Enemy HVTL • Civil considerations overlays/assessments • Combat information reports and intelligence	*IPB Steps 3 and 4* **Step 3** COA Development	• Enemy situation overlays • Enemy COA statements • Enemy HVTL • Event template • Event matrix • Initial information requirements

• Enemy situation overlays
• Enemy COA statements
• Enemy HVTL
• Civil considerations overlays/assessments
• Event template
• Event matrix
• Initial information requirements
	Step 4 COA Analysis/ Wargaming
	
	Step 5 COA Comparison
		• Priority intelligence requirements
		• Commander's guidance on—
		   - Information collection/intelligence collection
		   - Analysis

Note. For USMC, METOC forecasts and operational assessments are embedded within each step of the MCPP as well as the Rapid Response Planning Process	**Step 6** COA Approval/ Decision **Step 7** Orders Production, Dissemination, and Transition/ Development	Operation order input: • Paragraph 1B(1) (terrain) • Paragraph 1B(2) (weather) • Paragraph 1C (enemy forces) • Paragraph 1E (civil considerations) • Appendix 1/Annex B (intelligence) estimate • Annex H (METOC annex to operation order)

COA	course of action	MDMP	military decisionmaking process
HVTL	high-value target list	METOC	meteorological and oceanographic
IPB	intelligence preparation of the battlefield/battlespace	USMC	United States Marine Corps
MCPP	Marine Corps Planning Process		

See pp. 3-3 to 3-46 for complete discussion of the Intelligence Preparation of the Battlefield (IPB) process.

Staff Guidelines for Mission Analysis

Ref: Adapted from previous references (not provided in FM 6-0, C1).

During mission analysis, the commander and staff thoroughly analyze the higher headquarters plan or order and any planning directives pertaining to the situation. Their goal is to determine how their unit, by task and purpose, contributes to the mission, commander's intent, and concept of operations of the higher headquarters. They analyze their own unit capabilities and limitations, those of the enemy, and the terrain and weather. They also analyze civil considerations through the memory aid ASCOPE -- areas, structures, capabilities, organizations, people, and events. These considerations are also used when developing running estimates (pp. 2-4 to 2-5). Staff members bring technical knowledge, running estimates, and historical data to the mission analysis briefing to help the commander understand the situation and the unit's mission.

All Staff Officers

- Mission and commander's intent of higher headquarters one and two levels up
- Specified, implied, and essential tasks
- Area of operations
- Area of interest
- Enemy situation and capabilities
- Critical facts and assumptions
- Status of subordinate units
- Weapon systems capabilities and limitations
- Status of available assets within their functional area
- Constraints
- Risk considerations
- Time considerations
- Recommended commander's critical information requirements (CCIRs) and information requirements

Intelligence
ACOS, G-2 (S-2), Intelligence

- Managing intelligence preparation of the battlefield (IPB), to include integrating the IPB efforts of the rest of the staff and other echelons and supporting parallel planning during dynamic situations
- Performing situation development, to include updating the enemy, terrain and weather, and civil consideration portions of the common operational picture
- Conducting ISR synchronization, to include:
- Developing and continuously updating a list of intelligence gaps
- Recommending CCIR's and information requirements to develop initial collection tasks and requests for support from higher and adjacent commands
- Determining collection capabilities and limitations
- Determining unit intelligence production capabilities and limitations

- Facilitating ISR integration by giving the commander and G-3 (S-3) the initial ISR synchronization plan and helping the G-3 (S-3) develop the initial ISR plan
- Identifying enemy intelligence collection capabilities

Staff Weather Officer

The staff weather officer conducts mission analysis on how weather and the natural environment affect both the enemy and friendly forces:

- Developing and continuously updating current weather data
- Determining and continuously updating a long-term weather forecast
- Coordinating with the geospatial engineer to combine terrain and weather reports

Foreign Disclosure Officer

The foreign disclosure officer determines what may and may not be released to foreign partners.

Movement and Maneuver
ACOS, G-3 (S-3), Operations

The ACOS, G-3 (S-3), is the principal staff officer for operations and is the chief of movement and maneuver. This officer conducts mission analysis on all matters concerning training, operations, and plan:

- Managing the overall mission analysis effort of the staff to include:
- Consolidating facts and assumptions, specific and implied tasks, constraints, risk considerations, unit status, and recommended CCIR's
- Summarizing the current situation of subordinate units and activities
- Determining status of the task organization
- Developing the intelligence, surveillance, and reconnaissance (ISR) plan (with G-2 [S-2] and the rest of the staff). The ISR plan produces an initial ISR order to answer initial CCIRs and information requirements
- Developing the unit's recommended mission statement
- Developing the unit's operational timeline

ACOS, G-5 (S-5), Plans

The ACOS, G-5 (S-5), is the chief of plans, and conducts mission analysis on all matters concerning plans to include integration of all higher, lower, and supporting plans.

Aviation Coordinator

The aviation coordinator conducts mission analysis on all matters concerning Army aviation:

- Determining the status of the task organization
- Determining the current status of subordinate Army aviation units

Engineer Coordinator

- Identifying available information on routes and key facilities. Evaluate requirements for lines of communications, aerial ports of debarkation, and sea ports of debarkation
- Determining availability of construction and other engineering materials
- Reviewing availability of all engineer capabilities both civilian and military
- Identifying any obvious shortfalls in engineer forces or equipment and initiating requests for information or augmentation as early as possible
- Identifying available information on major roads, bridges, and key facilities in the area of operations
- Determining bed down requirements for supported force. Reviewing theater construction standards and base camp master planning.
- Reviewing existing geospatial data on potential sites; conducting site reconnaissance; and determining the threat (to include environmental)
- Obtaining necessary geologic, hydrologic, and climatic data
- Determining the level of interagency cooperation required
- Determining funding sources
- Determining terrain and mobility restraints, obstacle intelligence, threat engineer capabilities, and critical infrastructure
- Coordinating the integration of geospatial engineering into the MDMP
- Monitoring the production and distribution of maps and terrain products based on established priorities
- Integrating engineer reconnaissance
- Identifying gaps in geospatial data and nominating collection
- Synchronizing with the G-2 or S-2 and the geospatial information technician to prioritize requirements
- Coordinating engineer-related ISR requirements with the intel officer

Military Deception Officer

- Determining opportunities for military deception
- Identifying potential deception targets, objectives, and stories

Space Officer

- Identifying theater, strategic, national, and commercial space assets
- Determining global positioning system satellite coverage and accuracy data
- Providing Department of Defense and commercial satellite terrain and weather imagery
- Identifying the capabilities and vulnerabilities of enemy satellite systems
- Estimating the effects of space weather activities
- Identifying adversarial ground stations for possible targeting

Special Operations Coordinator

- Identifying status and capabilities of SOF available to the commander
- Identifying the status and capabilities of host-nation security forces
- Determining enemy SOF capabilities
- Identifying SOF aviation assets and status
- Determining SOF support requirements

Fires

Chief of Fires/Fire Support Officer (FSO)

- Higher HQ's specified and implied tasks
- A fires running estimate to identify capabilities and limitations including the status of: field artillery weapons, field artillery ammunition, field artillery target acquisition radars , close air support (CAS) and other related fixed-wing support, other assets allocated from higher headquarters
- Field artillery and mortar survey support
- Established and recommended fire support coordination measures
- The impact of rules of engagement
- The impact of geometry, terrain, and weather on friendly and enemy fires (such as smoke, CAS, and air interdiction)
- ISR support and requirements
- Initial high-payoff target list
- Fire support input to the IPB analysis
- Fire support tasks and purposes

Air Liaison Officer

The air liaison officer conducts mission analysis with regard to the availability and status of CAS, air interdiction, air reconnaissance, airlift, and joint suppression of enemy air defenses.

Electronic Warfare Officer

- Identifying enemy's electronic warfare capabilities and vulnerabilities
- Determining friendly electronic warfare capabilities and vulnerabilities
- Identifying electronic warfare targets
- Identifying electronic attack targets
- Determining electronic protection requirements

Continued on next page

Staff Guidelines (CONT)

Ref: Adapted from previous references (not provided in FM 6-0, C1).

Continued from previous page

MDMP
& TLP

Protection
Chief of Protection
The chief of protection is responsible for all mission analysis conducted by the protection section:

Air and Missile Defense Coordinator
- Air defense rules of engagement
- Weapons control status
- Current airspace control measures (current, planned, and required)
- Enemy air and missile capabilities (most likely air avenues of approach, types and numbers of sorties, and high-value target lists)
- Offensive counter-air, defensive counter-air, and theater missile defense targets and priorities
- Active and passive air defense measures
- Status of air and missile defense systems, air and missile defense sensor assets, and air defense artillery ammunition available

Chemical Officer
- Assets available, including reconnaissance, decontamination, and smoke
- Constraints related to CBRNE
- Mission-oriented protective posture status
- Troop safety criteria
- Enemy CBRNE capabilities and friendly vulnerabilities

Explosive Ordnance Disposal Officer
- Status of explosive ordnance disposal units
- Identifying the status of explosive ordnance disposal tools, equipment, and demolition materials
- Enemy explosive threats and capabilities

Operations Security Officer
- Assessing the commander's posture on operations security
- Determining essential elements of friendly information and OPSEC vulnerabilities
- Determining appropriate OPSEC measures
- Evaluating the potential effect of compromise to friendly information system, functions, and data

Personnel Recovery Officer
- Determining the time-distance relationship to interned, missing, detained, and captured for all units
- Assessing status of personnel recovery equipment
- Assessing ISR operations for effects on personnel recovery
- Assessing civilian and diplomatic capabilities to support personnel recovery

- Assessing how civilians and local security forces support and disrupt personnel recovery
- Identifying medical support to personnel recovery

Provost Marshal
- Route reconnaissance
- Dislocated civilian and straggler movement control
- Traffic regulation and enforcement
- Main supply route regulation
- Populace and resource control
- Tactical and police intelligence collecting and reporting

The provost marshal also considers area security operations, including activities associated with:

- Area and base security operations
- Command post access control
- Physical security procedures for critical assets, nodes, and sensitive materials
- Counter reconnaissance
- Protective services for key personnel
- Response force operations
- Antiterrorism
- Tactical and police intelligence collecting and reporting
- Criminal activity and trends within the operational area
- Host-nation law enforcement organization and capabilities
- Internment and resettlement of enemy prisoners of war and civilian internees, dislocated civilians, and U.S. military prisoners
- Law and order operations

Safety Officer
The safety officer provides technical advice and assistance to the staff as they complete their functional area risk assessments.

Sustainment
Chief of Sustainment
The chief of sustainment leads the mission analysis effort for the sustainment section.

ACOS, G-1/AG (S-1), Personnel
- Analyzing personnel strength data to determine current capabilities and project future requirements
- Analyzing unit strength maintenance, including monitoring, collecting, and analyzing data affecting Soldier readiness
- Preparing estimates for personnel replacement requirements based on estimated casualties, non-battle losses, and foreseeable administrative losses to include critical military occupational skill requirements

Continued from previous page

- Determining personnel services available to the force (current and projected)
- Determining personnel support available to the force (current and projected)

ACOS, G-4 (S-4), Logistics

- Determining current and projected supply status (classes I, II, III, IV, V, VII, and IX)
- Providing current equipment readiness status of the force and projected maintenance timelines
- Forecasting combat vehicle and weapons status
- Identifying availability of transportation assets
- Identifying availability and status of services
- Identifying contracted and host-nation support
- Reviewing availability of general engineer assets that enable logistics, to include units, host-nation support, and contract support

ACOS, G-8, Financial Management

- Determining current and projected funding levels, by type of appropriated funding
- Ensuring funding complies with laws and financial management regulations
- Determining current and projected currency requirements (U.S. and foreign) to support the procurement process
- Developing cost estimates and providing cost analyses (cost alternatives)
- Determining resource impact of contract and host-nation support

Command Surgeon

- Civilian and military medical assets available (treatment, evacuation, critical medical equipment, and personnel)
- Class VIII supply status including blood management, medical equipment maintenance and repair, and drug supply issues
- Environmental health effects on military forces
- Medical threats (to include occupational and environment health hazards)
- Patient estimates (medical workload)
- Theater evacuation policy
- Medical troop ceiling and availability of health service support medical treatment and evaluation resources
- Force health protection

Mission Command

ACOS, G-6 (S-6), Signal

- Determining communication and information systems operational status
- Determining available communications assets, including higher and host-nation support
- Ensuring integration with the higher headquarters communications plan

ACOS, G-7 (S-7), Information Engagement

- Identify higher themes and messages
- Analyze internal and external audience to inform, educate, and influence

ACOS, G-8, Financial Management

- Determining current and projected funding levels, by type of appropriated funding
- Ensuring funding complies with laws and financial management regulations
- Determining current and projected currency requirements (U.S. and foreign) to support the procurement process
- Developing cost estimates and providing cost analyses (cost alternatives)
- Determining resource impact of contract and host-nation support

ACOS, G-9 (S-9), Civil Affairs Operations

- Analyzing how civilian populations affect military operations
- Analyzing how military operations affect the host nation and its populace
- Determining dislocated civilian movement, routes, and assembly areas
- Identifying the host-nation ability to care for civilians
- Identifying host-nation resources to support military operations
- Determining a no-strike list, including cultural, religious, historical, and high-density civilian population areas
- Identifying NGO & other independent organizations in the operational area

Public Affairs Officer (PAO)

- The operation and information environment
- Level of U.S. public, host-nation, and international support
- The media presence and facilitation in the operational area
- Public affairs support to counter deception and counterpropaganda
- The status of public affairs units

Knowledge Management Officer

- Identifies knowledge gaps and additional knowledge requirements
- Identifies sources and solutions to fill knowledge gaps
- Determines what information and knowledge needs to be shared, who it needs to be shared with, and how best to share it
- Captures, organizes, and transfers new knowledge created by the staff

Chaplain

- The status of available unit ministry teams to include identified religious preferences
- Effects of indigenous religions on military operations

3. Determine Specified, Implied, and Essential Tasks

The staff analyzes the higher headquarters order and the higher commander's guidance to determine their specified and implied tasks. In the context of operations, a task is a clearly defined and measurable activity accomplished by Soldiers, units, and organizations that may support or be supported by other tasks. The "what" of a mission statement is always a task. From the list of specified and implied tasks, the staff determines essential tasks for inclusion in the recommended mission statement.

A. Specified Tasks

A specified task is a task specifically assigned to a unit by its higher headquarters. Paragraphs 2 and 3 of the higher headquarters' order or plan state specified tasks. Some tasks may be in paragraphs 4 and 5. Specified tasks may be listed in annexes and overlays. They may also be assigned verbally during collaborative planning sessions or in directives from the higher commander.

B. Implied Tasks

An implied task is a task that must be performed to accomplish a specified task or mission but is not stated in the higher headquarters' order. Implied tasks are derived from a detailed analysis of the higher headquarters' order, the enemy situation, the terrain, and civil considerations. Additionally, analysis of doctrinal requirements for each specified task might disclose implied tasks.

When analyzing the higher order for specified and implied tasks, the staff also identifies any be-prepared or on-order missions.

- A **be-prepared mission** is a mission assigned to a unit that might be executed. Generally a contingency mission, commanders execute it because something planned has or has not been successful. In planning priorities, commanders plan a be-prepared mission after any on-order mission.

- An **on-order mission** is a mission to be executed at an unspecified time. A unit with an on-order mission is a committed force. Commanders envisions task execution in the concept of operations; however, they may not know the exact time or place of execution. Subordinate commanders develop plans and orders and allocate resources, task-organize, and position forces for execution.

C. Essential Tasks

Once staff members have identified specified and implied tasks, they ensure they understand each task's requirements and purpose. The staff then identifies essential tasks. An essential task is a specified or implied task that must be executed to accomplish the mission. Essential tasks are always included in the unit's mission statement.

4. Review Available Assets and Identify Resource Shortfalls

The commander and staff examine additions to and deletions from the current task organization, command and support relationships, and status (current capabilities and limitations) of all units. This analysis also includes capabilities of civilian and military organizations (joint, special operations, and multinational) that operate within their unit's AO. They consider relationships among specified, implied, and essential tasks, and between them and available assets. From this analysis, staffs determine if they have the assets needed to complete all tasks. If shortages occur, they identify additional resources needed for mission success to the higher headquarters. Staffs also identify any deviations from the normal task organization and provide them to the commander to consider when developing the planning guidance. A more detailed analysis of available assets occurs during COA development.

5. Determine Constraints

The commander and staff identify any constraints placed on their command. A constraint is a restriction placed on the command by a higher command. A constraint dictates an action or inaction, thus restricting the freedom of action of a subordinate commander. Constraints are found in paragraph 3 of the OPLAN or OPORD. Annexes to the order may also include constraints. The operation overlay, for example, may contain a restrictive fire line or a no fire area. Constraints may also be issued verbally, in WARNOs, or in policy memoranda.

Constraints may also be based on resource limitations within the command, such as organic fuel transport capacity, or physical characteristics of the operational environment, such as the number of vehicles that can cross a bridge in a specified time.

The commander and staff should coordinate with the Staff Judge Advocate for a legal review of perceived or obvious constraints, restraints, or limitations in the OPLAN, OPORD, or related documents.

6. Identify Critical Facts and Develop Assumptions

Plans and orders are based on facts and assumptions. Commanders and staffs gather facts and develop assumptions as they build their plan.

A. Facts

A fact is a statement of truth or a statement thought to be true at the time. Facts concerning the operational and mission variables serve as the basis for developing situational understanding, for continued planning, and when assessing progress during preparation and execution.

B. Assumptions

An assumption is a supposition on the current situation or a presupposition on the future course of events, either or both assumed to be true in the absence of positive proof, necessary to enable the commander in the process of planning to complete an estimate of the situation and make a decision on the course of action. In the absence of facts, the commander and staff consider assumptions from their higher headquarters. They then develop their own assumptions necessary for continued planning.

Having assumptions requires commanders and staffs to continually attempt to replace those assumptions with facts. The commander and staff should list and review the key assumptions on which fundamental judgments rest throughout the MDMP. Rechecking assumptions is valuable at any time during the operations process prior to rendering judgments and making decisions.

7. Begin Risk Management

Risk management is the process of identifying, assessing, and controlling risks arising from operational factors and making decisions that balance risk cost with mission benefits (JP 3-0). During mission analysis, the commander and staff focus on identifying and assessing hazards. Developing specific control measures to mitigate those hazards occurs during course of action development.

The chief of protection (or operations staff officer [S-3] in units without a protection cell) in coordination with the safety officer integrates risk management into the MDMP. All staff sections integrate risk management for hazards within their functional areas. Units conduct the first four steps of risk management in the MDMP.

See following page and pp. 3-59 to 3-62 for further discussion of risk management.

Risk Management Process

Ref: ATP 5-19 (w/C1), Risk Management (Apr '2014), chap. 1. See pp. 3-59 to 3-62.

Risk Management is the process of identifying, assessing, and controlling risks arising from operational factors and making decisions that balance risk cost with mission benefits. (JP 3-0) *The Army no longer uses the term "composite risk management." Term replaced with joint term "risk management."*

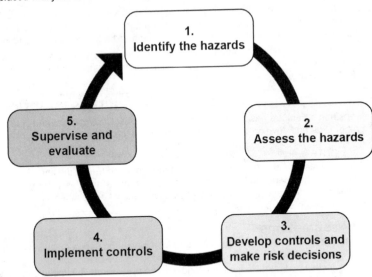

Ref: ATP 5-19, fig. 1-1. A cyclical, continuous process for managing risk.

1. Identify the hazards
A hazard is a condition with the potential to cause injury, illness, or death of personnel; damage to or loss of equipment or property; or mission degradation. Hazards exist in all environments—combat operations, stability operations, base support operations, training, garrison activities, and off-duty activities. The factors of mission, enemy, terrain and weather, troops and support available, time available, and civil considerations (METT-TC) serve as a standard format for identification of hazards, on-duty or off-duty.

2. Assess the hazards
This process is systematic in nature and uses charts, codes and numbers to present a methodology to assess probability and severity to obtain a standardized level of risk. Hazards are assessed and risk is assigned in terms of probability and severity of adverse impact of an event/occurrence.

3. Develop controls and make risk decisions
The process of developing and applying controls and reassessing risk continues until an acceptable level of risk is achieved or until all risks are reduced to a level where benefits outweigh the potential cost.

4. Implement controls
Leaders and staffs ensure that controls are integrated into SOPs, written and verbal orders, mission briefings, and staff estimates.

5. Supervise and evaluate

8. Develop Initial CCIR and EEFI

The mission analysis process identifies gaps in information required for further planning and decisionmaking during preparation and execution. During mission analysis, the staff develops information requirements (IRs). Some information requirements are of such importance to the commander that staffs nominate them to the commander to become a commander's critical information requirement (CCIR).

Commander's Critical Information Requirements (CCIR)

Commanders consider staff input when determining their CCIRs. CCIRs are situation-dependent and specified by the commander for each operation. Commanders continuously review CCIRs during the planning process and adjust them as situations change. The initial CCIRs developed during mission analysis normally focus on decisions the commander needs to make to focus planning. Once the commander selects a COA, the CCIRs shift to information the commander needs in order to make decisions during preparation and execution. Commanders designate CCIRs to inform the staff and subordinates what they deem essential for making decisions. Typically, commanders identify ten or fewer CCIRs; minimizing the number of CCIRs assists in prioritizing the allocation of limited resources. CCIR fall into one of two categories: PIRs and friendly force information requirements (FFIRs).

See pp. 1-18 to 1-19 for further discussion of CCIRs, to include FFIRs and PIRs.

- **Priority Intelligence Requirements (PIRs).** A PIR is an intelligence requirement, stated as a priority for intelligence support, that the commander and staff need to understand the adversary or the operational environment. PIRs identify the information about the enemy and other aspects of the operational environment that the commander considers most important. Lessons from recent operations show that intelligence about civil considerations may be as critical as intelligence about the enemy. Thus, all staff sections may recommend information about civil considerations as PIRs. The intelligence officer manages PIRs for the commander through planning requirements and assessing collection.

- **Friendly Force Information Requirements (FFIRs).** An FFIR is information the commander and staff need to understand the status of friendly force and supporting capabilities. FFIRs identify the information about the mission, troops and support available, and time available for friendly forces that the commander considers most important. In coordination with the staff, the operations officer manages FFIRs for the commander.

Essential Elements of Friendly Information (EEFI)

In addition to nominating CCIRs to the commander, the staff also identifies and nominates essential elements of friendly information (EEFIs). Although EEFIs are not CCIRs, they have the same priority as CCIRs and require approval by the commander. An EEFI establishes an element of information to protect rather than one to collect. EEFIs identify those elements of friendly force information that, if compromised, would jeopardize mission success. Like CCIRs, EEFIs change as an operation progresses.

See p. 1-19 for further discussion of EEFI.

Depending on the situation, the commander and selected staff members meet prior to the mission analysis brief to approve the initial CCIRs and EEFIs. This is especially important if the commander intends to conduct reconnaissance and collect information early in the planning process. The approval of the initial CCIRs early in planning assist the staff in developing the initial reconnaissance and surveillance synchronization plan and the subsequent reconnaissance and surveillance plan. Approval of an EEFI allows the staff to begin planning and implementing measures to protect friendly force information, such as military deception and operations security.

9. Develop the Initial Information Collection Plan

The initial information collection plan is crucial to begin or adjust the information collection effort to help answer information requirements necessary in developing effective plans. The initial information collection plan sets reconnaissance, surveillance, and intelligence operations in motion. It may be issued as part of a WARNORD, a fragmentary order (FRAGORD), or an OPORD. As more information becomes available, it is incorporated into a complete information collection plan (Annex L) to the OPORD.

The intelligence staff creates the requirements management tools for the information collection plan. The operations staff is responsible for the information collection plan. During this step, the operations and intelligence staff work closely to ensure they fully synchronize and integrate information collection activities into the overall plan.

The operations officer considers several factors when developing the initial information collection plan, including:

- Requirements for collection assets in subsequent missions.
- The time available to develop and refine the initial information collection plan.
- The risk the commander is willing to accept if information collection missions are begun before the information collection plan is fully integrated into the scheme of maneuver.
- Insertion and extraction methods for reconnaissance, security, surveillance, and intelligence collection assets.
- Contingencies for inclement weather to ensure coverage of key named areas of interest or target areas of interest.
- The communications plan for transmission of reports from assets to command posts.
- The inclusion of collection asset locations and movements into the fire support plan.
- The reconnaissance handover with higher or subordinate echelons.
- The sustainment support.
- Legal support requirements.

FM 3-55 contains additional information on information collection, planning requirements, and assessing collection.

10. Update Plan for the Use of Available Time

As more information becomes available, the commander and staff refine their initial plan for the use of available time. They compare the time needed to accomplish tasks to the higher headquarters' timeline to ensure mission accomplishment is possible in the allotted time. They compare the timeline to the assumed enemy timeline or the projected timelines within the civil sector with how they anticipate conditions will unfold. From this, they determine windows of opportunity for exploitation, times when the unit will be at risk for enemy activity, or when action to arrest deterioration in the civil sector is required.

The commander and COS (XO) also refine the staff planning timeline. The refined timeline includes the:

- Subject, time, and location of briefings the commander requires
- Times of collaborative planning sessions and the medium over which they will take place
- Times, locations, and forms of rehearsals

11. Develop Initial Themes and Messages

Gaining and maintaining the trust of key actors is an important aspect of operations. Faced with the many different actors (individuals, organizations, and the public) connected with the operation, commanders identify and engage those actors who matter to operational success. These actors' behaviors can help solve or complicate the friendly forces' challenges as commanders strive to accomplish missions.

Themes and messages support operations and military actions:

- A **theme** is a unifying or dominant idea or image that expresses the purpose for military action. Themes tie to objectives, lines of effort, and end state conditions. They are overarching and apply to capabilities of public affairs, military information support operations, and Soldier and leader engagements.

- A **message** is a verbal, written, or electronic communications that supports an information theme focused on a specific actor or the public and in support of a specific action (task).

Units transmit information themes and messages to those actors or the public whose perceptions, attitudes, beliefs, and behaviors matter to the success of an operation.

The public affairs officer adjusts and refines themes and messages received from higher headquarters for use by the command. These themes and messages are designed to inform specific domestic and foreign audiences about current or planned military operations. The military information support operations element receives approved themes and messages. This element adjusts or refines depending on the situation. It employs themes and messages as part of planned activities designed to influence specific foreign audiences for various purposes that support current or planned operations. The commander and the chief of staff approve all themes and messages used to support operations. The information operations officer assists the G-3 (S-3) and the commander to de-conflict and synchronize the use of information-related capabilities used specifically to disseminate approved themes and messages during operations.

12. Develop a Proposed Problem Statement

A problem is an issue or obstacle that makes it difficult to achieve a desired goal or objective. As such, a problem statement is the description of the primary issue or issues that may impede commanders from achieving their desired end states.

Note: The commander, staff, and other partners develop the problem statement as part of Army design methodology. During mission analysis, the commander and staff review the problem statement and revise it as necessary based on the increased understanding of the situation. If Army design methodology activities do not precede mission analysis, then the commander and staff develop a problem statement prior to moving to Step 3—COA Development.

How the problem is formulated leads to particular solutions. It is important that commanders dedicate the time in identifying the right problem to solve and describe it clearly in a problem statement. Ideally, the commander and members of the staff meet to share their analysis of the situation. They talk with each other, synthesize the results of the current mission analysis, and determine the problem. If the commander is not available, the staff members talk among themselves.

As part of the discussion to help identify and understand the problem, the staff:

- Compares the current situation to the desired end state
- Brainstorms and lists issues that impede the commander from achieving the desired end state

Based on this analysis, the staff develops a proposed problem statement—a statement of the problem to be solved—for the commander's approval.

13. Develop a Proposed Mission Statement

The COS (XO) or operations officer prepares a proposed mission statement for the unit based on the mission analysis. The commander receives and approves the unit's mission statement normally during the mission analysis brief. A mission statement is a short sentence or paragraph that describes the organization's essential task (or tasks) and purpose—a clear statement of the action to be taken and the reason for doing so. The mission statement contains the elements of who, what, when, where, and why, but seldom specifies how (JP 5-0). The five elements of a mission statement answer the questions:

- **Who** will execute the operation (unit or organization)?
- **What** is the unit's essential task (tactical mission task)?
- **When** will the operation begin (by time or event) or what is the duration of the operation?
- **Where** will the operation occur (area of operations, objective, grid coordinates)?
- **Why** will the force conduct the operations (for what purpose)?

The who, where, and when of a mission statement are straightforward. The what and why are more challenging to write and can confuse subordinates if not stated clearly. The what is a task and is expressed in terms of action verbs. These tasks are measurable and can be grouped as "actions by friendly forces" or "effects on enemy forces." The why puts the task into context by describing the reason for performing it. The why provides the mission's purpose—the reason the unit is to perform the task. It is extremely important to mission command and mission orders.

See facing page for further discussion.

14. Present the Mission Analysis Briefing

The mission analysis briefing informs the commander of the results of the staff's analysis of the situation. It helps the commander understand, visualize, and describe the operations. Throughout the mission analysis briefing, the commander, staff, and other partners discuss the various facts and assumptions about the situation. Staff officers present a summary of their running estimates from their specific functional area and how their findings impact or are impacted by other areas. This helps the commander and staff as a whole to focus on the interrelationships among the mission variables and to develop a deeper understanding of the situation. The commander issues guidance to the staff for continued planning based on situational understanding gained from the mission analysis briefing.

Ideally, the commander holds several informal meetings with key staff members before the mission analysis briefing, including meetings to assist the commander in developing CCIRs, the mission statement, and themes and messages. These meetings enable commanders to issue guidance for activities (such as reconnaissance, surveillance, security, and intelligence operations) and develop their initial commander's intent and planning guidance.

A comprehensive mission analysis briefing helps the commander, staff, subordinates, and other partners develop a shared understanding of the requirements of the upcoming operation. Time permitting, the staff briefs the commander on its mission analysis:

- Mission and commander's intent of the headquarters two levels up
- Mission, commander's intent, and concept of operations of the headquarters one level up
- A proposed problem statement
- A proposed mission statement
- Review of the commander's initial guidance

Proposed Mission Statement

Ref: FM 6-0 (C1), Commander and Staff Organization and Operations (May '15), pp. 9-12 to 9-13.

The mission statement contains the elements of who, what, when, where, and why, but seldom specifies how. The five elements of a mission statement answer the questions:

- **Who** will execute the operation (unit or organization)?
- **What** is the unit's essential task (tactical mission task)?
- **When** will the operation begin (by time or event) or what is the duration of the operation?
- **Where** will the operation occur (area of operations, objective, grid coordinates)?
- **Why** will the force conduct the operations (for what purpose or reason)?

The what is a task and is expressed in terms of action verbs. These tasks are measurable and can be grouped as "actions by friendly forces" or "effects on enemy forces." The why puts the task into context by describing the reason for performing it. The why provides the mission's purpose—the reason the unit is to perform the task. It is extremely important to mission command and mission orders.

Example 1. *Not later than 220400 Aug 09 (when), 1st Brigade (who) secures ROUTE SOUTH DAKOTA (what/task) in AREA OF OPERATIONS JACKRABBIT (where) to enable the movement of humanitarian assistance materials (why/purpose).*

Example 2. *1-505th Parachute Infantry Regiment (who) seizes (what/task) JACKSON INTERNATIONAL AIRPORT (where) not later than D-day, H+3 (when) to allow follow-on forces to air-land into AREA OF OPERATIONS SPARTAN (why/ purpose).*

The mission statement may have more than one essential task:

Example. *1-509th Parachute Infantry Regiment (who) seizes (what/task) JACKSON INTERNATIONAL AIRPORT (where) not later than D-day, H+3 (when) to allow follow-on forces to air-land into AREA OF OPERATIONS SPARTAN (why/purpose). On order (when), secures (what/task) OBJECTIVE GOLD (where) to prevent the 2nd Pandor Guards Brigade from crossing the BLUE RIVER and disrupting operations in AREA OF OPERATIONS SPARTAN (why/purpose).*

Tactical Mission Tasks

Commanders should use tactical mission tasks or other doctrinally approved tasks contained in combined arms field manuals or mission training plans in mission statements. These tasks have specific military definitions that differ from dictionary definitions. A tactical mission task is a specific activity performed by a unit while executing a form of tactical operation or form of maneuver. It may be expressed as either an action by a friendly force or effects on an enemy force (FM 7-15). FM 3-90-1 describes each tactical task. FM 3-07 provides a list of primary stability tasks which military forces must be prepared to execute. Commanders and planners should carefully choose the task that best describes the commander's intent and planning guidance.

The following is a list of commonly used tactical mission tasks; see pp. 7-31 to 7-34 for a listing of tactical mission tasks to include graphics and definitions:

- attack by fire
- block
- breach
- bypass
- canalize
- clear
- contain
- control
- counter reconnaissance
- defeat

- destroy
- disengage
- disrupt
- exfiltrate
- fix
- follow and assume
- follow and support
- interdict
- isolate
- neutralize

- occupy
- reduce
- retain
- secure
- seize
- support-by-fire
- suppress
- turn

- Initial IPB products, including civil considerations that impact the conduct of operations
- Specified, implied, and essential tasks
- Pertinent facts and assumptions
- Constraints
- Forces available and resource shortfalls
- Initial risk assessment
- Proposed themes and messages
- Proposed CCIRs and EEFIs
- Initial information collection plan
- Recommended timeline
- Recommended collaborative planning sessions

During the mission analysis briefing or shortly thereafter, commanders approve the mission statement and CCIRs. They then develop and issue their initial commander's intent and planning guidance.

15. Develop and Issue Initial Commander's Intent

The commander's intent is a clear and concise expression of the purpose of the operation and the desired military end state that supports mission command, provides focus to the staff, and helps subordinate and supporting commanders act to achieve the commander's desired results without further orders, even when the operation does not unfold as planned (JP 3-0). The initial commander's intent describes the purpose of the operation, initial key tasks, and the desired end state

See p. 1-8 for more details on commander's intent.

The higher commander's intent provides the basis for unity of effort throughout the force. Each commander's intent nests within the higher commander's intent. The commander's intent explains the broader purpose of the operation beyond that of the mission statement. This explanation allows subordinate commanders and Soldiers to gain insight into what is expected of them, what constraints apply, and most importantly, why the mission is being conducted.

Based on their situational understanding, commanders summarize their visualization in their initial commander's intent statement. The initial commander's intent links the operation's purpose with conditions that define the desired end state. Commanders may change their intent statement as planning progresses and more information becomes available. The commander's intent must be easy to remember and clearly understood by leaders two echelons lower in the chain of command. The shorter the commander's intent, the better it serves these purposes. Typically, the commander's intent statement is three to five sentences long and contains the purpose, key tasks, and end state.

16. Develop and Issue Initial Planning Guidance

Commanders provide planning guidance along with their initial commander's intent. Planning guidance conveys the essence of the commander's visualization. This guidance may be broad or detailed, depending on the situation. The initial planning guidance outlines an operational approach—a description of the broad actions the force must take to transform current conditions into those desired at end state (JP 5-0). The initial planning guidance outlines specific COAs the commander desires the staff to look at as well as rules out any COAs the commander will not accept. That clear guidance allows the staff to develop several COAs without wasting effort on things that the commander will not consider. It reflects how the commander sees the operation unfolding. It broadly describes when, where, and how the commander intends to employ combat power to accomplish the mission within the higher commander's intent.

Commander's Planning Guidance by Warfighting Function

Ref: FM 6-0 (C1), Commander and Staff Organization and Operations (May '15), table 9-1, p. 9-15.

The following list is not intended to meet the need of all situations. Commanders tailor planning guidance to meet specific needs based on the situation rather than address each item.

Mission Command	Commander's critical information requirements Rules of engagement Command post positioning Commander's location Initial themes and messages Succession of command	Liaison officer guidance Planning and operational guidance timeline Type of order and rehearsal Communications guidance Civil affairs operations Cyber electromagnetic considerations
Intelligence	Information collection guidance Information gaps Most likely and most dangerous enemy courses of action Priority intelligence requirements Most critical terrain and weather factors	Most critical local environment and civil considerations Intelligence requests for information Intelligence focus during phased operations Desired enemy perception of friendly forces
Movement and Maneuver	Commander's intent Course of action development guidance Number of courses of action to consider or not consider Critical events Task organization Task and purpose of subordinate units Forms of maneuver Reserve composition, mission, priorities, and control measures	Security and counterreconnaissance Friendly decision points Branches and sequels Task and direct collection Military deception Risk to friendly forces Collateral damage or civilian casualties Any condition that affects achievement of endstate Informatioroperations
Fires	Synchronization and focus of fires with maneuver Priority of fires High priority targets Special munitions Target acquisition zones Observer plan Air and missile defense positioning High-value targets	Task and purpose of fires Scheme of fires Suppression of enemy air defenses Fire support coordination measures Attack guidance Branches and sequels No strike list Restricted target list
Protection	Protection priorities Priorities for survivability assets Terrain and weather factors Intelligence focus and limitations for security Acceptable risk Protected targets and areas	Vehicle and equipment safety or security constraints Environmental considerations Unexploded ordnance Operations security risk tolerance Rules of engagement Escalation of force and nonlethal weapons Counterintelligence
Sustainment	Sustainment priorities—manning, fueling, fixing, arming, moving the force, and sustaining Soldiers and systems Health system support Sustainment of detainee and resettlement operations	Construction and provision of facilities and installations Detainee movement Anticipated requirements of Classes III, IV, V Controlled supply rates

Refer to The Army Operations & Doctrine SMARTbook (Guide to Unified Land Operations and the Six Warfighting Functions) for discussion of the fundamentals, principles and tenets of Army operations, plus chapters on each of the six warfighting functions: mission command, movement and maneuver, intelligence, fires, sustainment, and protection.

Commanders use their experience and judgment to add depth and clarity to their planning guidance. They ensure staffs understand the broad outline of their visualization while allowing the latitude necessary to explore different options. This guidance provides the basis for a detailed concept of operations without dictating the specifics of the final plan. As with their intent, commanders may modify planning guidance based on staff and subordinate input and changing conditions.

Commanders issue planning guidance initially after mission analysis. They continue to consider additional guidance throughout the MDMP including, but not limited, to the following::

- Upon receipt of or in anticipation of a mission (initial planning guidance)
- Following mission analysis (planning guidance for COA development)
- Following COA development (revised planning guidance for COAs)
- COA approval (revised planning guidance to complete the plan)

See previous page for a listing of commander's planning guidance by warfighting function.

17. Develop Course of Action Evaluation Criteria

Evaluation criteria are standards the commander and staff will later use to measure the relative effectiveness and efficiency of one COA relative to other COAs. Developing these criteria during mission analysis or as part of commander's planning guidance helps to eliminate a source of bias prior to COA analysis and comparison. Evaluation criteria address factors that affect success and those that can cause failure. Criteria change from mission to mission and must be clearly defined and understood by all staff members before starting the war game to test the proposed COAs. Normally, the COS (XO) initially determines each proposed criterion with weights based on the assessment of its relative importance and the commander's guidance. Commanders adjust criterion selection and weighting according to their own experience and vision. The staff member responsible for a functional area scores each COA using those criteria. The staff presents the proposed evaluation criteria to the commander at the mission analysis brief for approval.

18. Issue a Warning Order

Immediately after the commander gives the planning guidance, the staff sends subordinate and supporting units a WARNORD. It contains, at a minimum:

- The approved mission statement
- The commander's intent
- Changes to task organization
- The unit area of operations (sketch, overlay, or some other description)
- CCIRs and EEFIs
- Risk guidance
- Priorities by warfighting functions
- Military deception guidance
- Essential stability tasks
- Initial information collection plan
- Specific priorities
- Updated operational timeline
- Movements

See p. 4-21 for a sample warning order format.

MDMP Step III.
COA Development

Ref: FM 6-0 (C1), Commander and Staff Organization and Operations (May '15), pp. 9-16 to 9-25.

A COA is a broad potential solution to an identified problem. The COA development step generates options for follow-on analysis and comparison that satisfy the commander's intent and planning guidance. During COA development, planners use the problem statement, mission statement, commander's intent, planning guidance, and various knowledge products developed during mission analysis.

III. COA Development

Key Inputs	Key Outputs

▪ Mission statement
▪ Initial commander's intent, planning guidance, CCIRs, and EEFIs
▪ Updated IPB and running estimates
▪ Assumptions
▪ Evaluation Criteria for COAs
	▪ COA statements and sketches
	  - Tentative task organization
	  - Broad concept of operations
	▪ Revised planning guidance
	▪ Updated assumptions

1 Assess Relative Combat Power

2 Generate Options

3 Array Forces

4 Develop a Broad Concept

5 Assign Headquarters

6 Prepare COA Statements & Sketches

7 Conduct COA Briefing

8 Select or Modify COAs for Continued Analysis

Ref: FM 6-0 (C1), Commander and Staff Organization and Operations, fig. 9-4, p. 9-16.

1. Assess Relative Combat Power

Combat power is the total means of destructive, constructive, and information capabilities that a military unit/formation can apply at a given time. Army forces generate combat power by converting potential into effective action (ADP 3-0). Combat power is the effect created by combining the elements of intelligence, movement and maneuver, fires, sustainment, protection, mission command, information, and leadership. The goal is to generate overwhelming combat power to accomplish the mission at minimal cost.

To assess relative combat power, planners initially make a rough estimate of force ratios of maneuver units two levels down. For example, at division level, planners compare all types of maneuver battalions with enemy maneuver battalion equivalents. Planners then compare friendly strengths against enemy weaknesses, and vice versa, for each element of combat power. From these comparisons, they may deduce particular vulnerabilities for each force that may be exploited or may need protection. These comparisons provide planners insight into effective force employment.

In troop-to-task analysis for stability and defense support of civil authorities, staffs determine relative combat power by comparing available resources to specified or implied stability or civil support tasks. This analysis provides insight as available options and needed resources. In such operations, the elements of sustainment, movement and maneuver, non-lethal effects, and information may dominate. By analyzing force ratios and determining and comparing each force's strengths and weaknesses as a function of combat power, planners can gain insight into:

- Friendly capabilities that pertain to the operation
- The types of operations possible from both friendly and enemy perspectives
- How and where the enemy may be vulnerable
- How and where friendly forces are vulnerable
- Additional resources needed to execute the mission
- How to allocate existing resources

Planners must not develop and recommend COAs based solely on mathematical analysis of force ratios. Although the process uses some numerical relationships, the estimate is largely subjective. Assessing combat power requires assessing both tangible and intangible factors, such as morale and levels of training. A relative combat power assessment identifies exploitable enemy weaknesses, identifies unprotected friendly weaknesses, and determines the combat power necessary to conduct essential stability or defense support of civil authorities tasks.

2. Generate Options

Based on the commander's guidance and the initial results of the relative combat power assessment, the staff generates options. A good COA can defeat all feasible enemy COAs while accounting for essential stability tasks. In an unconstrained environment, planners aim to develop several possible COAs. Depending on available time, commanders may limit the options in the commander's guidance. Options focus on enemy COAs arranged in order of their probable adoption or on those stability tasks that are most essential to prevent the situation from deteriorating further.

Brainstorming is the preferred technique for generating options. It requires time, imagination, and creativity, but it produces the widest range of choices. The staff (and members of organizations outside the headquarters) remains unbiased and open-minded when developing proposed options.

In developing COAs, staff members determine the doctrinal requirements for each proposed operation, including doctrinal tasks for subordinate units. For example, a deliberate breach requires a breach force, a support force, and an assault force. Essential stability tasks require the ability to provide a level of civil security, civil control, and certain essential services. In addition, the staff considers the potential capabilities of attachments and other organizations and agencies outside military channels.

Course of Action (COA) Development

Ref: FM 6-0 (C1), Commander and Staff Organization and Operations (May '15), p. 9-17.

Embedded in COA development is the application of operational and tactical art. Planners develop different COAs by varying combinations of the elements of operational design, such as phasing, lines of effort, and tempo. (See ADRP 3-0.) Planners convert the approved COA into the concept of operations.

COA Screening Criteria

The commander's direct involvement in COA development greatly aids in producing comprehensive and flexible COA's within the available time. To save time, the commander may also limit the number of COA's to be developed or specify particular COA's not to explore. Planners examine each prospective COA for validity using the following screening criteria:

Feasible
The COA can accomplish the mission within the established time, space, and resource limitations

Acceptable
The COA must balance cost and risk with the advantage gained

Suitable
The COA can accomplish the mission within the commander's intent and planning guidance

Distinguishable
Each COA must differ significantly from the others (such as scheme or form of maneuver, lines of effort, phasing, day or night operations, use of reserves, and task organization)

Complete
A COA must incorporate:

- How the decisive operation or effort leads to mission accomplishment
- How shaping operations or efforts create and preserve conditions for success of the decisive operation or effort
- How sustaining operations enable shaping and decisive operations or efforts
- How offensive, defensive, and stability tasks are accounted for
- How to account for offensive, defensive, and stability or defense support of civil authorities tasks.
- Tasks to be performed and conditions to be achieved.

It is important in COA development that commanders and staffs appreciate the unpredictable and uncertain nature of the operational environment, and understand how to cope with ambiguity. Some problems that commanders face are straightforward, as when clearly defined guidance is provided from higher headquarters, or when resources required for a mission are available and can easily be allocated. In such cases, the COA is often self evident. However, for problems that are unfamiliar or ambiguous, Army design methodology may assist commanders in better understanding the nature of the problem, and afford both the commander and staff a level of comfort necessary to effectively advance through COA development. Commanders and staffs that are comfortable with ambiguity will often find that the Army design methodology provides flexibility in developing COAs that contain multiple options for dealing with changing circumstances. Staffs tend to focus on specific COAs for specific sets of circumstances, when it is usually best to focus on flexible COAs that provide the greatest options to account for the widest range of circumstances.

Army leaders are responsible for clearly articulating their visualization of operations in time, space, purpose, and resources in order to generate options. ADRP 3-0 describes in detail three established operational frameworks. Army leaders are not bound by any specific framework in organizing operations, but three operational frameworks, mentioned below, have proven valuable in the past. The higher headquarters will direct the specific framework or frameworks to be used by subordinate headquarters; the frameworks should be consistent throughout all echelons. The three operational frameworks are—

- Deep-close-security
- Main and supporting effort
- Decisive-shaping-sustaining

For example, when generating options for a decisive-shaping-sustaining operation, the staff starts with the decisive operation identified in the commander's planning guidance. The staff checks that the decisive operation nests within the higher headquarters' concept of operations. The staff clarifies the decisive operation's purpose and considers ways to mass the effects (lethal and nonlethal) of overwhelming combat power to achieve it.

Next, the staff considers shaping operations. The staff establishes a purpose for each shaping operation tied to creating or preserving a condition for the decisive operation's success. Shaping operations may occur before, concurrently with, or after the decisive operation. A shaping operation may be designated as the main effort if executed before or after the decisive operation.

The staff then determines sustaining operations necessary to create and maintain the combat power required for the decisive operation and shaping operation. After developing the basic operational organization for a given COA, the staff then determines the essential tasks for each decisive, shaping, and sustaining operation.

Once staff members have explored possibilities for each COA, they examine each COA to determine if it satisfies the pre-determined screening criteria. In doing so, they change, add, or eliminate COAs as appropriate. During this process, staffs avoid focusing on the development of one good COA among several throwaway COAs.

3. Array Forces

After determining the decisive and shaping operations and their related tasks and purposes, planners determine the relative combat power required to accomplish each task. Planners may use minimum historical planning ratios as a starting point:

Historical Minimum Planning Data

Friendly Mission	Position	Friendly:Enemy
Delay		1:6
Defend	Prepared or fortified	1:3
Defend	Hasty	1:2.5
Attack	Prepared or fortified	3:1
Attack	Hasty	2.5:1
Counterattack	Flank	1:1

FM 6-0 (C1), Commander & Staff Organization & Operations, table 9-2, p. 4-20.

For example, historically defenders have over a 50% probability of defeating an attacking force approximately three times their equivalent strength. Therefore, as a starting point, commanders may defend on each avenue of approach with roughly a 1:3 force ratio.

Planners determine whether these and other intangibles increase the relative combat power of the unit assigned the task to the point that it exceeds the historical planning ratio for that task. If it does not, planners determine how to reinforce the unit. Combat power comparisons are provisional at best. Arraying forces is tricky, inexact work, affected by factors that are difficult to gauge, such as impact of past engagements, quality of leaders, morale, maintenance of equipment, and time in position. Levels of electronic warfare support, fire support, close air support, civilian support, and many other factors also affect arraying forces.

In counterinsurgency operations, planners can develop force requirements by gauging troop density—the ratio of security forces (including host-nation military and police forces as well as foreign counterinsurgents) to inhabitants. Most density recommendations fall within a range of 20 to 25 counterinsurgents for every 1,000 residents in an AO. Twenty counterinsurgents per 1,000 residents are often considered the minimum troop density required for effective counterinsurgency operations; however, as with any fixed ratio, such calculations strongly depend on the situation.

Planners also determine relative combat power with regard to civilian requirements and conditions that require attention and then array forces and capabilities for stability tasks. For example, a COA may require a follow-on force to establish civil security, maintain civil control, and restore essential services in a densely populated urban area over an extended period. Planners conduct a troop-to-task analysis to determine the type of units and capabilities needed to accomplish these tasks.

Planners then proceed to initially array friendly forces starting with the decisive operation and continuing with all shaping and sustaining operations. Planners normally array ground forces two levels down. The initial array focuses on generic ground maneuver units without regard to specific type or task organization and then considers all appropriate intangible factors. During this step, planners do not assign missions to specific units; they only consider which forces are necessary to accomplish its task. In this step, planners also array assets to accomplish essential stability tasks.

The initial array identifies the total number of units needed and identifies possible methods of dealing with the enemy and stability tasks. If the number arrayed is less than the number available, planners place additional units in a pool for use when they develop the initial concept of the operation. If the number of units arrayed exceeds the number available and the difference cannot be compensated for with intangible factors, the staff determines whether the COA is feasible. Ways to make up the shortfall include requesting additional resources, accepting risk in that portion of the area of operations, or executing tasks required for the COA sequentially rather than simultaneously. Commanders should also consider requirements to minimize and relieve civilian suffering. Establishing civil security and providing essential services such as medical care, water, food, and shelter are implied tasks for commanders during any combat operation.

4. Develop a Broad Concept

In developing the broad concept of the operation, the commander describes how arrayed forces will accomplish the mission within the commander's intent. The broad concept concisely expresses the how of the commander's visualization and will eventually provide the framework for the concept of operations and summarizes the contributions of all warfighting functions. The staff develops the initial concept of the operation for each COA expressed in both narrative and graphic forms. A sound COA is more than the arraying of forces. It presents an overall combined arms idea that will accomplish the mission. The initial concept of the operation includes, but is not limited to, the following:

- The purpose of the operation
- A statement of where the commander will accept risk
- Identification of critical friendly events and transitions between phases (if the operation is phased)

- Designation of the reserve, including its location and composition
- Information collection activities
- Essential stability tasks
- Identification of maneuver options that may develop during an operation
- Assignment of subordinate areas of operations
- Scheme of fires
- Themes, messages, and means of delivery
- Military deception operations (on a need to know basis)
- Key control measures
- Designate the operational framework for this operation: deep-close-security, main and supporting effort, or decisive-shaping-sustaining
- Designation of the decisive operation, along with its task and purpose, linked to how it supports the higher headquarters' concept

Planners select control measures, including graphics, to control subordinate units during an operation. These establish responsibilities and limits that prevent subordinate units' actions from impeding one another. These measures also foster coordination and cooperation between forces without unnecessarily restricting freedom of action. Good control measures foster decision making and individual initiative.

Planners may use both lines of operations and lines of effort to build their broad concept. Lines of operations portray the more traditional links among objectives, decisive points, and centers of gravity. A line of effort, however, helps planners link multiple tasks with goals, objectives, and end state conditions. Combining lines of operations with lines of efforts allows planners to include nonmilitary activities in their broad concept. This combination helps commanders incorporate stability or defense support of civil authorities tasks that, when accomplished, help set end state conditions of the operation. Based on the commander's planning guidance (informed by the design concept if design preceded the MDMP), planners develop lines of effort by:

- Confirming end state conditions from the initial commander's intent and planning guidance
- Determining and describing each line of effort
- Identifying objectives (intermediate goals) and determining tasks along each line of effort

During COA development, lines of efforts are general and lack specifics, such as tasks to subordinate units associated to objectives along each line of effort. Units develop and refine lines of effort, to include specific tasks to subordinate units, during war-gaming. As planning progresses, commanders may modify lines of effort and add details while war-gaming. Operations with other instruments of national power support a broader, comprehensive approach to stability operations. Each operation, however, differs. Commanders develop and modify lines of effort to focus operations on achieving the end state, even as the situation evolves.

5. Assign Headquarters

After determining the broad concept, planners create a task organization by assigning headquarters to groupings of forces. They consider the types of units to be assigned to a headquarters and the ability of that headquarters to control those units. Generally, a headquarters controls at least two subordinate maneuver units (but not more than five) for fast-paced offensive or defensive operations. The number and type of units assigned to a headquarters for stability operations vary based on factors of the mission variables (known as METT-TC). If planners need additional headquarters, they note the shortage and resolve it later. Task organization takes into account the entire operational organization. It also accounts for the special mission command requirements for operations, such as a passage of lines, or air assault.

Sample COA Sketch and Statement

Ref: FM 6-0 (C1), Commander and Staff Organization and Operations (May '15), fig. 9-5, pp. 9-24 to 9-25.

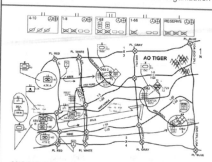

MISSION: On order, 3d ABCT clears remnants of the 72d Brigade in AO TIGER to establish security and enable the host-nation in reestablishing civil control in the region.

COMMANDER'S INTENT: The purpose of this operation is to provide a safe and secure environment in AO TIGER to enable the host-nation and other civilian organizations to reestablish civil control, restore essential services, and reestablish local governance within the area. The **key tasks** are: 1) destroy remnants of the 72nd BDE; 2) secure population centers vic OBHs 1, 2, and 3; 3) transition authority to the host nation. At **end state**, the BCT has destroyed remnant enemy forces in AO TIGER, secured population centers, and is prepared to transition responsibility for security to hostnnation authority.

INFORMATION COLLECTION: Priority of reconnaissance initially to locate enemy forces between PL RED (LD) and PL WHITE. Information collection operations subsequently focus on: 1) Identifying the location and disposition of enemy forces vic OBJ 1; 2) Observation of MSR HONDA between PL WHITE and PL BLUE; 3) observation of dislocated civilian traffic from CENTER CITY to EAST CITY.

SHAPING OPERATIONS:

4-10 CAV (ME) initially screens along PL WHITE IOT deny enemy reconnaissance and provide freedom of maneuver to follow on operations. On order, conducts FPOL at PL WHITE IOT move 1-8 CAB and 1-66 CAB(-) foward to conduct operations while maintaining contact with enemy.

O/O, **1-8 CAB (SE)** in the north moves from ATK A, crosses LD at PD1 on DIRECTION OF ATTACK ARES, conducts FPOL, and clears hostile gang vic OBJ 2 IOT enable NGO delivery of humanitarian assistance to WEST CITY and DODGE CITY.

TF 1-68 (SE) in the center occupies ATK B IOT prepare for follow on operations. On order, 1-66 CAB(-) (SE) in the south moves from ATK C, crosses LD at PD2, attacks along DIRECTION OF ATTACK NIKE, and clears enemy vic OBJ 3 IOT prevent disruption of DO vic OBJ 1.

588 BEB (SE) occupies BSA IOT set conditions for follow on operations.

RESERVE initially establishes vic ATK B. On order, displace to AA DOG (east). Priority of commitment to DO vic OBJ 1.

DECISIVE OPERATION:

4-10 CAV (SE) conducts FPOL vic PL WHITE IOT move 1-68 CAB (ME) forward to conduct operations

while maintaining enemy contact. On order, occupy AA DOG (south) IOT prepare for future operations. BPT conduct security operations in northeastern portion of AO TIGER IOT provide early and accurate warning of enemy or hostile threats to the security of the population centers.

1-8 CAB (SE) controls ASRs BUICK and FORD in assigned AO IOT facilitate sustaining operations and prevent civilians interference with DO vic OBJ 1.

O/O, TF -68 (ME) moves from ATK B along AXIS ZEUS, conducts FPOL, and attacks to destroy elements of 72nd BDE vic OBJ 1 IOT provide a secure environment for the CENTER CITY population. Bypass criteria is platoon-size or smaller.

1-66 CAB(-) (SE) controls DPRE camp vic EAST CITY IOT provide a secure environment and controls ASR BUICK in assigned AO IOT facilitate sustaining operations and prevent civilian intereference with DO vic OBJ 1.

588 BEB (SE) conducts operations as required IOT support DO.

RESERVE establishes in AA DOG (east). Priority of commitment is to reinforce DO vic OBJ 1.

FIRES:

(Shaping Operations): Priority of fires to 4-10 CAV, 1-8 CAB, 1-66 CAB, and TF 1-68 initially from PAA 9. O/O displace to PAA 10. HPTs are enemy reconnaissance forces, indirect fire systems, and mechanized enemy forces.

(Decisive Operations): Priority of fires to TF 1-68 (ME), 1-66 CAB, 1-8 CAB, and 4-10 CAB from PAA 10. HPTs are enemy armor, mechanized enemy forces, and indirect fire systems.

FSCM: CFL initially PL WHITE, O/O PL Gray, O/O PL BLUE (LOA).

SUSTAINING OPERATIONS:

(Shaping Operations): 64 BSB will initially establish operations in BSA. O/O, establish BSA in AA DOG vic WEST CITY using MSR HONDA, ASR FORD, and ASR BUICK as primary routes IOT sustain operations. Establish FLEs as required to support operations. Priority of support to 4-10 CAV (ME) will be class III, V, maintenance, and medical.

(Decisive Operations): Priority of support to TF 1-68 (ME) will be class III, V, maintenance, and medical. Coordinate with humanitarian relief agencies IOT facilitate rapid restoration of essential services in AO TIGER.

MISSION COMMAND:

(Command): 3rd ABCT commander located with TAC CP and executive officer located with MAIN CP throughout mission.

(Control/Signal): 3rd ABCT **MAIN CP** initially located vic ATK B. O/O displaces vic OBJ 2. 3rd ABCT **TAC CP** initially located vic ATK B. O/O, displaces vic OBJ 1.

RISK: Based on intelligence reports of negative enemy activity in the northeast mountainous portion of AO TIGER, risk is assumed with no ground maneuver forces initially allocated to conduct reconnaissance or surveillance operations. Mitigation will be accomplished by assigning a BPT mission to 4-10 CAV to conduct security operations IOT provide early and accurate warning of enemy or hostile threats to security of population centers.

6. Prepare COA Statements and Sketches

The G-3 (S-3) prepares a COA statement and supporting sketch for each COA. The COA statement clearly portrays how the unit will accomplish the mission. The COA statement briefly expresses how the unit will conduct the combined arms concept. The sketch provides a picture of the movement and maneuver aspects of the concept, including the positioning of forces. Together, the statement and sketch cover the who (generic task organization), what (tasks), when, where, and why (purpose) for each subordinate unit. The COA sketch includes the array of generic forces and control measures, such as:

- The unit and subordinate unit boundaries
- Unit movement formations (but not subordinate unit formations)
- The line of departure or line of contact and phase lines, if used
- Information collection graphics
- Ground and air axes of advance
- Assembly areas, battle positions, strong points, engagement areas, and objectives
- Obstacle control measures and tactical mission graphics
- Fire support coordination and airspace coordinating measures
- Main effort
- Location of command posts and critical information systems nodes
- Known or templated enemy locations
- Population concentrations

Planners can include identifying features (such as cities, rivers, and roads) to help orient users. The sketch may be on any medium. What it portrays is more important than its form.

7. Conduct a Course of Action Briefing

After developing COAs, the staff briefs them to the commander. A collaborative session may facilitate subordinate planning. The COA briefing includes:

- An updated IPB (if there are significant changes).
- As many threat COAs as necessary (or specified by the commander). At a minimum the most likely and most dangerous threat COAs must be developed.
- The approved problem statement and mission statement.
- The commander's and higher commander's intents.
- COA statements and sketches, including lines of effort if used.
- The rationale for each COA, including:
  - Considerations that might affect enemy COAs
  - Critical events for each COA
  - Deductions resulting from the relative combat power analysis
  - The reason units are arrayed as shown on the sketch
  - The reason the staff used the selected control measures
  - The impact on civilians
  - How the COA accounts for minimum essential stability tasks
  - New facts and new or updated assumptions
  - Refined COA evaluation criteria

8. Select or Modify COAs for Continued Analysis

After the COA briefing, the commander selects or modifies those COAs for continued analysis. The commander also issues planning guidance. If commanders reject all COAs, the staff begins again. If commanders accept one or more of the COAs, staff members begin COA analysis. The commander may create a new COA by incorporating elements of one or more COAs developed by the staff. The staff then prepares to war-game this new COA. The staff incorporates those modifications and ensures all staff members understand the changed COA.

MDMP Step IV. COA Analysis & War-Gaming

Ref: FM 6-0 (C1), Commander and Staff Organization and Operations (May '15), pp. 9-26 to 9-39.

COA analysis enables commanders and staffs to identify difficulties or coordination problems as well as probable consequences of planned actions for each COA being considered. It helps them think through the tentative plan. COA analysis may require commanders and staffs to revisit parts of a COA as discrepancies arise. COA analysis not only appraises the quality of each COA, but it also uncovers potential execution problems, decisions, and contingencies. In addition, COA analysis influences how commanders and staffs understand a problem and may require the planning process to restart.

IV. COA Analysis (War Game)

Key Inputs	Key Outputs
▪ Updated running estimates	▪ Refined COAs
▪ Revised planning guidance	▪ Potential decision points
▪ COA statements and sketches	▪ War-game results
▪ Updated assumptions	▪ Initial assessment measures
	▪ Updated assumptions

1 Gather the Tools

2 List all Friendly Forces

3 List Assumptions

4 List Known Critical Events & Decision Points

5 Select the War-Gaming Method

6 Select a Technique to Record and Display Results

7 War-Game the Operation and Assess the Results

8 Conduct a War-Game Briefing (Optional)

Ref: FM 6-0 (C1), Commander and Staff Organization and Operations, fig. 9-6, p. 9-26.

War-gaming is a disciplined process, with rules and steps that attempt to visualize the flow of the operation, given the force's strengths and dispositions, enemy's capabilities and possible COAs, impact and requirements of civilians in the AO, and other aspects of the situation. The simplest form of war-gaming is the manual method, often utilizing a tabletop approach with blowups of matrixes and templates. The most sophisticated form of war-gaming is modern, computer-aided modeling and simulation. Regardless of the form used, each critical event within a proposed COA should be war-gamed using the action, reaction, and counteraction methods of friendly and enemy forces interaction. This basic war-gaming method (modified to fit the specific mission and environment) applies to offensive, defensive, and stability or defense support of civil authorities operations. When conducting COA analysis, commanders and staffs perform the process actions and produce the outputs .

War-gaming results in refined COAs, a completed synchronization matrix, and decision support templates and matrixes for each COA. A synchronization matrix records the results of a war game. It depicts how friendly forces for a particular COA are synchronized in time, space, and purpose in relation to an enemy COA or other events in stability or defense support of civil authorities operations. The decision support template and matrix portray key decisions and potential actions that are likely to arise during the execution of each COA.

COA analysis allows the staff to synchronize the six war fighting functions for each COA. It also helps the commander and staff to:

- Determine how to maximize the effects of combat power while protecting friendly forces and minimizing collateral damage
- Further develop a visualization of the operation
- Anticipate operational events
- Determine conditions and resources required for success
- Determine when and where to apply force capabilities
- Identify coordination needed to produce synchronized results
- Determine the most flexible COA

During the war game, the staff takes each COA and begins to develop a detailed plan while determining its strengths or weaknesses. War-gaming tests and improves COAs. The commander, staff, and other available partners (and subordinate commanders and staffs if the war game is conducted collaboratively) may change an existing COA or develop a new COA after identifying unforeseen events, tasks, requirements, or problems.

General War-Gaming Rules

War gamers need to:

- Remain objective, not allowing personality or their sense of "what the commander wants" to influence them
- Avoid defending a COA just because they personally developed it
- Record advantages and disadvantages of each COA accurately as they emerge
- Continually assess feasibility, acceptability, and suitability of each COA. If a COA fails any of these tests, reject it
- Avoid drawing premature conclusions and gathering facts to support such conclusions
- Avoid comparing one COA with another during the war game. This occurs during Step 5—COA Comparison.

1. Gather the Tools

The first task for COA analysis is to gather the necessary tools to conduct the war game. The chief of staff or executive officer directs the staff to gather tools, materials, and data for the war game. Units war-game with maps, sand tables, computer simulations, or other tools that accurately reflect the terrain. The staff posts the COA on a map displaying the AO. Tools required include, but are not limited to:

- Running estimates
- Threat templates and models
- Civil considerations overlays, databases, and data files
- Modified combined obstacle overlays and terrain effects matrices
- A recording method
- Completed COAs, including graphics
- A means to post or display enemy and friendly unit symbols and other organizations
- A map of the area of operations

2. List All Friendly Forces

The commander and staff consider all units that can be committed to the operation, paying special attention to support relationships and constraints. This list must include assets from all participants operating in the AO. The friendly force list remains constant for all COA's.

3. List Assumptions

The commander and staff review previous assumptions for continued validity and necessity. Any changes resulting from this review are noted for record.

4. List Known Critical Events and Decision Points

A. Critical Events

A critical event is an event that directly influences mission accomplishment. Critical events include events that trigger significant actions or decisions (such as commitment of an enemy reserve), complicated actions requiring detailed study (such as a passage of lines), and essential tasks. The list of critical events includes major events from the unit's current position through mission accomplishment. It includes reactions by civilians that potentially affect operations or require allocation of significant assets to account for essential stability tasks.

B. Decision Points (DPs)

A decision point is a point in space and time when the commander or staff anticipates making a key decision concerning a specific course of action. Decision points may also be associated with the friendly force and the status of ongoing operations. A decision point will be associated with CCIRs that describe what information the commander requires to make the anticipated decision. The PIR describes what must be known about the enemy or the environment and often is associated with a named area of interest. A decision point requires a decision by the commander. It does not dictate what the decision is, only that the commander must make one, and when and where it should be made to maximally impact friendly or enemy COA's or the accomplishment of stability tasks.

War-Gaming Responsibilities

Ref: FM 6-0 (C1), Commander and Staff Organization and Operations (May '15), pp. 9-36 to 9-39.

Mission Command Responsibilities

The commander has overall responsibility for the war-gaming process, and the commander can determine the staff members who are involved in war-gaming. Traditionally, certain staff members have key and specific roles.

The COS (XO) coordinates actions of the staff during the war game. This officer is the unbiased controller of the process, ensuring the staff stays on a timeline and achieves the goals of the war-gaming session. In a time-constrained environment, this officer ensures that, at a minimum, the decisive operation is war-gamed.

The G-3 (S-3) assists the commander with the rehearsal. The G-3 (S-3)—

* Portrays the friendly scheme of maneuver, including the employment of information-related capabilities.
* Ensures subordinate unit actions comply with the commander's intent.
* Normally provides the recorder.

The assistant chief of staff, signal (G-6 [S-6]) assesses network operations, spectrum management operations, network defense, and information protection feasibility of each war-gamed COA. The G-6 (S-6) determines communications systems requirements and compares them to available assets, identifies potential shortfalls, and recommends actions to eliminate or reduce their effects The information operations officer assesses the information operations concept of support against the ability of information-related capabilities to execute tasks in support of each war-gamed COA and the effectiveness of integrated information-related capabilities to impact various audiences and populations in and outside the area of operations. The information operations officer, in coordination with the electronic warfare officer, also integrates information operations with cyber electromagnetic activities.

The assistant chief of staff, civil affairs operations (G-9 [S-9]) ensures each war-gamed COA effectively integrates civil considerations (the "C" of METT-TC). The civil affairs operations officer considers not only tactical issues but also sustainment issues. This officer assesses how operations affect civilians and estimates the requirements for essential stability tasks commanders might have to undertake based on the ability of the unified action partners. Host-nation support and care of dislocated civilians are of particular concern. The civil affairs operations officer's analysis considers how operations affect public order and safety, the potential for disaster relief requirements, noncombatant evacuation operations, emergency services, and the protection of culturally significant sites. This officer provides feedback on how the culture in the area of operations affects each COA. If the unit lacks an assigned civil affairs officer, the commander assigns these responsibilities to another staff member.

The red team staff section provides the commander and assistant chief of staff, intelligence (G-2) with an independent capability to fully explore alternatives. The staff looks at plans, operations, concepts, organizations, and capabilities of the operational environment from the perspectives of enemies, unified action partners, and others.

The electronic warfare officer provides information on the electronic warfare target list, electronic attack taskings, electronic attack requests, and the electronic warfare portion of the collection matrix and the attack guidance matrix. Additionally, the electronic warfare officer assesses threat vulnerabilities, friendly electronic warfare capabilities, and friendly actions relative to electronic warfare activities and other cyber electromagnetic activities not covered by the G-6 or G-2.

The staff judge advocate advises the commander on all matters pertaining to law, policy, regulation, good order, and discipline for each war-gamed COA. This officer provides legal advice across the range of military operations on law of war, rules of engagement, international agreements, Geneva Conventions, treatment and disposition of noncombatants, and the legal aspects of targeting.

The operations research and systems analysis staff section provides analytic support to the commander for planning and assessment of operations. The safety officer provides input to influence accident and incident reductions by implementing risk management procedures throughout the mission planning and execution process. The knowledge management officer assesses the effectiveness of the knowledge management plan for each course of action. The space operations officer provides and represents friendly, threat, and non-aligned space capabilities.

Intelligence Responsibilities

During the war game the G-2 (S-2) role-plays the enemy commander, other threat organizations in the area of operations, and critical civil considerations in the area of operations. This officer develops critical enemy decision points in relation to the friendly COAs, projects enemy reactions to friendly actions, and projects enemy losses. The intelligence officer assigns different responsibilities to available staff members within the section (such as the enemy commander, friendly intelligence officer, and enemy recorder) for war-gaming. The intelligence officer captures the results of each enemy, threat group, and civil considerations action and counteraction as well as the corresponding friendly and enemy strengths and vulnerabilities. By trying to realistically win the war game for the enemy, the intelligence officer ensures that the staff fully addresses friendly responses for each enemy COA.

Movemenent and Maneuver Responsibilities

During the war game, the G-3 (S-3) and assistant chief of staff, plans (G-5 [S-5]) are responsible for movement and maneuver. The G-3 (S-3) normally selects the technique for the war game and role-plays the friendly maneuver commander. Various staff officers assist the G-3 (S-3), such as the aviation officer and engineer officer. The G-3 (S-3) executes friendly maneuver as outlined in the COA sketch and COA statement. The G-5 (S-5) assesses warfighting function requirements, solutions, and concepts for each COA; develops plans and orders; and determines potential branches and sequels arising from various war-gamed COAs. The G-5 (S-5) also coordinates and synchronizes warfighting functions in all plans and orders. The planning staff ensures that the war game of each COA covers every operational aspect of the mission. The members of the staff record each event's strengths and weaknesses and the rationale for each action. They complete the decision support template and matrix for each COA. They annotate the rationale for actions during the war game and use it later with the commander's guidance to compare COAs.

Fires Responsibilities

The chief of fires (fire support officer) assesses the fire support feasibility of each war-gamed COA. This officer develops a proposed high-payoff target list, target selection standards, and attack guidance matrix. The chief of fires works with the intelligence officer to identify named and target areas of interest for enemy indirect fire weapon systems, and identifies high-payoff targets and additional events that may influence the positioning of field artillery and air defense artillery assets. The chief of fires should also offer a list of possible defended assets for air defense artillery forces and assist the commander in making a final determination about asset priority.

Protection Responsibilities

The chief of protection assesses protection element requirements, refines EEFIs, and develops a scheme of protection for each war-gamed COA.

Sustainment Responsibilities

During the war game, the assistant chief of staff, personnel (G-1 [S-1]) assesses the personnel aspect of building and maintaining the combat power of units. This officer identifies potential shortfalls and recommends COAs to ensure units maintain adequate manning to accomplish their mission. As the primary staff officer assessing the human resources planning considerations to support sustainment operations, the G-1 (S-1) provides human resources support for the operation.

The assistant chief of staff, logistics (G-4 [S-4]) assesses the logistics feasibility of each war-gamed COA. This officer determines critical requirements for each logistics function (classes I through VII, IX, and X) and identifies potential problems and deficiencies. The G-4 (S-4) assesses the status of all logistics functions required to support the COA, including potential support required to provide essential services to the civilians, and compares it to available assets. This officer identifies potential shortfalls and recommends actions to eliminate or reduce their effects. While improvising can contribute to responsiveness, only accurately predicting requirements for each logistics function can ensure continuous sustainment. The logistics officer ensures that available movement times and assets support each COA.

During the war game, the assistant chief of staff, financial management (G-8) assesses the commander's area of operations to determine the best COA for use of resources. This assessment includes both core functions of financial management: resource management and finance operations. This officer determines partner relationships (joint, interagency, intergovernmental, and multinational), requirements for special funding, and support to the procurement process.

The surgeon section coordinates, monitors, and synchronizes the execution of the health system activities for the command for each war-gamed COA to ensure a fit and healthy force.

Recorders

The use of recorders is particularly important. Recorders capture coordinating instructions, subunit tasks and purposes, and information required to synchronize the operation. Recorders allow the staff to write part of the order before they complete the planning. Automated information systems enable recorders to enter information into preformatted forms that represent either briefing charts or appendixes to orders. Each staff section keeps formats available to facilitate networked orders production.

5. Select the War-Game Method

Three recommended war-game methods exist: belt, avenue-in-depth, and box. Each considers the area of interest and all enemy forces that can affect the outcome of the operation. Planners can use the methods separately or in combination and modified for long-term operations dominated by stability.

See facing page (p. 2-43) for further discussion of the three war-game methods.

A. The Belt Method

The belt method divides the AO into belts (areas) running the width of the AO. The shape of each belt is based on the factors of METT-TC. The belt method works best when conducting offensive and defensive operations on terrain divided into well-defined cross-compartments, during phased operations (such as river crossings, air assaults, or airborne operations), or when the enemy is deployed in clearly defined belts or echelons. Belts can be adjacent to or overlap each other.

This method is based on a sequential analysis of events in each belt. It is preferred because it focuses simultaneously on all forces affecting a particular event. A belt might include more than one critical event. Under time-constrained conditions, the commander can use a modified belt method. The modified belt method divides the AO into not more than three sequential belts. These belts are not necessarily adjacent or overlapping but focus on the critical actions throughout the depth of the AO.

In stability tasks, the belt method can divide the COA by events, objectives (goals not geographic location), or events and objectives in a selected slice across all lines of effort. It consists of war-gaming relationships among events or objectives on all lines of effort in the belt.

B. Avenue-in-Depth Method

The avenue-in-depth method focuses on one avenue of approach at a time, beginning with the decisive operation. This method is good for offensive COA's or in the defense when canalizing terrain inhibits mutual support.

In stability tasks, planners can modify the avenue-in-depth method. Instead of focusing on a geographic avenue, the staff war-games a line of effort. This method focuses on one line of effort at a time, beginning with the decisive line. The avenue-in-depth method includes not only war-gaming events and objectives in the selected line, but also war-gaming relationships among events or objectives on all lines of effort with respect to events in the selected line.

C. The Box Method

The box method is a detailed analysis of a critical area, such as an engagement area, a river-crossing site, or a landing zone. It works best in a time-constrained environment, such as a hasty attack. It is particularly useful when planning operations in noncontiguous areas of operation. When using this method, the staff isolates the area and focuses on critical events in it. Staff members assume that friendly units can handle most situations in the AO's and focus their attention on essential tasks.

In stability tasks, the box method may focus analysis on a specific objective along a line of effort, such as development of local security forces as part of improving civil security.

War-Game Methods

Ref: FM 6-0 (C1), Commander and Staff Organization and Operations (May '15), pp. 9-28 to 9-31.

Belt Technique

The belt method divides the AO into belts (areas) running the width of the AO. The shape of each belt is based on the factors of METT-TC. The belt method works best when conducting offensive and defensive operations on terrain divided into well-defined cross-compartments, during phased operations or when the enemy is deployed in clearly defined belts or echelons.

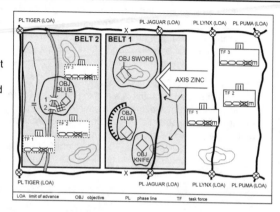

Avenue-in-Depth Technique

The avenue-in-depth method focuses on one avenue of approach at a time, beginning with the decisive operation. This method is good for offensive COA's or in the defense when canalizing terrain inhibits mutual support. In stability operations, this method can be modified. Instead of focusing on a geographic avenue, the staff war-games a line of effort.

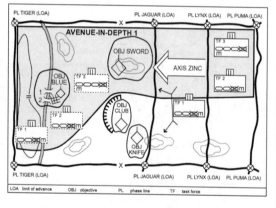

Box Technique

The box method is a detailed analysis of a critical area, such as an engagement area, a river-crossing site, or a landing zone. It is used when time is constrained. It is particularly useful when planning operations in noncontiguous AOs. The staff isolates the area and focuses on critical events in it. Staff members assume friendly units can handle most situations on the battlefield and focus on essential tasks.

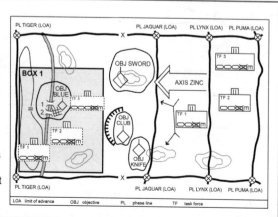

6. Select a Technique to Record and Display Results

The war-game results provide a record from which to build task organizations, synchronize activities, develop decision support templates, confirm and refine event templates, prepare plans or orders, and compare COA's. Two techniques are commonly used to record and display results: the synchronization matrix technique and the sketch note technique. In both techniques, staff members record any remarks regarding the strengths and weaknesses they discover. The amount of detail depends on the time available. Unit SOPs address details and methods of recording and displaying war-gaming results.

A. Synchronization Matrix

The synchronization matrix is a tool the staff uses to record the results of war-gaming and helps them synchronize a course of action across time, space, and purpose in relationship to potential enemy and civil actions. The first entry is time or phase of the operation. The second entry is the most likely enemy action. The third entry is the most likely civilian action. The fourth entry is the decision points for the friendly COA. The remainder of the matrix is developed around selected war fighting functions and their subordinate tasks and the unit's major subordinate commands.

Sample Synchronization Matrix

Time/Event		H – 24 hours	H-hour	H + 24
Enemy Action		Monitors movements	Defends from security zone	Commits reserve
Population		Orderly evacuation from area continues		
Decision Points		Conduct aviation attack of OBJ Irene		
Control Measures				
Movement and Maneuver	1st BCT	Move on Route Irish	Cross LD	Seize on OBJ Irene
	2d BCT	Move on Route Longstreet	Cross LD	Seize on OBJ Rose
	3d BCT			FPOL with 1st BCT
	Avn Bde	Attack enemy reserve on OBJ Irene		
	R&S			
Reserve				
Information Collection				
Fires		Prep fires initiated at H-5		
Protection	Engineer			
	PMO			
	CBRNE			
Sustainment				
Mission Command			MAIN CP with 1st BCT	
Close Air Support				
Electronic Warfare			Enemy C2 jammed	
Nonlethal Effects		Surrender broadcasts and leaflets		
Host Nation				
Interagency				
NGOs			Begins refugee relief	

Note: The first column is representative only and can be modified to fit formation needs.

AMD	air and missile defense	FPOL	forward passage of lines
Avn Bde	aviation brigade	LD	line of departure
BCT	brigade combat team	NGO	nongovernmental organization
C2	command and control	OBJ	objective
CBRNE	chemical, biological, radiological, nuclear, and high-yield explosives	PMO	provost marshal office
CP	command post	R&S	reconnaissance and surveillance

Ref: FM 6-0 (C1), Commander & Staff Organization & Operations, table 9-3, p. 9-32.

B. Sketch Note Technique

The sketch note technique uses brief notes concerning critical locations or tasks and purposes. These notes refer to specific locations or relate to general considerations covering broad areas. The commander and staff mark locations on the map and on a separate war-game work sheet. Staff members use sequence numbers to link the notes to the corresponding locations on the map or overlay. Staff members also identify actions by placing them in sequential action groups, giving each subtask a separate number. They use the war-game work sheet to identify all pertinent data for a critical event. They assign each event a number and title and use the columns on the work sheet to identify and list in sequence:

- Units and assigned tasks
- Expected enemy actions and reactions
- Friendly counteractions and assets
- Total assets needed for the task
- Estimated time to accomplish the task
- The decision point tied to executing the task
- CCIR's
- Control measures
- Remarks

Sample Sketch Note Technique

Critical Event	Seize OBJ Sword
Sequence number	1
Action	TF 3 attacks to destroy enemy company on OBJ Sword
Reaction	Enemy company on OBJ Club counterattacks
Counteraction	TF 1 suppresses enemy company on OBJ Club
Assets	TF 3, TF 1, and 1-78 FA (155-SP)
Time	H+1 to H+4
Decision point	DP 3a and 3b
Commander's Critical information Requirements	Location of enemy armor reserve west of PL Jaguar
Control measures	Axis Zinc and support by fire position 1
Remarks	

Ref: FM 6-0 (C1), Commander & Staff Organization & Operations, table 9-4, p. 9-33.

7. War-Game the Operation and Assess the Results

War-gaming is a conscious attempt to visualize the flow of operations, given the friendly force's strengths and disposition, enemy's capabilities and possible COA's, and civilians. During the war game, the commander and staff try to foresee the actions, reactions, and counteractions of all participants to include civilians. The staff analyzes each selected event. They identify tasks that the force must accomplish one echelon down, using assets two echelons down. Identifying strengths and weaknesses of each COA allows the staff to adjust the COA's as necessary.

The war game focuses not so much on the tools used but on the people who participate. Staff members who participate in war-gaming should be the individuals deeply involved in developing COA's. Red team members (who can provide alternative points of view) provide insight on each COA. In stability operations, subject matter experts in areas such as economic or local governance can also help assess results of planned actions to include identifying possible unintended effects.

The war game follows an action-reaction-counteraction cycle. Actions are those events initiated by the side with the initiative. Reactions are the opposing side's actions in response. With regard to stability operations, the war game tests the effects of actions including intended and unintended effects as they stimulate anticipated responses from civilians and civil institutions. Counteractions are the first side's responses to reactions. This sequence of action-reaction-counteraction continues until the critical event is completed or until the commander decides to use another COA to accomplish the mission.

The staff considers all possible forces, including templated enemy forces outside the AO, which can influence the operation. The staff also considers the actions of civilians in the AO and the diverse kinds of coverage of unfolding events and their consequences in the global media. The staff evaluates each friendly move to determine the assets and actions required to defeat the enemy at that point or to accomplish stability tasks. Then the staff continually considers branches to the plan that promote success against likely enemy counteractions or unexpected civilian reactions. Lastly, the staff lists assets used in the appropriate columns of the work sheet and lists the totals in the assets column (not considering any assets lower than two command levels down).

The commander and staff examine many areas in detail during the war game:

- All friendly capabilities
- All enemy capabilities and critical civil considerations that impact operations
- Global media responses to proposed actions
- Movement considerations
- Closure rates
- Lengths of columns
- Formation depths
- Ranges and capabilities of weapon systems
- Desired effects of fires

The commander and staff consider how to create conditions for success, protect the force, and shape the operational environment. Experience, historical data, SOPs, and doctrinal literature provide much of the necessary information. During the war game, staff officers perform a risk assessment for their functional area for each COA. They then propose appropriate controls. They continually assess the risk of adverse population and media reactions that result from actions taken by all sides in the operation. Staff officers develop ways to mitigate those risks.

The staff continually assesses the risk to friendly forces, balancing between mass and dispersion. When assessing the risk of weapons of mass destruction to friendly

Effective War Game Results

Ref: FM 6-0 (C1), Commander and Staff Organization and Operations (May '15), table 9-5, p. 9-35.

The commander and staff refine (or modify):
- Each course of action, to include identifying branches and sequels that become on-order or be-prepared missions.
- The locations and times of decisive points.
- The enemy event template and matrix.
- The task organization, including forces retained in general support.
- Control requirements, including control measures & updated operational graphics.
- CCIR and other information requirements—including the latest time information is of value—and incorporate them into the information collection plan.

The commander and staff identify:
- Key or decisive terrain and determining how to use it.
- Tasks the unit retains and tasks assigned to subordinates.
- Likely times and areas for enemy use of weapons of mass destruction and friendly chemical, biological, radiological, and nuclear defense requirements.
- Potential times or locations for committing the reserve.
- The most dangerous enemy course of action.
- The most likely enemy course of action.
- The most dangerous civilian reaction.
- Locations for the commander and command posts.
- Critical events.
- Requirements for support of each warfighting function.
- Effects of friendly and enemy actions on civilians and infrastructure and on military operations.
- Or confirming the locations of named areas of interest, target areas of interest, decision points, and intelligence requirements needed to support them.
- Analyzing, and evaluating strengths and weaknesses of each course of action.
- Hazards, assessing their risk, developing control measures for them, and determining residual risk.
- The coordination required for integrating and synchronizing interagency, host-nation, and nongovernmental organization involvement.

The commander and staff analyze:
- Potential civilian reactions to operations.
- Potential media reaction to operations.
- Potential impacts on civil security, civil control, and essential services in the area of operations.

The commander and staff develop:
- Decision points.
- A synchronization matrix.
- A decision support template and matrix.
- Solutions to achieving minimum essential stability tasks in the area of operations.
- The information collection plan and graphics.
- Themes and messages.
- Fires, protection, and sustainment plans and graphic control measures.

The commander and staff determine:
- The requirements for military deception and surprise.
- The timing for concentrating forces and starting the attack or counterattack.
- The movement times & tables for critical assets, including information systems nodes.
- The estimated the duration of the entire operation and each critical event.
- The projected percentage of enemy forces defeated in each critical event & overall.
- The percentage of minimum essential tasks that the unit can or must accomplish.
- The media coverage and impact on key audiences.
- The targeting requirements in the operation, to include identifying or confirming high-payoff targets and establishing attack guidance.
- The allocation of assets to subordinate commanders to accomplish their missions.

forces, planners view the target that the force presents through the eyes of an enemy target analyst. They consider ways to reduce vulnerability and determine the appropriate level of mission-oriented protective posture consistent with mission accomplishment.

The staff identifies the required assets of the warfighting functions to support the concept of operations, including those needed to synchronize sustaining operations. If requirements exceed available assets, the staff recommends priorities based on the situation, commander's intent, and planning guidance. To maintain flexibility, the commander may decide to create a reserve to maintain assets for unforeseen tasks or opportunities.

The commander can modify any COA based on how things develop during the war game. When doing this, the commander validates the composition and location of the decisive operation, shaping operations, and reserve forces. Control measures are adjusted as necessary. The commander may also identify situations, opportunities, or additional critical events that require more analysis. The staff performs this analysis quickly and incorporates the results into the war-gaming record.

An effective war game results in the commander and staff refining, identifying, analyzing, developing, and determining several effects.

See previous page for discussion of effective war game results.

8. Conduct a War-Game Briefing (Optional)

Time permitting, the staff delivers a briefing to all affected elements to ensure everyone understands the results of the war game. The staff uses the briefing for review and ensures that it captures all relevant points of the war game for presentation to the commander, COS (XO), or deputy or assistant commander. In a collaborative environment, the briefing may include selected subordinate staffs. A war-game briefing format includes the following:

- Higher headquarters mission, commander's intent, and military deception plan
- Updated IPB
- Assumptions
- Friendly and enemy COA's that were war-gamed, to include:
  - Critical events
  - Possible enemy actions and reactions
  - Possible impact on civilians
  - Possible media impacts
  - Modifications to the COA's
  - Strengths and weaknesses
  - Results of the war game
- War-gaming technique used

MDMP Step V.
COA Comparison

Ref: FM 6-0 (C1), Commander and Staff Organization and Operations (May '15), pp. 9-39 to 9-41.

COA comparison is an objective process to evaluate COA's independently of each other and against set evaluation criteria approved by the commander and staff. The goal to identify the strengths and weaknesses of COA's enable selecting a COA with the highest probability of success and further developing it in an OPLAN or OPORD. The commander and staff perform certain actions and processes that lead to the key outputs.

V. COA Comparison

Key Inputs	Key Outputs
▪ Updated running estimates ▪ Refined COAs ▪ Evaluation criteria ▪ War-game results ▪ Updated assumptions	▪ Evaluated COAs ▪ Recommended COAs ▪ Update running estimates ▪ Updated assumptions

1 Conduct Advantages and Disadvantages Analysis

2 Compare COAs

3 Conduct COA Decision Briefing

Ref: FM 6-0 (C1), Commander and Staff Organization and Operations, fig. 9-13, p. 9-39.

1. Conduct Advantages and Disadvantages Analysis

The COA comparison starts with all staff members analyzing and evaluating the advantages and disadvantages of each COA from their perspectives. Staff members each present their findings for the others' consideration. Using the evaluation criteria developed before the war game, the staff outlines each COA, highlighting its advantages and disadvantages. Comparing the strengths and weaknesses of the COAs identifies their advantages and disadvantages with respect to each other.

See following page for a sample advantages and disadvantages analysis.

Sample Advantages and Disadvantages

Course of Action	Advantages	Disadvantages
COA 1	Decisive operation avoids major terrain obstacles. Adequate maneuver space available for units conducting the decisive operation and the reserve.	Units conducting the decisive operation face stronger resistance at the start of the operation. Limited resources available to establishing civil control to Town X.
COA 2	Shaping operations provide excellent flank protection of the decisive operations. Upon completion of decisive operations, units conducting shaping operations can quickly transition to establish civil control and provide civil security to the population in Town X.	Operation may require the early employment of the division's reserve.

Ref: FM 6-0 (C1), Commander and Staff Organization and Operations, table 9-6, p. 9-40.

2. Compare Courses of Action

Comparison of COAs is critical. The staff uses any technique that helps develop those key outputs and recommendations and assists the commander to make the best decision. A common technique is the decision matrix. This matrix uses evaluation criteria developed during mission analysis and refined during COA development to help assess the effectiveness and efficiency of each COA.

See facing page for a sample decision matrix.

Commanders and staffs cannot solely rely on the outcome of a decision matrix, as it only provides a partial basis for a solution. During the decision matrix process, planners carefully avoid reaching conclusions from a quantitative analysis of subjective weights. Comparing and evaluating COAs by criterion is probably more useful than merely comparing totaled ranks. Judgments often change with regard to the relative weighting of criteria during close analysis of COAs, which will change weighted rank totals and possibly the most preferred COA.

The staff compares feasible COAs to identify the one with the highest probability of success against the most likely enemy COA, the most dangerous enemy COA, the most important stability task, or the most damaging environmental impact. The selected COA should also:

- Pose the minimum risk to the force and mission accomplishment
- Place the force in the best posture for future operations
- Provide maximum latitude for initiative by subordinates
- Provide the most flexibility to meet unexpected threats and opportunities
- Provide the most secure and stable environment for civilians in the AO
- Best facilitate information themes and messages

Staff officers often use their own matrix to compare COAs with respect to their functional areas. Matrixes use the evaluation criteria developed before the war game. Their greatest value is providing a method to compare COAs against criteria that, when met, produce operational success. Staff officers use these analytical tools to prepare recommendations. Commanders provide the solution by applying their judgment to staff recommendations and making a decision.

Sample Decision Matrix

Ref: FM 6-0 (C1), Commander and Staff Organization and Operations (May '15), pp. 9-40 to 9-41.

The decision matrix is a tool to compare and evaluate COAs thoroughly and logically. However, the process is based on highly subjective judgments that may change dramatically during the course of evaluation.

Sample Decision Matrix

Weight [1]	1	2	1	1	2	
Criteria [2]						
Course of Action	Simplicity	Maneuver	Fires	Civil control	Inform and influence activities	TOTAL
COA 1 [3]	2	2 (4)	2	1	1 (2)	8 (11)
COA 2 [3]	1	2 (2)	1	2	2 (4)	7 (10)

Notes:
[1] The COS (XO) may emphasize one or more criteria by assigning weights to them based on a determination of their relative importance.
[2] Criteria are those assigned in step 5 of COA analysis.
[3] COAs are those selected for war-gaming with values assigned to them based on comparison between them with regard to relative advantages and disadvantages of each, such as when compared for relative simplicity COA 2 is by comparison to COA 1 simpler and therefore is rated as 1 with COA 1 rated as 2.

Ref: FM 6-0 (C1), Commander & Staff Organization & Operations, table 9-7, p. 9-40.

In table 9-7, the numerical rankings reflect the relative advantages or disadvantages of each criterion for each COA as initially estimated by a COS (XO) during mission analysis. Rankings are assigned from 1 to however many COAs exist. Lower rankings are more preferred. At the same time, the COS (XO) determines weights for each criterion based on a subjective determination of their relative value. The lower weights signify a more favorable advantage, such as the lower the number, the more favorable the weight. After assigning ranks to COAs and weights to criteria, the staff adds the unweighted ranks in each row horizontally and records the sum in the Total column on the far right of each COA. The staff then multiplies the same ranks by the weights associated with each criterion and notes the product in parenthesis underneath the unweighted rank. No notation is required if the weight is 1. The staff adds these weighted products horizontally and records the sum in parenthesis underneath the unweighted total in the Total column to the right of each COA. The staff then compares the totals to determine the most preferred (lowest number) COA based on both unweighted and weighted ranks. Upon review and consideration, the commander—based on personal judgment—may elect to change either the weight or ranks for any criterion. Although the lowest total denotes a most preferred solution, the process for estimating relative ranks assigned to criterion and weighting may be highly subjective.

Commanders and staffs cannot solely rely on the outcome of a decision matrix, as it only provides a partial basis for a solution. During the decision matrix process, planners carefully avoid reaching conclusions from a quantitative analysis of subjective weights. Comparing and evaluating COAs by criterion is probably more useful than merely comparing totaled ranks. Judgments often change with regard to the relative weighting of criteria during close analysis of COAs, which will change weighted rank totals and possibly the most preferred COA.

3. Conduct a COA Decision Briefing

After completing its analysis and comparison, the staff identifies its preferred COA and makes a recommendation. If the staff cannot reach a decision, the COS (XO) decides which COA to recommend. The staff then delivers a decision briefing to the commander. The COS (XO) highlights any changes to each COA resulting from the war game. The decision briefing includes:

- The commander's intent of the higher and next higher commanders
- The status of the force and its components
- The current IPB
- The COAs considered, including:
  - Assumptions used
  - Results of running estimates
  - A summary of the war game for each COA, including critical events, modifications to any COA, and war-game results
  - Advantages and disadvantages (including risks) of each COA
  - The recommended COA. If a significant disagreement exists, then the staff should inform the commander and, if necessary, discuss the disagreement

MDMP Step VI. COA Approval

Ref: FM 6-0 (C1), Commander and Staff Organization and Operations (May '15), pp. 9-41 to 9-42.

After the decision briefing, the commander selects the COA to best accomplish the mission. If the commander rejects all COAs, the staff starts COA development again. If the commander modifies a proposed COA or gives the staff an entirely different one, the staff war-games the new COA and presents the results to the commander with a recommendation.

Note: These sub-steps are not delineated specifically in FM 6-0.

VI. COA Approval

Key Inputs	Key Outputs
▪ Updated running estimates ▪ Evaluated COAs ▪ Recommended COA ▪ Updated assumptions	▪ Commander approved COA and any modifications ▪ Refined commander's intent, CCIRs, and EEFIs ▪ Updated assumptions **WARNORD**

(Commander Approves a COA)

1 Commander's Decision

2 Issue Final Commander's Plannning Guidance

3 Issue Final Warning Order

Ref: FM 6-0 (C1), Commander and Staff Organization and Operations, fig. 9-14, p. 9-42.

1. Commander's Decision

After the decision briefing, the commander selects the COA to best accomplish the mission. If the commander rejects all COAs, the staff starts COA development again. If the commander modifies a proposed COA or gives the staff an entirely different one, the staff war-games the new COA and presents the results to the commander with a recommendation.

2. Issue Final Commander's Planning Guidance

After approves a COA, the commander issues the final planning guidance. The final planning guidance includes a refined commander's intent (if necessary) and new CCIRs to support execution. It also includes any additional guidance on priorities for the war fighting functions, orders preparation, rehearsal, and preparation. This guidance includes priorities for resources needed to preserve freedom of action and ensure continuous sustainment.

Commanders include the risk they are willing to accept in the final planning guidance. If there is time, commanders use a video teleconference to discuss acceptable risk with adjacent, subordinate, and senior commanders. However, commanders still obtain the higher commander's approval to accept any risk that might imperil accomplishing the higher commander's mission.

3. Issue Final Warning Order

Based on the commander's decision and final planning guidance, the staff issues a WARNO to subordinate headquarters. This WARNORD contains the information subordinate units need to refine their plans. It confirms guidance issued in person or by video teleconference and expands on details not covered by the commander personally. The WARNORD issued after COA approval normally contains:

- The area of operations
- Mission
- Commander's intent
- Updated CCIRs and EEFIs
- Concept of operations
- Principal tasks assigned to subordinate units
- Preparation and rehearsal instructions not included in the SOPs
- A final timeline for the operations

See p. 4-21 for a sample warning order format.

MDMP Step VII. Orders Production

Ref: FM 6-0 (C1), Commander and Staff Organization and Operations (May '15), pp. 9-42 to 9-44.

VII. Orders Production, Dissemination & Transition

Key Inputs	Key Outputs
▪ Commander approved COA and any modifications ▪ Refined commander's intent, CCIRs, and EEFIs ▪ Updated assumptions	▪ Approved operation plan or order ▪ Subordinates understand the plan or order

1 Produce and Disseminate Orders

2 Transition from Planning to Operations

Ref: FM 6-0 (C1), Commander and Staff Organization and Operations, fig. 9-15, p. 9-43.

1. Produce and Disseminate Orders

The staff prepares the order or plan by turning the selected COA into a clear, concise concept of operations and the required supporting information. The COA statement becomes the concept of operations for the plan. The COA sketch becomes the basis for the operation overlay. If time permits, the staff may conduct a more detailed war game of the selected COA to more fully synchronize the operation and complete the plan. The staff writes the OPORD or OPLAN using the Army's operation order format.

See chap. 4, Plans & Orders.

Normally, the COS (XO) coordinates with staff principals to assist the G-3 (S-3) in developing the plan or order. Based on the commander's planning guidance, the COS (XO) dictates the type of order, sets and enforces the time limits and development sequence, and determines which staff section publishes which attachments.

Prior to the commander approving the plan or order, the staff ensures the plan or order is internally consistent and is nested with the higher commander's intent. They do this through—

- Plans and orders reconciliation
- Plans and orders crosswalk

Plans and Orders Reconciliation

Plans and orders reconciliation occurs internally as the staff conducts a detailed review of the entire plan or order. This reconciliation ensures that the base plan or order and all attachments are complete and in agreement. It identifies discrepancies or gaps in planning. If staff members find discrepancies or gaps, they take corrective actions. Specifically, the staff compares the commander's intent, mission, and commander's CCIRs against the concept of operations and the different schemes of support (such as scheme of fires or scheme of sustainment). The staff ensures attachments are consistent with the information in the base plan or order.

Plans and Orders Crosswalk

During the plans and orders crosswalk, the staff compares the plan or order with that of the higher and adjacent commanders to achieve unity of effort and ensure the plan meets the superior commander's intent. The crosswalk identifies discrepancies or gaps in planning. If staff members find discrepancies or gaps, they take corrective action.

Approving the Plan or Order

The final action in plan and order development is the approval of the plan or order by the commander. Commanders normally do not sign attachments; however, they should review them before signing the base plan or order.

2. Plans-to-Operations Transition

Step 7 bridges the transition between planning and preparations. The plans-to-operations transition is a preparation activity that occurs within the headquarters. It ensures members of the current operations cell fully understand the plan before execution. During preparation, the responsibility for developing and maintaining the plan shifts from the plans (or future operations) cell to the current operations cell. This transition is the point at which the current operations cell becomes responsible for controlling execution of the operation order. This responsibility includes answering requests for information concerning the order and maintaining the order through fragmentary orders. This transition enables the plans cell to focus its planning efforts on sequels, branches, and other planning requirements directed by the commander.

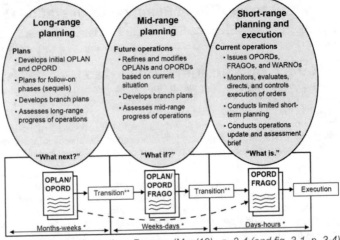

Ref: ADRP 5-0, The Operations Process (Mar '12), p. 3-4 (and fig. 3-1, p. 3-4).

The timing of the plans-to-operations transition requires careful consideration. It must allow enough time for members of the current operations cell to understand the plan well enough to coordinate and synchronize its execution. Ideally, the plans cell briefs the members of the current operations cell on the plans-to-operations transition before the combined arms rehearsal. This briefing enables members of the current operations cell to understand the upcoming operation as well as identify friction points and issues to solve prior to its execution. The transition briefing is a mission briefing that generally follows the five-paragraph operation order format.

Following the combined arms rehearsal, planners and members of the current operations cell review additional planning guidance issued by the commander and modify the plan as necessary. Significant changes may require assistance from the plans cell to include moving a lead planner to the current operations cell. The plans cell continues planning for branches and sequels.

Planning in a Time-Constrained Environment

Ref: FM 6-0 (C1), Commander and Staff Organization and Operations (May '15), pp. 9-44 to 9-46.

Any planning process aims to quickly develop a flexible, sound, and fully integrated and synchronized plan. However, any operation may "outrun" the initial plan. The most detailed estimates cannot anticipate every possible branch or sequel, enemy action, unexpected opportunity, or change in mission directed from higher headquarters. Fleeting opportunities or unexpected enemy action may require a quick decision to implement a new or modified plan. When this occurs, units often find themselves pressed for time in developing a new plan.

Quality staffs produce simple, flexible, and tactically sound plans in a time-constrained environment. Any METT-TC factor, but especially limited time, may make it difficult to complete every step of the MDMP in detail. Applying an inflexible process to all situations does not work. Anticipation, organization, and prior preparation are the keys to successful planning under time-constrained conditions. Staff can use the time saved on any step of the MDMP to:

- Refine the plan more thoroughly
- Conduct a more deliberate and detailed war game
- Consider potential branches and sequels in detail
- Focus more on rehearsing and preparing the plan
- Allow subordinate units more planning and preparation time

The Commander's Responsibility

The commander decides how to adjust the MDMP, giving specific guidance to the staff to focus on the process and save time. Commanders shorten the MDMP when they lack time to perform each step in detail. The most significant factor to consider is time. It is the only nonrenewable, and often the most critical, resource. Commanders (who have access to only a small portion of the staff or none at all) rely even more than normal on their own expertise, intuition, and creativity as well as on their understanding of the environment and of the art and science of warfare. They may have to select a COA, mentally war-game it, and confirm their decision to the staff in a short time. If so, they base their decision more on experience than on a formal, integrated staff process.

Effective commanders avoid changing their guidance unless a significantly changed situation requires major revisions. Commanders consult with subordinate commanders before making a decision, if possible. In situations where commanders must decide quickly, they advise their higher headquarters of the selected COA, if possible. However, commanders do not let an opportunity pass just because they cannot report.

The Staff's Responsibility

Staff members keep their running estimates current. When time constraints exist, they can provide accurate, up-to-date assessments quickly and move directly into COA development. Under time-constrained conditions, commanders and staffs use as much of the previously analyzed information and as many of the previously created products as possible. The importance of running estimates increases as time decreases. Decisionmaking in a time-constrained environment usually occurs after a unit has entered the area of operations and begun operations. Detailed planning provides the basis for information that the commander and staff need to make decisions during execution.

Time-Saving Techniques

Ref: FM 6-0 (C1), Commander and Staff Organization and Operations (May '15), pp. 9-45 to 9-46.

The following paragraphs discuss time-saving techniques to speed the planning process.

Increase Commander's Involvement
While commanders cannot spend all their time with the planning staff, the greater the commander's involvement in planning, the faster the staff can plan. In time-constrained conditions, commanders who participate in the planning process can make decisions (such as COA selection) without waiting for a detailed briefing from the staff.

Limit the Number of COAs to Develop
Limiting the number of COAs developed and war-gamed can save planning time. If time is extremely short, the commander can direct development of only one COA. In this case, the goal is an acceptable COA that meets mission requirements in the time available. This technique saves the most time. The fastest way to develop a plan has the commander directing development of one COA with branches against the most likely enemy COA or most damaging civil situation or condition. However, this technique should be used only when time is severely limited. In such cases, this choice of COA is often intuitive, relying on the commander's experience and judgment. The commander determines which staff officers are essential to assist in COA development. Normally commanders require the intelligence officer, operations officer, plans officer, chief of fires (fire support officer), engineer officer, civil affairs operations officer, inform and influence activities officer, and COS (XO). They may also include subordinate commanders, if available, either in person or by video teleconference. This team quickly develops a flexible COA that it feels will accomplish the mission. The commander mentally war-games this COA and gives it to the staff to refine.

Maximize Parallel Planning
Although parallel planning is the norm, maximizing its use in time-constrained environments is critical. In a time-constrained environment, the importance of WARNOs increases as available time decreases. A verbal WARNO now followed by a written order later saves more time than a written order one hour from now. The staff issues the same WARNOs used in the full MDMP when abbreviating the process. In addition to WARNOs, units must share all available information with subordinates, especially IPB products, as early as possible. The staff uses every opportunity to perform parallel planning with the higher headquarters and to share information with subordinates.

Increase Collaborative Planning
Planning in real time with higher headquarters and subordinates improves the overall planning effort of the organization. Modern information systems and a common operational picture shared electronically allow collaboration with subordinates from distant locations, can increase information sharing, and can improve the commander's visualization. Additionally, taking advantage of subordinates' input and knowledge of the situation in their AOs often results in developing better COAs quickly.

Use Liaison Officers (LNOs)
Liaison officers posted to higher headquarters allow the commander to have representation in their higher headquarters' planning session. These officers assist in passing timely information to their parent headquarters and directly to the commander. Effective liaison officers have the commander's full confidence and the necessary rank and experience for the mission. Commanders may elect to use a single individual or a liaison team.

See pp. 5-27 to 5-32 for discussion of liaison.

Troop Leading Procedures (TLP)

Ref: FM 6-0 (C1), Commander and Staff Organization and Operations (May '15), chap. 10.

Troop leading procedures extend the MDMP to the small-unit level. The MDMP and TLP are similar but not identical. They are both linked by the basic Army problem solving methodology explained. Commanders with a coordinating staff use the MDMP as their primary planning process. Company-level and smaller units lack formal staffs and use TLP to plan and prepare for operations. This places the responsibility for planning primarily on the commander or small-unit leader.

TLP - Planning at Company and Below

Troop Leading Procedures

1 **Receive Mission**

2 **Issue Warning Order**

3 **Make Tentative Plan**

4 **Initiate Movement**

5 **Conduct Recon**

6 **Complete Plan**

7 **Issue OPORD**

8 **Supervise and Refine**

METT-TC

Plan Development

Mission Analysis
• Analysis of the Mission
  ▪ Purpose
  ▪ Tasks – Specified, Implied, Essential
  ▪ Constraints
  ▪ Written Restated Mission
• Enemy Analysis
• Terrain and Weather Analysis
• Troops Available
• Time Available
• Risk Assessment

Course of Action Development
• Analyze Relative Combat Power
• Generate Options
• Develop a Concept of Operations
• Assign Responsibilities
• Prepare COA Statement and Sketch

COA Analysis
• Hasty War Game

COA Comparison

COA Selection

Troop leading procedures are a dynamic process used by small-unit leaders to analyze a mission, develop a plan, and prepare for an operation (ADP 5-0). These procedures enable leaders to maximize available planning time while developing effective plans and preparing their units for an operation. TLP consist of eight steps. The sequence of the steps of TLP is not rigid. Leaders modify the sequence to meet the mission, situation, and available time. Leaders perform some steps concurrently, while other steps may be performed continuously throughout the operation.

Leaders use TLP when working alone or with a small group to solve tactical problems. For example, a company commander may use the executive officer, first sergeant, fire support officer, supply sergeant, and communications sergeant to assist during TLP.

Refer to The Small Unit Tactics SMARTbook for further discussion of troop leading procedures and related activities/topics -- such as combat orders, preparation and pre-combat inspections (PCIs), and rehearsals -- from a small unit perspective.

Troop Leading Procedures (TLP)

Ref: FM 6-0 (C1), Commander and Staff Organization and Operations (May '15), pp. 10-3 to 10-9. Refer to The Small Unit Tactics SMARTbook for further discussion.

TLP provide small-unit leaders a framework for planning and preparing for operations. This occurs in steps 1 and 2 of TLP and is refined in plan development. Plan development occurs in step 3 and is completed in 6 of TLP. These tasks are similar to the steps of the military decisionmaking process (MDMP).

1. Receive the Mission

Receive the mission may occur in several ways. It may begin with the initial WARNO or OPORD from higher headquarters or when a leader anticipates a new mission. Frequently, leaders receive a mission in a FRAGO over the radio. Ideally, they receive a series of WARNO's, the OPORD, and a briefing from their commander. Normally after receiving an OPORD, leaders give a confirmation brief to their higher commander to ensure they understand the higher commander's intent and concept of operations. The leader obtains clarification on any portions of the higher headquarters plan as required.

When they receive the mission, leaders perform an initial assessment of the situation (METT-TC analysis) and allocate the time available for planning and preparation. (Preparation includes rehearsals and movement.) This initial assessment and time allocation forms the basis of their initial WARNO's.

Leaders complete a formal mission statement during TLP step 3 (make a tentative plan) and step 6 (complete the plan).

Based on what they know, leaders estimate the time available to plan and prepare for the mission. They begin by identifying the times at which major planning and preparation events, including rehearsals, must be complete. Reverse planning helps them do this. Leaders identify the critical times specified by higher headquarters and work back from them. Critical times might include aircraft loading times, the line of departure time, or the start point for movement.

Leaders ensure that all subordinate echelons have sufficient time for their own planning and preparation needs. A general rule of thumb for leaders at all levels is to use no more than one-third of the available time for planning and issuing the OPORD.

2. Issue a Warning Order

As soon as leaders finish their initial assessment of the situation and available time, they issue a WARNO. Leaders do not wait for more information. They issue the best WARNO possible with the information at hand and update it as needed with additional WARNO's.

The WARNO contains as much detail as possible. It informs subordinates of the unit mission and gives them the leader's timeline. Leaders may also pass on any other instructions or information they think will help subordinates prepare for the new mission. This includes information on the enemy, the nature of the higher headquarters' plan, and any specific instructions for preparing their units. The most important thing is that leaders not delay in issuing the initial WARNO. As more information becomes available, leaders can—and should—issue additional WARNO's. By issuing the initial WARNO as quickly as possible, leaders enable their subordinates to begin their own planning and preparation.

WARNO's follow the five-paragraph OPORD format. Normally an initial WARNO issued below battalion level includes:

- Mission or nature of the operation
- Time and place for issuing the OPORD
- Units or elements participating in the operation
- Specific tasks not addressed by unit SOPs
- Timeline for the operation

3. Make a Tentative Plan

Once they have issued the initial WARNO, leaders develop a tentative plan. This step combines the MDMP steps 2 through 6: mission analysis, COA development, COA analysis, COA comparison, and COA approval. At levels below battalion, these steps are less structured than for units with staffs. Often, leaders perform them mentally. They may include their principal subordinates—especially during COA development, analysis, and comparison:

- Mission analysis
- Course of action development
- Analyze courses of action (war game)
- Compare COA's & make a decision

4. Initiate Movement

Leaders initiate any movement necessary to continue mission preparation or position the unit for execution, sometimes before making a tentative plan. They do this as soon as they have enough information to do so, or when the unit is required to move to position itself for a task. This is also essential when time is short. Movements may be to an assembly area, a battle position, a new AO, or an attack position. They may include movement of reconnaissance elements, guides, or quartering parties. Leaders often initiate movement based on their tentative plan and issue the order to subordinates in the new location.

5. Conduct Reconnaissance

Whenever time and circumstances allow, leaders personally observe the AO for the mission prior to execution. No amount of intelligence preparation of the battlefield can substitute for firsthand assessment of METT-TC from within the AO. Unfortunately, many factors can keep leaders from performing a personal reconnaissance. The minimum action necessary is a thorough map reconnaissance, supplemented by imagery and intelligence products.

Leaders use results of the war game to identify information requirements. Reconnaissance operations seek to confirm or deny information that supports the tentative plan. They focus first on information gaps identified during mission analysis.

6. Complete the Plan

During this step, leaders incorporate the result of reconnaissance into their selected COA to complete the plan or order. This includes preparing overlays, refining the indirect fire target list, coordinating sustainment with command and control requirements, and updating the tentative plan as a result of the reconnaissance. At lower levels, this step may entail only confirming or updating information contained in the tentative plan. If time allows, leaders make final coordination with adjacent units and higher HQs before issuing the order.

7. Issue the Order

Small-unit orders are normally issued verbally and supplemented by graphics and other control measures. The order follows the standard five paragraph format OPORD format. Typically, leaders below company level do not issue a commander's intent. They reiterate the intent of their higher and next higher commander.

The ideal location for issuing the order is a point in the AO with a view of the objective and other aspects of the terrain. The leader may perform a leader's reconnaissance, complete the order, and then summon subordinates to a specified location to receive it. Sometimes security or other constraints make it infeasible to issue the order on the terrain. Then leaders use a sand table, detailed sketch, maps, and other products to depict the AO and situation.

8. Supervise and Refine

Throughout TLP, leaders monitor mission preparations, refine the plan, coordinate with adjacent units, and supervise and assess preparations. Normally unit SOPs state individual responsibilities and the sequence of preparation activities. Leaders supervise subordinates and inspect their personnel and equipment to ensure the unit is ready for the mission.

A crucial component of preparation is the rehearsal:

- Practice essential tasks
- Identify weaknesses or problems in the plan
- Coordinate subordinate element actions
- Improve Soldier understanding of the concept of operations
- Foster confidence among Soldiers

Company and smaller sized units use four types of rehearsals:

- Back brief
- Combined arms rehearsal
- Support rehearsal
- Battle drill or SOP rehearsal

Troop Leading Procedures and the MDMP

Ref: FM 6-0 (C1), Commander and Staff Organization and Operations (May '15), chap. 10.

MDMP & TLP

Troop leading procedures extend the MDMP to the small-unit level. The MDMP and TLP are similar but not identical. The type, amount, and timeliness of information passed from higher to lower headquarters directly impact the lower unit leader's TLP. The solid arrows depict when a higher headquarters' planning event could start TLP of a subordinate unit. However, events do not always occur in the order shown. For example, TLP may start with receipt of a warning order (WARNO), or they may not start until the higher headquarters has completed the MDMP and issues an operation order (OPORD). WARNO's from higher headquarters may arrive at any time during TLP. Leaders remain flexible. They adapt TLP to fit the situation rather than try to alter the situation to fit a preconceived idea of how events should flow.

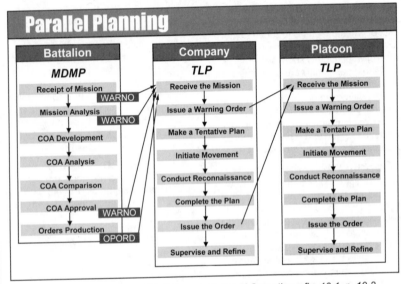

Ref: FM 6-0, Commander and Staff Organization and Operations, fig. 10-1, p. 10-2.
Normally, the first three steps (receive the mission, issue a WARNO, and make a tentative plan) of TLP occur in order. However, the sequence of subsequent steps is based on the situation. The tasks involved in some steps (for example, initiate movement and conduct reconnaissance) may occur several times. The last step, supervise and refine, occurs throughout.

A tension exists between executing current operations and planning for future operations. The small-unit leader must balance both. If engaged in a current operation, there is less time for TLP. If in a lull, transition, or an assembly area, there is more time to use TLP thoroughly. In some situations, time constraints or other factors may prevent leaders from performing each step of TLP as thoroughly as they would like. For example, during the step make a tentative plan, small-unit leaders often develop only one acceptable course of action (COA) vice multiple COA's. If time permits, leaders may develop, compare, and analyze several COA's before arriving at a decision on which one to execute.

Integrating Processes & Continuing Activities

Ref: ADRP 5-0, The Operations Process (Mar '12), pp. 1-11 to 1-12. See also pp. 1-26 to 1-27.

I. Integrating Processes

Throughout the operations process, commanders and staffs integrate the warfighting functions to synchronize the force in accordance with the commander's intent and concept of operations. Commanders and staffs use several integrating processes and continuing activities to do this. In addition to the major activities of the operations process, commanders and staffs use several integrating processes to synchronize specific functions throughout the operations process. The integrating processes are:

I. Intelligence Preparation of the Battlefield (IPB)

Intelligence preparation of the battlefield (IPB) is a systematic, continuous process of analyzing the threat and other aspects of an operational environment within a specific geographic area. Led by the intelligence officer, the entire staff participates in IPB to develop and sustain an understanding of the enemy, terrain and weather, and civil considerations. IPB helps identify options available to friendly and threat forces. IPB consists of four steps. Each step is performed or assessed and refined to ensure that IPB products remain complete and relevant. The four IPB steps are—

- Step 1—Define The Operational Environment
- Step 2—Describe Environmental Effects On Operations/*Describe The Effects On Operations*
- Step 3—Evaluate The Threat/*Adversary*
- Step 4—Determine Threat/*Adversary* Courses Of Action

See pp. 3-3 to 3-46.

II. Targeting

Targeting is the process of selecting and prioritizing targets and matching the appropriate response to them, considering operational requirements and capabilities (JP 3-0). The purpose of targeting is to integrate and synchronize fires into operations. Targeting begins in planning, and it is an iterative process that continues through preparation and execution. The steps of the Army's targeting process are—

- Decide
- Detect
- Deliver
- Assess

See pp. 3-47 to 3-58.

III. Risk Management

Risk management is the process of identifying, assessing, and controlling risks arising from operational factors and making decisions that balance risk cost with mission benefits (JP 3-0). Identifying and accepting prudent risk is a principle of mission command. Throughout the operations process, commanders and staffs use risk management to identify and mitigate risks associated with all hazards that have the potential to injure or kill friendly and civilian personnel, damage or destroy equipment, or otherwise impact mission effectiveness. Like targeting, risk management begins in planning and continues through preparation and execution.

See pp. 3-59 to 3-62.

II. Continuing Activities

While units execute numerous tasks throughout the operations process, commanders and staffs always plan for and coordinate the following continuing activities:

1. Liaison

Liaison is that contact or intercommunication maintained between elements of military forces or other agencies to ensure mutual understanding and unity of purpose and action (JP 3-08). Most commonly used for establishing and maintaining close communications, liaison continuously enables direct, physical communications between commands.

See pp. 5-29 to 5-34.

2. Information Collection

Information collection is an activity that synchronizes and integrates the planning and employment of sensors, assets, and processing, exploitation, and dissemination systems in direct support of current and future operations. For joint operations, this is referred to as intelligence, surveillance, and reconnaissance (ISR). The Army expands the joint ISR doctrine contained in JP 2-01 by defining information collection as an activity that focuses on answering the CCIRs. This highlights aspects that influence how the Army operates as a ground force in close and continuous contact with the threat and local populace. At the tactical level, reconnaissance, surveillance, security, and intelligence operations are the primary means by which a commander plans, organizes and executes tasks to answer the CCIR.

Refer to FM 3-55 for a detailed discussion of information collection.

3. Security Operations

Commanders and staffs continuously plan for and coordinate security operations throughout the conduct of operations. Security operations are those operations undertaken by a commander to provide early and accurate warning of enemy operations, to provide the force being protected with time and maneuver space within which to react to the enemy, and to develop the situation to allow the commander to effectively use the protected force (FM 3-90). The five forms of security operations are screen, guard, cover, area security, and local security.

Refer to The Small Unit Tactics SMARTbook and FM 3-90.

4. Terrain Management

Terrain management is the process of allocating terrain by establishing areas of operation, designating assembly areas, and specifying locations for units and activities to deconflict activities that might interfere with each other. Throughout the operations process, commanders assigned an area of operations manage terrain within their boundaries. Through terrain management, commanders identify and locate units in the area. The operations officer, with support from others in the staff, can then deconflict operations, control movements, and deter fratricide as units get in position to execute planned missions. Commanders also consider unified action partners located in their area of operations and coordinate with them for the use of terrain.

5. Airspace Control

Airspace control is the process used to increase operational effectiveness by promoting the safe, efficient, and flexible use of airspace (JP 3-52).Throughout the operations process, commanders and staffs must integrate and synchronize forces and war fighting functions within an area of operations (ground and air). Through airspace control, commanders and staffs establish both positive and procedural controls to maximize the use of air space to facilitate air-ground operations. Airspace is inherently joint, and the Army processes and systems used to control and manage airspace are joint compliant.

Refer to The Army Operations & Doctrine SMARTbook and FM 3-52.

I. Intelligence Preparation of the Battlefield (IPB)

Ref: ATP 2-01.3/MCRP 2-3A, Intelligence Preparation of the Battlefield/Battlespace (Nov '14).

Intelligence Preparation of the Battlefield (IPB) is the systematic process of analyzing the mission variables of enemy, terrain, weather, and civil considerations in an area of interest to determine their effect on operations. *Intelligence Preparation of the Battlespace (IPB) is the systematic, continuous process of analyzing the threat and environment in a specific geographic area.*

IPB Process

 Define the Operational Environment

 Describe Environmental Effects on Operations/ *Describe The Effects On Operations*

 Evaluate the Threat/*Adversary*

 Determine Threat/*Adversary* **Courses of Action**

The G-2/S-2 begins preparing for IPB during the generate intelligence knowledge task/*problem framing step*. The intelligence staff creates data files and/or databases based on the operational environment. Given the limited time available to collect and evaluate information, this information may not be specific enough to support the military decisionmaking process (MDMP)/*Marine Corps Planning Process (MCPP)*. However, this information helps create the operational environment frame during the design methodology.

Refer to MCWP 5-1 for a discussion on the MCPP.

IPB results in the creation of intelligence products that are used during the MDMP/ *MCPP* to aid in developing friendly courses of action (COAs) and decision points for the commander. Additionally, the conclusions reached and the products created during IPB are critical to planning information collection/intelligence collection and targeting operations.

Editor's Note: Since ATP -201/MCRP 2-3A is a dual-designated Army and Marine Corps manual, terms and phrasing specific to the Marine Corps are provided in italics.
*Change 1 to ATP 2-01.3 (dated Mar 2015) changed the distribution restriction notice of this source to "distribution unlimited;" because the posted cover remained dated Nov 2014, it is cited as such in The Battle Staff SMARTbook.

The G-2/S-2 leads this staff effort and begins preparing for IPB during the generate intelligence knowledge process associated with force generation and is incorporated into the Army design methodology. During generate intelligence knowledge, the intelligence staff creates data files on specific operational environments based on an evaluation of the information and intelligence related to the operational variables identified in the memory aid PMESII-PT (political, military, economic, social, information, infrastructure, physical environment, time)/*PMESII* (political, military, economic, social, information, and infrastructure). (For the Marine Corps, see MCWP 5-1 for more information on intelligence support to planning and problem framing.)

Given the limited time available to collect and evaluate information and intelligence on the operational variables, this information may not be specific enough to support the MDMP/*MCPP*. However, it can be used by the commander and the entire staff to aid the Army design methodology. Throughout the operations process, the commander and staff continue to collect information and analyze the operational variables in order to provide increased situational understanding. Upon receipt of a warning order or mission, they draw relevant information that was categorized by the operational variables and filter it into the mission variables used during mission analysis/*problem framing*. During IPB, the staff focuses on the relevant aspects of the operational environment as it pertains to their warfighting function and the mission variables. The intelligence staff is primarily focused on the mission variables of enemy, terrain, weather, and civil considerations.

To be effective, IPB must—

- Accurately define the commander's area of interest in order to focus collection and analysis on the relevant aspects of the mission variables of enemy, terrain, weather, and civil considerations. Relevant is defined as having significant effect on friendly operations and threat/*adversary* operations, and population in a unit's area of operations (AO).

- Describe how each of these four mission variables will affect friendly operations and how terrain, weather, and civil considerations will affect the enemy.

- Provide the IPB products necessary to aid each step of the MDMP/*MCPP* in accordance with the planning timelines and guidance provided by the commander.

- Determine how the interactions of friendly forces, enemy forces, and indigenous populations affect each other to continually create outcomes that affect friendly operations. This aspect of IPB is not the sole responsibility of the intelligence staff. This complex analysis involves the commander and the entire staff working together to determine these effects.

IPB is most effective and best aids the commander's decisionmaking when the intelligence staff integrates the expertise of the other staff and supporting elements, such as civil affairs teams and military information support personnel, into its analysis. This is especially true when operating in environments where the effects of the enemy, terrain, weather, and civil considerations are complex and not easily determined.

IPB aids commanders in reducing uncertainty by evaluating how the enemy, terrain, weather, and civil considerations may affect operations and decisionmaking. Most intelligence requirements are generated as a result of IPB and its interrelationship with decisionmaking.

A key aspect of IPB is refinement. The conclusions made and the products developed during IPB are continually refined throughout the operation. This information is incorporated into the running estimate as new information is obtained and further analysis is conducted during situation development. This refinement ensures that the commander's decisions are based on the most current information and intelligence available.

ATP 2-01.3/MCRP 2-3A (Nov '14) Changes

Ref: ATP 2-01.3/MCRP 2-3A, Intelligence Preparation of the Battlefield/Battlespace (Nov '14).

ATP 2-01.3/MCRP 2-3A is a dual-designated Army and Marine Corps manual that constitutes current doctrine on how to systematically evaluate the effects of significant characteristics of the operational environment for specific missions. It describes how the commander and staff examine mission variables to understand how these variables may affect operations. It discusses intelligence preparation of the battlefield/*intelligence preparation of the battlespace* (IPB) as a critical component of the military decision-making process (MDMP)/*Marine Corps Planning Process (MCPP)* and how IPB supports decisionmaking, as well as integrating processes and continuing activities.

The principal audience for ATP 2-01.3/MCRP 2-3A is Army/Marine Corps commanders and staffs. Commanders and staffs of Army/Marine Corps headquarters serving as a joint task force or a multinational headquarters also refer to applicable joint or multinational doctrine related to IPB. Trainers and educators throughout the Army/Marine Corps also use this publication.

Chapter 1 makes the following change: Redefines the Army's definition of IPB as "Intelligence Preparation of the Battlefield (IPB) is the systematic process of analyzing the mission variables of enemy, terrain, weather, and civil considerations in an area of interest to determine their effect on operations."

Chapter 3 replaces the sub-steps of step 1 with the following:
- Identify the limits of the commander's area of operations (AO).
- Identify the limits of the commander's area of interest.
- Identify significant characteristics within the AO and area of interest for further analysis.
- Evaluate current operations and intelligence holdings to determine additional information needed to complete IPB.
- Initiate processes necessary to acquire information necessary to complete IPB.

Chapter 4 replaces the sub-steps of step 2 with the following:
- Describe how the threat/*adversary* can affect friendly operations.
- Describe how terrain can affect friendly and threat/*adversary* operations.
- Describe how weather can affect friendly and threat/*adversary* operations.
- Describe how civil considerations can affect friendly & threat/*adversary* operations.

Chapter 5 replaces the sub-steps of step 3 with the following:
- Identify threat characteristics/*adversary order of battle.*
- Create or refine threat/*adversary* models.

Chapter 6 replaces the sub-steps of step 4 with the following:
- Develop threat/*adversary* courses of action (COAs).
- Develop the event template and matrix.

G-2/S-2 is used in cases when actions are conducted by both U.S. Army and Marine Corps.

Introductory table 1. Rescinded Army terms

Term	Remarks
event template	Rescinded Army definition. Adopts the joint definition.

Introductory table 2. Modified Army terms

Term	Remarks
intelligence preparation of the battlefield/battlespace	Modifies the definition.
latest time information is of value	Proponent publication changed to ATP 2-01.

IPB Process Activities (Overview)

Ref: ATP 2-01.3/MCRP 2-3A, Intelligence Preparation of the Battlefield/Battlespace (Nov '14), chap. 1.

The IPB process consists of the following four steps:

Step 1—Define The Operational Environment

Defining the operational environment results in the identification of significant characteristics of the operational environment that can affect friendly and enemy operations. This step also results in the identification of gaps in current intelligence holdings.

Step 1 is important because it assists the commander in defining relative aspects of the operational environment in time and space. During step 1, the intelligence staff must identify those significant characteristics related to the mission variables of enemy, terrain, weather, and civil considerations that are relevant to the mission and justify that analysis to the commander. Failure to identify or misidentify the effect these variables may have on operations can hinder decisionmaking and result in the development of an ineffective information collection strategy/*intelligence collection strategy* and targeting effort.

Understanding friendly and enemy forces is not enough; other factors, such as culture, languages, tribal affiliations, and operational and mission variables, can be equally important. Defining the significant characteristics of the operational environment is essential in identifying the additional information needed to complete IPB. Once approved by the commander, this information becomes the command's initial intelligence requirements. This focuses the command's initial information collection efforts/*intelligence collection efforts* and the remaining steps of the IPB process.

For the Marine Corps, the term "operational environment" is consistent with the need to study and learn as much as possible about a situation. Essentially, commanders analyze the operational environment in order to determine the physical dimensions of their battlespace in the form of areas of interest, influence, and operations. (See MCDP 1-0.)

Step 2—Describe Environmental Effects On Operations/ *Describe The Effects On Operations*

Once the intelligence staff has identified in step 1 of IPB the significant characteristics related to enemy, terrain, weather, and civil considerations of the operational environment, step 2 describes how these characteristics affect friendly operations. The intelligence staff also describes how terrain, weather, civil considerations, and friendly forces affect enemy forces. This evaluation focuses on the general capabilities of each force until threat/*adversary* COAs are developed in step 4 of IPB and friendly COAs are developed later in the MDMP/*MCPP*. Finally, the entire staff determines the impact and effects to the population of friendly and enemy force actions.

If the intelligence staff does not have the information it needs to form conclusions, it uses assumptions to fill information gaps—always careful to ensure the commander understands when assumptions are used in place of fact to form conclusions.

Step 3—Evaluate The Threat/*Adversary*

The purpose of evaluating the threat/*adversary* is to understand how a threat/*adversary* can affect friendly operations. Although threat/*adversary* forces may conform to some of the fundamental principles of warfare that guide Army/*Marine Corps* operations, these forces will have obvious, as well as subtle, differences in how they approach situations and problem solving. Understanding these differences is essential in understanding how a threat/*adversary* force will react in a given situation. Threat/*adversary* evaluation does not begin with IPB. The intelligence staff conducts threat/*adversary* evaluation and develops threat/*adversary* models as part of the generate intelligence knowledge task of support to force generation. Using this information, the intelligence staff refines threat/*adversary* models, as necessary, to support IPB. When analyzing a well-known threat/*adversary*, the intelligence staff may be able to rely on previously developed threat/*adversary* models. When analyzing a new or less well-known threat/*adversary*, the intelligence staff may need to evaluate the threat/*adversary* and develop models during the mission analysis step of the MDMP/*problem framing step of MCPP*. When this occurs, the intelligence staff relies heavily on the threat/*adversary* evaluation conducted by higher headquarters and other intelligence agencies.

In situations where there is no threat/*adversary* force, the intelligence analysis conducted and the products developed relating to terrain, weather, and civil considerations may be sufficient to support planning. An example of this type of situation is a natural disaster.

Step 4—Determine Threat/*Adversary* Courses Of Action
During step 4 the intelligence staff identifies and develops possible threat/*adversary* COAs that can affect accomplishing the friendly mission. The staff uses the products associated with determining threat/*adversary* COAs to aid in developing friendly COAs during the COA development and selecting a friendly COA during COA steps of the MDMP/*MCPP*. The identification and development of all valid threat/*adversary* COAs minimize the potential of the commander being surprised by an unanticipated enemy action.

Failure to fully identify and develop all valid threat/*adversary* COAs may lead to the development of an information collection strategy/*intelligence collection strategy* that does not provide the information necessary to confirm what COA the enemy has taken and may result in the commander being surprised. When needed, the staff should identify all significant civil considerations (this refers to those civil considerations identified as significant characteristics of the operational environment) so that the interrelationship of threat/*adversary*, friendly forces, and population activities is portrayed.

The staff develops threat/*adversary* COAs in the same manner friendly COAs are developed. Although written specifically as a guide to develop friendly COAs, the COA development discussion in ADRP 5-0/*MCWP 5-1* is an excellent model to use in developing valid threat/*adversary* COAs that are suitable, feasible, acceptable, unique, and consistent with threat/*adversary* doctrine. Although the intelligence staff has the primary responsibility for developing threat/*adversary* COAs, it needs assistance from the rest of the staff to ensure the most accurate and complete analysis is presented to the commander.

Intelligence Estimate
The intelligence estimate includes all the IPB products necessary to support planning and operations, such as—

- Enemy situation overlays with associated COA statements and high-value target lists (HVTLs)
- Event templates and associated event matrices
- Modified combined obstacle overlays (MCOOs), terrain effects matrices, and terrain assessments
- Weather forecast charts, weather effects matrices/*operational impacts charts*, light and illumination tables, and weather estimates
- Civil considerations overlays and assessments

Staff Integration Into IPB
Staff sections bring their own areas of expertise to IPB. Collaborative analysis among the staff facilitates a greater degree of situational understanding for the commander.

See following pages for discussion of additional intelligence products.

Types of Intelligence Products

Ref: ADRP 2-0, Intelligence (Aug '12), pp. 5-9 to 5-12.

In addition to IPB, the G-2/S-2 staff produces and maintains a broad variety of products tailored to its consumers. These products are developed and maintained in accordance with the commander's guidance. For all of these products, the primary focus of the G-2/S-2 staff's analysis is presenting predictive intelligence to support operations.

A. Intelligence Estimate

An intelligence estimate is the appraisal, expressed in writing or orally, of available intelligence relating to a specific situation or condition with a view to determining the courses of action open to the threat and the order of probability of their adoption. The G-2/S-2 staff develops and maintains the intelligence estimate. The primary purpose is to—

- Determine the full set of COAs open to the threat and the probable order of their adoption
- Disseminate information and intelligence
- Determine requirements concerning threats and other relevant aspects of the operational environment

The intelligence estimate is a logical and orderly examination of intelligence factors affecting the accomplishment of a mission (threats, terrain and weather, and civil considerations). It provides commanders with an analysis of the area of interest and threat strengths and capabilities that can influence their mission. An intelligence estimate may be prepared at any level. It may be formal or informal and detailed or summarized. It is normally written at division and higher levels and briefed down to the battalion level. The following is an example of the basic information and intelligence that could be included:

- **Mission.**
- **Analysis of the AO.** This analysis of the terrain is based on—
  - The military aspects of terrain (OAKOC)
  - Other significant characteristics
  - The effects of the terrain on friendly and threat operations and civil considerations
  - The effects of weather on friendly and threat operations and civil considerations:
    - Operational climatology data and information, light data, and predictive weather effects based on specific weather sensitivity thresholds
    - The current weather conditions based on the military aspects of weather (visibility, wind, precipitation, cloud cover, temperature, and humidity)
    - Projected weather forecasts with significant seasonal trends for that specific geographic location
  - An analysis of the civil considerations and projected effects of civil considerations on friendly and threat operations, and vice versa.
- **Current threat situation.** This is based on the threat characteristics (see FM 2-01.3) and includes estimates of the strength of threat forces, recent significant threat activities and trends, and threat peculiarities and weaknesses.
- **Threat capabilities.** These are the broad COAs and supporting operations that threats can take to achieve their goals and objectives. The G-2/S-2 staff considers each threat's ability to conduct each operation based on the mission variables (METT-TC) related to the current situation.
- **Threat characteristics.** These provide a framework for the consistent evaluation of any force. The G-2/S-2 staff considers composition, disposition, strengths, weaknesses, combat effectiveness, doctrine and tactics, command and support relationships, electronic technical data, capabilities and limitations, current operations, and historical data when analyzing threat characteristics.
- **Summary of the most significant points.** This includes:
  - The most significant terrain and weather and civil considerations effects on operations.
  - Potential impacts of operations on terrain and civil considerations.
  - At a minimum, the most likely and most dangerous threat COAs.
  - The most significant threat strengths and vulnerabilities.

The intelligence estimate also includes four tabs: Tab A (Terrain), Tab B (Weather), Tab C (Civil Considerations), and Tab D (IPB).

B. Intelligence Summary (INTSUM)

INTSUMs provide the context for commander's situational understanding. The INTSUM reflects the G-2's/S-2's interpretation and conclusions regarding threats, terrain and weather, and civil considerations over a designated period of time. This period will vary with the desires of the commander and the requirements of the situation. The INTSUM provides a summary of the threat situation, threat capabilities, the characteristics of terrain and weather and civil considerations, and COAs.

The INTSUM can be presented in written, graphic, or oral format, as directed by the commander. The INTSUM assists in assessing the current situation and updating other intelligence reports. It is disseminated to higher, lower, and adjacent units. The INTSUM has no prescribed format. The following is an example of the basic information and intelligence that should be included in an INTSUM:

- **Date-time group (DTG)** of the INTSUM and the period of time the INTSUM covers.
- **Weather and weather effects** that include current and forecast meteorological parameters and analysis based on the military aspects of weather and weather sensitivity thresholds.
- **Significant threat activities** over the reporting period and a near-term analysis of threat intent and activity.
- **Significant impacts of civil considerations** on operations and vice versa.
- **Subunit assessments of significant threat activities and civil considerations** in the AO over the reporting period and a near-term analysis of threat intent and activity.
- **Notable trends in threat activity** over a designated period of time (such as the previous 14 days). This may be presented as an all-source analysis product or focused on specific threat activities of interest to the commander—or both. This portion of the INTSUM should highlight new or emerging threats and the level of impact that each threat may present to the unit's operations.
- **Combat damage assessment roll-up** includes known or estimated threat unit strengths, significant threat systems degraded or destroyed, and all known captured, wounded, or killed threat personnel during the reporting period.
- **Written threat situation or situation template** (as of a specific DTG).
- **Assessments** include a near-term and long-term assessment of threat activities with as much detail as possible based on available information and current intelligence analysis. INTSUMs are predictive in nature. When specific intelligence or information is not available, INTSUMs must contain the G-2/S-2's best assessment of probabilities of threat actions based on experience and professional military judgment.
- **HVTLs** (in coordination with the targeting officer) may include high-value individuals, depending on the unit mission.
- **Current PIRs and projected PIRs** by phase.
- **Planning requirements tools and products.**
- **Special assessments** are developed for any unique circumstance that requires additional analysis.

C. Intelligence Running Estimate

Effective plans and successful execution hinge on accurate and current running estimates. A running estimate is the continuous assessment of the current situation used to determine if the current operation is proceeding according to the commander's intent and if the planned future operations are supportable (ADP 5-0). Failure to maintain accurate running estimates may lead to errors or omissions that result in flawed plans or bad decisions during execution. Running estimates are principal knowledge management tools used by the commander and staff throughout the operations process. In their running estimates, the commander and each staff section continuously consider the effect of new information and update the following: facts, assumptions, friendly force status, threat activities and capabilities, civil considerations, recommendations and conclusions.

D. Common Operational Picture (COP)

A common operational picture is a single display of relevant information within a commander's area of interest tailored to the user's requirements and based on common data and information shared by more than one command (ADRP 6-0). The COP is the primary tool for supporting the commander's situational understanding. All staff sections provide input from their area of expertise to the COP.

Step 1—Define the Operational Environment

Step 1 of the IPB process identifies for further analysis the significant characteristics of the operational environment that may influence friendly COAs and command decisions. Within an operational environment, an Army leader may be faced with major combat, military engagements, and humanitarian assistance simultaneously in the same AO.

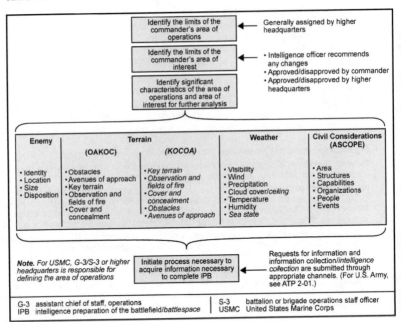

Desired End State

Step 1 of the IPB process focuses the IPB effort on the characteristics of the operational environment that can influence friendly and threat/*adversary* operations. The intelligence staff acquires the intelligence needed to complete IPB in the degree of detail required to support the decisionmaking process. The primary outputs associated with step 1 of the IPB process may include developing the—

- Determination of the AO and area of interest.
- Determination of the area of intelligence responsibility.
- Identification of general characteristics of the AO that could influence the unit's mission.
- Identification of gaps in current intelligence holdings, translating them into requirements for collection (requests for information, requests for collection) in order to complete IPB.

So What?

The "so what" in this step is clearly defining for the commanders what the relevant characteristics of their areas of interest are.

- Success results in saving time and effort by focusing only on those characteristics that will influence friendly COAs and command decisions.

Consequences of failure:

- Failure to focus on only the significant characteristics leads to wasted time and effort collecting and evaluating intelligence on characteristics of the operational environment that will not influence the operation.

- Failure to identify all the significant characteristics may lead to the command's surprise and unpreparedness when some overlooked feature of the operational environment has an effect on the operation for which the commander did not plan.

A. Identify the Limits of the Commander's Area of Operations

The area of operations is defined by the joint force commander for land and maritime forces that should be large enough to accomplish their missions and protect their forces (JP 3-0). The AO is comprised of an external boundary that delineates the AOs of adjacent units and includes subordinate unit AOs. Subordinate unit AOs may be contiguous or noncontiguous. Parts of an AO not assigned to subordinate units are called deep areas. The AO may be impacted due to political boundaries and/or other civil considerations. Once assigned, an AO can be subdivided by that command, as necessary, to support mission requirements.

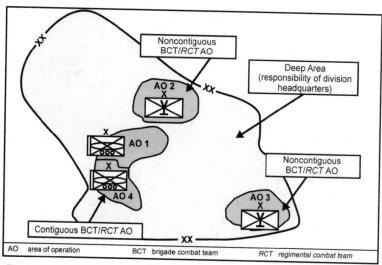

Figure 3-2. Example areas of operations

An area of influence is a geographical area where a commander is directly capable of influencing operations by maneuver or fire support systems normally under the commander's command or control (JP 3-0). The area of influence is—

- An area that includes terrain inside and outside the AO
- An area determined by both the G-2/S-2 and the G-3/S-3

B. Identify the Limits of the Commander's Area of Interest

An area of interest is that area of concern to the commander, including the area of influence, areas adjacent thereto and extending into enemy territory. This area also includes areas occupied by enemy forces who could jeopardize the accomplishment of the mission (JP 3-0). The area of interest is—

- Established by the commander with input from the G-2/S-2 or G-3/S-3. The mission, enemy, terrain and weather, troops and support available, time available, civil considerations (METT-TC)/*mission, enemy, terrain and weather, troops and support available, time available (METT-T)* factors must be considered.
- An area normally larger than the area of influence and may require more intelligence assets to monitor. It may include staging areas.

The area of interest is a geographical area from which information and intelligence are required to execute successful tactical operations and to plan for future operations. It includes any threat/*adversary* forces or characteristics that will significantly influence accomplishing the command's mission. In combat operations/*major operations*, the area of interest extends into enemy territory to the objectives of current or planned friendly operations if those objectives are located outside the assigned AO. In stability operations or defense support of civil authorities operations, the area of interest is typically much larger than that defined for combat operations/*major operations*.

An additional consideration would be to divide the area of interest into several components; for example, ground area of interest and air area of interest. Such a division accommodates the types of information relevant to each area of interest as well as their usually different geographical limits. At some point, it will likely become necessary to integrate the various areas of interest into a whole in order to present the commander with a complete, integrated picture.

An area of interest may be irregular in shape and overlap the areas of adjacent and subordinate unit AOs. The area will change as the situation changes and as commanders determine new information requirements. It is the geographical area from which information is required to facilitate planning and the successful conduct of the command's operation.

> By analyzing a commander's AO in terms of the area of influence and area of interest, a commander determines whether the assigned AO is appropriate. This analysis may include the forces' capabilities to conduct actions across the warfighting functions. Commanders consider the extent of subordinates' areas of influence when defining subordinates' AOs. In identifying an AO, the staff should avoid making it substantially larger than the unit's area of influence. Ideally, the entire AO is encompassed by the area of influence. The area of influence is useful to the commander in focusing information collection operations to shape the battlefield/battlespace to facilitate future operations.

For the Marine Corps, battlespace includes the area of interest, area of influence, and operational areas. Operational areas for Marine air-ground task forces (MAGTFs) are usually an AO. The staff may recommend battlespace refinements based on the analysis of the terrain and tasks as well as friendly and adversary centers of gravity, capabilities, and limitations. The size of the area of interest may change based on the commander's understanding of the situation. The area of influence is a geographical area wherein a commander is directly capable of influencing operations by maneuver or fire support systems normally under the commander's command or control (JP 3-0). The extent of the area of influence may change if forces are added or deleted, equipment capability (for example, the range of lethal and nonlethal weapon systems) and availability change, or rules of engagement change. The commander's AO may need to change based on the scope of the mission, the results of operations, operational reach, or to ensure sufficient battlespace to maneuver and protect his force.

C. Identify Significant Characteristics within the Area of Operations and Area of Interest for Further Analysis

In order to focus IPB and what is important to the commander, the staff identifies and defines the aspects of the enemy, terrain, weather, and civil considerations of the operational environment to determine the significance of each in relation to the mission; essentially building an environmental model as the framework to conduct and then present analysis to the commander. This prevents unnecessary analysis and allows the staff to maximize resources on critical areas. The initial analysis that occurs in this sub-step determines the amount of time and resources the intelligence staff commits to the detailed analysis that occurs in step 2 of the IPB process.

Enemy

An enemy is a party identified as hostile against which the use of force is authorized (ADRP 3-0). Analysis of the enemy includes not only the known enemy but also other threats/*adversaries* to mission success. Such threats/*adversaries* might include multiple *adversaries* posing with a wide array of political, economic, religious, and personal motivations. Additionally, threats/adversaries may wear uniforms and easily be identifiable. Or, they may not wear uniforms and blend into the population. To understand threat/*adversary* capabilities and vulnerabilities, commanders and staffs require detailed, timely, and accurate intelligence produced as a result of IPB.

Terrain and Weather

Terrain and weather are natural conditions that profoundly influence operations. Terrain and weather favor neither friendly nor enemy forces unless one is more familiar with—or better prepared to operate in—the physical environment. Terrain includes natural features (such as rivers and mountains) and manmade features (such as cities, airfields, and bridges). Terrain directly affects how commanders select objectives and locate, move, and control forces. Terrain also influences protective measures and the effectiveness of weapons and other systems.

Effective use of terrain reduces the effects of enemy fires, increases the effects of friendly fires, and facilitates surprise. Terrain appreciation—the ability to predict its impact on operations—is an important skill for every leader. For tactical operations, commanders analyze terrain using the five military aspects of terrain, expressed in the Army memory aid OAKOC (obstacles, avenues of approach, key terrain, observation and fields of fire, and cover and concealment) and the Marine Corps memory aid *KOCOA (key terrain, observation and fields of fire, cover and concealment, obstacles, and avenues of approach).*

See following pages for further discussion of OAKOC/KOCOA.

Climate refers to the average weather conditions for a location, area, or region for a specific time of the year as recorded for a period of years. Operational climatology is used to assess effects on weapon systems, collection systems, ground forces, tactics and procedures, enemy TTP, and other capabilities based on specific weather sensitivity thresholds when operational planning occurs more than 10 days prior to the execution. Climatological data is important at both the operational and tactical levels. Actual weather forecasts and/or predictions, using weather models and other tools, are used to assess weather effects on weapon systems, collection systems, ground forces, TTP, and other capabilities when operations occur within 10 days of operational planning.

Civil Considerations

Civil considerations reflect the influence of manmade infrastructure, civilian institutions, and attitudes and activities of the civilian leaders, populations, and organizations within the operational environment on the conduct of military operations. Com-

OAKOC - Military Aspects of the Terrain

Ref: Adapted from FM 34-130, Intelligence Preparation of the Battlefield (Jul '94), pp. 2-10 to 2-21 .

Terrain analysis consists of an evaluation of the military aspects of the battlefield's terrain to determine its effects on military operations. The military aspects of terrain are often described using the acronym OAKOC:

- O - Observation and Fields of Fire
- A - Avenues of Approach (AA)
- K - Key Terrain
- O - Obstacles
- C - Concealment and Cover

O - Observation and Fields of Fire

Observation. Observation is the ability to see the threat either visually or through the use of surveillance devices. Factors that limit or deny observation include concealment and cover.

Fields of fire. A field of fire is the area that a weapon or group of weapons may effectively cover with fire from a given position. Terrain that offers cover limits fields of fire.

Terrain that offers both good observation and fields of fire generally favors defensive COAs.

The evaluation of observation and fields of fire allows you to:

- Identify potential engagement areas, or "fire sacks" and "kill zones"
- Identify defensible terrain and specific system or equipment positions
- Identify where maneuvering forces are most vulnerable to observation and fire

Evaluate observation from the perspective of electronic and optical line-of-sight (LOS) systems as well as unaided visual observation. Consider systems such as weapon sights, laser range finders, radars, radios, and jammers.

While ground based systems usually require horizontal LOS, airborne systems use oblique and vertical LOS. The same is true of air defense systems.

If time and resources permit, prepare terrain factor overlays to aid in evaluating observation and fields of fire.

Consider the following:

- Vegetation or building height and density
- Canopy or roof closure
- Relief features, including micro-relief features such as defiles (elevation tinting techniques are helpful).
- Friendly and threat target acquisition and sensor capabilities
- Specific LOSs

A - Avenue of Approach (AA)

An Avenue of Approach (AA) is an air or ground route that leads an attacking force of a given size to its objective or to key terrain in its path.

During offensive operations, the evaluation of AAs leads to a recommendation on the best AAs to the command's objective and identification of avenues available to the threat for withdrawal or the movement of reserves.

During the defense, identify AAs that support the threat's offensive capabilities and avenues that support the movement and commitment of friendly reserves.

K - Key Terrain

Key terrain is any locality or area the seizure, retention, or control of which affords a marked advantage to either combatant. Key terrain is often selected for use as battle positions or objectives. Evaluate key terrain by assessing the impact of its seizure, by either force, upon the results of battle.

A common technique is to depict key terrain on overlays and sketches with a large "K" within a circle or curve that encloses and follows the contours of the designated terrain. On transparent overlays use a color, such as purple, that stands out.

In the offense, key terrain features are usually forward of friendly dispositions and are often assigned as objectives. Terrain features in adjacent sectors may be key terrain if their control is necessary for the continuation of the attack or the accomplishment of the mission. If the mission is to destroy threat forces, key terrain may include areas whose seizure helps ensure the required destruction. Terrain that gives the threat effective observation along an axis of friendly advance may be key terrain if it is necessary to deny its possession or control by the threat.

In the defense, key terrain is usually within the AO and within or behind the selected defensive area.

Some examples of such key terrain are:

- Terrain that gives good observation over AAs to and into the defensive position
- Terrain that permits the defender to cover an obstacle by fire
- Important road junctions or communication centers that affect the use of reserves, sustainment, or LOCs

Additional Considerations:

- **Key terrain varies with the level of command.** For example, to an army or theater commander a large city may afford marked advantages as a communications center. To a division commander the high ground which dominates the city may be key terrain while the city itself may be an obstacle.
- **Terrain which permits or denies maneuver may be key terrain.**
- **Major obstacles are rarely key terrain features.** The high ground dominating a river rather than the river itself is usually the key terrain feature for the tactical commander. An exception is an obstacle such as a built-up area which is assigned as an objective.
- **Key terrain is decisive** terrain if it has an **extraordinary impact** on the mission.
- **Decisive terrain is rare and will not be present in every situation.**

O - Obstacles

Obstacles are any natural or man-made terrain features that stop, impede, or divert military movement. An evaluation of obstacles leads to the identification of mobil-

ity corridors. This in turn helps identify defensible terrain and AAs. To evaluate obstacles:

- Identify pertinent obstacles in the AI
- Determine the effect of each obstacle on the mobility of the evaluated force
- Combine the effects of individual obstacles into an integrated product

If DMA products are unavailable, and time and resources permit, prepare terrain factor overlays to aid in evaluating obstacles. Some of the factors to consider are:

- Vegetation (tree spacing/diameter)
- Surface drainage (stream width, depth, velocity, bank slope, & height)
- Surface materials (soil types and conditions that affect mobility)
- Surface configuration (slopes that affect mobility)
- Obstacles (natural and man-made; consider obstacles to flight as well as ground mobility)
- Transportation systems (bridge classifications and road characteristics such as curve radius, slopes, and width)
- Effects of actual or projected weather such as heavy precipitation or snow

C - Concealment and Cover

Concealment is protection from observation. Woods, underbrush, snowdrifts, tall grass, and cultivated vegetation provide concealment.

Cover is protection from the effects of direct and indirect fires. Ditches, caves, river banks, folds in the ground, shell craters, buildings, walls, and embankments provide cover.

The evaluation of concealment and cover aids in identifying defensible terrain, possible approach routes, assembly areas, and deployment and dispersal areas. Use the results of the evaluation to:

- Identify and evaluate AAs
- Identify defensible terrain and potential battle positions
- Identify potential assembly and dispersal areas

manders and staffs analyze civil considerations in terms of the categories expressed in the memory aid ASCOPE (areas, structures, capabilities, organizations, people, and events).

Civil considerations help commanders understand the social, political, and cultural variables within the AO and their effect on the mission. Understanding the relationship between military operations and civilians, culture, and society is critical to conducting operations and is essential in developing effective plans. Operations often involve stabilizing the situation securing the peace, building host-nation capacity, and transitioning authority to civilian control. Combat operations/major operations directly affect the populace, infrastructure, and the force's ability to transition to host-nation authority. The degree to which the populace is expected to support or resist U.S. and friendly forces also affects offensive and defensive operational design.

Commanders and staffs use personal knowledge and running estimates to assess social, economic, and political factors. Commanders consider how these factors may relate to potential lawlessness, subversion, or insurgency. Their goal is to develop their understanding to the level of cultural awareness. At this level, they can estimate the effects of friendly actions and direct their subordinates with confidence. Cultural awareness improves how Soldiers/*Marines* interact with the populace and deters their false or unrealistic expectations. They have more knowledge of the society's common practices, perceptions, assumptions, customs, and values, giving better insight into the intent of individuals and groups.

Refer to FM 4-02 for extensive information on the medical aspects of IPB that relate mainly to civil considerations in the AO.

To improve the commander's sociocultural understanding, intelligence staffs can use sociocultural databases and repositories as well as HTTs/*foreign area officers, regional affairs officers, and other cultural enablers*, when available, to aid the intelligence analysis conducted as part of assessing civil considerations. Additionally, commanders and staffs continually seek to improve cultural understanding to improve their roles in IPB.

D. Evaluate Current Operations and Intelligence Holdings to Determine Additional Information Needed to Complete IPB

Not all the information needed to complete IPB will be in the data files and databases of the commands or their higher headquarters. Information gaps should be identified early and prioritized based on the commander's initial guidance and intent for intelligence and information collection/*intelligence collection*. The staff should ensure the commander is aware of any information gaps that cannot be answered within the time allotted for IPB. The staff develops reasonable assumptions to use in place of these answers and explains to the commander how they arrived at these assumptions.

E. Initiate Processes Necessary to Acquire the Information Needed to Complete IPB

After determining that information necessary to complete IPB is not contained within local and searchable external data files and databases, staff elements submit requests for information or requests for collection to obtain the information necessary to complete IPB. As information is received, IPB products are updated and intelligence gaps are eliminated. New intelligence gaps and information requirements may be developed as IPB continues.

Refer to FM 3-55/MCWP 2-2 for more information on information collection/ intelligence collection. Refer to ATP 2-01/MCWP 2-2 for more information on planning requirements and assessing collection.

Step 2. Describe Environmental Effects on Operations/*Describe the Effects on Operations*

Step 2 of the IPB process determines how significant characteristics of the operational environment can affect friendly and threat/*adversary* operations. The following example shows how the significant characteristic of the operational environment (specifically the terrain) impacts friendly operations.

Desired End State

Identify how the operational environment influences friendly and threat/*adversary* COAs. The primary outputs associated with step 2 of the IPB process may include ensuring—

* Terrain analysis for the AO and area of interest are completed, in particular:
* Ground and air avenues of approach (AAs)
* Key terrain
* Potential objectives, decision points, NAIs, and TAIs are identified
* The effects of weather and light data are integrated
* Any request for information on requests for collection are refined and updated

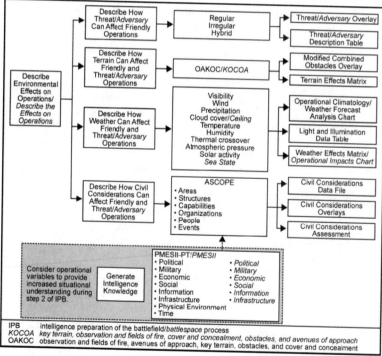

So What?

The "so what" in this step is identifying how relevant characteristics of the area of interest will affect friendly and threat/*adversary* operations:

* Success results in allowing the commander to quickly choose and exploit terrain, weather, and civil considerations to best support the mission.

Consequences of failure:
- The commander may not have the information needed to exploit the opportunities the operational environment provides.
- The enemy commander may have the information needed to exploit the opportunities the operational environment provides in a way the friendly commander did not anticipate.

A. Describe How The Threat/*Adversary* Can Affect Friendly Operations

Threats/*adversaries* are part of the operational environment. Commanders need to understand all the threats/*adversaries* to the operations within the AO and the area of interest. They may face one unified threat/*adversary* force or several disparate threat/*adversary* forces that must be engaged in order to accomplish the mission. Although detailed analysis of enemy forces occurs during steps 3 and 4 of the IPB process, the type of enemy forces and their general capabilities must be defined during step 2. This is done to place the existence of these forces in context with other variables to understand their relative importance as a characteristic of the operational environment. For example:

- When facing a regular force in major operations regardless of where the engagement occurs, that force is most likely the most important characteristic in that operational environment.
- When facing an irregular force conducting operations as part of an insurgency in a failing nation-state, the state of governance and other civil considerations may be more significant than the threat/*adversary* posed by these irregular forces.

The threat/*adversary* overlay and threat/*adversary* description table focus the analysis of threat/*adversary* at this point and aid in communicating that analysis to the commander.

Threat/*Adversary* Overlay

The threat/*adversary* overlay is a depiction of the current physical location of all potential threats/*adversaries* in the AO and the area of interest. This graphic includes the identity, size, location, strength, and AO for each potential threat/*adversary*. Figure 4-2 is an example of a threat/*adversary* overlay for irregular forces.

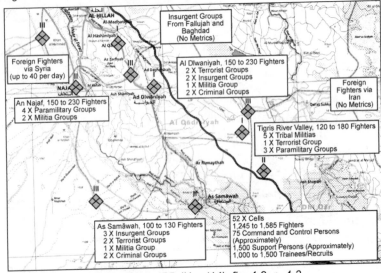

Ref: ATP 2-01.3/MCRP 2-3A, IPB (Nov '14), fig. 4-2, p. 4-3.

Threat/*Adversary* Description Table

The threat/*adversary* description table supports the threat/*adversary* overlay by classifying the type of threats/*adversaries* identified on the overlay and describing the broad capabilities of each threat/*adversary*.

B. Describe How Terrain Can Affect Friendly and Threat/*Adversary* Operations

Terrain analysis is the evaluation of geographic information on the natural and manmade features of the terrain, combined with other relevant factors, to predict the effect of the terrain on friendly and enemy operations. It involves the study and interpretation of natural and manmade features of an area, their effects on military operations, and the effects of weather and climate on these features. Terrain analysis is a continuous process as changes in the operational environment may alter the analysis of its effect on operations.

There are two types of terrain in which a command may operate—natural and urban. Both of these terrain types are analyzed based on military aspects using the OAKOC/KOCOA considerations. Analysis of natural terrain focuses on surface area, airspace, and subsurface areas. Analysis of urban terrain also focuses on surface area and airspace, but must also consider subsurface as well as internal and external supersurface areas.

See pp. 3-14 to 3-15 for an overview of military aspects of terrain (OAKOC).

See pp. 3-14 to 3-15 for an overview of military aspects of terrain (OAKOC).

Analyze the Military Aspects of Terrain

Generally in the Army, detailed terrain analysis is conducted by geospatial intelligence cells assigned to brigade combat teams, division headquarters, corps headquarters, and theater headquarters based on priorities established by the intelligence officer. These cells have state-of-the-art digital mapping tools and access to national-level support from agencies like the National Geospatial Intelligence Agency. *Generally in the Marine Corps, geospatial intelligence capability resides within the intelligence battalion and the Marine aircraft wing (MAW). During the conduct of operations, this capability can be deployed down to the regimental combat team or Marine aircraft group level.* The result of terrain analysis is the evaluation of the military aspects of terrain on operations.

Analyzing the military aspects of terrain involves the collection, processing, evaluation, and interpretation of geographic information on natural and manmade features of the terrain, combined with other relevant factors, to determine potential effects of the terrain on military operations. It involves the study and interpretation of natural and manmade features of an area, effects on military operations, and the effects of weather and climate on these features. Terrain analysis is a continuous process.

Terrain Effects

After determining terrain characteristics, the staff must determine the effect that the terrain will have on friendly and threat/*adversary* operations. The primary analytic tools used to aid in determining this effect are the MCOO and the terrain effects matrix.

Modified Combined Obstacle Overlay (MCOO)

The MCOO is a graphic product that portrays the effects of natural and urban terrain on military operations. The MCOO normally depicts military significant aspects of the terrain and other aspects of the terrain that can affect mobility. Though not all inclusive, some of these aspects are—

- AAs
- Mobility corridors
- Natural and manmade obstacles
- Terrain mobility classifications
- Key terrain

See following pages for further discussion of the MCOO.

See following pages for further discussion of the MCOO.

Modified Combined Obstacle Overlay (MCOO)

Ref: ATP 2-01.3/MCRP 2-3A, Intelligence Preparation of the Battlefield/Battlespace (Nov '14), pp. 4-14 to 4-17.

The MCOO is a graphic product that portrays the effects of natural and urban terrain on military operations. The MCOO normally depicts military significant aspects of the terrain and other aspects of the terrain that can affect mobility. Though not all inclusive, some of these aspects are—

- AAs
- Mobility corridors
- Natural and manmade obstacles
- Terrain mobility classifications
- Key terrain

The combined obstacle overlay provides a basis for identifying ground AAs and mobility corridors. Unlike the cross-country mobility, the combined obstacle overlay integrates all obstacles to vehicular movement, such as built-up areas, slope, soils, vegetation, and hydrology into one overlay. The overlay depicts areas that impede movement (severely restricted and restricted areas) and areas where friendly and enemy forces can move unimpeded (unrestricted areas).

The MCOO is tailored to the mission and is a collaborative effort involving input from the entire staff. The MCOO depicts the terrain according to mobility classification. These classifications are severely restricted, restricted, and unrestricted:

- **Severely restricted terrain** severely hinders or slows movement in combat formations unless some effort is made to enhance mobility. This could take the form of committing engineer assets to improving mobility or deviating from doctrinal tactics, such as moving in columns instead of line formations, or at speeds much lower than those preferred. For example, severely restricted terrain for armored and mechanized forces is typically characterized by steep slopes and large or densely spaced obstacles with little or no supporting roads. A common technique is to depict this type of severely restricted terrain on overlays and sketches by marking the areas with cross¬hatched diagonal lines. Another technique is to color code the areas in red.

- **Restricted terrain** hinders movement to some degree. Little effort is needed to enhance mobility, but units may have difficulty maintaining preferred speeds, moving in combat formations, or transitioning from one formation to another. Restricted terrain slows movement by requiring zigzagging or frequent detours. Restricted terrain for armored or mechanized forces typically consists of moderate-to-steep slopes or moderate-to-densely spaced obstacles, such as trees, rocks, or buildings. Swamps or rugged terrain are examples of restricted terrain for dismounted infantry forces. Logistical or sustainment area movement may be supported by poorly developed road systems. A common and useful technique is to depict restricted terrain on overlays and sketches by marking the areas with diagonal lines. Another technique is to color code the areas in yellow.

- **Unrestricted terrain** is free of any restriction to movement. Nothing needs to be done to enhance mobility. Unrestricted terrain for armored or mechanized forces is typically flat to moderately sloping terrain with scattered or widely spaced obstacles such as trees or rocks. Unrestricted terrain allows wide maneuver by the forces under consideration and unlimited travel supported by well-developed road networks. No symbology is needed to show unrestricted terrain on overlays and sketches.

Terrain mobility classifications are not absolute but reflect the relative effect of terrain on the different types and sizes of movement formations. They are based on the ability of a force to maneuver in combat formations or to transition from one type of formation to another.

The staff should consider the following:

- Obstacles are only effective if they are covered by observation and fire. However, even undefended obstacles may canalize an attacker into concentrations, which are easier to detect and target or defend against.

- When evaluating the terrain's effect on more than one type of organization (for example, mounted or dismounted), the obstacle overlays reflect the mobility of the particular force.

- The cumulative effects of individual obstacles in the final evaluation. For example, individually a gentle slope or a moderately dense forest may prove to be an unrestrictive obstacle to vehicular traffic. Taken together, the combination may prove to be restrictive.

- Account for the weather's effects on factors that affect mobility.

- The classification of terrain into various obstacle types reflects only its relative impact on force mobility. There are many examples of a force achieving surprise by negotiating supposedly "impassable" terrain.

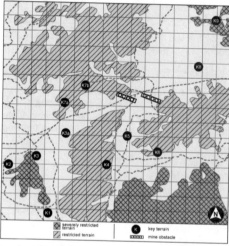

Figure 4-14 is an example of a MCOO developed for natural terrain.

For urban terrain, graphics typically depict population status overlays (population centers, urban areas, political boundaries); logistics sustainability overlays; LOCs; route overlays (street names, patterns, and widths); bridges, underpass and overpass information; potential sniper and ambush locations (likely this data will be a separate overlay); and key navigational landmarks. In developing urban terrain overlays, the following should be depicted:

- **Natural terrain**—the underlying natural terrain on which manmade terrain is superimposed, such as rivers, streams, hills, valleys, forests, desert, bogs, swamps.

- **Manmade terrain**—streets, bridges, buildings, railways, canals, traffic control points; building density, construct, dimensions; functional zone disposition; and street construct, materials, disposition, dimensions.

- **Key facilities, targets and/or terrain**—banks, bridges, airports, electric power grids, oil facilities, military facilities, key residences and places of employment, waterways; tall structures (skyscrapers); choke points; intersections; bridges; industrial complexes; other facilities; density of construction or population; street patterns.

- **Obstacles**—rubble and vehicles in the road; fixed barriers; masking of fires; burning of buildings and other fire hazards; rivers and lakes; power lines; cell phone towers; population; trenches; minefields; certain religious or cultural sites; wire obstacles (concertina wire, barb wire).

Evaluate Terrain Effects on Operations

Using the MCOO as a guide, the terrain effects matrix describes the effect each aspect of OAKOC/*KOCOA* has on friendly and threat/*adversary* operations. Table 4-3 is an example of a terrain effects matrix using a table format.

OAKOC aspects	Terrain effects
Obstacles	Wadis throughout the area of operations with an average depth of 5 to 10 feet and an average width of 20 feet that runs 6 to 10 kilometers long. Above-ground oil and transport pipeline that runs through the central width of the area of operations.
Avenues of approach	Primary and secondary road systems for high avenues of approach. Generally flat terrain with brigade-sized mobility corridors between small villages. Railroad in the north running east to west.
Key terrain	Airfield used as resupply and troop movements. Dam control waterflow on the river and is the primary objective of the threat/adversary.
Observation and fields of fire	Sparse vegetation on generally flat desert terrain with observation of 3 to 5 kilometers. There are 10 kilometers between intervisibility lines. Air support observation is unlimited due to sparse terrain and curve of the earth. Fields of fire for direct fire is 300 to 500 meters for small arms.
Cover and concealment	Cover is provided by intervisibility lines. Concealment is limited by the open terrain and sparse vegetation.

Note. For table 4-3, the Marine Corps uses KOCOA (key terrain, observation and fields of fire, cover and concealment, obstacles, and avenues of approach) aspects.

C. Describe How Weather Can Affect Friendly and Threat/*Adversary* Operations

Weather analysis is the collection, processing, evaluation, and interpretation of relevant military aspects of weather. There are two sub-steps in weather analysis: analyze the military aspects (characteristics) of weather; and evaluate the weather's effects on military operations.

Analyze the Military Aspects of Weather

The following are military aspects of weather:

- Visibility
- Wind
- Precipitation
- Cloud cover/*ceiling*
- Temperature
- Humidity
- Atmospheric pressure (as required)
- *Sea state*

Evaluate the Weather's Effects on Military Operations

Weather has both direct and indirect effects on military operations. The following are examples of direct and indirect effects on military operations:

- Temperature inversions might cause some battle positions to be more at risk to the effects of chemical agents as a result of atmospheric ducting, a process that occurs when strong high pressure influences an area and prevents particulates from dispersing into the upper atmosphere.
- Local visibility restrictions, such as fog, can have an effect on observation for both friendly and threat/*adversary* forces. Severe restrictions to visibility often restrict aviation operations.
- Hot, dry weather might force friendly and threat/*adversary* forces to consider water sources as key terrain.
- Dense, humid air limits the range of loudspeaker broadcasts affecting sonic deception, surrender appeals to enemy forces, and the ability to provide instruction to friendly or neutral audiences.
- Sandstorms with high silica content may decrease the strength and clarity of radio and television signals.

Weather and climate effects have an impact on seasonal outlooks, which have utility for seasonal decisionmaking.

D. Describe How Civil Considerations Can Affect Friendly and Threat/*Adversary* Operations

An understanding of civil considerations—the ability to analyze their impact on operations— enhances several aspects of operations: among them, the selection of objectives; location, movement, and control of forces; use of weapons; and protection measures. The intelligence staff should leverage the rest of the staff, as well as outside agencies, who have expertise in civil considerations to aid the intelligence analysis in this area. Building knowledge during Army force generation is an opportunity to leverage agencies which are not deploying with the unit, but which have relevant regional knowledge.

Civil considerations comprise six characteristics, expressed in the memory aid ASCOPE. Civil considerations encompass the manmade infrastructure, civilian institutions, and attitudes and activities of the civilian leaders, populations, and organizations within an AO and how these elements influence military operations. Tactical Army/*Marine Corps* staffs use ASCOPE to analyze civil considerations that are essential to support the development of effective plans for operations.

Sociocultural factors are the social, cultural, and behavioral factors characterizing the relationships and activities of the population of a specific region or operational environment (JP 2-01.3) must be closely analyzed during irregular warfare and hybrid conflicts. This cultural information incorporated into the IPB process provides the backdrop against which an analysis of social and political factors will allow for successful operations. The MCIA produced a cultural GIRH and Cultural Intelligence Indicator Guide that will assist Marine forces in understanding foreign cultures. Both documents are available on MCIA's SIPRNET Web site. Used in conjunction with ASCOPE analysis, an appreciation of cultural intelligence enables Marines to understand the environment in which they operate and ultimately lead to mission accomplishment.

Due to the complexity and volume of data involving civil considerations, there is no simple model for presenting civil considerations analysis. Rather, it comprises a series of intelligence products composed of overlays and assessments.

See table 4-4 on the following pages, which provides a cross-walk of the operational variables PMESII and some examples for each ASCOPE characteristic.

Civil Considerations Data Files, Overlays, and Assessments

The intelligence staff maintains a civil considerations data file that organizes all the information it has collected and analyzed based on the ASCOPE characteristics. This data file organizes the raw data the intelligence staff uses to assess civil considerations during IPB, as well as to support targeting and civil affairs operations. The data file includes all the information related in the ASCOPE characteristics.

One way of maintaining civil considerations data is in a data file and/or database; this contributes to the continuous evaluation of civil considerations as part of the running estimate by organizing the vast amount of information necessary to analyze civil considerations.

Civil considerations overlays are graphic depictions of the data file and aids planning throughout the MDMP/*MCPP*, as well as aiding situation development during operations. These overlays aid the intelligence staff in describing civil considerations effects, as assessed in the data file, to the commander and rest of the staff.

The civil considerations data file and associated overlays aids the commander and staff in identifying information and intelligence requirements not normally identified through the event templating process associated with determining threat/*adversary* COAs. In contingency operations, or when conducting stability tasks, these work aids are critical in assisting the intelligence staff in determining and assessing threat/*adversary* COAs.

Integrating Processes

Civil Considerations (PMESII and ASCOPE)

Ref: ATP 2-01.3/MCRP 2-3A, Intelligence Preparation of the Battlefield/Battlespace (Nov '14), table 4-4, PMESII and ASCOPE Examples, pp. 4-29 to 4-30.

An understanding of civil considerations—the ability to analyze their impact on operations—enhances several aspects of operations: among them, the selection of objectives; location, movement, and control of forces; use of weapons; and protection measures. The intelligence staff should leverage the rest of the staff, as well as outside agencies, who have expertise in civil considerations to aid the intelligence analysis in this area. Building knowledge during Army force generation is an opportunity to leverage agencies which are not deploying with the unit, but which have relevant regional knowledge.

Civil considerations comprise six characteristics, expressed in the memory aid ASCOPE. Civil considerations encompass the manmade infrastructure, civilian institutions, and attitudes and activities of the civilian leaders, populations, and organizations within an AO and how these elements influence military operations. Tactical Army/Marine Corps staffs use ASCOPE to analyze civil considerations that are essential to support the development of effective plans for operations. Table 4-4 lists one method of cross-walking the operational variables PMESII and some examples for each ASCOPE characteristic.

Sociocultural factors are the social, cultural, and behavioral factors characterizing the relationships and activities of the population of a specific region or operational environment (JP 2-01.3) must be closely analyzed during irregular warfare and hybrid conflicts. This cultural information incorporated into the IPB process provides the backdrop against which an analysis of social and political factors will allow for successful operations. The MCIA produced a cultural GIRH and Cultural Intelligence Indicator Guide that will assist Marine forces in understanding foreign cultures. Both documents are available on MCIA's SIPRNET Web site. Used in conjunction with ASCOPE analysis, an appreciation of cultural intelligence enables Marines to understand the environment in which they operate and ultimately lead to mission accomplishment.

	AREAS	STRUCTURES	CAPABILITIES	ORGANIZATIONS	PEOPLE	EVENTS
POLITICAL	• Enclaves • Municipalities • Provinces • Districts • Political districts • Voting • National boundaries • Party affiliation areas • Shadow government influence areas	• Courts (court houses, mobile courts) • Government centers • Provincial/district centers • Meeting halls • Polling sites	• Public administration: ∘ Civil authority, practices, and rights ∘ Political system ∘ Political stability ∘ Political traditions ∘ Standards and effectiveness • Executive: ∘ Administration ∘ Policies ∘ Powers ∘ Organization • Legislative: ∘ Administration ∘ Policies ∘ Powers ∘ Organization • Judicial/legal: ∘ Administration ∘ Capacity ∘ Policies ∘ Civil and criminal codes ∘ Powers ∘ Organization ∘ Law enforcement • Dispute resolution, grievances • Local leadership • Degrees of legitimacy	• Major political parties: ∘ Formal ∘ Informal • Nongovernment organizations • Host government • Insurgent group affiliations • Court system • Covert political power • Partnerships: foreign	• United Nations representatives • Political leaders • Governors • Councils • Elders • Community leaders • Paramilitary members • Judges • Prosecutors	• Elections • Council meetings • Speeches (significant) • Security and military training sessions • Significant trials • Distribution of power • Political motivation • Treaties • Will
MILITARY	• Area of influence • Area of interest • Area of operation • Safe havens or sanctuary • Multinational/local nation bases • Historic ambush/ improvised explosive device sites/insurgent bases	• Bases • Headquarters (police) • Known leader houses/businesses	• Doctrine • Organization • Training • Materiel • Leadership • Personnel manpower • Facilities • History • Nature of civil-military relationships • Resource constraints • Local security forces • Quick reaction force • Insurgent strength • Enemy recruiting	• Host-nation forces present • Insurgent groups present and networks • Multinational forces • Paramilitary organizations • Terrorists • Multinational forces present • Fraternal organizations • Civic organizations	• Key leaders • Multinational, insurgent, military	• Combat • Historical • Noncombat • Kinetic events • Unit reliefs • Loss of leadership

	AREAS	STRUCTURES	CAPABILITIES	ORGANIZATIONS	PEOPLE	EVENTS

ECONOMIC	• Commercial
	• Fishery
	• Forestry
	• Industrial
	• Livestock dealers
	• Markets
	• Mining
	• Movement of goods/
	  services
	• Smuggling routes
	• Trade routes
	• Black market areas
		• Banking
		• Fuel:
		  ◦ Distribution
		  ◦ Refining
		  ◦ Source
		• Industrial plants
		• Manufacturing
		• Mining
		• Warehousing
		• Markets
		• Silos, granaries,
		  warehouses
		• Farms/ranches
		• Auto repair shops
			• Fiscal:
			  ◦ Access to banks
			  ◦ Currency
			  ◦ Monetary policy
			• Ability to withstand drought
			• Black market
			• Energy
			• Imports/exports
			• External support/aid
			• Food:
			  ◦ Distributing
			  ◦ Marketing
			  ◦ Production
			  ◦ Processing
			  ◦ Rationing
			  ◦ Security
			  ◦ Storing
			  ◦ Transporting
			• Inflation
			• Market prices
			• Raw materials
			• Tariffs
				• Banks
				• Business organizations
				• Cooperatives
				• Economic
				  nongovernment
				  organizations
				• Guilds
				• Labor unions
				• Major illicit industries
				• Large landholders
				• Volunteer groups
					• Bankers
					• Employers/employees
					• Labor occupations
					• Consumption patterns
					• Unemployment rate
					• Underemployment
					  rate (if this exists)
					• Job lines
					• Landholders
					• Merchants
					• Money lenders
					• Black marketers
					• Gang members
					• Smuggling chain
						• Drought, harvest, yield,
						  domestic animals,
						  livestock (cattle, sheep)
						  and market cycles
						• Labor migration events
						• Market days
						• Payday
						• Business openings
						• Loss of business

SOCIAL	• Refugee camps
	• Enclaves:
	  ◦ Ethnic
	  ◦ Religious
	  ◦ Social
	  ◦ Tribal
	  ◦ Families or clans
	• Neighborhoods
	• Boundaries of
	  influence
	• School districts
	• Parks
	• Traditional picnic areas
	• Markets
	• Outdoor religious sites
		• Clubs
		• Jails
		• Historical buildings/
		  houses
		• Libraries
		• Religious
		• Schools/universities
		• Stadiums
		• Cemeteries
		• Bars and tea shops
		• Social gathering places
		  (meeting places)
		• Restaurants
			• Medical:
			  ◦ Traditional
			  ◦ Modern
			• Social networks
			• Academic
			• Strength of tribal/village
			  traditional structures
			• Judicial
				• Clan
				• Community councils and
				  organizations
				• School councils
				• Criminal organizations
				• Familial
				• Patriotic/service
				  organizations
				• Religious groups
				• Tribes
					• Community leaders,
					  councils and their
					  members
					• Education
					• Ethnicity/racial:
					  ◦ Biases
					  ◦ Dominant group
					  ◦ Percentages
					  ◦ Role in conflict
					• Key figures:
					  ◦ Criminals
					  ◦ Entertainment
					  ◦ Religious leaders
					  ◦ Chiefs/elders
					• Language/dialects
					• Vulnerable populations
					• Displaced persons
					• Sports
					• Influential families
					• Migration patterns
					• Culture:
					  ◦ Artifacts
					  ◦ Behaviors
					  ◦ Customs
					  ◦ Shared beliefs/values
						• Celebrations
						• Civil disturbances
						• National holidays
						• Religious holidays and
						  observance days
						• Food line
						• Weddings
						• Birthdays
						• Funerals
						• Sports events
						• Market days
						• Family gatherings
						• History: Major wars/
						  conflicts

INFORMATION	• Broadcast
	  coverage area
	  (newspaper, radio,
	  television)
	• Word of mouth
	• Gathering points
	• Graffiti
	• Posters
		• Communications:
		  ◦ Lines
		  ◦ Towers (cell, radio,
		    television)
		• Internet service:
		  ◦ Satellite
		  ◦ Hard wire
		  ◦ Cafes
		• Cellular phone
		• Postal service
		• Print shops
		• Telephone
		• TV stations
		• Radio stations
			• Availability of electronic
			  media
			• Indigenous
			  communications networks
			• Internet access
			• Intelligence services
			• Printed material:
			  ◦ Journals
			  ◦ Newspapers
			  ◦ Flyers
			• Propaganda mechanisms
			• Radio
			• Television
			• Social media
			• Literacy rate
			• Word of mouth
				• Media groups and news
				  organizations
				• Religious groups
				• Insurgent inform and
				  influence activities
				  groups
				• Government groups
				• Public relations and
				  advertising agencies
					• Decisionmakers
					• Media personalities
					• Media groups and
					  news organizations
					• Community leaders
					• Elders
					• Heads of families
						• Disruption of services
						• Censorship
						• Religious observance
						  days
						• Publishing dates
						• Inform and influence
						  activities campaigns
						• Project openings

INFRASTRUCTURE	• Commercial
	• Industrial
	• Residential
	• Rural
	• Urban
	• Road systems
	• Power grids
	• Irrigation networks
	• Water tables
		• Emergency shelters
		• Energy:
		  ◦ Distribution system
		  ◦ Electrical lines
		  ◦ Natural gas
		  ◦ Power plants
		• Medical:
		  ◦ Hospitals
		  ◦ Veterinary
		• Public buildings
		• Transportation:
		  ◦ Airfields
		  ◦ Bridges
		  ◦ Bus stations
		  ◦ Ports and harbors
		  ◦ Railroads
		  ◦ Roadways
		  ◦ Subways
		• Waste distribution,
		  storage, and treatment:
		  ◦ Dams
		  ◦ Sewage
		  ◦ Solid
		• Construction sites
			• Construction
			• Clean water
			• Communications systems
			• Law enforcement
			• Fire fighting
			• Medical:
			  ◦ Basic
			  ◦ Intensive
			  ◦ Urgent
			  ◦ Sanitation
			• Maintain roads, dams,
			  irrigation, sewage systems
			• Environmental
			  management
				• Construction companies
				• Government
				• Contract
					• Builders
					• Road contractors
					• Local development
					  councils
						• Scheduled
						  maintenance
						  (road/bridge
						  construction)
						• Natural/manmade
						  disasters
						• Well digging
						• Community center
						  construction
						• School construction

Due to the complexity and volume of data involving civil considerations, there is no simple model for presenting civil considerations analysis. Rather, it comprises a series of intelligence products composed of overlays and assessments. The six characteristics of ASCOPE are discussed in ATP 2-01.3/MCRP 2-3A, paragraphs 4-89 through 4-116.

See p. 1-16 for related discussion of operational and mission variables.

Integrating Processes

Step 3—Evaluate the Threat/*Adversary*

Step 3 of the IPB process determines threat/*adversary* force capabilities and the doctrinal principles and TTP threat/*adversary* forces prefer to employ. This may include threats/*adversaries* that create multiple dilemmas for our maneuver forces by simultaneous employment of regular, irregular, terrorist forces, and criminal elements, using an ever-changing variety of traditional and nontraditional tactics.

Desired end state

The G-2/S-2 develops threat/*adversary* models which accurately portray how threat/*adversary* forces normally execute operations and how they have reacted to similar situations in the past for the threats/*adversaries* specific to the mission and environment. The primary output associated with step 3 of the IPB process is a compilation of threat/*adversary* models for each identified threat/*adversary* in the AO that the intelligence staff uses to guide the development of threat/*adversary* COA. This may include—

- Creating and updating threat characteristics/*adversary order of battle* files
- Developing the situation template
- Creating threat/*adversary* capabilities statement
- Determining the HVTL
- Updating the intelligence estimate
- Any request for information on requests for collection, which are refined and updated

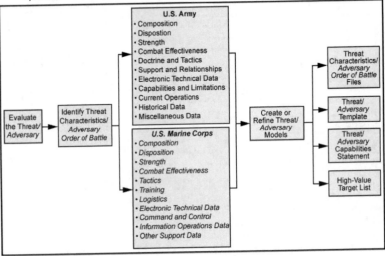

So What?

The "so what" in this step is enhancing the commander's understanding of the regular, irregular, catastrophic, or disruptive threat/*adversary* force within the commander's area of interest:

- Success results in threat/*adversary* COAs developed in the next step of IPB to reflect what the threat/*adversary* is capable of and trained to do in similar situations.

Consequences of failure:

- The staff will lack the intelligence needed for planning.

- The threat/*adversary* will surprise the friendly force with capabilities that the G-2/S-2 failed to account for.
- The staff may waste time and effort planning against threat/*adversary* capabilities that do not exist.

Threats/*adversaries* are a fundamental part of an overall operational environment for any operation but are discussed separately here simply for emphasis. A threat is any combination of actors, entities, or forces that have the capability and intent to harm United States forces, United States national interests, or the homeland (ADRP 3-0). Threats/*adversaries* may include individuals, groups of individuals (organized or not organized), paramilitary or military forces, nation-states, or national alliances.

Threats/*adversaries* are generally nation-states, organizations, people, groups, or conditions that can damage or destroy life, vital resources, or institutions. Army/*Marine Corps* doctrine divides these threats/*adversaries* into the following categories: regular, irregular, hybrid, disruptive, catastrophic, and hazards. This publication only discusses the evaluation of regular, irregular, and hybrid threat/*adversary* forces. Evaluating the threat/*adversary* should begin with identifying there is a threat/*adversary*, followed by the analysis of the threat's characteristics/*adversary's order of battle,* and ultimately leading to the identification of the threat/*adversary* model (regular, irregular, or hybrid structure).

- **Regular threats/*adversary* forces** are part of nation-states employing recognized military capabilities and forces in understood forms of military competition and conflict. The Islamic Republic of Iran Army and the Peoples Liberation Army of China are examples of regular forces.

- **Irregular threat/*adversary* forces** are an opponent employing unconventional, asymmetric methods and means to counter U.S. advantages. A weaker enemy often uses unconventional methods to exhaust the U.S. collective will through protracted conflict. Unconventional methods include such means as terrorism, insurgency, and guerrilla warfare. Economic, political, informational, and cultural initiatives usually accompany and may even be the chief means of irregular attacks on U.S. influence. The Revolutionary Army Forces of Columbia-People's Army and Al Qaeda are examples of irregular forces.

- **Hybrid threats/*adversary* forces** are the diverse and dynamic combination of regular forces, irregular forces, terrorist forces, and/or criminal elements unified to achieve mutually benefitting effects.

The analysis of any enemy force involves understanding that enemy through the de-aggregation of its component parts (threat characteristics/*adversary order of battle*).

A commander's understanding of the threat/*adversary* is based in part on the intelligence staff's research and analysis on threat/*adversary* characteristics. To ensure this understanding is as complete as possible, the intelligence staff considers the following when assessing these factors:

- Threat characteristics/*adversary order of battle* form a framework for the consistent evaluation of any force.
- The threat characteristics/*adversary order of battle* evaluation framework should be adapted to the mission and a unit's needs.
- Properly maintained files are sources of information on the threat's/*adversary's* operations, capabilities, and weaknesses.
- Threat characteristics/*adversary order of battle* are analyzed as a whole.

Although threat/*adversary* forces may conform to some of the fundamental principles of warfare that guide Army/*Marine Corps* operations, these forces all have obvious and subtle differences in how they approach situations and problem solving. Understanding these differences is essential in understanding how a threat/*adversary* force will react in a given situation.

Refer to ADRP 2-0 for additional information on threat capabilities. See MCWP 2-3 for a discussion on adversary capabilities.

A. Identify Threat Characteristics/*Adversary Order of Battle*

There are 11 broad areas the intelligence staff considers when analyzing threat characteristics/*adversary order of battle*: composition, disposition, strength, combat effectiveness, doctrine and tactics, support and relationships, electronic technical data, capabilities and limitations, current operations, historical data, and miscellaneous data.

See following pages (3-30 to 3-31) for discussion and an overview of these 11 broad areas.

During steps 1 and 2 of the IPB process, the intelligence staff identified and defined each individual threat/*adversary* within the commander's area of interest. During step 3, the intelligence staff analyzes the characteristics associated with each of these threats/*adversaries*. The intelligence staff also develops threat/*adversary* models for each of these threats/*adversaries*.

When operating against a new or emerging threat/*adversary* that is not identified and described in the unit's enemy data files, the intelligence staff has to develop new data files for each of these threats/*adversaries*.

B. Create or Refine Threat/*Adversary* Models

Threat/*adversary* models accurately portray how threat/*adversary* forces normally execute operations and how they have reacted to similar situations in the past. This also includes knowledge of threat/*adversary* capabilities based on the current situation. Threat/*adversary* models are initially created by analyzing information contained in various databases. Some threat/*adversary* models are created and developed by higher agencies and organizations; but in immature operational environments or when a new threat/*adversary* emerges, analysts have to develop threat/*adversary* models.

Identify Threat/*Adversary* Capabilities

Threat/*adversary* capabilities are options and supporting operations that the threat/*adversary* can take to influence accomplishing friendly missions. The analysts define capabilities with the use of statements. The following are examples of capability statements:

- "The threat/*adversary* has the capability to attack with up to 8 divisions supported by 150 daily sorties of fixed-wing aircraft."
- "The criminal organization has the ability to pay off local law enforcement agencies."
- "The terrorists have the capability to send destructive viruses over the Internet, which can destroy computer files and archives."
- "The threat/*adversary* can establish a prepared defense by 14 May."
- "The terrorists have the capability of using CBRN weapons."
- "The drug smugglers have the ability to conduct three drug-smuggling operations at the same time."
- "The terrorists have the ability to conduct multiple car bombings simultaneously."
- "The threat/*adversary* has the ability to target friendly convoys along main supply routes using remotely detonated IEDs."

Threat/Adversary Models

Ref: ATP 2-01.3/MCRP 2-3A, Intelligence Preparation of the Battlefield/Battlespace (Nov '14), pp. 5-21 to 5-23.

A threat/*adversary* model is a three-part analytical work aid designed to assist in the development of situation templates during step 4 of the IPB process. Threat/adversary models consist of three parts:

1. Convert Threat/*Adversary* Doctrine or Patterns of Operation to Graphics

Threat/*adversary* templates graphically portray how the threat/adversary might utilize its capabilities to perform the functions required to accomplish its objectives. Threat/*adversary* templates are scaled to depict the threat's/*adversary's* disposition and actions for a particular type of operation (for example, offense, defense, insurgent ambush, or terrorist kidnapping operation). When possible, templates should be depicted graphically as an overlay, on a supporting system or through some other means. Threat/*adversary* templates are tailored to the needs of the unit or staff creating them. They may depict, but are not limited to, unit frontages, unit depths, boundaries, engagement areas, and obstacles.

2. Describe the Threat's/*Adversary's* Tactics and Options

The threat/*adversary* model includes a description of the threat's/*adversary's* preferred tactics. A description is still needed even if the threat/adversary has preferred tactics are depicted in a graphic form. The description—

- Lists the options available to the threat/*adversary* should the operation fail or succeed.

- Prevents the threat/*adversary* model from becoming more than a "snapshot in time" of the operation being depicted.

- Aids in mentally wargaming the operation over its duration and during the development of threat/*adversary* COAs and situation templates.

- Addresses typical timelines and phases of operation, points where unit's transition from one form of maneuver to the next and how each warfighting function contributes to the success of the operation.

The analyst describes the actions of the supporting warfighting function in enough detail to allow for identification and development of HVTs. The analyst also examines each phase separately because target values may change from phase to phase.

3. Identify High-Value Targets (HVTs)

The following techniques may be useful in identifying and evaluating HVTs:

- Identify HVTs from existing intelligence studies, evaluation of the databases, patrol debriefs, and SALUTE reports. A review of threat/*adversary* TTP and previous threat/*adversary* operations as well as understanding the threat's/*adversary's* objective, tasks, purpose, and intent will be useful.

- Identify assets that are key to executing the primary operation or sequels.

- Determine how the threat/*adversary* might react to the loss of each identified HVT. Consider the threat's/*adversary's* ability to substitute other assets as well as adopt branches or sequels.

After identifying the set of HVTs, place them in order of their relative worth to the threat's/*adversary's* operation and record them as part of the threat/*adversary* model. A HVTs value will vary over the course of an operation. Staffs should identify and annotate changes in value by phase of operations. The identification of HVTs assists the staff in the creation of HPTs.

Threat Characteristics/Adversary Order of Battle (Considerations)

Ref: ATP 2-01.3/MCRP 2-3A, Intelligence Preparation of the Battlefield/Battlespace (Nov '14), table 4-4, pp. 5-3 to 5-20.

There are 11 broad areas the intelligence staff considers when analyzing threat characteristics/*adversary order of battle*: composition, disposition, strength, combat effectiveness, doctrine and tactics, support and relationships, electronic technical data, capabilities and limitations, current operations, historical data, and miscellaneous data.

Refer to MCWP 2-3 for a discussion on adversary order of battle factors such as composition, disposition, strength, tactics, training, logistics, combat effectiveness, electronic technical data, information operations data, and other support data.

1. Composition
Composition is the identification and organization of a threat/*adversary*. It applies to specific units or commands as opposed to types of units. Regular forces are normally self-identified and organized similar to friendly forces. Irregular forces may follow similar rules but most often are organized based on a cellular structure.

2. Disposition
Disposition refers to how threat/*adversary* forces are arrayed on the battlefield/*battlespace*. It includes the recent, current, and projected movements or locations of tactical forces. Regular threat/*adversary* forces are generally conducting some form of offensive or defensive maneuver. Irregular threat/*adversary* forces are generally in some part of the plan, prepare, execute, and assess phases for an operation such as a raid or ambush. Understanding how the threat/adversary doctrinally arrays itself on the battlefield/*battlespace* is essential in developing threat/adversary models in step 3 of the IPB process and threat/*adversary* situation overlays in step 4 of the IPB process. The intelligence staff familiarizes themselves with graphic training aids that visually depict range fans with weapons' fire limits and direct and indirect weapons capabilities to better understand enemy weapon systems.

3. Strength
Strength describes a unit in terms of personnel, weapons, and equipment. Information concerning strength provides the commander with an indication of enemy capabilities and helps determine the probable COAs or options open to threat/*adversary* commanders. A lack of strength or a preponderance of strength has the effect of lowering or raising the estimate of the capabilities of an enemy force. Likewise, a marked concentration or build-up of units in an area gives the commander certain indications of enemy objectives and probable COAs. During peacetime, changes in the strength of potential threat/*adversary* forces are important factors which may indicate changes in the threat's/*adversary's* intention. Strength is determined by comparing how a threat/*adversary* organization is doctrinally staffed and equipped with what the organization actually has on hand.

4. Combat Effectiveness
Combat effectiveness describes the abilities and fighting quality of a unit. Numerous tangible and intangible factors affect it.

5. Doctrine and Tactics
Doctrine and tactics include tactical doctrine as well as tactics employed by specific units. While tactical doctrine refers to the enemy's accepted organization and employment principles, tactics refer to the threat/*adversary* force's conduct of operations. Based on knowledge of a threat's/*adversary's* tactical doctrine, the intelligence staff can

determine how the threat/adversary force may employ its forces in the offense and defense under various conditions. Analysts integrate tactics in threat/adversary templates and other intelligence products. *Identify the adversary force's possible actions (defend, reinforce, attack, withdraw, delay [DRAW-D]).*

6. Support and Relationships
The threat/*adversary* force's adoption of a COA should depend on the ability of its support system to support that action. However, depending on the threat/*adversary* force's objectives, possible time constraints, and/or willingness to assume risk—especially as dictated by political leaders or dynamics of political-military circumstances—this could substantially alter adoption of a COA. With knowledge of these factors, analysts can better evaluate the threat/*adversary* force capabilities, strength, and combat effectiveness.

7. Electronic Technical Data
Electronic technical data derived from targeting and electronic warfare are required to conduct electronic warfare. For U.S. Army, it is also derived from cyber electromagnetic activities. This data includes communications and noncommunications equipment parameters, such as emitter type and nomenclature, modulation, multiplex capability, pulse duration, pulse repetition frequency, bandwidth, associated weapons systems, and other technical characteristics of electronic emissions. This information can be developed into an overlay. In order to produce the overlay, signal intelligence personnel require the assistance and input of the targeting and electronic warfare staff.

8. Capabilities and Limitations
Capabilities are the broad COAs and supporting operations that the enemy can take to achieve its goals and objectives. The following four tactical COAs are generally open to military forces in conventional operations: attack, defend, reinforce, retrograde/*DRAW-D*.

9. Current Operations
Current operations are those operations in which an enemy force is currently engaged. This includes operations against U.S. military forces or interests or against the military forces or interests of other nation-states. Analyzing current operations provides up-to-date information on all other threat/*adversary* characteristics.

10. Historical Data
Compiling the history of any threat/*adversary* organization involves conducting the research necessary to gather all relevant information regarding the threat/*adversary* and producing the materials needed to communicate that information to the commander and staff. Information briefings and papers are the two most common methods used for this purpose. Both of these methods can be used to support intelligence training, officer professional development, and noncommissioned officer professional development. The history component of the threat/*adversary* data file includes the original sources of information used to compile information briefings and papers. These sources form part of the professional reading required by all of the unit's intelligence personnel.

11. Miscellaneous Data
Intelligence staffs use supporting information to develop threat/*adversary* force characteristics and to construct comprehensive intelligence estimates. This information includes biographic data, personalities, and biometric data, as well as other information important to mission accomplishment. Biographic data contains information on characteristics and attributes of a threat/*adversary* force's members. Knowledge of personalities is important in identifying units and, in some cases, predicting a unit's COA. Personality data is valuable because the tactics and combat efficiency of particular units are closely tied to the commander's character, schooling, and personality traits. In counterinsurgency operations, supporting data may include tribal, clan, or ethnic group traits and their effects on the combat capabilities or limitations of the threat/*adversary* force, as well as biometric data.

Other capabilities include support to COAs (attack, defend, reinforce, retrograde/ DRAW-D) or specific types of operations, as well as operations that would allow the threat/adversary force to use a COA that would not normally be available or would be severely hindered if the supporting operation were not conducted. Examples of these types of operations include—

- Use of CBRN weapons
- Intelligence collection
- Electronic warfare operations
- Use of air assets (fixed-and rotary-wing)
- Engineering operations
- Air assault or airborne operations
- Amphibious operations
- River operations
- Propaganda
- Deception operations
- Car bombings, bomb scares, and suicide bombers
- Raids on weapon storage facilities
- Carjacking or hijacking of vehicles used in transporting personnel, weapons, or drugs
- Theft of chemicals related to drug manufacturing

When identifying threat/adversary capabilities and COAs, start with a full set of threat/adversary models and consider the threat's/adversary's ability to conduct each operation based on the current situation and the threat's/adversary's own METT-TC/ METT-T conditions. Most situations will not present the threat/adversary with ideal conditions envisioned by their doctrine. As a result, the threat's/adversary's actual capabilities usually will not mirror the ideal capabilities represented by the complete set of threat/adversary models.

The threat/adversary could be under-strength in personnel and equipment, may be short of logistic support, or the personnel may be inexperienced or poorly trained. For example, a terrorist group's normal tactics may call for the use of car bombs as a diversionary tactic in order to conduct other operations elsewhere. The evaluation of the threat's/adversary's logistics might indicate a critical shortage of explosives. Analysts should consider the following:

- Avoid limiting the threat/adversary models and capabilities strictly to the threat/ adversary's conventional forces. For example, student rioters during a noncombatant evacuation operation may be or may become a threat/adversary during the operation.
- Avoid overstating the threat/adversary model and threat/adversary capabilities. The proper use of findings and recommendations developed from threat/adversary assessments will in turn develop realistic threat/adversary models.
- During any discussion of the threat/adversary, cultural awareness is an important factor. By developing an awareness of the culture, friendly units can identify groups or individual members of the population that may be friendly, a threat/adversary, somewhere in between, or both.

1. Threat/Adversary Template
As operations commence, it is imperative to develop foundationally sound and accurate threat/adversary models through careful analysis. The analyst analyzes a threat's/adversary's capability, vulnerabilities, doctrinal principles, and preferred TTP. It is from the threat's/adversary's doctrine, training practices, and observed patterns and activities that analysts construct threat/adversary templates.

A threat/*adversary* template is a graphic that depicts the time and distance of relationships of threat/*adversary* forces conducting a specific operation or activity. Depending on the mission variables, developing templates can be time intensive.

Threat/*adversary* templates show the deployment pattern and disposition preferred by the threat/*adversary* when not constrained by the effects of the operational environment. These templates are normally scaled depictions. They include—

- The location of all enemy units two levels down. For example, an infantry battalion in the defense template would depict platoon and specialty team locations.
- The distance and/or time between enemy units.
- Graphic control measures associated with the operation (boundaries, routes, etc.).

Threat/*adversary* templates graphically portray how the threat/*adversary* prefers to utilize its capabilities to perform the functions required to accomplish its objectives. Threat/*adversary* templates are scaled to depict the threat's/*adversary's* disposition and actions for a particular type of operation (for example, offense, defense, insurgent ambush, or terrorist kidnapping operation).

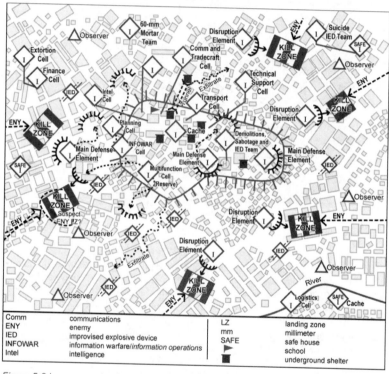

Figure 5-8 is an example of a threat/adversary template for counterinsurgency operations.

When possible, templates are depicted graphically as an overlay, on a supporting system, or through some other means. Threat/*adversary* templates are tailored to the needs of the unit or staff creating them. They may depict, but are not limited to—

- Unit frontages
- Unit depths
- Boundaries
- Engagement areas
- Obstacles

Threat/*adversary* templates allow analysts and the staff to—

- Fuse all relevant combat information
- Assist in identifying intelligence gaps
- Predict threat/*adversary* activities and adapt COAs
- Synchronize information collection

2. Threat/*Adversary* Capabilities Statement

Threat/*adversary* capabilities are the broad options the threat/*adversary* has to counter friendly operations and supporting operations the threat/*adversary* can take based on the conclusions made when determining threat characteristics/*adversary order of battle* at the beginning of step 3 of the IPB process. A threat/*adversary* capabilities statement is a narrative that identifies a particular action for which the threat/*adversary* has the capability to complete and the tactics the threat/*adversary* prefers to use to accomplish its objectives. It addresses operations of major units that will be portrayed on the threat/*adversary template* and the activities of each warfighting function.

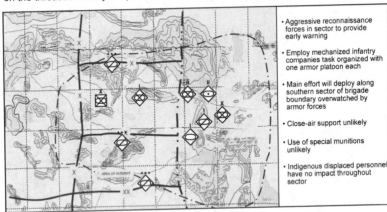

- Aggressive reconnaissance forces in sector to provide early warning
- Employ mechanized infantry companies task organized with one armor platoon each
- Main effort will deploy along southern sector of brigade boundary overwatched by armor forces
- Close-air support unlikely
- Use of special munitions unlikely
- Indigenous displaced personnel have no impact throughout sector

Figure 5-10 is an example of a threat/adversary capability statement that illustrates the capabilities of the 231st Brigade Tactical Group.

3. High-Value Target List (HVTL)

The HVTs identified during step 3 of the IPB process are initially refined during step 4 of the IPB process, and are refined again during the COA analysis step of the MDMP/*COA wargaming step of MCPP*. This data is used to develop the HPTL that is continually refined during execution by targeting groups and boards.

HVTs are determined based on analysis of the threat/*adversary* capabilities statement, an analysis of the threat/*adversary* template, and tactical judgment. Mentally wargaming and thinking through the threat/*adversary* operation is the quickest and most efficient method to determine HVTs at this point. Determining how the threat/*adversary* will employ its assets aids in determining the assets critical to the operation. For example, when mentally wargaming a threat/*adversary* air attack against friendly targets supported by a well-prepared air defense system, it is logical to conclude that the threat/*adversary* will need a substantial air defense suppression package as part of its operation to ensure the success of the attack. In this case, the artillery and air assets that form this suppression package are HVTs.

In identifying and evaluating HVTs, it may be useful to—

- Identify HVTs from existing intelligence studies, evaluation of the databases, patrol debriefs, and SALUTE reports. A review of threat/*adversary* TTP and previous threat/*adversary* operations as well as understanding the threat's/*adversary's* objective, tasks, purpose, and intent will be useful.

- Identify assets that are key to executing the primary operation or sequels.
- Determine how the threat/*adversary* might react to the loss of each identified HVT. Consider the threat's/*adversary's* ability to substitute other assets as well as to adopt branches or sequels.

After identifying the set of HVTs, place them in order of their relative worth to the threat/*adversary* operation and record them as part of the threat/*adversary* model. An HVT's value varies over the course of an operation. The staff should identify and annotate changes in value by the phase of operation. The following are additional considerations:

- Use all available intelligence sources (for example, patrol debriefs, SALUTE reports) to update and refine the threat/*adversary* models.
- Categorize the updates to reach a conclusion concerning the threat's/*adversary's* operations, capabilities, and vulnerabilities.

HPTs can include various threat/*adversary* considerations that can be detrimental to the success of friendly missions. During targeting, HVTs are identified and prioritized during the wargaming phase of planning. In addition, it identifies the subset of HVTs that must be acquired and attacked for the friendly mission to succeed. HVTs may be nominated as HPTs when these targets can be successfully acquired, vulnerable to attacks, and such an attack supports the commander's scheme of maneuver.

To ensure all HVTs are identified, the staff determines which assets are critical to the success of the threat's/*adversary's* main and supporting efforts, as well as those critical to the success of possible threat/*adversary* branches and sequels. Determining how the threat/*adversary* will react to the loss of an asset and its ability to substitute other assets will also aid in this process. HVTs should be prioritized by their relative worth to the threat's/*adversary's* operation. Target value analysis aids in prioritizing HVTs.

Marine Corps staffs conduct a center of gravity analysis based on the understanding gained through design and task analysis to identify or refine adversary and friendly centers of gravity and to determine which friendly and adversary weaknesses may become critical vulnerabilities. A critical vulnerability is some aspect of the center of gravity that is, or can be made, vulnerable to attack.

Target-Value Analysis (TVA)

The TVA is a process led by the fires cell as part of targeting that quantifies the relative value of HVTs with each other in relation to a particular enemy operation. (See FM 3-60 and FM 6-20-40 for more discussion on TVA.) This analysis is based in part on the conclusions the intelligence staff reaches as it evaluates threat characteristics/*adversary order of battle* during IPB. The IPB products required to support TVA are the threat/*adversary* template, the threat/*adversary* capabilities statement, and the HVTL. These products aid the fires cell and the rest of the staff in—

- Providing a focus for the commander's target acquisition effort
- Identifying priorities for the engagement of enemy targets that will facilitate the success of the mission
- Identifying effects criteria

Note. While TVA is conducted initially during IPB, it is a separate process that is repeated throughout the operations process as part of targeting. To be effective, TVA depends on the most current intelligence related to the enemy. Initially based on the threat/adversary templates developed during step 3 of the IPB process, TVA should be refined based on the threat/adversary COAs developed during step 4 of the IPB process, and refined continually based on changes to the enemy situation overlay during operations. Whenever conducted, the intelligence staff supports TVA with the most up-to-date enemy-related intelligence it has. Refer to JP 3-60 for more information on TVA.

Step 4—Determine Threat/*Adversary* Courses of Action

Step 4 of the IPB process identifies and describes threat/*adversary* COAs that can influence friendly operations.

Desired End State

The desired end state of step 4 of the IPB process is the development of graphic overlays (enemy situation templates) and narratives (enemy COA statements) for each possible enemy COA that has been identified. The staff uses these products during the friendly COA development and friendly COA analysis steps of MDMP/ *COA wargaming step of MCPP:*

- Replicate the set of COAs that the enemy commander and staff are considering.
- Identify all COAs that will influence the friendly command's mission
- Identify those areas and activities that, when observed, will discern which COA the enemy commander has chosen. The primary outputs associated with step 4 may include—
- Representing the enemy action or enemy COAs with associated COA statements and HVTLs
- Developing an event template and associated event matrix
- Determining the HVTL and providing input to HPTs and the HPTL
- Providing input into the collection plan
- Updating the intelligence estimate
- Providing input into PIRs
- Providing input into OPORDs and/or OPLANs (annexes and/or appendixes)

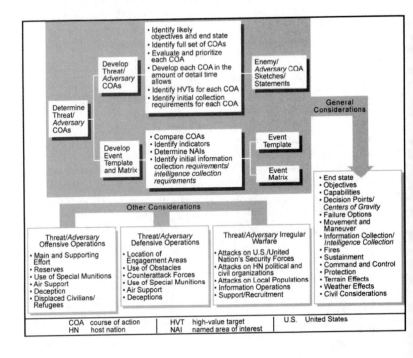

So What?

The "so what" in this step is determining the enemy COAs necessary to aid the development of friendly COAs.

- Success results in the friendly commander will avoid being surprised with an unanticipated enemy action, thus quickly narrowing the set of possible threat/*adversary* COAs to the one the enemy has chosen.

Consequences of failure:

- Failure to identify which of the possible COAs the enemy has chosen, leading to surprise of the friendly command.
- The enemy commander may have the information needed to exploit the opportunities the operational environment provides in a way the friendly commander did not anticipate.

Determining threat/*adversary* COAs is a two-step process:

A. Develop Threat/*Adversary* Courses Of Action

Threat/*adversary* COA development is a six-step process that requires an understanding of the threat characteristics/*adversary order of battle*, and the effects of terrain, weather, and civil considerations on operations. Population effects to operations will be clearly annotated with full details so that during the wargame the population and the effects and threat/*adversary* actions will be portrayed during the wargame. The most important element in determining enemy COAs is in understanding enemy operational art and tactics. There are three types of threat/*adversary* forces that U.S. forces may encounter: regular, irregular, and hybrid. The process to determine COAs these forces may employ is identical, mirrors friendly COA development, and consists of the following:

- Identify likely objectives and end state
- Identify the full set of COAs available to the threat/*adversary*
- Evaluate and prioritize each threat/*adversary* COA
- Develop each COA in the amount of detail time allows
- Identify HVTs for each COA
- Identify initial collection requirements for each COA

See following pages for further discussion.

In order to plan for all possible contingencies, the commander understands all COAs a threat/*adversary* commander can use to accomplish his objectives. To aid in this understanding, the staff determines all valid threat/*adversary* COAs and prioritizes them from most to least likely. The staff also determines which threat/*adversary* COA action is the most dangerous to friendly forces. To be valid, threat/**adversary** COAs should be feasible, acceptable, suitable, distinguishable, and complete—the same criteria used to validate friendly COAs.

When determining COAs for regular and hybrid threats/*adversaries* where the threat/*adversary* operates under the command and control of a unified command structure, the staff will develop COAs focused on the objectives and end state of that command structure. However, when faced with multiples threats/*adversaries* with varied and competing objectives, such as those encountered during stability tasks, the staff will have to develop COAs for each of these threats/*adversaries*.

Develop Threat/Adversary COAs (Overview)

Ref: ATP 2-01.3/MCRP 2-3A, Intelligence Preparation of the Battlefield/Battlespace (Nov '14), chap. 6.

Threat/*adversary* COAs are developed in the same manner as friendly COAs. When developing a threat/*adversary* COA, the intelligence staff accounts for all relevant enemy activity; this includes all possible branches and sequels the threat/*adversary* commander may adopt.

Refer to ADRP 5-0/MCWP 5-1 for discussion of the development of friendly COAs.

1. Identify Likely Objectives and End State

Based on the results of analysis of mission variables conducted earlier in the IPB process, the staff now identifies the enemy's likely immediate and subsequent objectives and desired end state. These elements are included in the threat/*adversary* COA statement developed for each COA.

An objective is a clearly defined, decisive, and attainable goal toward which every operation is directed. The end state is a set of required conditions that define achievement of the commander's objectives. Enemy objectives are normally terrain or force oriented. For example, an enemy may attack to destroy a friendly force or to seize key terrain; defend to delay a friendly force or retain control of key terrain; or conduct guerrilla operations to disrupt friendly operations.

The end state is the desired conditions that, if achieved, meet the conditions of policy, orders, guidance, and directives issued by the commander. For example, the end state for an attack to destroy may be the destruction of all friendly forces down to platoon level and friendly forces incapable of conducting a coordinated defense.

For regular forces, objectives can be either terrain or force oriented, and the end state is usually based on effect and time. For irregular forces, while the end state remains based on effect, objectives are not always linear or time-based. Often, the objectives for irregular forces are driven by event rather than time.

2. Identify Full Set of COAs Available to the Threat/*Adversary*

A regular force has two primary types of operations it can conduct: attack or defend. Based on its objectives, the enemy must select one of these options. Once selected, the threat/*adversary* generally has multiple options to consider when developing its plan.

An irregular force can conduct an attack or defend on a small scale, for short periods, or in complex terrain, but it is difficult to sustain these types of operations without degradation to their effectiveness and their operations. The primary types of operations irregular forces can conduct are activities associated with insurgent or guerilla operations, raids, ambushes, sabotage, and acts of terror.

A hybrid force can combine the capabilities of regular and irregular forces to engage U.S. forces from all points in order to overwhelm U.S. capabilities.

Regardless of the type of force and the type of operation being conducted, enemy forces may plan operations based on task, purpose, method, and end state. Activities within its operations are planned to support that task and purpose. The staff identifies the tasks, purpose, and end state for each COA developed. By identifying these for each COA, the intelligence staff will be better able to determine the chosen threat/*adversary* COA during the conduct of operations.

Once the staff has identified all valid threat/adversary COAs, it compares each COA to the others and prioritizes them by number. For example, if four COAs have been developed, COA 1 is the enemy's most likely COA and COA 4 is the least likely. Additionally, the staff determines which COA is the most dangerous to U.S. forces. The most likely COA may also be the most dangerous. Additionally, a COA needs to answer six basic questions:

- **Who**—the organizational structure of the threat/*adversary* organization, including external organizations providing support
- **What**—the type of operation: attack, defend, other
- **When**—the earliest time the action can begin
- **Where**—the battlefield/*battlespace* geometry that frames the COA (boundaries, objectives, routes, other)
- **How**—the threat/*adversary* will employ its assets to achieve its objectives
- **Why**—the threat's/*adversary's* objectives

3. Evaluate and Prioritize Each Enemy/*Adversary* COA

6-23. The commander approves a plan that is optimized to counter the most likely enemy COA, while allowing for contingency options should the threat/*adversary* choose another COA. Therefore, the staff evaluates each enemy COA and prioritizes it according to how likely it is that the threat/*adversary* adopts that option. Generally, threat/*adversary* forces are more likely to use a COA that offers the greatest advantage while minimizing risk. However, based on the situation and its objectives, the threat/*adversary* may choose to accept risk to achieve a desired end state. It is impossible to predict what COA the threat/*adversary* will choose. Therefore, the staff develops and prioritizes as many valid threat/*adversary* COAs as time allows but at a minimum develops the most likely and most dangerous COAs.

4. Develop Each COA in the Amount of Detail Time Allows

A threat/adversary COA consists of the following products:
- Situation template for the threat/*adversary* COA *(see p. 3-40)*
- Threat/*adversary* COA statement *(see p. 3-44)*
- HVTs and HVTL for the threat/*adversary* COA *(see p. 3-44)*

5. Identify Initial Collection Requirements for Each COA

After identifying the full set of potential threat/*adversary* COAs, the staff develops the tools necessary to determine which COA the threat/*adversary* will implement. Because the threat/*adversary* has not acted yet, this determination cannot be made during IPB. However, the staff can develop the information requirements and indicators necessary to support the construction of an information collection plan/*intelligence collection plan* that can provide the information necessary to confirm or deny threat/*adversary* COAs and locate enemy targets. Information requirements are those items of information that need to be collected and processed in order to meet the intelligence requirements of the commander. An indicator is an item of information which reflects the intention or capability of a threat/*adversary* to adopt or reject a COA.

For the Marine Corps, after identifying potential adversary COAs, the analyst must determine which one the enemy will adopt. Initial collection requirements are designed to help answer the challenge. The identification of initial intelligence collection requirements revolves around predicting specific areas and activities, which, when observed, will reveal which COAs the adversary has chosen. The areas where the analyst expects key events to occur are designated NAIs. The activities that reveal the selected COA are called indicators.

Refer to ATP 2-01.3, chapters 7, 8, and 9 for discussion of the types of information needed to support offensive, defensive, and stability tasks. These requirements are generally related to confirming or denying a threat/adversary COA and locating enemy HVTs.

Situation Template for the Threat/ Adversary COA

Ref: ATP 2-01.3/MCRP 2-3A, Intelligence Preparation of the Battlefield/Battlespace (Nov '14), pp. 6-6 to 6-8.

When constructing a situation template, the staff uses the threat/*adversary* template developed as part of the threat/*adversary* model during step 3 of the IPB process as a base. That template is modified based on the significant effects the operational environment will have on the threat/*adversary* COA. For example, an enemy may prefer to establish battle positions 1 to 1.5 kilometers apart. The terrain, however, may force the enemy to increase this distance in order to protect its flanks. Another example is, the enemy prefers to attack on high speed AAs but also prefers to avoid complex terrain. Therefore, the location of an urban area along a high speed, optimal AA may force the threat/adversary to use a suboptimal approach.

A threat/*adversary* situation template is a depiction of a potential threat/*adversary* COA as part of a particular threat/*adversary* operation. Situation templates are developed using the threat's/*adversary's* current situation, based on threat/adversary doctrine and the effects of terrain, weather, and civil considerations. Situation templates can be simple sketches, reserving in-depth development and analysis for later when more time is available.

A technique is to design a sketch to depict an enemy action or COA which is a graphic representation that will show key outputs or a graphic representation of an enemy action or enemy COA. Each enemy COA has a corresponding situation template.

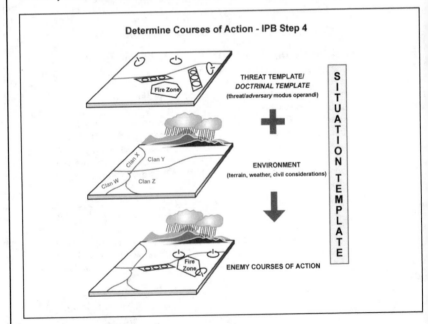

Figure 6-2 is an example of a situation template.

A threat/*adversary* situation template is a graphic depiction along with the analysis of expected enemy dispositions related to a specific COA. Situation overlays usually depict the most critical point in the operation as determined by the commander, the operations officer, and the intelligence officer. However, the operation may require several overlays representing different "snapshots in time." This is especially true when developing overlays for enemy offensive tasks where there may be several critical points in the engagement.

Generally, there will not be enough time during the MDMP/*MCPP* to develop enemy situation overlays for all COAs. A good technique is to develop alternate or secondary COAs, write a COA statement, and produce a HVTL to use during the mission analysis briefing and COA development. Once these tools and products are complete, the staff constructs overlays depicting the enemy's most likely and most dangerous COA to use during friendly COA analysis.

There are three primary types of enemy situation overlays the staff may have to develop: enemy in the offense, enemy in the defense, and irregular forces conducting guerrilla or terror operations. During IPB, these overlays are largely based on assumption and depict enemy locations and activities that are usually templated. This is especially true of overlays depicting enemy offensive tasks or guerilla and/or terror activities. Because the enemy is more static in defensive tasks, the staff may have information related to enemy locations that aids the development of the overlay.

When developing an overlay depicting regular forces conducting offensive or defensive tasks, the staff should template enemy locations and activities two levels down. For example, a friendly brigade combat team/unit would construct an overlay showing maneuver companies and specialty platoons. One of that brigade's battalions/*an element two levels down* from the unit would refine that overlay for its zone or sector showing maneuver platoons and specialty teams.

When developing an overlay depicting irregular forces, the staff at every echelon templates enemy locations and activities at the cellular level. For example, whether at corps, division, brigade, or battalion/*regardless of the level of the unit* the staff templates enemy cells where these cells are believed to be operating. Staffs template where they believe the activity associated with each cell can occur. This activity is determined by evaluating enemy activity through predictive and pattern analysis.

For the Marine Corps, once the complete set of adversary COAs has been identified, analysts develop each COA in as much detail as the situation requires and time allows. The order in which each COA is developed is based on its probability of adoption and the commander's guidance. To ensure completeness, each COA must answer the following five questions:

- *What (type of operation)?*
- *When (time the action will begin)?*
- *Where (sectors, zones, axis of attack)?*
- *How (method by which the adversary will employ his assets)?*
- *Why (objective or end state of the adversary)?*

Preparing Overlays

Ref: ATP 2-01.3/MCRP 2-3A, *Intelligence Preparation of the Battlefield/Battlespace (Nov '14)*, pp. 6-8 to 6-12.

Overlays Depicting the Enemy in Offensive Tasks

The staff constructs an enemy offensive overlay using an 11-step process that includes the following steps:

- **Step 1**—Draw the enemy line of departure. This graphic-control measure is normally placed where the friendly limit of advance is. H-Hour is the time the enemy crosses the enemy line of departure or friendly limit of advance. When the enemy begins movement from assembly areas, to the line of departure or limit of advance, its actions in time and space occur on an H-countdown. Enemy movement that occurs past the line of departure or limit of advance happens on an H+ countdown. This information will be depicted on the enemy attack timeline accompanying the overlay.

- **Step 2**—Draw the enemy's immediate and subsequent objectives as identified in the enemy COA statement. Enemy offensive objectives are normally terrain or force oriented. For example, a force-oriented immediate objective may be to defeat first echelon defending forces and facilitate the passage of second echelon forces. A subsequent objective for this operation may be the destruction of friendly second echelon defending forces. Reverse IPB can aid in determining these objectives. Although the commander has not approved the plan yet, the staff will already have a rough idea of how to construct the defense based on the results of IPB so far.

- **Step 3**—Draw the enemy left and right boundaries. This determination is made on the doctrinal frontage for the enemy attack and the effects of terrain on movement. The MCOO developed during step 2 of the IPB process will show AAs, as well as the optimal and suboptimal movement routes, available to the enemy attacking force.

- **Step 4**—Draw all available attack routes the enemy may use to conduct its attack and secure its immediate and subsequent objectives. The MCOO and weather effects matrix/*operational impacts chart* will aid this analysis also.

- **Step 5**—Template the point of penetration. This area is where the enemy's main effort will attempt to move through the main defensive line. This area will most likely be at the end of a high-speed optimal attack route that allows the enemy to use speed and mass to quickly overwhelm the defense. It may also be at perceived weak points in the defense.

- **Step 6**—Template the locations of enemy ground reconnaissance assets from the line of departure along attack routes to the immediate and subsequent objectives. These locations will normally be associated with the enemy commander's decision points and locations where reconnaissance assets can provide observation in support of targeting.

- **Step 7**—Template the initial and subsequent field artillery firing positions the enemy will use to support the attack. Templating where the range fans for each type of enemy indirect fire system need to be to support actions on each enemy objective aids in this analysis.

- **Step 8**—Template potential locations the enemy may employ special munitions to isolate part of the friendly defense; delaying reorientation of the defense or the use of counterattack forces.

- **Step 9**—Template air AAs that enable the enemy's use of close air support on immediate and subsequent objectives.

- **Step 10**—Template enemy movement formation and attack timeline. There are several ways to do this. One way is to template how the enemy movement formation looks as the advance guard main body enters the defense's engagement area.

Another technique is to show how the enemy movement formation looks at different points along attack routes. This technique requires the development of multiple enemy attack formations as it moves through the defense's sector.

- **Step 11**—Label enemy commander's decision points. Indicate on the overlay the areas where the enemy commander has to make a decision regarding the movement of forces to achieve the desired objectives and end state associated with the COA.

Overlays Depicting the Enemy in Defensive Tasks

The staff constructs an enemy defensive overlay using a 10-step process that includes the following steps:

- **Step 1**—Template the location of enemy battle positions. Enemy battle positions are determined based on the assessed locations of enemy units, what is known about enemy operational art and tactics, and the effects of terrain and weather on the construction of a defense.
- **Step 2**—Template the location of enemy obstacles. The location of obstacles is determined based on assessed locations of enemy obstacles and unit locations, what is known about enemy operational art and tactics, and the methods available to the enemy to tie its obstacle plan into the terrain.
- **Step 3**—Template the location of enemy engagement areas. The templated location of enemy battle positions and obstacles aids in determining the location of engagement areas.
- **Step 4**—Draw the control measures (internal and external boundaries) associated with the defense. The frontage of the enemy defense can be determined by the structure presented by the configuration of battle positions, obstacles, and engagement areas templated in steps 1 through 3.
- **Step 5**—Template the field artillery firing positions the enemy will use to support the defense. Templating where the range fans for each type of enemy indirect fire system need to be to support enemy forces in the security zone and in the main battle area aids in this analysis.
- **Step 6**—Template the locations of enemy observation posts, antitank ambushes, and forward positions located in the security zone. These locations will normally be associated with the enemy commander's decision points, locations where reconnaissance assets can provide observation in support of targeting, and locations where the enemy can disrupt or deceive attacking forces.
- **Step 7**—Template potential locations where the enemy may employ special munitions to channel attacking forces into engagement areas; separate echelons or force attacking forces to adopt a protective posture from CBRN attack.
- **Step 8**—Template air AAs that enable the enemy's use of close air support on the main defensive belt to support the defense.
- **Step 9**—Template the location of enemy counterattack forces and the movement routes these forces can use to support the defense. When templating movement routes, identify the movement times associated with each route.
- **Step 10**—Label enemy commander's decision points. Indicate on the overlay the areas where the enemy commander has to make a decision regarding the movement of forces to achieve the desired objectives and end state associated with the COA.

Overlays Depicting Irregular Forces

Overlays depicting irregular forces conducting operations typically focus on armed forces in a tactical array. Staffs consider whether they need to create overlays that depict the less visible elements of the threat/adversary to include auxiliary support networks, and popular support groups as well as the activities they engage in. Additionally, staffs should capture the process they use to template the overlay so that they and subordinate staffs can replicate the process as required.

Threat/*Adversary* COA Statements

As stated previously, every threat/*adversary* COA includes a threat/*adversary* COA statement, which is a narrative that describes the situation overlay.

Figure 6-7 is an example of a threat/adversary COA statement.

Current enemy situation.
Enemy mission.
Enemy objectives and end state.
Enemy task organization.
Capabilities.
Vulnerabilities.
Decision points.
Decisive point/*Center of gravity.*
Failure options.
Commander's intent for—
  • Movement and maneuver.
  • Information collection/*Intelligence collection.*
  • Fires.
  • Sustainment.
  • Threat/*adversary* command and control.
  • Protection.
  • Information activities.
  • Denial and deception

HVTs and HVTL for the Threat/*Adversary* COA

An HVT is an asset an enemy commander requires for the successful completion of a mission. Identifying HVTs involves mentally wargaming an enemy COA to determine what assets are required to complete the mission. This process involves—

  • Using the HVTL developed as part of the threat/*adversary* model in step 3 of the IPB process as a guide

  • Determining the effect on the threat/*adversary* COA if each of these targets is lost

  • Identifying possible threat/*adversary* responses if the target is lost

B. Develop the Event Template and Matrix

An event template is a graphic overlay used to confirm or deny enemy COAs. The event template is used as a guide during the COA analysis step of the MDMP/*COA wargaming step of MCPP* to describe enemy actions throughout wargaming. Additionally, the event template is used to develop the information collection overlay/*intelligence collection overlay* and the decision support template during COA analysis. The event template is used during the execution phase of the operations process to aid in determining which COA the enemy has adopted. An event template is always accompanied by an event matrix.

The event template is comprised of the following elements: time-phase lines, NAIs, and enemy decision points. Time-phase lines are linear geographic areas that depict when enemy activity will occur. NAIs are usually selected to capture indications of enemy COAs, but also may be related to conditions of the operational environment. A decision point is a point in time and space when the enemy commander anticipates making a decision regarding a specific COA.

An event matrix is a table that associates the NAI and enemy decision points identified on the event template with indicators to aid in determining which COA the enemy commander is implementing. An indicator is an item of information which reflects the intention or capability of an enemy to adopt or reject a COA.

Constructing an Event Template

Ref: ATP 2-01.3/MCRP 2-3A, Intelligence Preparation of the Battlefield/Battlespace (Nov '14), fig. 6-8 and 6-9, p. 6-16.

Constructing an event template is an analytical process that involves comparing the multiple enemy COAs developed earlier in step 4 of the IPB process to determine the time or event and the place or condition in which the enemy commander must make a decision on a particular COA.

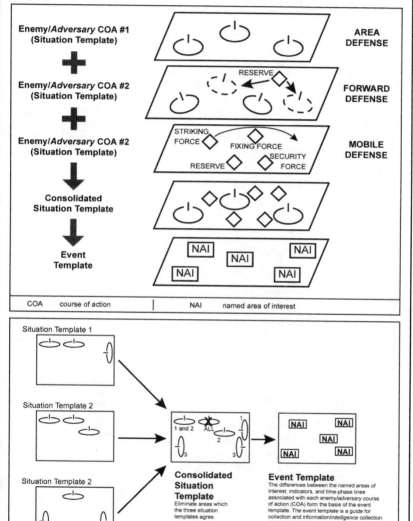

Figure 6-8 and figure 6-9 on page 6-16 are examples of how to illustrate the basic mechanics of this process. The figures only display some minimal, but not all-inclusive information, for what is included on the event template.

The initial event template and matrix are normally developed prior to COA analysis, refined during COA analysis, and further refined during execution as the situation changes. In addition to using the event template and matrix to support its own planning, the staff normally disseminates the event template to subordinate units to aid in the development of subordinate unit information collection plans/*intelligence collection plans*.

Event Template

Constructing an event template is an analytical process that involves comparing the multiple enemy COAs developed earlier in step 4 of the IPB process to determine the time or event and the place or condition in which the enemy commander must make a decision on a particular COA.

Figure 6-8 and figure 6-9 on the previous page 6-16 are examples of how to illustrate the basic mechanics of this process.

Event Matrix

Constructing an event matrix is an analytical process that involves determining the indicators of enemy activity that aid in identifying the decisions the enemy commander has made. Table 6-1 below illustrates the basic mechanics of this process.

Named area of interest	Indicators	Enemy decision point	Time (Hour)	Enemy course of action (COA) indicated
1, 2, 3	• Establishment of battle positions and obstacles • Presence of armored vehicles • Presence of engineer assets	1	H–12	COA 1 area defense
1, 3 4	• Establishment of battle positions and obstacles • Presence of armored vehicles • Presence of engineer assets • Identification of company (+) sized reserve	2	H–12	COA 2 forward defense
1, 2, 3 5, 6	• Absence of maneuver and engineer assets • Presence of mobile armored formation	3	H–3	COA 3 mobile defense

Figure 6-10 below is an example of a completed event template for an enemy conducting offensive operations. This figure is for illustrative purposes and is not based on a tactical scenario.

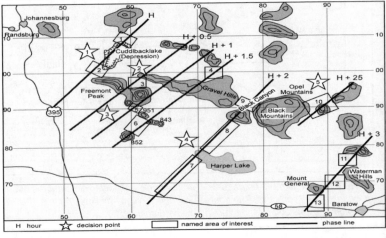

II. Fires and Targeting (D3A)

Ref: ADRP 3-09, Fires (Aug '12); ATP 3-60, Targeting (May '15); and FM 3-09, Field Artillery Operations and Fire Support (Apr '14).

Army targeting uses the functions decide, detect, deliver, and assess (D3A) as its methodology. Its functions complement the planning, preparing, executing, and assessing stages of the operations process. Army targeting addresses two targeting categories—deliberate and dynamic.

Targeting Methodology

I Decide	II Detect	III Deliver	IV Assess
▪ Target Development ▪ TVA ▪ HPT and HVT ▪ TSS ▪ Attack Options ▪ Attack Guidance	▪ Target Deception Means ▪ Detection Procedures ▪ Target Tracking	▪ Attack ▪ Planned Targets ▪ Targets of Opportunity ▪ Desired Effects ▪ Attack Systems	▪ Tactical Level ▪ Operational Level ▪ Restrike ▪ Feedback

Deliberate Targeting

Deliberate targeting prosecutes planned targets. These targets are known to exist in an operational area and have actions scheduled against them. There are two types of planned targets: scheduled and on-call–

  • **Scheduled targets** exist in the operational environment and are located in sufficient time or prosecuted at a specific, planned time.
  • **On-call targets** have actions planned, but not for a specific delivery time. The commander expects to locate these targets in sufficient time to execute planned actions. These targets are unique in that actions are planned against them using deliberate targeting, but execution will normally be conducted using dynamic targeting such as close air support missions and time-sensitive targets (TST).

Dynamic Targeting

Dynamic targeting prosecutes targets of opportunity and changes to planned targets or objectives. Targets of opportunity are targets identified too late, or not selected for action in time, to be included in deliberate targeting. Targets prosecuted as part of dynamic targeting are previously unanticipated, unplanned, or newly detected. There are two types of targets of opportunity:

  • **Unplanned targets** are known to exist in the operational environment, but no action has been planned against them. The target may not have been detected or located in sufficient time to meet planning deadlines. Alternatively, the target may have been located, but not previously considered of sufficient importance to engage.
  • **Unanticipated targets** are unknown or not expected to exist in the operational environment.

I. Decide

Decide is the first function in targeting and occurs during the planning portion of the operations process. The "decide" function continues throughout the operation. The staff develops "decide" information to address:

- What targets should be acquired and attacked/engaged?
- When and where are the targets likely to be found?
- How do the rules of engagement impact target selection?
- How long will the target remain once acquired?
- Who or what can locate/track the targets?
- What accuracy of target location will be required to attack/engage the target?
- What are the priorities for reconnaissance, surveillance, target acquisition, sensor allocation, and employment?
- What intelligence requirements are essential to the targeting effort and how and by when must the information be collected, processed, and disseminated?
- When, where, how, and in what priority should the targets be attacked/engaged?
- What are the measures of performance and measure of effectiveness that determine whether the target has been successfully attacked/engaged and whether the commander's desired effects have been generated by doing so?
- Who or what can attack/engage the targets, and how should the attack/engagement be conducted (for example, number/type of attack/engagement assets, ammunition to be used) to generate desired effects and what are the required assets/resources based on commander's guidance?
- What or who will obtain assessment or other information required for determining the success or failure of each attack/engagement? Who must receive and process that information, how rapidly, and in what format?
- Who has the decisionmaking authority to determine success or failure, and how rapidly must the decision be made and disseminated?
- What actions will be required if an attack/engagement is unsuccessful and who has the authority to direct those actions?

Decide Products

1. High-Payoff Target List (HPTL)
2. Intelligence Collection Plan
3. Target Selection Standards (TSSs)
4. Attack Guidance Matrix (AGM)

A. High-Payoff Target List (HPTL)

The high-payoff target list (HPTL) is a prioritized list of high-payoff targets (HPTs) whose loss to the enemy will contribute to the success of the friendly course of action. Target value is usually the greatest factor contributing to target payoff. However, other things to be considered include the following:

- The sequence or order of appearance
- The ability to detect identify, classify, locate, and track the target. (This decision must include sensor availability and processing time-line considerations.)
- The degree of accuracy available from the acquisition system(s)
- The ability to engage the target
- The ability to suppress, neutralize, or destroy on the basis of attack guidance
- The resources required to do all of the above

Targeting Interrelationships

Ref: ATP 3-60, Targeting (May '15), table 1-1, p. 1-9.

Army targeting uses the functions decide, detect, deliver, and assess (D3A) as its methodology. Its functions complement the planning, preparing, executing, and assessing stages of the operations process. Army targeting addresses two targeting categories—deliberate and dynamic. Deliberate targeting prosecutes planned targets. Dynamic targeting prosecutes targets of opportunity and changes to planned targets or objectives.

While the targeting process may be labeled differently at the joint level the same targeting tasks are being accomplished, as demonstrated in table 1-1.

Operations Process		Joint Targeting Cycle	D3A	MDMP	Targeting Task
Continuous Assessment	Planning	1. The End State and Commanders Objectives	Decide	Mission Analysis	• Perform target value analysis to develop fire support (including cyber/electromagnetic and inform/influence activities) high- value targets. • Provide fire support, inform/influence, and cyber/electromagnetic activities input to the commander's targeting guidance and desired effects.
		2. Target Development and Prioritization		Course of Action Development	• Designate potential high-payoff targets. • Deconflict and coordinate potential high-payoff targets. • Develop high-payoff target list. • Establish target selection standards. • Develop attack guidance matrix. • Develop fire support and cyber/electromagnetic activities tasks. • Develop associated measures of performance and measures of effectiveness.
		3. Capabilities Analysis		Course of Action Analysis	• Refine the high-payoff target list. • Refine target selection standards. • Refine the attack guidance matrix. • Refine fire support tasks. • Refine associated measures of performance and measures of effectiveness. • Develop the target synchronization matrix. • Draft airspace control means requests.
		4. Commander's Decision and Force Assignment		Orders Production	• Finalize the high-payoff target list. • Finalize target selection standards. • Finalize the attack guidance matrix. • Finalize the targeting synchronization matrix. • Finalize fire support tasks. • Finalize associated measures of performance and measures of effectiveness. • Submit information requirements to S-2.
	Preparation	5. Mission Planning and Force Execution	Detect		• Execute ISR Plan. • Update information requirements as they are answered. • Update the high-payoff target list, attack guidance matrix, and targeting synchronization matrix. • Update fire support and cyber/electromagnetic activities tasks. • Update associated measures of performance and measures of effectiveness.
	Execution		Deliver		• Execute fire support and electronic attacks in accordance with the attack guidance matrix and the targeting synchronization matrix.
		6. Assessment	Assess		• Assess task accomplishment (as determined by measures of performance). • Assess effects (as determined by measures of effectiveness).

Table 1-1. Crosswalk of the operations process, joint targeting cycle, D3A, and MDMP.

High-Payoff Target List (HPTL) Example

Event or Phase:		
Priority	Category	Target

Ref: FM 34-8-2. Intelligence Officer's Handbook. fig. F-5. p. F-9.

B. Intelligence Collection Plan

The intelligence collection plan answers the commander's PIRs, to include those HPTs designated as PIR. The plan, within the availability of additional collection assets, supports the acquisition of more HPTs. Determining the intelligence requirements is the first step in the collection management process.

The collection plan provides a framework that collection managers use to determine, evaluate, and satisfy intelligence needs. Because of the diversity of missions, capabilities, and requirements, the collection plan has no prescribed doctrinal format. However, a dynamic collection plan should:

- Have as its basis the commander's priority intelligence requirements, to include those HPTs approved as PIRs
- Help the commander see his area of interest
- Provides synchronized coverage of the commander's area of operations
- Have a five-dimensional battlefield approach: width, length, depth or altitude, time, and electromagnetic spectrum
- Cover the collection capabilities of higher and adjacent units. Identify assets for acquiring and tracking HPTs and determining BDA on HPTs
- Be flexible enough to allow response to changes as they occur
- Cover only priority requirements
- Be a working document
- Contain precise and concise information

C. Target Selection Standards (TSS)

Target selection standards address accuracy or other specific criteria that must be met before targets can be attacked. TSS are criteria applied to enemy activity (acquisitions and battlefield information) used in deciding whether the activity is a target. TSS break nominations into two categories: targets, which meet accuracy and timeliness requirements for attack; and suspected targets, which must be confirmed before any attack.

- **HPT**. This refers to the designated HPTs which the collection manager is tasked to acquire.
- **Timeliness**. Valid targets are reported to attack systems within the designated timeliness criteria.
- **Accuracy**. Valid targets must be reported to the attack system meeting the required TLE criteria. The criteria is the least restrictive TLE considering the capabilities of available attack systems.

D3A Methodology and the MDMP

Ref: ATP 3-60, Targeting (May '15), pp. 1-7 to 1-10 (fig. 1-3, p. 1-7).

The D3A methodology is an integral part of the military decisionmaking process (MDMP) from receipt of the mission through operation order (OPORD) execution and assessment. Like MDMP, targeting is a leadership driven process. Targeting frequently begins simultaneously with receipt of mission, and may even begin based on a warning order. As the MDMP is conducted, targeting becomes more focused based on the commander's guidance and intent. The composite risk management process is an integral tool in the MDMP and is compatible process that aligns with MDMP.

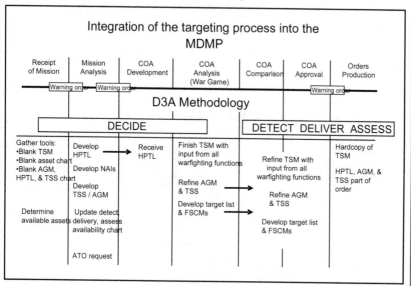

Integrating Processes

The commander is responsible for mission analysis but may have his staff conduct a detailed mission analysis for his approval. The mission analysis considers intelligence preparation of the battlefield (IPB), environmental considerations, enemy situation, and potential enemy course of action (COA). The commander provides his initial planning guidance and intent for further COA developments. The initial guidance and intent is given in a warning order. A warning order is sent to subordinate units to allow them to begin planning, providing them as much lead time as possible.

The plans cell develops potential friendly COAs based on facts and assumptions identified during IPB and mission analysis. These developed friendly COAs are usually checked by the commander or chief of staff to ensure they comply with the commander's initial guidance and intent and meet considerations for COA development. The intelligence staff develops as many possible enemy COAs as time allows.

The rules are developed by the rules of engagement cell under the supervision of the operations offices and assisted by staff judge advocate, based on commander's guidance, during the planning phase of the operations process.

Once approved for further development, a friendly COA is war gamed against the most likely and/or most threatening enemy COA to determine their suitability, acceptability, and feasibility. These results are normally briefed to the commander in a decision briefing. Following a decision by the commander, adjustments are made, if necessary, to the selected COA and orders preparation begins. A warning order is with as much information as possible to expedite their planning.

Example TSS Matrix

Target Selections Standards		
HPT	Timeliness	Accuracy
COPs	3 hr	150 m
RISTA	30 min	150 m
2S3	30 min	500 m
M-46	30 min	500 m
ADA	15 min	500 m
CPs	3 hr	500 m
Ammunition	6 hr	1 km
Maneuver	1 hr	150 m

Ref: FM 34-8-2, Intelligence Officer's Handbook, fig. F-6, p. F-10.

Considering these factors, different TSS may exist for a given enemy activity on the basis of different attack systems. For example, an enemy artillery battery may have a 150-meter TLE requirement for attack by cannon artillery and a 1 km require-ment for attack helicopters. TSS are developed by the FSE in conjunction with MI personnel. Intelligence analysts use TSS to quickly determine targets from battlefield information and pass the targets to the FSE.

Attack system managers, such as FSEs, FCEs, or FDCs, use TSS to quickly identify targets for attack. Commands can develop standard TSS based on anticipated en-emy OB and doctrine matched with the normally available attack systems.

D. Attack Guidance Matrix (AGM)

The attack guidance matrix (AGM), approved by the commander, addresses which targets will be attacked, how, when, and the desired effects. The products of the decide function are briefed to the commander. Upon his approval, his decisions are translated into the OPORD with annexes.

Knowing target vulnerabilities and the effect an attack will have on enemy operations allows a staff to propose the most efficient available attack option. Key guidance is whether the commander wishes to disrupt, delay, limit damage, or destroy the enemy. During wargaming, DPs linked to events, areas (NAIs and TAIs), or points on the battlefield are developed. These DPs cue the command decisions and staff actions where tactical decisions are needed.

On the basis of commander's guidance, the targeting team recommends how each target should be engaged in terms of the effects of fire and attack options to use. Effects of fire *(see Joint Pub 1-02)* can be to **harass, suppress, neutralize,** or **de-stroy** the target. The subjective nature of what is meant by these terms means the commander must ensure the targeting team understands his use of them. Applying FS automation system default values further complicates this understanding.

Example Attack Guidance Matrix (AGM)

PHASE/EVENT: ATTACK THROUGH THE SECURITY ZONE				
HPTL	**WHEN**	**HOW**	**EFFECT**	**REMARKS**
COPs	P	GS ARTY	N	PLAN IN INITIAL PREP
RISTA and OPs	P	GS ARTY	N	P
2S1 and 2S3	P	MLRS	N	
2S6, S9 and SA13	P	GS ARTY	S	SEAD FOR AVN OPS
REGT CP	A	MLRS	N	
RESERVE BN	P	AVN BDE	D	INTENT TO ATTACK RESERVE BN IN EA HOT

LEGEND I = IMMEDIATE   S = SUPPRESS
           A = AS ACQUIRED N = NEUTRALIZE
           P = PLANNED   D = DESTROY

Ref: FM 34-8-2, Intelligence Officer's Handbook, fig. F-7, p. F-13.

1. Harassing Fire

Harassing fire is designed to disturb the rest of the enemy troops, to curtail movement, and, by threat of losses, to lower morale. The decision to employ harassing fires needs careful consideration. Harassing fire has little real effect on the enemy, subjects gun crews to an additional workload, and increases the threat of counter-battery fires. ROE or the potential for adverse public opinion may prohibit its use. However, harassing fires may be a combat multiplier in some situations. Consider their use in SASO , delaying actions, and economy of force operations.

2. Suppressive Fire

Suppressive fire on or about a weapons system degrades its performance below the level needed to fulfill its mission objectives. Suppression lasts only as long as the fires continue. The duration of suppressive fires is either specified in the call for fire or established by SOP. Suppression is used to prevent effective fire on friendly forces. It is typically used to support a specified movement of forces. The FSCOORD needs to ask or calculate the *when* and *how long* questions.

3. Neutralization Fire

Neutralization fire is delivered to render the target ineffective or unusable temporarily. Neutralization fire results in enemy personnel or material becoming incapable of interfering with an operation or COA. Key questions the FSCOORD must ask are when and how long does the commander want the target to be neutralized. Most planned missions are neutralization fires.

4. Destructive Fire

Destruction fire is delivered for the sole purpose of destroying material objects. It physically renders the target permanently combat-ineffective unless it is restored, reconstituted, or rebuilt. Setting automated FS default values for destruction of 30 percent does not guarantee achieving the commander's intent. The surviving 70 percent may still influence the operation. Destruction missions are expensive in terms of time and material. Consider whether neutralization or suppression may be more efficient.

Which Attack System to Use?

The decision of what attack system to use is made at the same time as the decision on when to acquire and attack the target. Coordination is required when deciding to attack with two different means (such as EW and combat air operations). Coordination requirements are recorded during the wargame process.

The attack guidance must be approved by the commander and detail the following:

- A prioritized list of HPTs
- When, how, and desired effects of attack
- Any special instructions
- HPTs that require BDA

This information is developed during the wargame. Attack guidance:

- Applies to planned targets and targets of opportunity
- May address specific or general target descriptions
- Is provided to attack system managers via the AGM
- May change as the operation progresses

The AGM must be updated during staff planning meetings and as the enemy situation changes. Consider separate AGMs for each phase of an operation.

II. Detect

Detect is the second function in targeting and occurs primarily during the prepare portion of the operations process. A key resource for fires planning and targeting is the intelligence generated through reconnaissance, surveillance, and intelligence operations to answer the targeting information requirements. Requirements for target detection and action are expressed as PIR and information requirements. Their priority depends on the importance of the target to the friendly course of action and tracking requirements. PIR and information requirements that support detection of HPTs are incorporated into the overall unit information collection plan. Named areas of interest and target areas of interest are focal points particularly for this effort and are integrated into the information collection plan.

The detect function continues during the execution of the operations order (OPORD). Target acquisition assets gather information and report their findings back to their controlling headquarters, which in turn pass pertinent information to the tasking agency. Some collection assets provide actual targets, while other assets must have their information processed to produce valid targets. The target priorities developed in the decide function are used to expedite the processing of targets. Situations arise where the attack, upon location and identification, of a target is either impossible (for example out of range) or undesirable (outside of but moving toward an advantageous location for the attack). Critical targets that we cannot or choose not to attack in accordance with the attack guidance must be tracked to ensure they are not lost. Tracking suspected targets expedites execution of the attack guidance. Tracking suspected targets keeps them in view while they are validated. Planners and executors must keep in mind that assets used for target tracking may be unavailable for target acquisition. As targets are developed, appropriate weapon systems are tasked in accordance with the attack guidance and location requirements of the system.

III. Deliver

Deliver is the third function in targeting and occurs primarily during the execution stage of the operations process. The main objective is to attack/engage targets in accordance with the commander's guidance. The selection of a weapon system or a combination of weapons systems leads to a technical solution for the selected weapon.

Attack of Targets

The attack of targets must satisfy the attack guidance developed in the decide function. Target attack requires several decisions and actions. These decisions fall into two categories—tactical and technical.

Attack of Targets (Decision Categories)

A. Tactical Decisions
- The time of attack
- The desired effect, or degree of damage
- The attack system to be used

B. Technical Decisions
- Number and type of munitions
- Unit to conduct the attack
- Response time of the attacking unit

A. Tactical Decisions

1. Time of Attack

The time of attack is determined according to the type of target-planned target or target of opportunity.

2. Planned Targets

Some targets will not appear as anticipated. Target attack takes place only when the forecasted enemy activity occurs in the projected time or place. The detection and tracking of activities associated with the target becomes the trigger for target attack. Once the designated activity is detected the targeting team does the following:

- The G2 verifies the enemy activity as the planned target to be attacked. This is done by monitoring decision points and TAIs/NAIs associated with HPTs.

- The G2 validates the target by conducting a final check of the reliability of the source and the accuracy (time and location) of the target. Then he passes the target to the FSE.

- The current operations officer checks the legality of the target in terms of the rules of engagement (ROE)

- The FSE determines if the attack system(s) planned is available and still the best system for the attack

- The FSE coordinates as required with higher, lower, and adjacent units, other services, allies, and host nation. This is particularly important where potential fratricide situations are identified.

- The FSE issues the fire mission request to the appropriate executing unit(s)
- The FSE informs the G2 of target attack
- The G2 alerts the appropriate system responsible for BDA (when applicable)

3. Targets of Opportunity

High-payoff targets of opportunity are processed the same as planned HPTs. Targets of opportunity not on the HPTL are first evaluated to determine when or if they should be attacked. The decision to attack targets of opportunity follows the attack guidance and is based on a number of factors such as the following:

- Activity of the target
- Dwell time
- Target payoff compared to other targets currently being processed for engagement

If the decision is made to attack immediately, the target is processed further. The availability and capabilities of attack systems to engage the target are assessed. If the target exceeds the capabilities or availability of the unit attack systems, the target should be sent to a higher headquarters for immediate attack. If the decision is to defer the attack, continue tracking, determine decision point(s) for attack, and modify collection taskings as appropriate.

4. Desired Effects

Effects of fires can only be properly assessed by an observer or with an analysts. At brigade and TF, it is important that each target has a primary and alternate observer. The observers must understand the desired effects, when and for how long they are required. When in doubt about the commander's intent, ask—never assume. Emphasis on this issue during training will enhance the effectiveness and efficiency of fire support.

5. Attack System

The last tactical decision to be made is the selection of the appropriate attack system. For planned targets, this decision should have been made during the decide function of the targeting process. A check must be made to ensure that the selected attack system is available and can conduct the attack. If not, the targeting team must determine the best system available to attack the target. All available attack assets should be considered. In some cases, the target attach must be coordinated among two or more attack systems.

B. Technical Decisions

Once the tactical decisions have been made, the FS cell directs the attack system to attack the target. The FS cell provides the attack system manager with the following:

- Selected time of attack
- Effects desired in accordance with previous discussion
- Any special restraints or requests for particular munitions types

The attack system manager (FSCOORD, ALO, avn bde LO, NGLO, and so on) determines if his system can meet the requirements. If his system is unable to meet the requirements, he notifies the FS cell. There are various reasons an attack system may not be able to meet the requirements. Some are:

- System not available at the specified time
- Required munitions not available
- Target out of range

The FS cell must decide if the selected system should attack under different criteria or if a different system should be used.

IV. Assess

Assess is the fourth function of targeting and occurs throughout the operations process. The commander and staff assess the results of mission execution. If assessment reveals that the commander's guidance has not been met, the targeting must continue to focus on the target(s) involved. This feedback may result in changes to original decisions made during the target selection. These changes may influence the continued execution of the plan.

Combat assessment is the determination of the effectiveness of force employment during military operations. Combat assessment is composed of three elements:

Combat Assessment

 A Battle Damage Assessment (BDA)

 B Munitions Effects Assessment (MEA)

 C Reattack Recommendation

Integrating Processes

A. Battle Damage Assessment (BDA)

In combination, BDA and MEA inform the commander of effects against targets and target sets. Based on this, the threat's ability to make and sustain war and centers of gravity are continuously estimated. During the review of the effects of the campaign, restrike recommendations are proposed or executed. BDA pertains to the results of attacks on targets designated by the commander.

B. Munitions Effectiveness Assessment (MEA)

The G3 through the targeting team conducts MEA concurrently and interactively with BDA as a function of combat assessment. MEA is used as the basis for recommending changes to increase effectiveness in:

- Methodology
- Tactics
- Weapon systems
- Munitions
- Weapon delivery parameters

The G3 develops MEA by determining the effectiveness of tactics, weapons systems, and munitions. Munitions effect on targets can be calculated by obtaining rounds fired on specific targets by artillery assets. The targeting team may generate modified commander's guidance concerning:

- Unit Basic Load (UBL)
- Required Supply Rate (RSR)
- Controlled Supply Rate (CSR)

The need for BDA for specific HPTs is determined during the decide function. Record BDA on the AGM and intelligence collection plan. The resources used for BDA are the same resources used for target development and TA. An asset used for BDA may not be available for target development and TA. The ACE receives, processes, and disseminates the results of attack (in terms of desired effects).

Each BDA has three assessment components:

1. Physical Damage Assessment
Physical damage assessment estimates the quantitative extent of physical damage through munitions blast, fragmentation, and/or fire damage effects to a target. This assessment is based on observed or interpreted damage.

2. Functional Damage Assessment
Functional damage assessment estimates the effect of attack on the target to perform its intended mission compared to the operational objective established against the target. This assessment is inferred on the basis of all-source intelligence and includes an estimate of the time needed to replace the target function. A functional damage assessment is a temporary assessment (compared to target system assessment) used for specific missions.

3. Target System Assessment
Target system assessment is a broad assessment of the overall impact and effectiveness of all types of attack against an entire target systems capability; for example, enemy ADA systems. It may also be applied against enemy unit combat effectiveness. A target system assessment may also look at subdivisions of the system compared to the commander's stated operational objectives. It is a relatively permanent assessment (compared to a functional damage assessment) that will be used for more than one mission.

BDA is more than determining the number of casualties or the amount of equipment destroyed. The targeting team can use other information, such as:

- Whether the targets are moving or hardening in response to the attack
- Changes in deception efforts and techniques
- Increased communication efforts as the result of jamming
- Whether the damage achieved is affecting the enemy's combat effectiveness as expected

BDA may also be passive by compiling information regarding a particular target or area (e.g., the cessation of fires from an area). If BDA is to be made, the targeting team must give intelligence acquisition systems adequate warning for sensors to be directed at the target at the proper time. BDA results may change plans and earlier decisions. The targeting team must periodically update the decisions made during the decide function concerning:

- IPB products
- HPTLs
- TSS
- AGMs
- Intelligence collection plans
- OPLANs

C. Reattack Recommendation
Based on BDA and MEA, the G2/G3 consider the level to which operational objectives have been achieved and make recommendations to the commander. Reattack and other recommendations should address operational objectives relative to the:

- Target
- Target critical elements
- Target systems
- Enemy combat force strengths

III. Risk Management (RM)

Ref:ATP 5-19 (w/C1), Risk Management (Apr '14).

Risk management is the process of identifying, assessing, and controlling risks arising from operational factors and making decisions that balance risk cost with mission benefits (JP 3-0). The Army uses risk management (RM) to help maintain combat power while ensuring mission accomplishment in current and future operations. RM applies to operations and to nonoperational activities.

RM is the Army's process for helping organizations and individuals make informed decisions to reduce or offset risk. Using this process increases operational effectiveness and the probability of mission accomplishment. It is a systematic way of identifying hazards, assessing them, and managing the associated risks.

Commanders, staffs, Army leaders, Soldiers, and Army civilians integrate RM into all planning, preparing, executing, and assessing of operations. The process applies to all types of operations, tasks, and activities.

RM outlines a disciplined approach to express a risk level in terms readily understood at all echelons. Except in time-constrained situations, planners complete the process in a deliberate manner—systematically applying all the steps and recording the results on the prescribed form (*see DD Form 2977 on following pages*).

RM Principles

The principles of RM are—

- Integrate RM into all phases of missions and operations
- Make risk decisions at the appropriate level
- Accept no unnecessary risk
- Apply RM cyclically and continuously

Army forces must integrate RM throughout planning, preparation, execution, and assessment activities. Army units should use RM for on- and off-duty activities. Commanders must emphasize RM in planning processes; they must dedicate sufficient time and other resources to RM during planning to ensure Army forces manage risk effectively throughout all phases of missions and operations.

A *risk decision* is a commander, leader, or individual's determination to accept or not accept the risk(s) associated with an action he or she will take or will direct others to take. RM is only effective when the specific information about hazards and risks is passed to the appropriate level of command for a risk decision. Subordinates must pass specific risk information up the chain of command. Conversely, the higher command must provide subordinates making risk decisions or implementing controls with the established *risk tolerance*—the level of risk the responsible commander is willing to accept. RM application must be inclusive; those executing an operation and those directing it participate in an integrated process.

In the context of RM, a *control* is an action taken to eliminate a hazard or to reduce its risk. If a commander, Army leader, or any individual responsible for executing a task determines that the controls available will not reduce risk to a level within the risk tolerance, that person must elevate the risk decision to the next level in the chain of command.

Risk Management Worksheet (DD Form 2977)

Ref: ATP 5-19 (w/C1), Risk Management (Apr '14), app. A.

DD Form 2977 is the Army's standard form for deliberate risk assessment. Aviation; explosive; chemical, biological, radiological, or nuclear; and other highly technical activities may require additional specialized documentation. However, when coordination may occur across sections or commands, DD Form 2977 is the standard for the majority of Army operations. It allows units to track haz ards and risks in a logical manner. Army forces use this form to document risk management (RM) steps taken during planning, preparation, and execution of any type of operation, including training and combat.

DELIBERATE RISK ASSESSMENT WORKSHEET

1. MISSION/TASK DESCRIPTION	2. DATE *(DD/MM/YYYY)*

3. PREPARED BY

a. Name *(Last, First, Middle Initial)*		b. Rank/Grade	c. Duty Title/Position
d. Unit		e. Work Email	f. Telephone *(DSN/Commercial (Include Area Code))*
g. UIC/CIN *(as required)*		h. Training Support/Lesson Plan or OPORD *(as required)*	i. Signature of Preparer

Five steps of Risk Management: (1) Identify the hazards (2) Assess the hazards (3) Develop controls & make decisions (4) Implement controls (5) Supervise and evaluate *(Step numbers not equal to numbered items on form)*

4. SUBTASK/SUBSTEP OF MISSION/TASK	5. HAZARD	6. INITIAL RISK LEVEL	7. CONTROL	8. HOW TO IMPLEMENT/ WHO WILL IMPLEMENT	9. RESIDUAL RISK LEVEL
				How: Who:	
				How: Who:	
				How: Who:	
				How: Who:	
				How: Who:	

Additional entries for items 5 through 9 are provided on page 2.

10. OVERALL RESIDUAL RISK LEVEL *(All controls implemented)*:
☐ EXTREMELY HIGH ☐ HIGH ☐ MEDIUM ☐ LOW

11. OVERALL SUPERVISION PLAN AND RECOMMENDED COURSE OF ACTION

12. APPROVAL OR DISAPPROVAL OF MISSION OR TASK ☐ APPROVE ☐ DISAPPROVE

a. Name *(Last, First, Middle Initial)*	b. Rank/Grade	c. Duty Title/Position	d. Signature of Approval Authority
e. Additional Guidance:			

DD FORM 2977, JAN 2014

Page 1 of ____ Pages
Adobe Professional X

DD Form 2977 is designed for the entire Army and the other Services. It provides standardization for joint operations and assignments. It may be filled out electronically or free hand. It is the standard way of capturing the information analyzed during the five steps of RM. It helps the user in thinking through the five steps and then sharing the resulting assessment. It is a living document. Pen and pencil changes on hard copies are acceptable and encouraged since changes will occur during operations.

RM is a universal process used for managing risk at every level of effort from the individual to large units or organizations. Its application is blind to the cause of the hazard.

Refer to ATP 5-19, app. A for sample general, notional examples of completed DD Form 2977.

DELIBERATE RISK ASSESSMENT WORKSHEET

Risk Assessment Matrix		Probability *(expected frequency)*				
		Frequent: Continuous, regular, or inevitable occurrences	**Likely:** Several or numerous occurrences	**Occasional:** Sporadic or intermittent occurrences	**Seldom:** Infrequent occurrences	**Unlikely:** Possible occurrences but improbable
Severity *(expected consequence)*		**A**	**B**	**C**	**D**	**E**
Catastrophic: *Death, unacceptable loss or damage, mission failure, or unit readiness eliminated*	I	EH	EH	H	H	M
Critical: *Severe injury, illness, loss, or damage; significantly degraded unit readiness or mission capability*	II	EH	H	H	M	L
Moderate: *Minor injury, illness, loss, or damage; somewhat degraded unit readiness or mission capability*	III	H	M	M	L	L
Negligible: *Minimal injury, loss, or damage; little or no impact to unit readiness or mission capability*	IV	M	L	L	L	L

Legend:
EH – extremely high risk   H – high risk   M – medium risk   L – low risk

13. RISK ASSESSMENT REVIEW *(Required when assessment applies to ongoing operations or activities)*

a. Date	b. Last Name	c. Rank/Grade	d. Duty Title/Position	e. Signature of Reviewer

14. FEEDBACK AND LESSONS LEARNED

15. ADDITIONAL COMMENTS OR REMARKS

DD FORM 2977, JAN 2014

Page ____ of ____ Pages

Risk Management Process

Ref: ATP 5-19 (w/C1), Risk Management (Apr '14), chap. 1.

Risk Management is the process of identifying, assessing, and controlling risks arising from operational factors and making decisions that balance risk cost with mission benefits. (JP 3-0) *The Army no longer uses the term "composite risk management." Term replaced with joint term "risk management."*

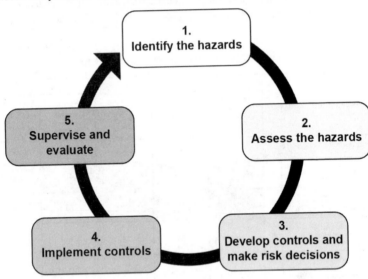

Ref: ATP 5-19, fig. 1-1. A cyclical, continuous process for managing risk.

1. Identify the hazards
A hazard is a condition with the potential to cause injury, illness, or death of personnel; damage to or loss of equipment or property; or mission degradation. Hazards exist in all environments—combat operations, stability operations, base support operations, training, garrison activities, and off-duty activities. The factors of mission, enemy, terrain and weather, troops and support available, time available, and civil considerations (METT-TC) serve as a standard format for identification of hazards, on-duty or off-duty.

2. Assess the hazards
This process is systematic in nature and uses charts, codes and numbers to present a methodology to assess probability and severity to obtain a standardized level of risk. Hazards are assessed and risk is assigned in terms of probability and severity of adverse impact of an event/occurrence.

3. Develop controls and make risk decisions
The process of developing and applying controls and reassessing risk continues until an acceptable level of risk is achieved or until all risks are reduced to a level where benefits outweigh the potential cost.

4. Implement controls
Leaders and staffs ensure that controls are integrated into SOPs, written and verbal orders, mission briefings, and staff estimates.

5. Supervise and evaluate

I. Plans & Orders

Ref: FM 6-0 (C1), Commander and Staff Organization and Operations (May '15), app.C.

Planning is the art and science of understanding a situation, envisioning a desired future, and laying out an operational approach to achieve that future. Based on this understanding and operational approach, planning continues with the development of a fully synchronized operation plan or order that arranges potential actions in time, space, and purpose to guide the force during execution (see ADP 5-0).

A product of planning is a plan or order—a directive for future action. Commanders issue plans and orders to subordinates to communicate their understanding of the situation and their visualization of an operation. Plans and orders direct, coordinate, and synchronize subordinate actions and inform those outside the unit how to coop- erate and provide support.

Prepare the Order or Plan

The staff prepares the order or plan by turning the selected COA into a clear, concise concept of operations and the required supporting information. The COA statement becomes the concept of operations for the plan. The COA sketch becomes the basis for the operation overlay. If time permits, the staff may conduct a more detailed war game of the selected COA to more fully synchronize the operation and complete the plan. The staff writes the OPORD or OPLAN using the Army's operation order format.

See pp. 2-55 to 2-56, step VII of the MDMP, Orders Production.

Normally, the COS (XO) coordinates with staff principals to assist the G-3 (S-3) in de- veloping the plan or order. Based on the commander's planning guidance, the COS (XO) dictates the type of order, sets and enforces the time limits and development sequence, and determines which staff section publishes which attachments.

Prior to the commander approving the plan or order, the staff ensures the plan or order is internally consistent and is nested with the higher commander's intent. They do this through—

- Plans and orders reconciliation
- Plans and orders crosswalk

Verbal Orders

Commanders use verbal orders when operating in an extremely time-constrained environment. These orders offer the advantage of being distributed quickly but risk important information being overlooked or misunderstood. Verbal orders are usually followed by written FRAGORDs.

Written Orders

Commanders issue written plans and orders that contain both text and graphics. Graphics convey information and instructions through military symbols. (FM 1-02 lists approved symbols.) They complement the written portion of a plan or an order and promote clarity, accuracy, and brevity. Staffs often develop and disseminate written orders electronically to shorten the time needed to gather and brief the orders group. Staffs can easily edit and modify electronically produced orders. They can send the same order to multiple recipients simultaneously. Using computer programs to develop and disseminate precise, corresponding graphics adds to the efficiency and clarity of the orders process. Electronic editing makes importing text and graphics into orders easy. Unfortunately, such ease can result in orders becoming unneces- sarily large without added operational value. Commanders need to ensure that orders contain only that information needed to facilitate effective execution. Orders should not regurgitate unit standard operating procedures (SOPs). They should be clear, concise, and relevant to the mission.

I. Guidance for Plans

Planning is the art and science of understanding a situation, envisioning a desired future, and laying out an operational approach to achieve that future. Based on this understanding and operational approach, planning continues with the development of a fully synchronized operation plan or order that arranges potential actions in time, space, and purpose to guide the force during execution (see FM 5-0).

A product of planning is a plan or order—a directive for future action. Commanders issue plans and orders to subordinates to communicate their understanding of the situation and their visualization of an operation. Plans and orders direct, coordinate, and synchronize subordinate actions and inform those outside the unit how to cooperate and provide support. To properly understand and execute the joint commander's plan, Army commanders and staffs must be familiar with joint planning processes, procedures, and orders formats. (Refer to JP 3-33 and JP 5-0.)

Building Simple, Flexible Plans

Simplicity is a principle of war and vital to effective planning. Effective plans and orders are simple and direct. Staffs prepare clear, concise, and complete plans and orders to ensure thorough understanding. They use doctrinally correct operational terms and graphics. Doing this minimizes chances of misunderstanding. Shorter rather than longer plans aid in simplicity. Shorter plans are easier to disseminate, read, and remember.

Complex plans have a greater potential to fail in execution since they often rely on intricate coordination. Operations are always subject to the fog of war and friction. The more detailed the plan, the greater the chances it will no longer be applicable as friendly, enemy, and civilian actions change the situation throughout an operation.

Simple plans require an easily understood concept of operations. Planners also promote simplicity by minimizing details where possible and by limiting the actions or tasks to what the situation requires. Subordinates can then develop specifics within the commander's intent. For example, instead of assigning a direction of attack, planners can designate an axis of advance.

Simple plans are not simplistic plans. Simplistic refers to something made overly simple by ignoring the situation's complexity. Good plans simplify complicated situations. However, some situations require more complex plans than others do. Commanders at all levels weigh the apparent benefits of a complex concept of operations against the risk that subordinates will be unable to understand or follow it adequately. Commanders prefer simple plans that are easy to understand and execute.

Flexible plans help units adapt quickly to changing circumstances. Commanders and planners build opportunities for initiative into plans by anticipating events that allow them to operate inside of the enemy's decision cycle or react promptly to deteriorating situations. Identifying decision points and designing branches ahead of time—combined with a clear commander's intent—help create flexible plans. Incorporating control measures to reduce risk also makes plans more flexible. For example, a commander may hold a large, mobile reserve to compensate for the lack of information concerning an anticipated enemy attack.

II. Mission Orders

Ref: FM 6-0 (C1), Commander and Staff Organization and Operations (May '15), p. C-2.

Commanders stress the importance of mission orders as a way of building simple, flexible plans. Mission orders are directives that emphasize to subordinates the results to be attained, not how they are to achieve them (ADP 6-0). Mission orders focus on what to do and the purpose of doing it without prescribing exactly how to do it. Commanders establish control measures to aid cooperation among forces without imposing needless restrictions on freedom of action. Mission orders contribute to flexibility by allowing subordinates the freedom to seize opportunities or react effectively to unforeseen enemy actions and capabilities.

Mission orders follow the five-paragraph format (situation, mission, execution, sustainment, and command and signal) and are as brief and simple as possible. Mission orders clearly convey the unit's mission and commander's intent. They summarize the situation (current or anticipated starting conditions), describe the operation's objectives and end state (desired conditions), and provide a simple concept of operations to accomplish the unit's mission. When assigning tasks to subordinate units, mission orders include all components of a task statement: who, what, when, where, and why. However, commanders particularly emphasize the purpose (why) of the tasks to guide (along with the commander's intent) individual initiative. Effective plans and orders foster mission command by:

- Describing the situation to create a common situational understanding
- Conveying the commander's intent and concept of operations
- Assigning tasks to subordinate units and stating the purpose for conducting the task
- Providing the control measures necessary to synchronize the operation while retaining the maximum freedom of action for subordinates
- Task-organizing forces and allocating resources
- Directing preparation activities and establishing times or conditions for execution

Mission orders contain the proper level of detail; they are neither so detailed that they stifle initiative nor so general that they provide insufficient direction. The proper level depends on each situation and is not easy to determine. Some phases of operations require tighter control over subordinate elements than others require. An air assault's air movement and landing phases, for example, require precise synchronization. Its ground maneuver plan requires less detail. As a rule, the base plan or order contains only the specific information required to provide the guidance to synchronize combat power at the decisive time and place while allowing subordinates as much freedom of action as possible. Commanders rely on individual initiative and coordination to act within the commander's intent and concept of operations. The attachments to the plan or order contain details regarding the situation and instructions necessary for synchronization.

III. Types of Plans and Orders

Ref: FM 6-0 (C1), Commander and Staff Organization and Operations (May '15), pp. C-3 to C-4.

Plans

Plans come in many forms and vary in scope, complexity, and length of planning horizons. Strategic plans establish national and multinational military objectives and include ways to achieve those objectives. Operational-level or campaign plans cover a series of related military operations aimed at accomplishing a strategic or operational objective within a given time and space. Tactical plans cover the employment of units in operations, including the ordered arrangement and maneuver of units in relation to each other and to the enemy within the framework of an operational-level or campaign plan. There are several types of plans:

1. Campaign Plan

A campaign plan is a joint operation plan for a series of related major operations aimed at achieving strategic or operational objectives within a given time and space (JP 5-0). Developing and issuing a campaign plan is appropriate when the contemplated simultaneous or sequential military operations exceed the scope of a single major operation. Only joint force commanders develop campaign plans.

2. Operation Plan (OPLAN)

An operation plan is 1. Any plan for the conduct of military operations prepared in response to actual and potential contingencies. 2. A complete and detailed joint plan containing a full description of the concept of operations, all annexes applicable to the plan, and a time-phased force and deployment data. (JP 5-0). An OPLAN may address an extended period connecting a series of objectives and operations, or it may be developed for a single part or phase of a long-term operation. An OPLAN becomes an operation order when the commander sets an execution time or designates an event that triggers the operation.

3. Supporting Plan

A supporting plan is an operation plan prepared by a supporting commander, a subordinate commander, or an agency to satisfy the requests or requirements of the supported commander's plan (JP 5-0). For example, the ARFOR commander develops a supporting plan as to how Army forces will support the joint force commander's campaign plan or OPLAN.

4. Concept Plan

In the context of joint operation planning level 3 planning detail, a concept plan is an operation plan in an abbreviated format that may require considerable expansion or alteration to convert it into a complete operation plan or operation order (JP 5-0). Often branches and sequels are written as concept plans. As time and the potential allow for executing a particular branch or sequel, these concept plans are developed in detail into OPLANs.

5. Branch

A branch describes the contingency options built into the base plan. A branch is used for changing the mission, orientation, or direction of movement of a force to aid success of the operation based on anticipated events, opportunities, or disruptions caused by enemy actions and reactions. Branches are also used in stability operations to address potential actions and reactions of populations.

6. Sequel

A sequel is the subsequent major operation or phase based on the possible outcomes (success, stalemate, or defeat) of the current major operation or phase (JP 5-0). For every action or major operation that does not accomplish a strategic or operational objective, there should be a sequel for each possible outcome, such as win, lose, draw, or decisive win.

Orders

An order is a communication—verbal, written, or signaled—which conveys instructions from a superior to a subordinate. Commanders issue orders verbally or in writing. The five-paragraph format (situation, mission, execution, sustainment, and command and signal) remains the standard for issuing orders. The technique used to issue orders (verbal or written) is at the discretion of the commander; each technique depends on time and the situation. Army organizations use three types of orders:

1. Operation Order (OPORD)

An operation order is a directive issued by a commander to subordinate commanders for the purpose of effecting the coordinated execution of an operation (JP 5-0). Commanders issue OPORDs to direct the execution of long-term operations as well as the execution of discrete short-term operations within the framework of a long-range OPORD.

See pp. 4-22 to 4-27 for a sample format.

2. Fragmentary Order (FRAGORD)

A fragmentary order is an abbreviated form of an operation order issued as needed after an operation order to change or modify that order or to execute a branch or sequel to that order (JP 5-0). FRAGORDs include all five OPORD paragraph headings and differ from OPORDs only in the degree of detail provided. An example of the proper naming convention for a FRAGORD to an OPORD is "FRAGORD 11 to OPORD 3411 (OPERATION DESERT DRAGON) (UNCLASSIFIED)." If a FRAGORD contains an entire annex, then the proper naming convention for the annex would be "Annex A (Task Organization) to FRAGORD 12 to OPORD 3411 (OPERATION DESERT DRAGON) (UNCLASSIFIED)."

See p. 4-32 for a sample format.

3. Warning Order (WARNORD)

A warning order is a preliminary notice of an order or action that is to follow (JP 3-33). WARNOs help subordinate units and staffs prepare for new missions by describing the situation, providing initial planning guidance, and directing preparation activities. For example, the proper naming convention for WARNORD number 8 is "WARNORD #8."

See p. 4-21 for a sample format.

In addition to these types of orders, Army forces may receive the following types of orders from a joint headquarters:

- Planning order
- Alert order
- Execute order
- Prepare-to-deploy order

Joint Planning Processes, Procedures and Orders

To properly understand and execute the joint commander's plan, Army commanders and staffs must be familiar with joint planning processes, procedures, and orders formats. An Army headquarters that forms the base of a joint task force uses the joint operation planning process and publishes plans and orders in accordance with the joint format. An Army HQs that provides the base of a joint force or coalition forces land component command headquarters will participate in joint planning and receive a joint formatted plan or order. This headquarters then has the option to use the MDMP or joint operations planning process to develop its own supporting plan or order. Refer to the Joint Forces Operations & Doctrine SMARTbook.

IV. Characteristics of Plans and Orders

The amount of detail provided in a plan or order depends on several factors, including the cohesion and experience of subordinate units and complexity of the operation. Effective plans and orders encourage subordinates' initiative by providing the "what" and "why" of tasks to subordinate units; they leave how to perform the tasks to subordinates. To maintain clarity and simplicity, planners keep the base plan or order as short and concise as possible. They address detailed information and instructions in attachments as required.

Effective plans and orders are simple and direct to reduce misunderstanding and confusion. The situation determines the degree of simplicity required. Simple plans executed on time are better than detailed plans executed late. Commanders at all echelons weigh potential benefits of a complex concept of operations against the risk that subordinates will fail to understand it. Multinational operations mandate simplicity due to the differences in language, doctrine, and culture. The same applies to operations involving interagency and nongovernmental organizations.

Effective plans and orders reflect authoritative and positive expression through the commander's intent. As such, the language is direct and affirmative. An example of this is, "The combat trains will remain in the assembly area" instead of "The combat trains will not accompany the unit." Effective plans and orders directly and positively state what the commander wants the unit and its subordinate units to do and why.

Effective plans and orders avoid meaningless expressions, such as "as soon as possible." Indecisive, vague, and ambiguous language leads to uncertainty and lack of confidence.

Effective plans and orders possess brevity and clarity. These plans use short words, sentences, and paragraphs. Plans use acronyms unless clarity is hindered. They do not include material covered in SOPs, but refer to those SOPs instead. Brief and clear orders use doctrinally correct terms and symbols, avoid jargon, and eliminate every opportunity for misunderstanding the commander's exact, intended meaning.

Effective plans and orders contain assumptions. This helps subordinates and others better understand the logic behind a plan or order and facilitates the preparation of branches and sequels.

Effective plans and orders incorporate flexibility. There is room built into the plan to adapt and make adjustments to counter unexpected challenges and seize opportunities. Effective plans and orders identify decision points and proposed options at those decision points to build flexibility.

Effective plans and orders exercise timeliness. Plans and orders sent to subordinates promptly allow subordinates to collaborate, plan, and prepare their own actions.

II. Task Organization (Annex A)

Ref: FM 6-0 (C1), Commander and Staff Organization and Operations (May '15), app. D.

This section discusses the fundamentals of task organization and provides the format and instructions for developing Annex A (Task Organization) to the base plan or order. This annex does not follow the five-paragraph attachment format. Unit standard operating procedures (SOPs) will dictate development and format for this annex.

Task-organizing is the act of designing an operating force, support staff, or sustainment package of specific size and composition to meet a unique task or mission (ADRP 3-0). Characteristics to examine when task-organizing the force include, but are not limited to, training, experience, equipment, sustainability, operational environment, (including enemy threat), and mobility. For Army forces, it includes allocating available assets to subordinate commanders and establishing their command and support relationships. Command and support relationships provide the basis for unity of command in operations. The assistant chief of staff, plans (G-5) or assistant chief of staff, operations (G-3 [S-3]) develops Annex A (Task Organization).

I. Fundamental Considerations

Military units consist of organic components. Organic parts of a unit are those forming an essential part of the unit and are listed in its table of organization and equipment (TOE). Commanders can alter organizations' organic unit relationships to better allocate assets to subordinate commanders. They also can establish temporary command and support relationships to facilitate exercising mission command.

Establishing clear command and support relationships is fundamental to organizing any operation. These relationships establish clear responsibilities and authorities between subordinate and supporting units. Some command and support relationships (for example, tactical control) limit the commander's authority to prescribe additional relationships. Knowing the inherent responsibilities of each command and support relationship allows commanders to effectively organize their forces and helps supporting commanders to understand their unit's role in the organizational structure.

Commanders designate command and support relationships to weight the decisive operation and support the concept of operations. Task organization also helps subordinate and supporting commanders support the commander's intent. These relationships carry with them varying responsibilities to the subordinate unit by the parent and gaining units. Commanders consider two organizational principles when task-organizing forces:

1. **When possible, commanders maintain cohesive mission teams.** They organize forces based on standing headquarters, their assigned forces, and habitual associations when possible. When not feasible and ad hoc organizations are created, commanders arrange time for training and establishing functional working relationships and procedures. Once commanders have organized and committed a force, they keep its task organization unless the benefits of a change clearly outweigh the disadvantages.

2. **Commanders carefully avoid exceeding the span of control capabilities of subordinates.** Span of control refers to the number of subordinate units under a single commander. This number is situation dependent and may vary. As a rule, commanders can effectively command two to six subordinate units. Allocating subordinate commanders more units gives them greater flexibility and increases options and combinations. However, increasing the number of subordinate units increases the number of decisions for commanders to make in a timely fashion. This slows down the reaction time among decisionmakers.

Running Estimates and Course of Action (COA) Analysis

Running estimates and course of action (COA) analysis of the military decisionmaking process provide information that helps commanders determine the best task organization. An effective task organization:

- Facilitates the commander's intent and concept of operations
- Retains flexibility within the concept of operations
- Adapts to conditions imposed by mission variables
- Accounts for the requirements to conduct essential stability tasks for populations within an area of operations
- Creates effective combined arms teams
- Provides mutual support among units
- Ensures flexibility to meet unforeseen events and to support future operations
- Allocates resources with minimum restrictions on their employment
- Promotes unity of command
- Offsets limitations and maximizes the potential of all forces available
- Exploits enemy vulnerabilities

Creating an appropriate task organization requires understanding:

- The mission, including the higher commander's intent and concept of operations
- The fundamentals of offense, defense, stability, and defense support of civil authorities tasks (ADRP 3-0) and basic tactical concepts (ADRP 3-90)
- The roles and relationships among the warfighting functions
- The status of available forces, including morale, training, and equipment capabilities
- Specific unit capabilities, limitations, strengths, and weaknesses
- The risks inherent in the plan

During COA analysis, commanders identify what resources they need, and where, when, and how frequently they will need them. Formal task organization and the change from generic to specific units begin after COA analysis when commanders assign tasks to subordinate commanders. The staffs assign tasks to subordinate headquarters and determine if subordinate headquarters have enough combat power, reallocating combat power as necessary. They then refine command and support relationships for subordinate units and decide the priorities of support. Commanders approve or modify the staff's recommended task organization based on their evaluation of the factors and information from running estimates and COA analysis.

In allocating assets, the commander and staff consider the:

- Task organization for the ongoing operation
- Potential adverse effects of breaking up cohesive teams by changing the task organization
- Time necessary to realign the organization after receipt of the task organization
- Limits on control over supporting units provided by higher headquarters

II. Army Command and Support Relationships

Ref: FM 6-0 (C1), Commander and Staff Organization and Operations (May '15), app. B.

Establishing clear command and support relationships is a key task in task organizing for any operation. (See ADRP 5-0.) These relationships establish clear responsibilities and authorities between subordinate and supporting units. Some command and support relationships limit the commander's authority to prescribe additional relationships.

Army commanders build combined arms organizations using command and support relationships.

- **Command relationships** define command responsibility and authority.
- **Support relationships** define the desired purpose, scope, and effect when one capability supports another.

Refer to The Joint Forces Operations & Doctrine SMARTbook and/or JP1 for discussion of the four types of joint command relationships (combatant command, operational control, tactical control, and support).

Army Command Relationships

Command relationships define superior and subordinate relationships between unit commanders. By specifying a chain of command, command relationships unify effort and enable commanders to use subordinate forces with maximum flexibility. Army command relationships identify the degree of control of the gaining Army commander. The type of command relationship often relates to the expected longevity of the relationship between the headquarters involved and quickly identifies the degree of support that the gaining and losing Army commanders provide. Army command relationships include:

See table B-1 on the following pages for Army command relationships.

Organic. Organic forces are those assigned to and forming an essential part of a military organization as listed in its table of organization for the Army, Air Force, and Marine Corps, and are assigned to the operating forces for the Navy (JP 1). Joint command relationships do not include organic because a joint force commander is not responsible for the organizational structure of units. That is a Service responsibility. The Army establishes organic command relationships through organizational documents such as tables of organization and equipment and tables of distribution and allowances. If temporarily task-organized with another headquarters, organic units return to the control of their organic headquarters after completing the mission.

Assigned. Assign is to place units or personnel in an organization where such placement is relatively permanent, and/or where such organization controls and administers the units or personnel for the primary function, or greater portion of the functions, of the unit or personnel (JP 3-0). Unless specifically stated, this relationship includes administrative control.

Attached. Attach is the placement of units or personnel in an organization where such placement is relatively temporary (JP 3-0). A unit that is temporarily placed into an organization is attached.

Operational Control. Operational control is the authority to perform those functions of command over subordinate forces involving organizing and employing commands and forces, assigning tasks, designating objectives, and giving authoritative direction necessary to accomplish the mission (JP 1).

Tactical Control. Tactical control is the authority over forces that is limited to the detailed direction and control of movements or maneuvers within the operational area necessary to accomplish missions or tasks assigned (JP 1). Tactical control allows commanders below combatant command level to apply force and direct tactical use of logistic assets but does not provide authority to change organizational structure or direct administrative and logistical support.

Army Command & Support Relationships

Ref: FM 6-0 (C1), Commander and Staff Organization and Operations (May '15), app. B.

Army command and support relationships are similar but not identical to joint command authorities and relationships. Differences stem from the way Army forces task-organize internally and the need for a system of support relationships between Army forces. Another important difference is the requirement for Army commanders to handle the administrative support requirements that meet the needs of Soldiers

A. Command Relationships

Army command relationships define superior and subordinate relationships between unit commanders. By specifying a chain of command, command relationships unify effort and enable commanders to use subordinate forces with maximum flexibility. Army command relationships identify the degree of control of the gaining Army commander. The type of command relationship often relates to the expected longevity of the relationship between the headquarters involved and quickly identifies the degree of support that the gaining and losing Army commanders provide.

If relation-ship is:	Then inherent responsibilities:							
	Have command relation-ship with:	May be task-organized by: [1]	Unless modified, ADCON have responsi-bility through:	Are assigned position or AO by:	Provide liaison to:	Establish/maintain communi-cations with:	Have priorities establish-ed by:	Can impose on gaining unit further command or support relationship of:
Organic	All organic forces organized with the HQ	Organic HQ	Army HQ specified in organizing document	Organic HQ	N/A	N/A	Organic HQ	Attached; OPCON; TACON; GS; GSR; R; DS
Assigned	Combatant command	Gaining HQ	Gaining Army HQ	OPCON chain of command	As required by OPCON	As required by OPCON	ASCC or Service-assigned HQ	As required by OPCON HQ
Attached	Gaining unit	Gaining unit	Gaining Army HQ	Gaining unit	As required by gaining unit	Unit to which attached	Gaining unit	Attached; OPCON; TACON; GS; GSR; R; DS
OPCON	Gaining unit	Parent unit and gaining unit; gaining unit may pass OPCON to lower HQ[1]	Parent unit	Gaining unit	As required by gaining unit	As required by gaining unit and parent unit	Gaining unit	OPCON; TACON; GS; GSR; R; DS
TACON	Gaining unit	Parent unit	Parent unit	Gaining unit	As required by gaining unit	As required by gaining unit and parent unit	Gaining unit	TACON; GS GSR; R; DS

Note: [1] In NATO, the gaining unit may not task-organize a multinational force. (See TACON.)

ADCON	administrative control	HQ	headquarters
AO	area of operations	N/A	not applicable
ASCC	Army Service component command	NATO	North Atlantic Treaty Organization
DS	direct support	OPCON	operational control
GS	general support	R	reinforcing
GSR	general support–reinforcing	TACON	tactical control

Ref: FM 6-0 (C1), Commander and Staff Organization and Operations, table B-2, p. B-5.

B. Support Relationships

Table B-3 on the following page lists Army support relationships. Army support relationships are not a command authority and are more specific than the joint support relationships. Commanders establish support relationships when subordination of one unit to another is inappropriate. Commanders assign a support relationship when—

- The support is more effective if a commander with the requisite technical and tactical expertise controls the supporting unit, rather than the supported commander. The echelon of the supporting unit is the same as or higher than that of the supported unit. For example, the supporting unit may be a brigade, and the supported unit may be a battalion. It would be inappropriate for the brigade to be subordinated to the battalion, hence the use of an support relationship.
- The supporting unit supports several units simultaneously. The requirement to set support priorities to allocate resources to supported units exists. Assigning support relationships is one aspect of mission command.

If relation-ship is:	Then inherent responsibilities:							
	Have command relation-ship with:	May be task-organized by:	Receive sustain-ment from:	Are assigned position or an area of operations by:	Provide liaison to:	Establish/ maintain communi-cations with:	Have priorities established by:	Can impose on gaining unit further command or support relation-ship by:
Direct support[1]	Parent unit	Parent unit	Parent unit	Supported unit	Supported unit	Parent unit; supported unit	Supported unit	See note[1]
Reinforc-ing	Parent unit	Parent unit	Parent unit	Reinforced unit	Reinforced unit	Parent unit; reinforced unit	Reinforced unit; then parent unit	Not applicable
General support– reinforc-ing	Parent unit	Parent unit	Parent unit	Parent unit	Reinforced unit and as required by parent unit	Reinforced unit and as required by parent unit	Parent unit; then reinforced unit	Not applicable
General support	Parent unit	Parent unit	Parent unit	Parent unit	As required by parent unit	As required by parent unit	Parent unit	Not applicable

Note: [1] Commanders of units in direct support may further assign support relationships between their subordinate units and elements of the supported unit after coordination with the supported commander.

Ref: FM 6-0 (C1), Commander and Staff Organization and Operations, table B-3, p. B-6.

Army support relationships allow supporting commanders to employ their units' capabilities to achieve results required by supported commanders. Support relationships are graduated from an exclusive supported and supporting relationship between two units—as in direct support—to a broad level of support extended to all units under the control of the higher headquarters—as in general support. Support relationships do not alter administrative control. Commanders specify and change support relationships through task organization.

Direct support is a support relationship requiring a force to support another specific force and authorizing it to answer directly to the supported force's request for assistance (ADRP 5-0). A unit assigned a direct support relationship retains its command relationship with its parent unit, but is positioned by and has priorities of support established by the supported unit.

General support is that support which is given to the supported force as a whole and not to any particular subdivision thereof (JP 3-09.3). Units assigned a GS relationship are positioned and have priorities established by their parent unit.

Reinforcing is a support relationship requiring a force to support another supporting unit (ADRP 5-0). Only like units (for example, artillery to artillery) can be given a reinforcing mission. A unit assigned a reinforcing support relationship retains its command relationship with its parent unit, but is positioned by the reinforced unit. A unit that is reinforcing has priorities of support established by the reinforced unit, then the parent unit.

General support-reinforcing is a support relationship assigned to a unit to support the force as a whole and to reinforce another similar-type unit (ADRP 5-0). A unit assigned a general support-reinforcing (GSR) support relationship is positioned and has priorities established by its parent unit and secondly by the reinforced unit.

III. Unit Listing Sequence

Ref: FM 6-0 (C1), Commander and Staff Organization and Operations (May '15), pp. D-3 to D-6.

Order writers group units by headquarters. They list major subordinate maneuver units first (for example, 2d ABCT; 1-77th IN; A/4-52d CAV). Order writers place them by size in numerical order. They list brigade combat teams (BCTs) ahead of combat aviation brigades. In cases where two BCTs are numbered the same, order writers use the division number (by type). For example, 1st ABCT (armored brigade combat team) 1st Infantry Division (Mechanized) is listed before the 1st ABCT 1st Armored Division (AD). In turn, the 1st ABCT 1st Armored Division is listed before the 1st ABCT 1st Cavalry Division. Combined arms battalions are listed before battalions, and company teams before companies. Order writers follow maneuver units with multifunctional supporting units in the following order: fires, battlefield surveillance, maneuver enhancement, and sustainment. Supporting units (in alpha-numerical order) follow multifunctional supporting units. The last listing should be any special troops units under the command of the force headquarters.

Order writers use a plus (+) symbol when attaching one or more subordinate elements of a similar function to a headquarters. They use a minus symbol (–) when deleting one or more subordinate elements of a similar function to a headquarters. Order writers always show the symbols in parenthesis. They do not use a plus symbol when the receiving headquarters is a combined arms task force or company team. Order writers do not use plus and minus symbols together (as when a headquarters detaches one element and receives attachment of another); they use the symbol that portrays the element's combat power with respect to other similar elements. Order writers do not use either symbol when two units swap subordinate elements and their combat power is unchanged.

If applicable, order writers list task organizations according to phases of the operation. When the effective attachment time of a nonorganic unit to another unit differs from the effective time of the plan or order, order writers add the effective attachment time in parentheses after the attached unit—for example, 1-80 IN (OPCON 2 ABCT Phase II). They list this information either in the task organization (preferred) or in paragraph 1c of the plan or order, but not both. For clarity, order writers list subsequent command or support relationships under the task organization in parentheses following the affected unit—for example, "...on order, OPCON (operational control) to 2 ABCT" is written (O/O OPCON 2 ABCT).

Long or complex task organizations are displayed in outline format in Annex A (Task Organization) of the OPLAN or OPORD in lieu of being placed in the base plan or order. Units are listed under the headquarters to which they are allocated or that they support in accordance with the organizational taxonomy previously provided in this chapter. The complete unit task organization for each major subordinate unit should be shown on the same page. Order writers only show command or support relationships if they are other than organic or attached. Other Services and multinational forces recognize and understand this format. Planners should use it during joint and multinational operations.

Order writers list subordinate units under the higher headquarters to which they are assigned, attached, or in support. They place direct support (DS) units below the units they support. Order writers indent subordinate and supporting units two spaces. They identify relationships other than attached with parenthetical terms—for example, (GS) or (DS).

Order writers provide the numerical designations of units as Arabic numerals, unless they are shown as Roman numerals. For example, an Army corps is numbered in series beginning with Roman numeral "I"—for example, I Corps or XVIII Airborne Corps.

During multinational operations, order writers insert the country code between the numeric designation and the unit name—for example, 3d (DE) Corps. (Here, DE designates that the corps is German. ADRP 1-02 contains authorized country codes.)

Order writers use abbreviated designations for organic units. They use the full designation for nonorganic units—for example, 1-52 FA (MLRS) (GS), rather than 1-52 FA. They specify a unit's command or support relationship only if it differs from that of its higher headquarters.

Order writers designate task forces with the last name of the task force (TF) commander (for example, TF WILLIAMS), a code name (for example, TF DESERT DRAGON), or a number.

For unit designation at theater army level, order writers list major subordinate maneuver units first, placing them in alpha-numerical order, followed by multifunctional brigades in the following order: fires, intelligence, maneuver enhancement, sustainment, then followed by functional brigades in alpha-numerical order, and any units under the command of the force headquarters. For each function following maneuver, they list headquarters in the order of commands, brigades, groups, battalions, squadrons, companies, detachments, and teams.

	Corps	Division	Brigade	Battalion	Company
Movement and Maneuver	Divisions Separate maneuver brigades or battalions Combat aviation brigades or battalions Special operations forces - Ranger - Special forces MISO	Brigade-size ground units in alpha-numerical order - Infantry - Armor - Stryker Battalion TF - Named TFs in alphabetical order - Numbered TFs in numerical order MISO Combat aviation brigade Special operations forces - Ranger - Special forces	Battalion TFs Battalions or squadrons - Combined arms - Infantry - Reconnaissance Company teams Companies Air cavalry squadrons MISO	Company teams - Named teams in alphabetical order - Letter designated teams in alphabetical order Companies or troops (in alphabetical order) - Infantry - Armor - Stryker MISO	Platoons - Organic platoons - Attached platoons - Weapons squads
Fires	Fires brigade USAF air support unit - Air defense	Fires brigade USAF air support unit - Air defense	Fires battalion USAF air support unit - Air defense	FA batteries Fire support team Mortar platoon USAF air support unit - Air defense	FA firing platoons Fire support team Mortar section - Air defense
Intelligence	Battlefield surveillance brigade - MI - Recon squads - Human terrain team	Battlefield surveillance brigade - MI - Recon squads - Human terrain team	CI teams Ground sensor teams Human terrain team HUMINT teams Scout platoon TUAS platoon	CI teams Ground sensor teams HUMINT teams Scout platoon TUAS platoon	CI teams Ground sensor teams HUMINT teams
Protection	MEB Functional brigades - Air defense - CBRN - Engineer - EOD - Military police	MEB Functional brigades - Air defense - CBRN - Engineer - EOD - Military police	Functional battalions or companies or batteries and detachments - Air defense - CBRN - Engineer - EOD - Military police	Functional companies or batteries and detachments - Air defense - CBRN - Engineer - EOD - Military police	Functional platoons and detachments - Air defense - CBRN - Engineer - EOD - Military police
Sustainment	Sustainment brigade (attached functional units are listed in alpha-numerical order) - Contracting - Finance - Ordnance - Personnel services - Transportation - Quartermaster Medical brigade (support)	Sustainment brigade (attached functional units are listed in alpha-numerical order) - Contracting - Finance - Ordnance - Personnel services - Transportation - Quartermaster Medical brigade (support)	Brigade support battalion (attached or supporting functional units are listed first by branch in alphabetical order and then in numerical order)	Forward support company (attached or supporting functional units are listed first by branch in alphabetical order and then in numerical order)	Attached or supporting functional platoons and teams listed in alpha-numerical order

Ref: FM 6-0 (C1), Commander and Staff Organization and Operations (May '15), table D-1, pp. D-3 to D-4.

Plans & Orders

IV. Outline Format (Sample)

Ref: FM 6-0 (C1), Commander and Staff Organization and Operations (May '15), pp. D-8 to D-9.

Use the outline format for listing units as shown in the example below. (An acronym list is helpful if attached units are unfamiliar with Army acronyms.) If applicable, list task organization according to the phases of the operation during which it applies.

[CLASSIFICATION]
ANNEX A (TASK ORGANIZATION) TO OPERATION PLAN/ORDER [number] [(code name)]—[issuing headquarters] [(classification of title)]
(sample task organization)

2/52 ABCT	2/54 ABCT	116 ABCT (+)
1-31 IN (-)	4-77 IN	3-116 AR
1-30 AR (-)	8-40 AR	1-163 IN
1-20 CAV	3-20 CAV	2-116 AR
A/4-52 CAV (ARS) (DS)	2/C/4-52 CAV (ARS) (DS)	1-148 FA
2-606 FA (2x8)	2-607 FA	145 BSB
TACP/52 ASOS (USAF)	TACP/52 ASOS (USAF)	4/B/2-52 AV (GSAB) (TACON)
521 BSB	105 BSB	4/2/311 QM CO (MA)
2/2/311 QM CO (MA)	3/2/311 QM CO (MA)	4/577 MED CO (GRD AMB)
1/B/2-52 AV (GSAB) (TACON)	2/B/2-52 AV (GSAB) (TACON)	844 FST
2/577 MED CO (GRD AMB)	843 FST	116 BSTB
(attached)	3/577 MED CO (GRD AMB)	366 EN CO (SAPPER) (DS)
842 FST	3 BSTB	1/401 EN CO (ESC) (DS)
2 BSTB	A 388 CA BN	2/244 EN CO (RTE CL) (DS)
31 EN CO (MRBC) (DS)	1/244 EN CO (RTE CL) (DS)	52 EOD
63 EOD	763 EOD	1/301 MP CO
2/244 EN CO (RTE CL) (DS)	2/2/1/55 SIG CO (COMCAM)	1/3/1/55 SIG CO (COMCAM)
1/2/1/55 SIG CO (COMCAM)	3D MP PLT	1/467 CM CO (MX) (S)
2D MP PLT	52 CAB AASLT	C/388 CA BN
RTS TM 1/A/52 BSTB	HHC/52 CAB	116 MP PLT
RTS TM 2/A/52 BSTB	1/B/1-31 IN (DIV QRF) (OPCON)	52 SUST BDE
RTS TM 3/A/52 BSTB	1-52 AV (ARB) (-)	52 BTB
RTS TM	4-52 CAV (ARS) (-)	520 CSSB
87 IBCT	3-52 AV (ASLT) (-)	521 CSSB
1-80 IN	2-52 AV (GSAB)	10 CSH
2-80 IN	1 (TUAS)/B/52 BSTB (-) (GS)	168 MMB
3-13 CAV	2/694 EN CO (HORIZ) (DS)	
A/3-52 AV (ASLT) (DS)		52 HHB
B/1-52 AV (ARB) (DS)	52 FIRES BDE	A/1-30 AR (DIV RES)
C/4-52 CAV (ARS) (-) (DS)	HHB	35 SIG CO (-) (DS)
2-636 FA	TAB (-)	154 LTF
A/3-52 FA (+)	1-52 FA (MLRS)	2/1/55 SIG CO (-)
TACP/52 ASOS (USAF)	3-52 FA (-) (M109A6)	14 PAD
Q37 52 FA BDE (GS)	1/694 EN CO (HORIZ) (DS)	388 CA BN (-) (DS)
99 BSB		
845 FST	17 MEB 52 ID	
1/577 MED CO (GRD AMB)	25 CM BN (-)	
3/B/2-52 AV (GSAB) (TACON)	700 MP BN	
1/2/311 QM CO (MA)	7 EN BN	
87 BSTB	2/2/1/55 SIG CO (COMCAM)	
53 EOD	11 ASOS (USAF)	
3/2/1/55 SIG CO (COMCAM)		
B/420 CA BN		
2 HCT/3/B/52 BSTB		
745 EN CO (MAC) (DS)		
1/1/52 CM CO (R/D) (R)		
2/467 CM CO (MX) (S)		
1/1102 MP CO (DS)		
4/A/52 BSTB		

[page number]
[CLASSIFICATION]

Ref: FM 6-0 (C1), Commander and Staff Organization and Operations, fig. D-1, p. D-8.

III. Administrative Instructions & Examples

Ref: FM 6-0 (C1), Commander and Staff Organization and Operations (May '15), pp. C-5 to C-10.

I. Administrative Instructions

The following information pertains to administrative instructions for preparing all plans and orders. Unless otherwise stated, the term order refers to both plans and orders. The term base order refers to the main body of a plan or order without annexes.

Regardless of echelon, all orders adhere to the same guidance. Show all paragraph headings on written orders. A paragraph heading with no text will state "None" or "See [attachment type] [attachment letter or number]." In this context, attachment is a collective term for annex, appendix, tab, and exhibit.

The base order and all attachments follow a specific template for the paragraph layout. The paragraph title begins with a capital letter and is underlined. For example, "situation" is <u>Situation</u>. All subparagraphs and subtitles begin with capital letters and are underlined. For example, "concept of operations" is <u>Concept of Operations</u>.

When a paragraph is subdivided, it must have at least two subdivisions. The tabs are 0.25 inches and the space is doubled between paragraphs. Subsequent lines of text for each paragraph may be flush left or equally indented at the option of the chief of staff or executive officer, as long as consistency is maintained throughout the order.

A. Acronyms and Abbreviations

Order writers use acronyms and abbreviations to save time and space, if these acronyms and abbreviations do not cause confusion. However, order writers do not sacrifice clarity for brevity. Order writers keep acronyms and abbreviations consistent throughout the order and its attachments. They do not use acronyms and abbreviations not found in ADRP 1-02 or JP 1-02. Before using an entire acronym or abbreviation, at its first use in the document order writers use the full form of the term and then place the acronym or abbreviation between parentheses immediately after the term. After this first use, they use the acronym or abbreviation throughout the document.

B. Digital Display and Common Access to Information

To ensure standardization and the ability to understand the common operational picture (COP), commanders must designate the standardized system to display, access, and share information. Commanders also designate which COP the command will use to gain shared understanding.

B. Place and Direction Designations

Order writers describe locations or points on the ground by:
- Providing the map datum used throughout the order
- Referring to military grid reference system coordinates.
- Referring to longitude and latitude, if available maps do not have the military grid reference system.

Order writers designate directions in one of two ways:
- As a point of the compass. For example, north or northeast
- As a magnetic, grid, or true bearing, stating the unit of measure. For example, 85 degrees (magnetic)

When first mentioning a place or feature on a map, order writers print the name in capital letters exactly as spelled on the map and show its complete grid coordinates (grid zone designator, 100-kilometer grid square, and four-, six-, eight-, or ten-digit grid coordinates) in parentheses after it. When first using a control measure (such as a contact point), order writers print the name or designation of the point followed by its complete grid coordinates in parentheses. Thereafter, they repeat the coordinates only for clarity.

Order writers describe areas by naming the northernmost (12 o'clock) point first and the remaining points in clockwise order. They describe positions from left to right and from front to rear, facing the enemy. To avoid confusion, order writers identify flanks by compass directions, rather than right or left of the friendly force.

If the possibility of confusion exists when describing a route, order writers add a compass direction for clarity (for example, "The route is northwest along the road LAPRAIRIE–DELSON."). If a particular route already has a planning name, such as main supply route SPARTAN, order writers refer to the route using only that designator.

Order writers designate trails, roads, and railroads by the names of places along them or with grid coordinates. They precede place names with a trail, road, or railroad (for example, "road GRANT– CODY"). Order writers designate the route for a movement by listing a sequence of grids from the start point to the release point. Otherwise, they list the sequence of points from left to right or front to rear, facing the enemy.

Order writers identify riverbanks as north, south, east, or west. In wet gap-crossing operations, they identify riverbanks as either near or far.

C. Naming Conventions

Unit SOPs normally designate naming conventions for graphics. Otherwise, planners select them. For clarity, avoid multiword names, such as "Junction City." Simple names are better than complex ones. To ensure operations security, avoid assigning names that could reveal unit identities, such as the commander's name or the unit's home station. Do not name sequential phase lines and objectives in alphabetical order. For memory aids, use sets of names designated by the type of control measure or subordinate unit. For example, the division might use colors for objective names and minerals for phase line names.

D. Classification Markings

AR 380-5 contains a detailed description of marking techniques, transmitting procedures, and other classification instructions. Each page and portions of the text on that page will be marked with the appropriate abbreviation ("TS" for TOP SECRET, "S" for SECRET, "C" for CONFIDENTIAL, or "U for UNCLASSIFIED). Place classification markings at the top and bottom of each page. All paragraphs must have the appropriate classification marking immediately following the alphanumeric designation of the paragraph (preceding the first word if the paragraph is not numbered).

The abbreviation "FOUO" will be used in place of "U" when a portion is UNCLASSIFIED but contains "For Official Use Only" information. AR 25-55 contains the definition and policy application of FOUO markings.

Leaders may have to handle Department of State information. Sensitive But Unclassified (SBU) information is information originating from within the Department of State.

The Army continues its involvement in numerous multinational commitments and operations. This involves an understanding of how commanders may release to or withhold information from select unified action partners. Intelligence information previously marked "Not Releasable To Foreign Nationals" (NOFORN) continues to be non-releasable to foreigners and must be referred to the originator. NOFORN is not authorized for new classification decisions. A limited amount of information will contain the marking "U.S. ONLY". This information cannot be shared with any foreign government.

E. Expressing Unnamed Dates and Hours

Ref: FM 6-0 (C1), Commander and Staff Organization and Operations (May '15), pp. C-6 to C-9.

Order writers use specific letters to designate unnamed dates and times in plans and orders.

Term	Designates
C-Day	The unnamed day on which a deployment operation commences or is to commence (JP 5-0).
D-day	The unnamed day on which a particular operation commences or is to commence (JP 3-02).
F-hour	The effective time of announcement by the Secretary of Defense to the Military Departments of a decision to mobilize reserve units (JP 3-02).
H-hour	The specific hour on D-Day at which a particular operation commences (JP 5-0).
L-hour	The specific hour on C-day at which a deployment operation commences or is to commence (JP 5-0).
M-day	The term used to designate the unnamed day on which full mobilization commences or is due to commence (JP 3-02).
N-day	The unnamed day an active duty unit is notified for deployment or redeployment (JP 3-02).
P-hour	The specific hour on D-day at which a parachute assault commences with the exit of the first Soldier from an aircraft over a designated drop zone. P-hour may or may not coincide with H-hour.
R-day	Redeployment day. The day on which redeployment of major combat, combat support, and combat service support forces begins in an operation (JP 3-02).
S-day	The day the President authorizes Selective reserve callup (not more than 200,000) (JP 3-02).
T-day	The effective day coincident with Presidential declaration of national emergency and authorization of partial mobilization (not more than 1,000,000 personnel exclusive of the 200,000 callup) (JP 3-02).
W-day	Declared by the President, W-day is associated with an adversary decision to prepare for war (unambiguous strategic warning) (JP 3-02).

Ref: FM 6-0 (C1), Commander and Staff Organization &Operations, table C-1, p. C-8.

The effective time for implementing the plan or order is the same as the date-time group of the order. Order writers express the date and time as a six-digit date-time group. The first two digits indicate the day of the month; the next four digits indicate the time. The letter at the end of the time indicates the time zone. Staffs add the month and year to the date-time group to avoid confusion. For example, a complete date-time group for 6 August 20XX at 1145 appears as 061145Z August 20XX.

If the effective time of any portion of the order differs from that of the order, staffs identify those portions at the beginning of the coordinating instructions (in paragraph 3). For example, order writers may use "Effective only for planning on receipt" or "Task organization effective 261300Z May 20XX."

Order writers express all times in a plan or order in terms of one time zone, for example ZULU (Z) or LOCAL. (Order writers do not abbreviate local time as [L]. The abbreviation for the LIMA time is L.) Staffs include the appropriate time zone indicator in the heading data and mission statement. For example, the time zone indicator for Central Standard Time in the continental United States is SIERRA. When daylight savings time is in effect, the time zone indicator for Central Standard Time is ROMEO. The relationship of local time to ZULU time, not the geographic location, determines the time zone indicator to use.

When using inclusive dates, staffs express them by writing both dates separated by a dash (6–9 August 20XX or 6 August–6 September 20XX). They express times in the 24-hour clock system by means of four-digit Arabic numbers, including the time zone indicator.

Plans & Orders

F. Attachments (Annexes, Appendixes, Tabs, and Exhibits)

Ref: FM 6-0 (C1), Commander and Staff Organization and Operations (May '15), pp. C-6 to C-9 and table C-2, pp. C-17 to C-21.

Attachments (annexes, appendixes, tabs, and exhibits) are information management tools. They simplify orders by providing a structure for organizing information. However, even when attachments are used, an effective base order contains enough information to be executed without them. The organizational structure for attachments to Army OPLANs and OPORDs is in table C-2 on page C-17 through C-21.

Attachments are part of an order. Using them increases the base order's clarity and usefulness by keeping the base order or plan short. Attachments include information (such as sustainment), administrative support details, and instructions that expand upon the base order.

Commanders and staffs are not required to develop all attachments listed in table C-2. The number and type of attachments depend on the commander, level of command, and complexity or needs of a particular operation. Minimizing the number of attachments keeps the order consistent with completeness and clarity. If the information relating to an attachment's subject is brief, the order writer places the information in the base order and "omits" the attachment. (See paragraph C-64 for information on omitting attachments.)

Staffs list attachments under an appropriate heading at the end of the document they expand. For example, they list annexes at the end of the base order, appendixes at the end of annexes, and so forth.

Army OPLANs or OPORDs do not use Annexes I and O as attachments. Army orders label these annexes "Not Used." Annexes T, X, and Y are available for use and are labeled as "Spare." If the commander needs to use any of these three spare annexes (T, X, Y), orders writers use the same attachment format as described as figure C-3 on page C-22 and C-23. When an attachment required by doctrine or an SOP is unnecessary, staffs indicate this by stating, "Type of attachment and its alphanumeric identifier omitted."

Staffs refer to attachments by letter or number and title using the following naming conventions:

Annexes. Staffs designate annexes with capital letters, for example, Annex D (Fires) to OPORD 09 06—1 ID.

Appendixes. Staffs designate appendixes with Arabic numbers, for example, Appendix 1 (Intelligence Estimate) to Annex B (Intelligence) to OPORD 09-06—1 ID.

Tabs. Staffs designate tabs with capital letters, for example, Tab B (Target Synchronization Matrix) to Appendix 3 (Targeting) to Annex D (Fires) to OPORD 09-06—1 ID.

Exhibits. Staffs designate exhibits with Arabic numbers, for example, Exhibit 1 (Traffic Circulation and Control) to Tab C (Transportation) to Appendix 1 (Logistics) to Annex F (Sustainment) to OPORD 09-06—1 ID.

If an attachment has wider distribution than the base order or is issued separately, the attachment requires a complete heading and acknowledgment instructions. When staffs distribute attachments with the base order, these elements are not required.

ANNEX A – TASK ORGANIZATION (G-5 or G-3 [S-3])
ANNEX B – INTELLIGENCE (G-2 [S-2])
  Appendix 1 – Intelligence Estimate
    Tab A – Terrain (Engineer Officer)
    Tab B – Weather (Staff Weather Officer)
    Tab C – Civil Considerations
    Tab D – Intelligence Preparation of the Battlefield
    Products
  Appendix 2 – Counterintelligence
  Appendix 3 – Signals Intelligence
  Appendix 4 – Human Intelligence
  Appendix 5 – Geospatial Intelligence
  Appendix 6 – Measurement and Signature Intelligence
  Appendix 7 – Open Source Intelligence
ANNEX C – OPERATIONS (G-5 or G-3 [S-3])
  Appendix 1 – Army Design Methodology Products
  Appendix 2 – Operation Overlay

  Appendix 3 – Decision Support Products
    Tab A – Execution Matrix
    Tab B – Decision Support Template and Matrix
  Appendix 4 – Gap Crossing Operations
    Tab A – Traffic Control Overlay
  Appendix 5 – Air Assault Operations
    Tab A – Pickup Zone Diagram
    Tab B – Air Movement Table
    Tab C – Landing Zone Diagram
  Appendix 6 – Airborne Operations
    Tab A – Marshalling Plan
    Tab B – Air Movement Plan
    Tab C – Drop Zone/Extraction Zone Diagram
  Appendix 7 – Amphibious Operations
    Tab A – Advance Force Operations
    Tab B – Embarkation Plan
    Tab C – Landing Plan

Tab D – Rehearsal Plan
Appendix 8 – Special Operations (G-3 [S-3])
Appendix 9 – Battlefield Obscuration (CBRN Officer)
Appendix 10 – Airspace (G-3 [S-3] or Airspace Control Officer)
Tab A – Air Traffic Services
Appendix 11 – Rules of Engagement (Staff Judge Advocate)
Tab A – No Strike List
Tab B – Restricted Target List (G-3 [S-3] with Staff Judge Advocate)
Appendix 12–Cyber Electromagnetic Activities (Electronic Warfare Officer)
Tab A–Offensive Cyberspace Operations
Tab B–Defensive Cyberspace Operations–Response Actions
Tab C–Electronic Attack
Tab D–Electronic Protection
Tab E–Electronic Warfare Support
Appendix 13–Military Information Support Operations (Military Information Support Officer)
Appendix 14–Military Deception (Military Deception Officer)
Appendix 15–Information Operations (Information Operations Officer)
ANNEX D – FIRES (Chief of Fires/Fire Support Officer)
Appendix 1 – Fire Support Overlay
Appendix 2 – Fire Support Execution Matrix
Appendix 3 – Targeting
Tab A – Target Selection Standards
Tab B – Target Synchronization Matrix
Tab C – Attack Guidance Matrix
Tab D – Target List Worksheets
Tab E – Battle Damage Assessment (G-2 [S-2])
Appendix 4 – Field Artillery Support
Appendix 5 – Air Support
Appendix 6 – Naval Fire Support
Appendix 7–Air and Missile Defense (Air and Missile Defense Officer)
Tab A–Enemy Air Avenues of Approach
Tab B–Enemy Air Order of Battle
Tab C–Enemy Theater Ballistic Missile Overlay
Tab D–Air and Missile Defense Protection Overlay
ANNEX E – PROTECTION (Chief of Protection/Protection Officer as designated by the commander)
Appendix 1–Operational Area Security
Appendix 2–Safety (Safety Officer)
Appendix 3–Operations Security
Appendix 4–Intelligence Support to Protection
Appendix 5–Physical Security
Appendix 6–Antiterrorism
Appendix 7–Police Operations (Provost Marshal)
Appendix 8–Survivability Operations
Appendix 9–Force Health Protection (Surgeon)
Appendix 10–Chemical, Biological, Radiological, and Nuclear Defense (CBRN Officer)
Appendix 11–Explosive Ordnance Disposal (EOD Officer)
Appendix 12–Coordinate Air and Missile Defense (Air Defense Officer)
Appendix 13–Personnel Recovery (Personnel Recovery Officer)
Appendix 14–Detainee and Resettlement
ANNEX F – SUSTAINMENT (Chief of Sustainment [S-4])
Appendix 1 – Logistics (G-4 [S-4])
Tab A – Sustainment Overlay
Tab B – Maintenance
Tab C – Transportation
Exhibit 1 – Traffic Circulation and Control (Provost Marshal)
Exhibit 2 – Traffic Circulation Overlay
Exhibit 3 – Road Movement Table
Exhibit 4 – Highway Regulation (Provost Marshal)
Tab D – Supply
Tab E – Field Services

Tab F – Distribution
Tab G – Contract Support Integration
Tab H – Mortuary Affairs
Tab I – Internment and Resettlement Support
Appendix 2 – Personnel Services Support (G-1 [S-1])
Tab A – Human Resources Support (G-1 [S-1])
Tab B – Financial Management (G-8)
Tab C – Legal Support (Staff Judge Advocate)
Tab D – Religious Support (Chaplain)
Tab E – Band Operations (G-1 [S-1])
Appendix 3 – Army Heath System Support (Surgeon)
ANNEX G – Engineer (Engineer Officer)
Appendix 1 – Mobility/Countermobility
Tab A – Obstacle Overlay
Appendix 2 – Survivability (Engineer Officer)
Appendix 3 – General Engineering
Appendix 4 – Geospatial Engineering
Appendix 5 – Environmental Considerations
Tab A – Environmental Assessments
Tab B – Environmental Assessment Exemptions
Tab C – Environmental Baseline Survey
ANNEX H – SIGNAL (G-6 [S-6])
Appendix 1–Defensive Cyberspace Operations
Appendix 2–Information Network Operations
Appendix 3–Voice, Video, and Data Network Diagrams
Appendix 4–Satellite Communications
Appendix 5–Foreign Data Exchanges
Appendix 6–Spectrum Management Operations
Appendix 7–Information Services
ANNEX I – Not Used
ANNEX J – PUBLIC AFFAIRS
Appendix 1–Public Affairs Running Estimate
Appendix 2–Public Affairs Guidance
ANNEX K – CIVIL AFFAIRS OPERATIONS (G-9 [S-9])
Appendix 1 – Execution Matrix
Appendix 2 – Populace and Resources Control Plan
Appendix 3 – Civil Information Management Plan
ANNEX L – INFORMATION COLLECTION (G-3 [S-3])
Appendix 1–Information Collection Plan
Appendix 2–Information Collection Overlay
ANNEX M – ASSESSMENT (G-5 [S-5] or G-3 [S-3])
Appendix 1 – Nesting of Assessment Efforts
Appendix 2 – Assessment Framework
Appendix 3 – Assessment Working Group
ANNEX N – SPACE OPERATIONS
ANNEX O – Not Used
ANNEX P – HOST-NATION SUPPORT (G-4 [S-4])
ANNEX Q – KNOWLEDGE MANAGEMENT (Knowledge Management Officer)
Appendix 1–Knowledge Management Decision Support Matrix
Appendix 2–Common Operational Picture Configuration Matrix
Appendix 3–Mission Command Information Systems Integration Matrix
Appendix 4–Content Management
Appendix 5–Battle Rhythm
ANNEX R – REPORTS (G-3 [S-3], G-5 [S-5], G-7, and Knowledge Management Officer)
ANNEX S – SPECIAL TECHNICAL OPERATIONS
Appendix 1 – Special Technical Operations Capabilities Integration Matrix
Appendix 2 – Functional Area I Program and Objectives
Appendix 3 – Functional Area II Program and Objectives
ANNEX T – Spare
ANNEX U – INSPECTOR GENERAL
ANNEX V – INTERAGENCY COORDINATION (G-3 [S-3] and G-9 [S-9])
ANNEX W – OPERATIONAL CONTRACT SUPPORT (G-4 [S-4])
ANNEX X – Spare
ANNEX Y –Spare
ANNEX Z – DISTRIBUTION (G-3 [S-3] and Knowledge Management Officer)

Plans & Orders

G. Expressing Time

The effective time for implementing the plan or order is the same as the date-time group of the order. Order writers express the date and time as a six-digit date-time group. The first two digits indicate the day of the month; the next four digits indicate the time. The letter at the end of the time indicates the time zone. Staffs add the month and year to the date-time group to avoid confusion. For example, a complete date-time group for 6 August 20XX at 1145 appears as 061145Z August 20XX.

If the effective time of any portion of the order differs from that of the order, staffs identify those portions at the beginning of the coordinating instructions (in paragraph 3). For example, order writers may use "Effective only for planning on receipt" or "Task organization effective 261300Z May 20XX."

Order writers express all times in a plan or order in terms of one time zone, for example ZULU (Z) or LOCAL. (Order writers do not abbreviate local time as [L]. The abbreviation for the LIMA time is L.) Staffs include the appropriate time zone indicator in the heading data and mission statement. For example, the time zone indicator for Central Standard Time in the continental United States is SIERRA. When daylight savings time is in effect, the time zone indicator for Central Standard Time is ROMEO. The relationship of local time to ZULU time, not the geographic location, determines the time zone indicator to use.

When using inclusive dates, staffs express them by writing both dates separated by a dash (6–9 August 20XX or 6 August–6 September 20XX). They express times in the 24-hour clock system by means of four-digit Arabic numbers, including the time zone indicator.

H. Identifying Pages

Staffs identify pages following the first page of plans and orders with a short title identification heading located two spaces under the classification marking. They include the number (or letter) designation of the plan, and the issuing headquarters. For example, OPLAN 09-15–23d AD (U) or Annex B (Intelligence) to OPLAN 09-15–23rd AD (U).

I. Numbering Pages

Order writers use the following convention to indicate page numbers:

- Order writers number the pages of the base order and each attachment separately beginning on the first page of each attachment. They use a combination of alphanumeric designations to identify each attachment.

- Order writers use Arabic numbers only to indicate page numbers. They place page numbers after the alphanumeric designation that identifies the attachment. (Use Arabic numbers without any proceeding alphanumeric designation for base order page numbers.) For example, the designation of the third page to Annex C is C-3. Order writers assign each attachment either a letter or Arabic number that corresponds to the letter or number in the attachment's short title. They assign letters to annexes, Arabic numbers to appendixes, letters to tabs, and Arabic numbers to exhibits. For example, the designation of the third page to Appendix 5 to Annex C is C-5-3.

- Order writers separate elements of the alphanumeric designation with hyphens. For example, the designation of the third page of exhibit 2 to Tab B to Appendix 5 to Annex C is C-5-B-2-3.

II. Example Plan & Order Formats

All plans and orders follow the five-paragraph order format. Attachments also follow the five-paragraph format except matrixes, overlays, and lists.

See following pages for examples.

Warning Order (WARNORD) Format

Ref: FM 6-0 (C1), Commander and Staff Organization and Operations (May '15), fig. C-4, p. C-24.

[Classification]
(Change from verbal orders, if any) (Optional)

Copy ## of ## copies
Issuing headquarters
Place of issue
Date-time group of signature
Message reference number

WARNING ORDER [number] Example: **WARNING ORDER #8**

(U) References: *Refer to higher headquarters' OPLAN/OPORD and identify map sheets for operation (Optional).*

(U) Time Zone Used Throughout the OPLAN/OPORD: (Optional)

(U) Task Organization: (Optional)

1. (U) <u>Situation</u>. *The situation paragraph describes the conditions and circumstances of the operational environment that impact operations in the following subparagraphs:*

    a. (U) <u>Area of Interest</u>.

    b. (U) <u>Area of Operations</u>.

    c. (U) <u>Enemy Forces</u>.

    d. (U) <u>Friendly Forces</u>.

    e. (U) <u>Interagency, Intergovernmental, and Nongovernmental Organizations</u>.

    f. (U) <u>Civil Considerations</u>.

    g. (U) <u>Attachments and Detachments</u>. *Provide initial task organization.*

    h. (U) <u>Assumptions</u>. *List any significant assumptions for order development.*

2. (U) <u>Mission</u>. *State the issuing headquarters' mission.*

3. (U) <u>Execution</u>.

    a. (U) <u>Initial Commander's Intent</u>. *Provide brief commander's intent statement.*

    b. (U) <u>Concept of Operations</u>. *This may be "to be determined" for an initial WARNORD.*

    c. (U) <u>Task to Subordinate Units</u>. *Include any known tasks at time of issuance of WARNORD.*

    d. (U) <u>Coordinating Instructions</u>.

4. (U) <u>Sustainment.</u> *Include known logistics, personnel, or health system prep tasks.*

5. (U) <u>Command and Signal</u>. *Include changes to existing order or state "no change."*

ACKNOWLEDGE:

                         [Commander's last name]
                         [Commander's rank]

OFFICIAL:
[Authenticator's name]
[Authenticator's position]
ANNEXES: *List annexes by letter and title.*
DISTRIBUTION: *List recipients.*

[page number]
[CLASSIFICATION]

Annotated OPLAN/OPORD Format

Ref: FM 6-0 (C1), Commander and Staff Organization and Operations (May '15), fig. C-2, pp. C-11 to C-17.

[CLASSIFICATION]

Place the classification at the top and bottom of every page of the OPLAN or OPORD. Place the classification marking at the front of each paragraph and subparagraph in parentheses. Refer to AR 380-5 for classification and release marking instructions.

Copy ## of ## copies
Issuing headquarters
Place of issue
Date-time group of signature
Message reference number ⁓

The first line of the heading is the copy number assigned by the issuing headquarters. A log is maintained of specific copies issued to addressees. The second line is the official designation of the issuing headquarters (for example, 1st Infantry Division). The third line is the place of issue. It may be a code name, postal designation, or geographic location. The fourth line is the date or date-time group that the plan or order was signed or issued and becomes effective unless specified otherwise in the coordinating instructions. The fifth line is a headquarters internal control number assigned to all plans and orders in accordance with unit standing operating procedures (SOPs).

OPERATION PLAN/ORDER [number] [(code name)] [(classification of title)]
Example: **OPORD 3411 (OPERATION DESERT DRAGON) (UNCLASSIFIED)**

Number plans and orders consecutively by calendar year. Include code name, if any.

(U) References: *List documents essential to understanding the OPLAN/OPORD. List references concerning a specific function in the appropriate attachments.*

(a) List maps and charts first. Map entries include series number, country, sheet names, or numbers, edition, and scale.

(b) List other references in subparagraphs labeled as shown.

(U) Time Zone Used Throughout the OPLAN/OPORD: *State the time zone used in the area of operations during execution. When the OPLAN/OPORD applies to units in different time zones, use Greenwich Mean (ZULU) Time.*

(U) Task Organization: *Describe the organization of forces available to the issuing headquarters and their command and support relationships. Refer to Annex A (Task Organization) if long or complicated.*

1. (U) Situation. *The situation paragraph describes the conditions of the operational environment that impact operations in the following subparagraphs:*

a. (U) Area of Interest. Describe the area of interest. Refer to Annex B (Intelligence) as required.

b. (U) Area of Operations. Describe the area of operations (AO). Refer to the appropriate map by its subparagraph under references, for example, "Map, reference (b)." Refer to the Appendix 2 (Operation Overlay) to Annex C (Operations).

(1) (U) Terrain. Describe the aspects of terrain that impact operations. Refer to Annex B (Intelligence) as required.

(2) (U) Weather. Describe the aspects of weather that impact operations. Refer to Annex B (Intelligence) as required.

[page number]
[CLASSIFICATION]

OPLAN/OPORD [number] [(code name)]—[issuing headquarters] [(classification of title)]
Place the classification and title of the OPLAN/OPORD and the issuing headquarters at the top of the second and any subsequent pages of the base plan or order.

Continued on next page

c. (U) <u>Enemy Forces</u>. *Identify enemy forces and appraise their general capabilities. Describe the enemy's disposition, location, strength, and probable courses of action. Identify known or potential terrorist threats and adversaries within the AO. Refer to Annex B (Intelligence) as required.*

d. (U) <u>Friendly Forces</u>. *Briefly identify the missions of friendly forces and the objectives, goals, and missions of civilian organizations that impact the issuing headquarters in following subparagraphs:*

(1) (U) <u>Higher Headquarters' Mission and Intent</u>. *Identify and state the mission and commander's intent for headquarters two levels up and one level up from the issuing headquarters.*

(a) (U) <u>Higher Headquarters Two Levels Up</u>. *Identify the higher headquarters two levels up the paragraph heading (for example, Joint Task Force-18).*

1 (U) Mission.

2 (U) Commander's Intent.

(b) (U) <u>Higher Headquarters</u>. *Identify the higher headquarters one level up in the paragraph heading (for example, 1st (US) Armored Division).*

1 (U) Mission.

2 (U) Commander's Intent.

(2) (U) <u>Missions of Adjacent Units</u>. *Identify and state the missions of adjacent units and other units whose actions have a significant impact on the issuing headquarters.*

e. (U) <u>Interagency, Intergovernmental, and Nongovernmental Organizations</u>. *Identify and state the objective or goals and primary tasks of those non-Department of Defense organizations that have a significant role within the AO. Refer to Annex V (Interagency Coordination) as required.*

f. (U) <u>Civil Considerations</u>. *Describe the critical aspects of the civil situation that impact operations. Refer to Appepndix 1 (Intelligence Estimate) to Annex B (Intelligence) as required.*

g. (U) <u>Attachments and Detachments</u>. *List units attached to or detached from the issuing headquarters. State when each attachment or detachment is effective (for example, on order, on commitment of the reserve) if different from the effective time of the OPLAN/OPORD. Do not repeat information already listed in Annex A (Task Organization).*

h. (U) <u>Assumptions</u>. *List assumptions used in the development of the OPLAN/OPORD*

2. (U) Mission. *State the unit's mission—a short description of the who, what (task), when, where, and why (purpose) that clearly indicates the action to be taken and the reason for doing so.*

3. (U) Execution. *Describe how the commander intends to accomplish the mission in terms of the commander's intent, an overarching concept of operations, schemes of employment for each warfighting function, assessment, specified tasks to subordinate units, and key coordinating instructions in the subparagraphs below.*

Continued on next page

Plans & Orders

a. (U) <u>Commander's Intent</u>. *Commanders develop their intent statement personally. The commander's intent is a clear, concise statement of what the force must do and the conditions the force must establish with respect to the enemy, terrain, and civil considerations that represent the desired end state. It succinctly describes what constitutes the success of an operation and provides the purpose and conditions that define that desired end state. The commander's intent must be easy to remember and clearly understood two echelons down. The commander's intent includes:*

Purpose–an expanded description of the operation's purpose beyond the "why" of the mission statement.

Key tasks–those significant activities the force as a whole must perform to achieve the desired end state.

End state–a description of the desired future conditions that represent success.

b. (U) <u>Concept of Operations</u>. *The concept of operations is a statement that directs the manner in which subordinate units cooperate to accomplish the mission and establishes the sequence of actions the force will use to achieve the end state. It is normally expressed in terms of the commander's desired operational framework as discussed in ADRP 3-0. It states the principal tasks required, the responsible subordinate units, and how the principal tasks complement one another. Normally, the concept of operations projects the status of the force at the end of the operation. If the mission dictates a significant change in tasks during the operation, the commander may phase the operation. The concept of operations may be a single paragraph, divided into two or more subparagraphs, or if unusually lengthy, summarize here with details located in Annex C (Operations). If the concept of operations is phased, describe each phase in a subparagraph. Label these subparagraphs as "Phase" followed by the appropriate Roman numeral, for example, "Phase I." If the operation is phased, all paragraphs and subparagraphs of the base order and all annexes must mirror the phasing established in the concept of operations. The operation overlay and graphic depictions of lines of effort help portray the concept of operations and are located in Annex C (Operations).*

c. (U) <u>Scheme of Movement and Maneuver.</u> *Describe the employment of maneuver units in accordance with the concept of operations. Provide the primary tasks of maneuver units conducting the decisive operation and the purpose of each. Next, state the primary tasks of maneuver units conducting shaping operations, including security operations, and the purpose of each. For offensive tasks, identify the form of maneuver. For defensive tasks, identify the type of defense. For stability tasks, describe the role of maneuver units by primary stability tasks. If the operation is phased, identify the main effort.*

(1) (U) <u>Scheme of Mobility/Countermobility</u>. *State the scheme of mobility/countermobility including priorities by unit or area. Refer to Annex G (Engineer) as required.*

(2) (U) <u>Scheme of Battlefield Obscuration</u>. *State the scheme of battlefield obscuration, including priorities by unit or area. Refer to Appendix 9 (Battlefield Obscuration) to Annex C (Operations) as required.*

(3) (U) <u>Scheme of Information Collection.</u> *Describe how the commander intends to use reconnaissance missions and surveillance tasks to support the concept of operations. Include the primary reconnaissance objectives. Refer to Annex L (Information Collection) as required.*

(Note: Army forces do not conduct reconnaissance and surveillance within the United States and its territories. For domestic operations, this paragraph is titled "Information Awareness and Assessment" and the contents of this paragraph comply with Executive Order 12333.)

[page number]
[CLASSIFICATION]

d. (U) <u>Scheme of Intelligence</u>. *Describe how the commander envisions intelligence supporting the concept of operations. Include the priority of effort to situation development, targeting, and assessment. State the priority of intelligence support to units and areas. Refer to Annex B (Intelligence) as required.*

e. (U) <u>Scheme of Fires</u>. *Describe how the commander intends to use fires (lethal and nonlethal) to support the concept of operations with emphasis on the scheme of maneuver. State the fire support tasks and the purpose of each task. State the priorities for, allocation of, and restrictions on fires. Refer to Annex D (Fires) as required.*

f. (U) <u>Scheme of Protection</u>. *Describe how the commander envisions protection supporting the concept of operations. Include the priorities of protection by unit and area. Include survivability. Address the scheme of operational area security, including security for routes, bases, and critical infrastructure. Identify tactical combat forces and other reaction forces. Use subparagraphs for protection categories (for example, air and missile defense and explosive ordnance disposal) based on the situation. Refer to Annex E (Protection) as required.*

g. (U) <u>Cyber Electromagnetic Activities</u>. *Describe how cyber electromagnetic activities (including cyberspace operations, electronic warfare and spectrum management operations), supports the concept of operations. Refer to Appendix 12 (Cyber Electromagnetic Activities) to Annex C (Operations) as required. Refer to Annex H (Signal) for defensive cyberspace operations, network operations and spectrum management operations as required.*

h. (U) <u>Stability Tasks</u>. *Describe how stability tasks support the concept of operations. Describe how the commander envisions the conduct of stability tasks in coordination with other organizations. (See ADRP 3-07.) If other organizations or the host nation cannot provide for civil security, restoration of essential services, and civil control, then commanders with an assigned area of operations must do so with available resources, request additional resources, or request relief for these requirements from higher headquarters. Commanders assign specific responsibilities for stability tasks to subordinate units in paragraph 3j (Tasks to Subordinate Units) and paragraph 3k (Coordinating Instructions). Refer to Annex C (Operations) and Annex K (Civil Affairs Operations) as required.*

i. (U) <u>Assessment</u>. *Describe the priorities for assessment and identify the measures of effectiveness used to assess end state conditions and objectives. Refer to Annex M (Assessment) as required.*

j. (U) <u>Tasks to Subordinate Units</u>. *State the task assigned to each unit that reports directly to the headquarters issuing the order. Each task must include who (the subordinate unit assigned the task), what (the task itself), when, where, and why (purpose). Use a separate subparagraph for each unit. List units in task organization sequence. Place tasks that affect two or more units in paragraph 3k (Coordinating Instructions).*

k. (U) <u>Coordinating Instructions</u>. *List only instructions and tasks applicable to two or more units not covered in unit SOPs.*

(1) (U) <u>Time or condition when the OPORD becomes effective</u>.

(2) (U) <u>Commander's Critical Information Requirements</u>. *List commander's critical information requirements (CCIRs) here.*

(3) (U) <u>Essential Elements of Friendly Information</u>. *List essential elements of friendly information (EEFIs) here.*

(4) (U) <u>Fire Support Coordination Measures</u>. *List critical fire support coordination or control measures.*

Continued on next page

Continued on next page

Plans & Orders

(5) (U) <u>Airspace Coordinating Measures</u>. *List critical airspace coordinating or control measures.*

(6) (U) <u>Rules of Engagement</u>. *List rules of engagement here. Refer to Appendix 11 (Rules of Engagement) to Annex C (Operations) as required.* *(Note: For operations within the United States and its territories, title this paragraph "Rules for the Use of Force").*

(7) (U) <u>Risk Reduction Control Measures</u>. *State measures specific to this operation not included in unit SOPs. They may include mission-oriented protective posture, operational exposure guidance, troop-safety criteria, and fratricide prevention measures. Refer to Annex E (Protection) as required.*

(8) (U) <u>Personnel Recovery Coordination Measures</u>. *Refer to Appendix 13 (Personnel Recovery) to Annex E (Protection) as required.*

(9) (U) <u>Environmental Considerations</u>. *Refer to Appendix 5 (Environmental Considerations) to Annex G (Engineer) as required.*

(10) (U) <u>Soldier and Leader Engagement.</u> *State commander's guidance for target audiences and reporting requirements.*

(11) (U) <u>Other Coordinating Instructions</u>. *List in subparagraphs any additional coordinating instructions and tasks that apply to two or more units, such as the operational timeline and any other critical timing or events.*

4. (U) <u>Sustainment.</u> *Describe the concept of sustainment, including priorities of sustainment by unit or area. Include instructions for administrative movements, deployments, and transportation—or references to applicable appendixes—if appropriate. Use the following subparagraphs to provide the broad concept of support for logistics, personnel, and health service support. Provide detailed instructions for each sustainment subfunction in the appendixes to Annex F (Sustainment).*

a. (U) <u>Logistics</u>. *Refer to Annex F (Sustainment) as required.*

b. (U) <u>Personnel</u>. *Refer to Annex F (Sustainment) as required.*

c. (U) <u>Health System Support</u>. *Refer to Annex F (Sustainment) as required.*

5. (U) <u>Command and Signal</u>.

a. (U) <u>Command</u>.

(1) (U) <u>Location of Commander and Key Leaders</u>. *State where the commander and key leaders intend to be during the operation, by phase if the operation is phased.*

(2) (U) <u>Succession of Command</u>. *State the succession of command if not covered in the unit's SOPs.*

(3) (U) <u>Liaison Requirements</u>. *State liaison requirements not covered in the unit's SOPs.*

b. (U) <u>Control</u>.

(1) (U) <u>Command Posts</u>. *Describe the employment of command posts (CPs), including the location of each CP and its time of opening and closing, as appropriate. State the primary controlling CP for specific tasks or phases of the operation (for example, "Division tactical command post will control the air assault").*

(2) (U) <u>Reports</u>. *List reports not covered in SOPs. Refer to Annex R (Reports) as required.*

c. (U) <u>Signal</u>. *Describe the concept of signal support, including location and movement of key signal nodes and critical electromagnetic spectrum considerations throughout the operation. Refer to Annex H (Signal) as required.*

Continued from previous page

Continued from previous page

Plans & Orders

[Classification]

OPLAN/OPORD [number] [(code name)]—[issuing headquarters] [(classification of title)]

ACKNOWLEDGE: *Include instructions for the acknowledgement of the OPLAN/OPORD by addressees. The word "acknowledge" may suffice. Refer to the message reference number if necessary. Acknowledgement of a plan or order means that it has been received and understood.*

[Commander's last name]

[Commander's rank]

The commander or authorized representative signs the original copy. If the representative signs the original, add the phrase "For the Commander." The signed copy is the historical copy and remains in the headquarters' files.

OFFICIAL:

[Authenticator's name]

[Authenticator's position]

Use only if the commander does not sign the original order. If the commander signs the original, no further authentication is required. If the commander does not sign, the signature of the preparing staff officer requires authentication and only the last name and rank of the commander appear in the signature block.

ANNEXES: *List annexes by letter and title. Army and joint OPLANs or OPORDs do not use Annexes I and O as attachments and in Army orders label these annexes "Not Used." Annexes T, X, and Y are available for use in Army OPLANs or OPORDs and are labeled as "Spare." When an attachment required by doctrine or an SOP is unnecessary, label it "Omitted." (See pp. 4-18 to 4-19 for further discussion of annexes).*

Annex A–Task Organization
Annex B –Intelligence
Annex C –Operations
Annex D–Fires
Annex E –Protection
Annex F –Sustainment
Annex G–Engineer
Annex H–Signal
Annex I–Not Used
Annex J–Public Affairs
Annex K–Civil Affairs Operations
Annex L –Information Collection
Annex M–Assessment
Annex N–Space Operations
Annex O–Not Used
Annex P –Host-Nation Support
Annex Q–Knowledge Management
Annex R –Reports
Annex S –Special Technical Operations
Annex T –Spare
Annex U–Inspector General
Annex V–Interagency Coordination
Annex W–Operational Contract Support
Annex X–Spare
Annex Y–Spare
Annex Z –Distribution

DISTRIBUTION: *Furnish distribution copies either for action or for information. List in detail those who are to receive the plan or order. Refer to Annex Z (Distribution) if lengthy.*

[page number]
[CLASSIFICATION]

Attachment Format (OPLANS/OPORDS)

Ref: FM 6-0 (C1), Commander and Staff Organization and Operations (May '15), fig. C-3, pp. C-22 to C-23. See pp. 4-16 to 4-17 for discussion of attachments (annexes, appendixes, tabs, and exhibits).

[CLASSIFICATION]

(Change from verbal orders, if any)

Copy ## of ## copies
Issuing headquarters
Place of issue
Date-time group of signature
Message reference number

Include heading if attachment is distributed separately from the base order or higher-level attachment.

[Attachment type and number/letter] [(attachment title)] TO [higher-level attachment type and number/letter, if applicable] [(higher-level attachment title, if applicable)] TO OPERATION PLAN/ORDER [number] [(code name)] [(classification of title)]

References: *Refer to higher headquarters' OPLAN or OPORD and identify map sheets for operation (Optional).*

Time Zone Used Throughout the Order:

1. (U) Situation. *Include information affecting the functional area that paragraph 1 of the OPLAN/OPORD does not cover or that needs to be expanded.*

   a. (U) Area of Interest. *Refer to Annex B (Intelligence) as required.*

   b. (U) Area of Operations. *Refer to Appendix 2 (Operation Overlay) to Annex C (Operations).*

      (1) (U) Terrain. *Describe aspects of terrain that impact functional area operations. Refer to Annex B (Intelligence) as required.*

      (2) (U) Weather. *Describe aspects of weather that impact functional area operations. Refer to Annex B (Intelligence) as required.*

   c. (U) Enemy Forces. *List known and templated locations and activities of enemy functional area units for one echelon up and two echelons down. List enemy maneuver and other area capabilities that will impact friendly operations. State expected enemy courses of action and employment of enemy functional area assets. Refer to Annex B (Intelligence) as required.*

   d. (U) Friendly Forces. *Outline the higher headquarters' plan as it pertains to the functional area. List designation, location, and outline of plan of higher, adjacent, and other functional area assets that support or impact the issuing headquarters or require coordination and additional support.*

   e. (U) Interagency, Intergovernmental, and Nongovernmental Organizations. *Identify and describe other organizations in the area of operations that may impact the conduct of functional area operations or implementation of functional area-specific equipment and tactics.*

   f. (U) Civil Considerations. *Describe critical aspects of the civil situation that impact functional area operations. Refer to Annex K (Civil Affairs Operations) as required.*

   g. (U) Attachments and Detachments. *List units attached or detached only as necessary to clarify task organization. Refer to Annex A (Task Organization) as required.*

   h. (U) Assumptions. *List any functional area-specific assumptions that support the annex development.*

[page number]
[CLASSIFICATION]

[Attachment type and number/letter] [(attachment title)] TO [higher-level attachment type and number/letter, if applicable] [(higher-level attachment title, if applicable)] TO OPERATION PLAN/ORDER [number] [(code name)]—[issuing headquarters] [(classification of title)]

2. (U) Mission. *State the mission of the functional area in support of the base plan or order.*

3. (U) Execution.

    a. (U) Scheme of Support. *Describe how the functional area supports the commander's intent and concept of operations. Establish the priorities of support to units for each phase of the operation. Refer to Annex C (Operations) as required.*

    b. (U) Tasks to Subordinate Units. *List functional area tasks assigned to specific subordinate units not contained in the base order.*

    c. (U) Coordinating Instructions. *List only instructions applicable to two or more subordinate units not covered in the base order.*

4. (U) Sustainment. *Identify priorities of sustainment for functional area key tasks and specify additional instructions as required. Refer to Annex F (Sustainment) as required.*

5. (U) Command and Signal.

    a. (U) Command. *State the location of key leaders.*

    b. (U) Control. *State the functional area liaison requirements not covered in the base order.*

    c. (U) Signal. *Address any functional area-specific communications requirements or reports. Refer to Annex H (Signal) as required.*

ACKNOWLEDGE: *Include only if attachment is distributed separately from the base order.*

OFFICIAL:

[Authenticator's name]

[Authenticator's position]

Either the commander or coordinating staff officer responsible for the functional area may sign attachments.

ATTACHMENT: *List lower-level attachments.*

DISTRIBUTION: *Show only if distributed separately from the base order or higher-level attachments.*

Note. See pp. 4-18 to 4-19 for discussion of administrative instructions for preparing attachments (annexes, appendixes, tabs, and exhibits).

Plans & Orders

Overlay Order Format (Example)

Ref: FM 6-0 (C1), Commander and Staff Organization and Operations (May '15), fig. C-6, p. C-27

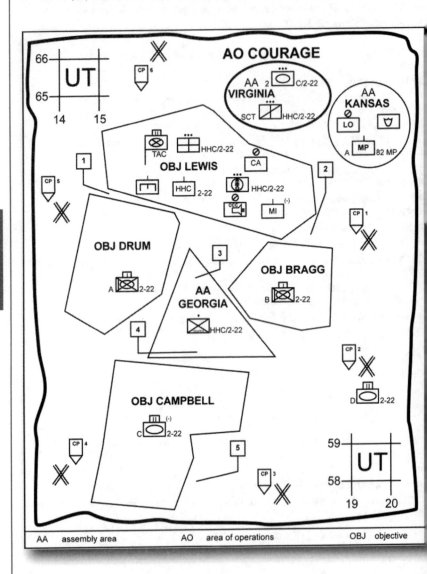

AA	assembly area	AO area of operations	OBJ objective

TASK ORGANIZATION

TF Control	A/2-22 IN	B/2-22 IN	C/2-22 AR	D/2-22 AR
Sniper Sqd/HHC/2-22	1/A/2-22 IN 2/A/2-22 IN 3/C/2-22 AR	1/B/2-22 IN 2/B/2-22 IN 3/D/2-22 AR	1/C/2-22 AR 2/C/2-22 AR 3/A/2-22 IN	1/D/2-22 AR 2/D/2-22 AR 3/B/2-22 IN
HHC	HN Civil Authorities (DIRLAUTH)			
Scout PLT/2-22 IN Mortars/HHC/2-22 Medical/HHC/2-22	None			

MISSION:

TF 2-22 conducts a cordon and search in AO COURAGE NLT 120900ZJAN07 to capture anti-coalition forces (ACF) and seize weapons caches in order to limit the attacks on coalition forces.

COMMANDER'S INTENT:

Simultaneous occupation of outer cordon checkpoints (CKPs) to isolate search objectives and prevent ACF exfiltration or infiltration. Lead with information dissemination of information themes and messages. Exercise patience, discipline, and respect for host-nation population and property while conducting thorough searches. Immediate evacuation of ACF personnel to BCT Detainee Collection Point for processing and evacuation. End state is OBJ's LEWIS, DRUM, BRAGG and CAMPBELL free of ACF and companies postured for future operations.

EXECUTION – TASKS TO SUBORDINATE UNITS:

A/2-22 IN	**TF Decisive Operation:** Secure OBJ DRUM (inner cordon) and conduct search to capture ACF and seize weapons caches in order to limit the attacks on coalition forces.
B/2-22 IN	Secure OBJ BRAGG (inner cordon) and conduct search to capture ACF and seize weapons caches in order to limit the attacks on coalition forces.
C/2-22 AR	1. Secure OBJ CAMPBELL (inner cordon) and conduct search to capture ACF and seize weapons caches in order to limit the attacks on coalition forces.
D/2-22 AR	1. Secure the outer cordon at CKPs 1-6. 2. Secure AA KANSAS, for HNCA occupation.
HHC (-)/2-22	1. Secure TF tactical command post and TF Forward Aid Station in OBJ LEWIS.
Sniper/HHC/2-22	1. Occupy AA GEORGIA and provide observation and surveillance of OBJs DRUM, BRAGG, and CAMPBELL. 2. O/O deliver precision fires to destroy ACF.

Acknowledge: A/2-22 IN, B/2-22 IN, C/2-22 AR, D/2-22 AR, HHC/2-22, Sniper/2-22 IN

Fragmentary Order (FRAGORD) Format

Ref: FM 6-0 (C1), Commander and Staff Organization and Operations (May '15), fig. C-5, p. C-25.

(Change from verbal orders, if any) (Optional)

Copy ## of ## copies
Issuing headquarters
Place of issue
Date-time group of signature
Message reference number

FRAGMENTARY ORDER [number] to OPERATION PLAN/ORDER [number] [(code name)]—[(classification of title)]

(U) References: *Refer to higher the order being modified.*

(U) Time Zone Used Throughout the OPLAN/OPORD: *(Optional)*

1. (U) <u>Situation</u>. *Include any changes to the existing order or state "No change." For example, "No change to OPORD 03-XX."*

2. (U) <u>Mission</u>. *State "No change."*

3. (U) <u>Execution</u>. *Include any changes or state "No change."*

    a. (U) <u>Commander's Intent</u>. *Include any changes or state "No change."*

    b. (U) <u>Concept of Operations</u>. *Include any changes or state "No change."*

    c. (U) <u>Scheme Movement and Maneuver</u>. *Include changes or state "No change."*

    d. (U) <u>Scheme of Intelligence</u>. *Include changes or state "No change."*

    e. (U) <u>Scheme of Fires</u>. *Include any changes or state "No change."*

    f. (U) <u>Scheme of Protection</u>. *Include any changes or state "No change."*

    g. (U) <u>Cyber Electromagnetic Activities.</u> *Include changes or state "No change."*

    h. (U) <u>Stability Tasks</u>. *Include any changes or state "No change."*

    i. (U) <u>Assessment</u>. *Include any changes or state "No change."*

    j. (U) <u>Tasks to Subordinate Units</u>. *Include any changes or state "No change."*

    k. (U) <u>Coordinating Instructions</u>. *Include any changes or state "No change"*

4. (U) <u>Sustainment.</u> *Include any changes or state "No change."*

5. (U) <u>Command and Signal</u>. *Include any changes or state "No change."*

ACKNOWLEDGE:

                    [Commander's last name]
                    [Commander's rank]

OFFICIAL:

[Authenticator's name]

[Authenticator's position]

ANNEXES: *List annexes by letter and title. Army and joint OPLANs or OPORDs do not use Annexes I and O as attachments and in Army orders label these annexes "Not Used." Annexes T, X, and Y are available for use in Army OPLANs or OPORDs and are labeled as "Spare." When an attachment required by doctrine or an SOP is unnecessary, label it "Omitted."*

DISTRIBUTION:

                    [page number]

Plans & Orders

I. Mission Command Overview

Ref: ADRP 6-0, Mission Command (May '12), preface and chap. 1.

Historically, military commanders have employed variations of two basic concepts of command: mission command and detailed command. While some have favored detailed command, the nature of operations and the patterns of military history point to the advantages of mission command. Mission command has been the Army's preferred style for exercising command since the 1980s. The concept traces its roots back to the German concept of Auftragstaktik, which translates roughly to mission-type tactics. Auftragstaktik held all German commissioned and noncommissioned officers duty bound to do whatever the situation required, as they personally saw it. Understanding and achieving the broader purpose of a task was the central idea behind this style of command. Commanders expected subordinates to act when opportunities arose.

I. Mission Command

Mission command is the exercise of authority and direction by the commander using mission orders to enable disciplined initiative within the commander's intent to empower agile and adaptive leaders in the conduct of unified land operations (ADP 6-0). Mission command is one of the foundations of unified land operations. This philosophy of command helps commanders capitalize on the human ability to take action to develop the situation and integrate military operations to achieve the commander's intent and desired end state. Mission command emphasizes centralized intent and dispersed execution through disciplined initiative. This precept guides leaders toward mission accomplishment.

Disciplined initiative fosters agile and adaptive forces. Throughout operations, unexpected opportunities and threats rapidly present themselves. The nature of military operations requires responsibility and decision making at the point of action. Leaders and subordinates who exercise initiative, within the commander's intent, create opportunity by taking action to develop the situation. Agile leaders are comfortable with uncertainty and understand that disciplined initiative is an important part of being adaptive. Successful Army leaders adapt their thinking, their formations, and their employment techniques to the specific situation they face. Adaptive leaders realize that concrete answers or perfect solutions to operational problems are rarely apparent. They understand that there may be periods of reduced uncertainty as the situation evolves. Agile and adaptive leaders use initiative to set and dictate the terms of action. They accept they will often have to act despite significant gaps in their understanding. Agile and adaptive leaders make timely adjustments in response to changes in their operational environment.

Through mission command, commanders integrate and synchronize operations. Commanders understand they do not operate independently but as part of a larger force. They integrate and synchronize their actions with the rest of the force to achieve the overall objective of the operation. Commanders create and sustain shared understanding and purpose through collaboration and dialogue within their organizations and with unified action partners to facilitate unity of effort. They provide a clear commander's intent and use mission orders to assign tasks, allocate resources, and issue broad guidance. Guided by the commander's intent and the mission purpose, subordinates take actions that will best accomplish the mission. They take appropriate actions and perform the necessary coordination without needing new orders.

II. The Exercise of Mission Command

Ref: ADRP 6-0, Mission Command (May '12), pp. 1-2 to 1-5.

To function effectively and have the greatest chance for mission accomplishment, commanders, supported by their staffs, exercise mission command throughout the conduct of operations. In this discussion, the "exercise of mission command" refers to an overarching idea that unifies the mission command philosophy of command and the mission command war fighting function. The exercise of mission command encompasses how Army commanders and staffs apply the foundational mission command philosophy together with the mission command war fighting function, guided by the principles of mission command.

An effective approach to mission command must be comprehensive, without being rigid. Military operations are affected by human interactions and as a whole defy orderly, efficient, and precise control. People are the basis of all military organizations. Commanders understand that some decisions must be made quickly and are better made at the point of action. Mission command concentrates on the objectives of an operation, not how to achieve it. Commanders provide subordinates with their intent, the purpose of the operation, the key tasks, the desired end state, and resources. Subordinates then exercise disciplined initiative to respond to unanticipated problems. Mission command is based on mutual trust and shared understanding and purpose. It demands every Soldier be prepared to assume responsibility, maintain unity of effort, take prudent action, and act resourcefully within the commander's intent.

Mission Command as a Philosophy

As the Army's philosophy of command, mission command emphasizes that command is essentially a human endeavor. Successful commanders understand that their leadership directs the development of teams and helps to establish mutual trust and shared understanding throughout the force. Commanders provide a clear intent to their forces that guides subordinates' actions while promoting freedom of action and initiative. Subordinates, by understanding the commander's intent and the overall common objective, are then able to adapt to rapidly changing situations and exploit fleeting opportunities. They are given the latitude to accomplish assigned tasks in a manner that best fits the situation. Subordinates understand that they have an obligation to act and synchronize their actions with the rest of the force. Likewise, commanders influence the situation and provide direction and guidance while synchronizing their own operations. They encourage subordinates to take action, and they accept prudent risks to create opportunity and to seize the initiative. Commanders at all levels need education, rigorous training, and experience to apply these principles effectively. Mission command operates more on self-discipline than imposed discipline.

Mission Command as a Warfighting Function

Mission command—as a warfighting function—assists commanders in balancing the art of command with the science of control, while emphasizing the human aspects of mission command. A war fighting function is a group of tasks and systems (people, organizations, information, and processes) united by a common purpose that commanders use to accomplish missions (ADRP 3-0). The mission command war fighting function consists of the mission command war fighting function tasks and the mission command system.

See pp. 5-7 to 5-14 for further discussion of mission command as a warfighting function.

Mission Command System

Commanders need support to exercise mission command effectively. At every echelon of command, each commander establishes a mission command system—the arrangement of personnel, networks, information systems, processes and procedures, and facilities and equipment that enable commanders to conduct operations (ADP 6-0). Commanders organize the five components of their mission command system to support decision making and facilitate communication. The most important of these components is personnel.

The Exercise of Mission Command

Unified Land Operations

How the Army seizes, retains, and exploits the initiative to gain and maintain a position of relative advantage in sustained land operations through simultaneous offensive, defensive, and stability operations in order to prevent or deter conflict, prevail in war, and create the conditions for favorable conflict resolution.

One of the foundations is...

Nature of Operations

Military operations are human endeavors.

They are contests of wills characterized by continuous and mutual adaptation by all participants.

Army forces conduct operations in complex, ever-changing, and uncertain operational environments.

To account for this, the Army exercises...

Mission Command Philosophy

Exercise of authority and direction by the commander using mission orders to enable disciplined initiative within the commander's intent to empower agile and adaptive leaders in the conduct of unified land operations.

Guided by the principles of...

- Build cohesive teams through mutual trust
- Create shared understanding
- Provide a clear commander's intent
- Exercise disciplined initiative
- Use mission orders
- Accept prudent risk

The principles of mission command assist commanders and staff in balancing the **art of command** *with the* **science of control.**

Executed through the...

Mission Command Warfighting Function

The related tasks and systems that develop and integrate those activities enabling a commander to balance the art of command and the science of control in order to integrate the other warfighting functions.

A series of mutually supported tasks...

Commander Tasks:
- Drive the operations process through the activities of understand, visualize, describe, direct, lead, and assess
- Develop teams, both within their own organizations and with unified action partners
- Inform and influence audiences, inside and outside their organizations

Leads

Supports

Staff Tasks:
- Conduct the operations process (plan, prepare, execute, and assess)
- Conduct knowledge management and information management
- Conduct inform and influence activities
- Conduct cyber electromagnetic activities

Additional Tasks:
- Conduct military deception
- Conduct civil affairs operations
- Conduct airspace control
- Install, operate, and maintain the network
- Conduct information protection

Enabled by a system...

Mission Command System:
- Personnel
- Networks
- Information systems
- Processes and procedures
- Facilities and equipment

Together, the mission command philosophy and warfighting function guide, integrate, and synchronize Army forces throughout the conduct of unified land operations.

Ref: ADRP 6-0, Mission Command, fig. 1-1, p. 1-3.

Mission Command

III. Principles of Mission Command

Ref: ADP 6-0, Mission Command (May '12), pp. 2 to 5.

1. Build Cohesive Teams Through Mutual Trust

Mutual trust is shared confidence among commanders, subordinates, and partners. Effective commanders build cohesive teams in an environment of mutual trust. There are few shortcuts to gaining the trust of others. Trust takes time and must be earned. Commanders earn trust by upholding the Army values and exercising leadership, consistent with the Army's leadership principles. (See the Army leadership publication for details on the leadership principles.)

Effective commanders build teams within their own organizations and with unified action partners through interpersonal relationships. Unified action partners are those military forces, governmental and nongovernmental organizations, and elements of the private sector with whom Army forces plan, coordinate, synchronize, and integrate during the conduct of operations (ADRP 3-0). Uniting all the diverse capabilities necessary to achieve success in operations requires collaborative and cooperative efforts that focus those capabilities toward a common goal. Where military forces typically demand unity of command, a challenge for building teams with unified action partners is to forge unity of effort. Unity of effort is coordination and cooperation toward common objectives, even if the participants are not necessarily part of the same command or organization—the product of successful unified action (JP 1).

2. Create Shared Understanding

A defining challenge for commanders and staffs is creating shared understanding of their operational environment, their operation's purpose, its problems, and approaches to solving them. Shared understanding and purpose form the basis for unity of effort and trust. Commanders and staffs actively build and maintain shared understanding within the force and with unified action partners by maintaining collaboration and dialogue throughout the operations process (planning, preparation, execution, and assessment). (See ADP 5-0 for a discussion of the operations process.)

Commanders use collaboration to establish human connections, build trust, and create and maintain shared understanding and purpose. Collaborative exchange helps commanders increase their situational understanding, resolve potential misunderstandings, and assess the progress of operations. Effective collaboration provides a forum. It allows dialogue in which participants exchange information, learn from one another, and create joint solutions. Establishing a culture of collaboration is difficult but necessary. Creating shared understanding of the issues, concerns, and abilities of commanders, subordinates, and unified action partners takes an investment of time and effort. Successful commanders talk with Soldiers, subordinate leaders, and unified action partners. Through collaboration and dialogue, participants share information and perspectives, question assumptions, and exchange ideas to help create and maintain a shared understanding and purpose.

3. Provide a Clear Commander's Intent

The commander's intent is a clear and concise expression of the purpose of the operation and the desired military end state that supports mission command, provides focus to the staff, and helps subordinate and supporting commanders act to achieve the commander's desired results without further orders, even when the operation does not unfold as planned (JP 3-0). Commanders establish their own commander's intent within the intent of their higher commander. The higher commander's intent provides the basis for unity of effort throughout the larger force.

Commanders articulate the overall reason for the operation so forces understand why it is being conducted. A well-crafted commander's intent conveys a clear image of the operation's purpose, key tasks, and the desired outcome. It expresses the broader purpose of the operation—beyond that of the mission statement. This helps subordinate commanders and Soldiers to gain insight into what is expected of them, what constraints apply, and, most important, why the mission is being undertaken. A clear commander's intent that lower-level leaders can understand is key to maintaining unity of effort. (See ADRP 5-0 for the format of the commander's intent.)

4. Exercise Disciplined Initiative

Disciplined initiative is action in the absence of orders, when existing orders no longer fit the situation, or when unforeseen opportunities or threats arise. Leaders and subordinates exercise disciplined initiative to create opportunities. Commanders rely on subordinates to act, and subordinates take action to develop the situation. This willingness to act helps develop and maintain operational initiative that sets or dictates the terms of action throughout an operation.

The commander's intent defines the limits within which subordinates may exercise initiative. It gives subordinates the confidence to apply their judgment in ambiguous and urgent situations because they know the mission's purpose, key task, and desired end state. They can take actions they think will best accomplish the mission. Using disciplined initiative, subordinates strive to solve many unanticipated problems. They perform the necessary coordination and take appropriate action when existing orders no longer fit the situation.

Commanders and subordinates are obligated to follow lawful orders. Commanders deviate from orders only when they are unlawful, needlessly risk the lives of Soldiers, or no longer fit the situation. Subordinates inform their superiors as soon as possible when they have deviated from orders. Adhering to applicable laws and regulations when exercising disciplined initiative builds credibility and legitimacy. Straying beyond legal boundaries undermines trust and jeopardizes tactical, operational, and strategic success.

5. Use Mission Orders

Mission orders are directives that emphasize to subordinates the results to be attained, not how they are to achieve them. Commanders use mission orders to provide direction and guidance that focus the forces' activities on the achievement of the main objective, set priorities, allocate resources, and influence the situation. They provide subordinates the maximum freedom of action in determining how best to accomplish missions. Mission orders seek to maximize individual initiative, while relying on lateral coordination between units and vertical coordination up and down the chain of command. The mission orders technique does not mean commanders do not supervise subordinates in execution. However, they do not micromanage. They intervene during execution only to direct changes, when necessary, to the concept of operations.

6. Accept Prudent Risk

Commanders accept prudent risk when making decisions because uncertainty exists in all military operations. Prudent risk is a deliberate exposure to potential injury or loss when the commander judges the outcome in terms of mission accomplishment as worth the cost. Opportunities come with risks. The willingness to accept prudent risk is often the key to exposing enemy weaknesses.

Making reasonable estimates and intentionally accepting prudent risk are fundamental to mission command. Commanders focus on creating opportunities rather than simply preventing defeat—even when preventing defeat appears safer. Reasonably estimating and intentionally accepting risk are not gambling. Gambling, in contrast to prudent risk taking, is staking success on a single event without considering the hazard to the force should the event not unfold as envisioned. Therefore, commanders avoid taking gambles. Commanders carefully determine risks, analyze and minimize as many hazards as possible, and then take prudent risks to exploit opportunities.

Mission
Command

IV. Information

Ref: ADRP 6-0, Mission Command (May '12), pp. 2-13 to 2-14.

Commanders use the science of control to manage information. Information fuels understanding and decision making. Commanders establish information requirements to set priorities for collecting relevant information. An information requirement is any information element the commander and staff require to successfully conduct operations. Relevant information that answers information requirements is:

- **Accurate**: it conveys the true situation
- **Timely**: it is available in time to make decisions
- **Usable**: it is portrayed in common, easily understood formats and displays
- **Complete**: it provides all information necessary
- **Precise**: it contains sufficient detail
- **Reliable**: it is trustworthy and dependable

Commanders balance the art of command with the science of control as they assess information against these criteria. For example, in some situations, relevant information that is somewhat incomplete or imprecise may be better than no information at all, especially when time for execution is limited. However, effective commanders use the science of control to reduce the likelihood of receiving inaccurate, late, or unreliable information, which is of no value to the exercise of mission command.

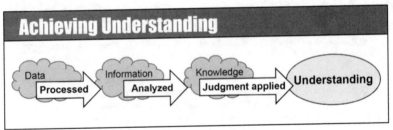

Ref: ADRP 6-0, Mission Command, fig. 2-1, p. 2-7.

Information can come in many forms, such as feedback and electronic means. Feedback comes from subordinates, higher headquarters, or adjacent, supporting, and supported forces and unified action partners. For feedback to be effective, a commander's mission command system must process it into knowledge, identifying any differences between the desired end state and the situation that exists. Commanders and staffs interpret information received to gain situational understanding and to exploit fleeting opportunities, respond to developing threats, modify plans, or reallocate resources.

Staffs provide commanders and subordinates information relevant to their operational environment and the progress of operations. They use the operational variables (political, military, economic, social, information, infrastructure, physical environment, and time—known as PMESII-PT) and the mission variables (mission, enemy, terrain and weather, troops and support available, time available and civil considerations—known as METT–TC) as major subject categories to group relevant information. Commanders and staffs develop a common operational picture (known as a COP), a single display of relevant information within a commander's area of interest tailored to the user's requirements and based on common data and information shared by more than one command. They choose any appropriate technique to develop and display the COP, such as graphical representations, verbal narratives, or written reports. Development of the COP is ongoing throughout operations. This tool supports developing knowledge and understanding.

II. Mission Command Warfighting Function

Ref: ADP 6-0, Mission Command (May '12), chap. 3.

Commanders, assisted by their staffs, conceptualize and apply capabilities in terms of combat power to accomplish the mission. Combat power consists of eight elements: leadership, information, and the six warfighting functions—mission command, movement and maneuver, intelligence, fires, sustainment, and protection. Each war fighting function consists of related tasks and a system, united by a common purpose that commanders use to achieve objectives and accomplish missions.

See p. 1-7 for an overview of the six warfighting functions from ADRP 3-0.

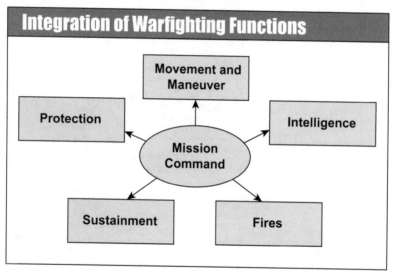

Ref: ADRP 6-0, Mission Command, fig. 3-1, p. 3-1.

The mission command warfighting function is the related tasks and systems that develop and integrate those activities enabling a commander to balance the art of command and the science of control in order to integrate the other war fighting functions (ADRP 3-0). It consists of the related tasks and a mission command system that support the exercise of authority and direction by the commander. Through the mission command warfighting function, commanders integrate the other warfighting functions into a coherent whole to mass the effects of combat power at the decisive place and time.

Refer to The Army Operations & Doctrine SMARTbook (Guide to Unified Land Operations and the Six Warfighting Functions) for discussion of the fundamentals, principles and tenets of Army operations, plus chapters on each of the six warfighting functions: mission command, movement and maneuver, intelligence, fires, sustainment, and protection.

I. Mission Command Warfighting Function Tasks

The mission command warfighting function tasks define what commanders and staffs do to integrate the other warfighting functions. They include mutually support- ing commander, staff, and additional tasks. The commander leads the staff tasks, and the staff tasks fully support the commander in executing the commander tasks. Commanders, assisted by their staffs, integrate numerous processes and activities within the headquarters and across the force as they exercise mission command.

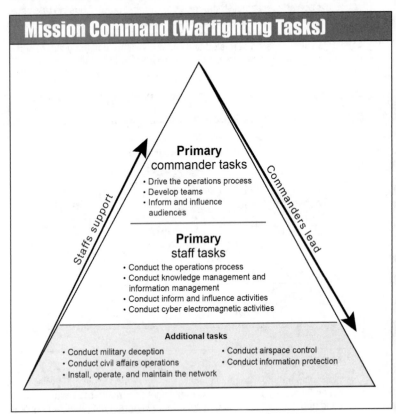

Ref: ADRP 6-0, Mission Command, fig. 3-2, p. 3-2.

Commanders are the central figures in mission command. Throughout operations, commanders balance their time between leading their staffs through the operations process and providing purpose, direction, and motivation to subordinate command- ers and Soldiers. Commanders encourage disciplined initiative through a clear commander's intent while providing enough direction to integrate and synchronize the actions of the force at the decisive place and time. Commanders create positive command climates that foster mutual trust and shared understanding within their command and with unified action partners.

The staff supports the commander and subordinate commanders in understanding situations, decision making, and implementing decisions throughout the conduct of operations.

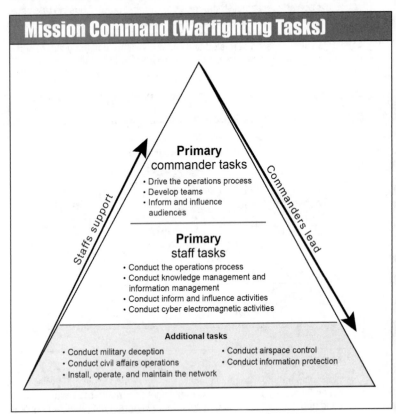 — inside: **Mission Command (Warfighting Tasks)**

Staffs support / Commanders lead

Primary commander tasks
- Drive the operations process
- Develop teams
- Inform and influence audiences

Primary staff tasks
- Conduct the operations process
- Conduct knowledge management and information management
- Conduct inform and influence activities
- Conduct cyber electromagnetic activities

Additional tasks
- Conduct military deception
- Conduct civil affairs operations
- Install, operate, and maintain the network
- Conduct airspace control
- Conduct information protection

II. Mission Command System

Ref: ADP 6-0, Mission Command (May '12), pp. 11 to 12.

At every echelon of command, each commander establishes a mission command system—the arrangement of personnel, networks, information systems, processes and procedures, and facilities and equipment that enable commanders to conduct operations. Commanders organize their mission command system to support decision making and facilitate communication.

1. Personnel

A commander's mission command system begins with people. Therefore, commanders base their mission command system on human characteristics and abilities more than on equipment and procedures. An effective mission command system requires trained personnel; commanders must not underestimate the importance of providing training. Key personnel dedicated to mission command include seconds in command, command sergeants major, and staff.

2. Networks

Social and technical networks enable commanders to communicate information and control forces, leading to successful operations. Generally, a network is a grouping of people or things interconnected for a purpose. Commanders develop and leverage various social networks—individuals and organizations interconnected by a common interest—to exchange information and ideas, build teams, and promote unity of effort. Technical networks also connect people and allow sharing of resources and information. For example, LandWarNet (the Army's portion of the Global Information Grid) is a technical network. It encompasses all Army information management systems and information systems that collect, process, store, display, disseminate, and protect information worldwide.

3. Information Systems

Commanders determine their information requirements and focus their staffs and organizations on using information systems to meet these requirements. An information system consists of equipment that collects, processes, stores, displays, and disseminates information. This includes computers—hardware and software—and communications, as well as policies and procedures for their use. Staffs use information systems to process, store, and disseminate information according to the commander's priorities. These capabilities relieve the staff of handling routine data. Information systems—especially when merged into a single, integrated network—enable extensive information sharing.

4. Processes and Procedures

Processes and procedures help commanders organize the activities within the headquarters and throughout the force. Processes and procedures govern actions within a mission command system to make it more effective and efficient. A process is a series of actions directed to an end state. One example is the military decision making process. Procedures are standard, detailed steps, often used by staffs, which describe how to perform specific tasks to achieve the desired end state. One example is a standard operating procedure. Adhering to processes and procedures minimizes confusion, misunderstanding, and hesitation as commanders make frequent, rapid decisions to meet operational requirements.

5. Facilities and Equipment

Facilities and equipment include command posts, signal nodes, and all mission command support equipment, excluding information systems. A facility is a structure or location that provides a work environment and shelter for the personnel within the mission command system. Facilities range from a command post composed of vehicles and tentage to hardened buildings. Examples of equipment needed to sustain a mission command system include vehicles, generators, and lighting.

Mission Command

A. Commander Tasks

Ref: ADRP 6-0, Mission Command (May '12), pp. 3-2 to 3-5.

Commanders are the central figures in mission command. Throughout operations, commanders balance their time between leading their staffs through the operations process and providing purpose, direction, and motivation to subordinate commanders and Soldiers. Commanders encourage disciplined initiative through a clear commander's intent while providing enough direction to integrate and synchronize the actions of the force at the decisive place and time. Commanders create positive command climates that foster mutual trust and shared understanding within their command and with unified action partners. The commander tasks are:

- Drive the operations process through their activities of understanding, visualizing, describing, directing, leading, and assessing operations
- Develop teams, both within their own organizations and with joint, interagency, and multinational partners
- Inform and influence audiences, inside and outside their organizations

1. Drive the Operations Process through Understanding, Visualizing, Describing, Directing, Leading and Assessing

The Army's overarching framework for exercising mission command is the operations process—the major mission command activities performed during operations: planning, preparing, executing, and continuously assessing the operation (ADP 5-0). Commanders, assisted by their staffs, integrate activities within the headquarters and across the force, as they exercise mission command. Commanders drive the operations process through the activities of understanding, visualizing, describing, directing, leading, and assessing operations. Throughout the operations process, commanders apply leadership to translate decisions into action. They do this by synchronizing forces and war fighting functions in time, space, and purpose, to accomplish the mission.

Commanders understand, visualize, describe, direct, lead, and assess throughout operations. Commanders continuously develop, test, and update their understanding throughout the conduct of operations. They actively collaborate with other commanders, the staff, and unified action partners, to create a shared understanding. As commanders begin to develop an understanding of the operational environment, they start visualizing the operation's end state and potential solutions to solve problems. After commanders visualize an operation, they describe it to their staffs and subordinates. This description facilitates shared understanding of the situation, mission, and intent. Based on this understanding, commanders make decisions and direct action throughout the operations process. Commanders use the operations process to lead Soldiers and forces by providing direction and guidance. Commanders assess operations continuously to better understand current conditions and determine how operations are progressing. Commanders incorporate the assessments of the staff, subordinate commanders, and unified action partners into their personal assessment of the situation. Based on their assessment, commanders modify plans and orders to better accomplish the mission. If their assessment reveals a significant variance from their original commander's visualization, commanders reframe the problem and develop a new operational approach.

The commander's focus on understanding, visualizing, describing, directing, leading, or assessing throughout operations varies during different operations process activities. For example, during planning commanders focus more on understanding, visualizing, and describing while directing, leading, and assessing. During execution, commanders often focus more on directing, leading, and assessing—while improving their understanding and modifying their visualization as needed.

2. Develop Teams within Their Own Organizations and with Joint, Interagency, and Multinational Partners

Successful mission command relies on teams and teamwork. A team is a group of individuals or organizations that work together toward a common goal. Teams range from informal groups of peers to structured, hierarchical groups. Teams may form in advance or gradually as the situation develops.

Commanders cannot always rely on habitual or pre-established relationships, and they must be able to build teams. In some cases, commanders must overcome biases that inhibit trust and cooperation. Commanders use their teambuilding skills to form effective teams and foster unity of effort. Successful team builders establish mutual trust, shared understanding, and cohesion. They instill a supportive attitude and a sense of responsibility among the team, and they appropriately distribute authority. Additionally, commanders expect to join pre-existing teams as host-nation and civilian organizations often are present before military forces arrive and remain long after forces leave. Overall, team building is a worthwhile investment because good teams complete missions on time with given resources and a minimum of wasted effort.

Effective teams synchronize individual efforts toward a common goal. They promote the exchange of ideas, creativity, and the development of collective solutions. They collaborate across the team to develop and improve processes. The variety of knowledge, talent, expertise, and resources in a team can produce better understanding and alternative options faster than one individual can achieve alone. Successful mission command fosters a greater understanding of the operational environment and solution development through teamwork. This results in teams that:

- Are adaptive and anticipate transitions
- Accept risks to create opportunities
- Influence friendly, neutrals, adversaries, enemies, and unified action partners

The ultimate team outcome is successful mission accomplishment.

3. Inform and Influence Audiences, Inside and Outside Their Organizations

Commanders use inform and influence activities to ensure actions, themes, and messages compliment and reinforce each other to accomplish objectives. Inform and influence activities are the integration of designated information-related capabilities in order to synchronize themes, messages, and actions with operations to inform United States and global audiences, influence foreign audiences, and affect adversary and enemy decision making (ADRP 3-0). An information theme is a unifying or dominant idea or image that expresses the purposes for an action. A message is a verbal, written, or electronic communication that supports an information theme focused on an audience. It supports a specific action or objective.

Actions, themes, and messages are inextricably linked. Commanders use inform and influence activities to ensure actions, themes, and messages compliment and reinforce each other and support operational objectives. They keep in mind that every action implies a message, and they avoid apparently contradictory actions, themes, or messages.

Throughout operations, commanders inform and influence audiences, both inside and outside of their organizations. Some commanders inform and influence through Soldier and leader engagements, conducting radio programs, command information programs, operations briefs, and unit Web site posts. Inform and influence activities assist commanders in creating shared understanding and purpose both inside and outside their organizations and among all affected audiences. This supports the commander's operational goals by synchronizing words and actions.

Mission
Command

B. Staff Tasks

Ref: ADRP 6-0, Mission Command (May '12), pp. 3-5 to 3-6.

The staff supports the commander and subordinate commanders in understanding situations, decision making, and implementing decisions throughout the conduct of operations. The staff does this through the four staff tasks:

- Conduct the operations process: plan, prepare, execute, and assess
- Conduct knowledge management and information management
- Conduct inform and influence activities
- Conduct cyber electromagnetic activities

1. Conduct the Operations Process: Plan, Prepare, Execute, and Assess

The operations process consists of the major activities of mission command conducted during operations: planning, preparing, executing and assessing operations. Commanders drive the operations process, while remaining focused on the major aspects of operations. Staffs conduct the operations process; they assist commanders in the details of planning, preparing, executing, and assessing.

Upon receipt of a mission, planning starts a cycle of the operations process that results in a plan or operation order to guide the force during execution. After the completion of the initial order, however, the commander and staff revise the plan based on changing circumstances. While units and Soldiers always prepare for potential operations, preparing for a specific operation begins during planning and continues through execution. Execution puts plans into action. During execution, staffs focus on concerted action to seize and retain operational initiative, build and maintain momentum, and exploit success. As the unit executes the current operation, the commander and staff are planning future operations based on assessments of progress. Assessment is continuous and affects the other three activities. Subordinate units of the same command may be conducting different operations process activities.

The continuous nature of the operations process allows commanders and staffs to make adjustments enabling agile and adaptive forces. Commanders, assisted by their staffs, integrate activities within the headquarters and across the force as they exercise mission command. Throughout the operations process, they develop an understanding and appreciation of their operational environment. They formulate a plan and provide purpose, direction, and guidance to the entire force. Commanders then adjust operations as changes to the operational environment occur. It is this cycle that enables commanders and forces to seize, retain, and exploit the initiative to gain a position of relative advantage over the enemy. (See ADRP 5-0 for a detailed explanation of the operations process.)

2. Conduct Knowledge Management and Information Management

Knowledge management is the process of enabling knowledge flow to enhance shared understanding, learning, and decision making. Knowledge management facilitates the transfer of knowledge between staffs, commanders, and forces. Knowledge management aligns people, processes, and tools within an organization to distribute knowledge and promote understanding. Commanders apply judgment to the information and knowledge provided to understand their operational environment and discern operational advantages. (See Army doctrine on knowledge management for more information.)

Commanders are constantly seeking to understand their operational environment in order to facilitate decision making. The staff uses information management to assist the commander in building and maintaining understanding. Information management is the science of using procedures and information systems to collect, process, store, display, disseminate, and protect data, information, and knowledge products. The staff studies the operational environment, identifies information gaps, and helps the commander develop and answer information requirements. Collected data are then organized and processed into information for development into and use as knowledge. Information becomes knowledge, and that knowledge also becomes a source of information. As this happens, new knowledge is created, shared, and acted upon. During the course of operations, knowledge constantly flows between individuals and organizations. Staffs help manage this constant cycle of exchange. (See Army doctrine on information management for more information.)

Staffs use information and knowledge management to provide commanders the information they need to create and maintain their understanding and make effective decisions. Information is disseminated, stored, and retrieved according to established information management practices. Information management practices allow all involved to build on each other's knowledge to further develop a shared understanding across the force. Knowledge management practices enable the transfer of knowledge between individuals and organizations. Knowledge transfer occurs both formally—through established processes and procedures—and informally—through collaboration and dialogue. Participants exchange perspectives along with information. They question each other's assumptions and exchange ideas. In this way, they create and maintain shared understanding and develop new approaches. Teams benefit, and forces enhance integration and synchronization.

3. Conduct Inform and Influence Activities

Throughout the operations process, staffs assist commanders in developing themes and messages to inform domestic audiences and influence foreign friendly, neutral, adversary, and enemy populations. They coordinate the activities and operations of information-related capabilities to integrate and synchronize all actions and messages into a cohesive effort. Staffs assist the commander in employing those capabilities to inform and influence foreign target audiences to shape the operational environment, exploit success, and protect friendly vulnerabilities. (See Army doctrine on inform and influence activities for more information.)

All assets and capabilities at a commander's disposal have the capacity to inform and influence to varying degrees. Some examples of resources commanders may use include combat camera, counter intelligence, maneuver and fires, and network operations. The primary information-related capabilities of inform and influence activities are:

- Public affairs
- Military information support operations
- Soldier and leader engagement

4. Conduct Cyber Electromagnetic Activities

Cyber electromagnetic activities are activities leveraged to seize, retain, and exploit an advantage over adversaries and enemies in both cyberspace and the electromagnetic spectrum, while simultaneously denying and degrading adversary and enemy use of the same and protecting the mission command system (ADRP 3-0).

To succeed in unified land operations, cyber electromagnetic activities must be integrated and synchronized across all command echelons and war fighting functions. Commanders, supported by their staff, integrate cyberspace operations, electromagnetic spectrum operations and electronic warfare. The electronic warfare working group or similar staff organization coordinates cyber electromagnetic activities. These activities may employ the same technologies, capabilities, and enablers to accomplish assigned tasks. Cyber electromagnetic activities also enable inform and influence activities, signals intelligence, and network operations. (See Army doctrine on cyber electromagnetic activities for more information.)

Continued on next page

Primary Staff Responsibilities

Ref: FM 6-0 (C1), Commander and Staff Organization and Operations (May '15), pp. 2-1 to 2-3.

Continued from previous page

The staff is a key component of the mission command system. In addition to executing the mission command staff tasks (see ADRP 6-0), the primary responsibilities of any staff are to:

- Support the commander
- Assist subordinate commanders, staffs, and units
- Inform units and organizations outside the headquarters

Support The Commander

Staffs support the commander in understanding, visualizing, and describing the operational environment; making and articulating decisions; and directing, leading, and assessing military operations. Staffs make recommendations and prepare plans and orders for the commander. Staff products consist of timely and relevant information and analysis. Staffs use knowledge management to extract that information from the vast amount of available information. Staffs synthesize this information and provide it to commanders in the form of running estimates to help commanders build and maintain their situational understanding.

Staffs support and advise the commander within their area of expertise. While commanders make key decisions, they are not the only decisionmakers. Trained and trusted staff members, given decisionmaking authority based on the commander's intent, free commanders from routine decisions. This enables commanders to focus on key aspects of operations. Staffs support the commander in communicating the commander's decisions and intent through plans and orders.

Assist Subordinate Commanders, Staffs, and Units

Effective staffs establish and maintain a high degree of coordination and cooperation with staffs of higher, lower, supporting, supported, and adjacent units. Staffs help subordinate headquarters understand the larger context of operations. They do this by first understanding their higher headquarters' operations and commander's intent, and nesting their own operations with higher headquarters. They then actively collaborate with subordinate commanders and staffs to facilitate a shared understanding of the operational environment. Examples of staffs assisting subordinate units include performing staff coordination, staff assistance visits, and staff inspections.

Inform Units and Organizations Outside the Headquarters

The staff keeps its units well informed. The staff also keeps civilian organizations informed with relevant information according to their security classification, as well as their need to know. As soon as a staff receives information and determines its relevancy, that staff passes that information to the appropriate headquarters. The key is relevance, not volume. Masses of data are worse than meaningless data; they inhibit mission command by distracting staffs from relevant information. Effective knowledge management helps staffs identify the information the commander and each staff element need, and its relative importance.

Information should reach recipients based on their need for it. Sending incomplete information sooner is better than sending complete information too late. When forwarding information, the sending staff highlights key information for each recipient and clarifies the commander's intent. Such highlighting and clarification assists receivers in analyzing the content of the information received in order to determine that information that may be of particular importance to the higher and subordinate commanders. The sending staff may pass information directly, include its analysis, or add context to it. Common, distributed databases can accelerate this function; however, they cannot replace the personal contact that adds perspective.

Continued from previous page

Common Staff Duties and Responsiblities

In addition to the mission command staff tasks, each staff element has specific duties and responsibilities by area of expertise. However, all staff sections share a set of common duties and responsibilities:

- Advising and informing the commander
- Building and maintaining running estimates
- Providing recommendations
- Preparing plans, orders, and other staff writing
- Assessing operations
- Managing information within area of expertise
- Identifying and analyzing problems
- Conducting staff assistance visits
- Performing risk management
- Performing intelligence preparation of the battlefield
- Conducting staff inspections
- Conducting staff research
- Performing staff administrative procedures
- Exercising staff supervision over their area of expertise
- Consulting and working with the servicing legal representative

Staff Relationships

Staff effectiveness depends in part on relationships of the staff with commanders and other staff. Collaboration and dialogue aids in developing shared understanding and visualization among staffs at different echelons. A staff acts on behalf of, and derives its authority from, the commander. Although commanders are the principal decisionmakers, individual staff officers make decisions within their authority based on broad guidance and unit standard operating procedures (SOPs). Commanders insist on frank dialogue between themselves and their staff officers. A staff gives honest, independent thoughts and recommendations, so commanders can make the best possible decisions. Once the commander makes a decision, staff officers support and implement the commander's decision even if the decision differs from their recommendations.

Teamwork within a staff and between staffs produces the staff integration essential to synchronized operations. A staff works efficiently with complete cooperation from all staff sections. A force operates effectively in cooperation with all headquarters. Commanders and staffs contribute to foster this positive climate during training and sustain it during operations. However, frequent personnel changes and augmentation to the headquarters adds challenges to building and maintaining the team. While all staff sections have clearly defined functional responsibilities, none can operate effectively in isolation. Therefore, coordination is extremely important. Commanders ensure staff sections are properly equipped and manned. This will allow staffs to efficiently work within the headquarters and with their counterparts in other headquarters. Commanders ensure staff integration through developing the unit's battle rhythm, including synchronizing various meetings, working groups, and boards.

C. Additional Tasks

Ref: ADRP 6-0, Mission Command (May '12), p. 3-7.

Commanders, assisted by their staffs, integrate five additional mission command warfighting function tasks. These are:

1. Conduct Military Deception

Commanders may use military deception to establish conditions favorable to success. Military deception is actions executed to deliberately mislead adversary military decision makers as to friendly military capabilities, intentions, and operations, thereby causing the adversary to take specific actions (or inactions) that will contribute to the accomplishment of the friendly mission (JP 3-13.4). Commanders use military deception to confuse an adversary, to deter hostile actions, and to increase the potential of successful friendly actions. It targets adversary decision makers and affects their decision making process. Military deception can enhance the likelihood of success by causing an adversary to take (or not to take) specific actions, not just to believe certain things.

2. Conduct Civil Affairs Operations

Commanders use civil affairs operations to engage the civil component of the operational environment. Military forces interact with the civilian populace during operations. A supportive civilian population can provide resources and information that facilitate friendly operations. A hostile civilian population can threaten the operations of deployed friendly forces. Commanders use civil affairs operations to enhance the relationship between military forces and civil authorities in areas where military forces are present. Civil affairs operations are usually conducted by civil affairs forces due to the complexities and demands for specialized capabilities. (See Army doctrine on civil affairs for more information.)

3. Install, Operate, and Maintain the Network

Commanders rely on technical networks to communicate information and control forces. Technical networks facilitate information flow by connecting information users and information producers and enable effective and efficient information flow. Technical networks help shape and influence operations by getting information to decision makers, with adequate context, enabling them to make better decisions. They also assist commanders in projecting their decisions across the force. (See Army doctrine on network operations for more information.)

4. Conduct Airspace Control

Commanders conduct airspace control to increase combat effectiveness. Airspace control promotes the safe, efficient, and flexible use of airspace with minimum restraint on airspace users, and includes the coordination, integration, and regulation of airspace to increase operational effectiveness. Effective airspace control reduces the risk of fratricide, enhances air defense operations, and permits greater flexibility of operations. (See Army doctrine on airspace control for more information.)

5. Conduct Information Protection

Information protection is active or passive measures used to safeguard and defend friendly information and information systems. It denies enemies, adversaries, and others the opportunity to exploit friendly information and information systems for their own purposes. It is accomplished through active and passive means designed to help protect the force and preserve combat power.

III. Command Post (CP) Organization/Operations

Ref: FM 6-0 (C1), Commander and Staff Organization and Operations (May '15), chap. 1.

This section describes how commanders organize their headquarters into command posts during the conduct of operations. This section defines the different types of command posts and describes their purposes. Next, this section discusses the effectiveness and survivability factors commanders consider when organizing their command posts. This section also describes how commanders cross-functionally organize their staffs within command posts into functional and integrating cells. The section concludes by providing guidelines for command post operations, including the importance of establishing standard operating procedures (SOPs) for the headquarters.

Refer to JP 3-33 for more information on an Army headquarters serving as a joint headquarters.

I. Command Post Organization

In operations, effective mission command requires continuous, close coordination, synchronization, and information sharing across staff sections. To promote this, commanders cross-functionally organize elements of staff sections in command posts (CPs) and CP cells. Additional staff integration occurs in meetings, including working groups and boards.

A. Command Posts

A command post is a unit headquarters where the commander and staff perform their activities. The headquarters' design, combined with robust communications, gives commanders a flexible mission command structure consisting of a main CP, a tactical CP, and a command group for brigades, divisions, and corps. Combined arms battalions are also resourced with a combat trains CP and a field trains CP. Theater army headquarters are resourced with a main CP and a contingency CP. See appropriate echelon manuals for doctrine on specific CP and headquarters' organization. Each CP performs specific functions by design as well as tasks the commander assigns. Activities common in all CPs include, but are not limited to:

- Maintaining running estimates and the common operational picture
- Controlling operations
- Assessing operations
- Developing and disseminating orders
- Coordinating with higher, lower, and adjacent units
- Conducting knowledge management and information management
- Conducting network operations
- Providing a facility for the commander to control operations, issue orders, and conduct rehearsals
- Maintaining the common operational picture
- Performing CP administration (examples include sleep plans, security, and feeding schedules)
- Supporting the commander's decisionmaking process

1. Main Command Post (Main CP)

The main command post is a facility containing the majority of the staff designed to control current operations, conduct detailed analysis, and plan future operations. The main CP is the unit's principal CP. It includes representatives of all staff sections and a full suite of information systems to plan, prepare, execute, and assess operations. It is larger in size and in staffing and less mobile than the tactical CP. The chief of staff (COS) or executive officer (XO) leads and provides staff supervision of the main CP. Functions of the main CP include, but are not limited to:

- Controlling and synchronizing current operations
- Monitoring and assessing current operations (including higher and adjacent units) for their impact on future operations
- Planning operations, including branches and sequels
- Assessing the overall progress of operations
- Preparing reports required by higher headquarters and receiving reports for subordinate units

2. Tactical Command Post (Tactical CP)

The tactical command post is a facility containing a tailored portion of a unit head-quarters designed to control portions of an operation for a limited time. Commanders employ the tactical CP as an extension of the main CP to help control the execution of an operation or a specific task, such as a gap crossing, a passage of lines, or an air assault operation. Commanders may employ the tactical CP to direct the operations of units close to each other, such as during a relief in place. The tactical CP may also control a special task force or a complex task, such as reception, staging, onward movement, and integration. The tactical CP is fully mobile and includes only essential Soldiers and equipment. The tactical CP relies on the main CP for planning, detailed analysis, and coordination. A deputy commander or operations officer leads the tactical CP. When employed, tactical CP functions include the following:

- Monitoring and controlling current operations
- Monitoring and assessing the progress of higher and adjacent units
- Performing short-range planning
- Providing input to targeting and future operations planning

When the commander does not employ the tactical CP, the staff assigned to it reinforces the main CP. Unit standard operating procedures (SOPs) should address the specifics for this, including procedures to quickly detach the tactical CP from the main CP.

B. Command Group

A command group consists of commander and selected staff members who assist the commander in controlling operations away from a command post. The command group is organized and equipped to suit the commander's decision making and leadership requirements. It does this while enabling the commander to accomplish critical mission command tasks anywhere in the area of operations.

Command group personnel includes staff representation that can immediately affect current operations, such as maneuver, fires (including the air liaison officer), and intelligence. The mission and available staff, however, dictate the command group's makeup. For example, during a deliberate breach, the command group may include an engineer and an air defense officer. When visiting a dislocated civilians' collection point, the commander may take a translator, civil affairs operations officer, a medical officer, and a chaplain.

Divisions and corps headquarters are equipped with a mobile command group. The mobile command group serves as the commander's mobile CP. It consists of ground and air components equipped with information systems. The mobile command group's mobility allows commanders to move to critical locations to personally assess a situation, make decisions, and influence operations. The mobile command group's information systems and small staff allow commanders to do this while retaining communication with the entire force.

C. Early Entry Command Post (EECP)

While not part of the unit's table of organization and equipment, commanders can establish an early-entry command post to assist them in controlling operations during the deployment phase of an operation. An early-entry command post is a lead element of a headquarters designed to control operations until the remaining portions of the headquarters are deployed and operational. The early-entry command post normally consists of personnel and equipment from the tactical CP with additional intelligence analysts, planners, and other staff officers from the main CP based on the situation. The early-entry command post performs the functions of the main and tactical CPs until those CPs are deployed and fully operational. A deputy commander, COS (XO), or operations officer normally leads the early-entry command post.

II. Command Post Operations

Units must man, equip, and organize command posts to control operations for extended periods. Effective CP personnel use information systems and equipment to support 24-hour operations while they ontinuously communicate with all subordinate, higher, and adjacent units. Commanders arrange CP personnel and equipment to facilitate internal coordination, information sharing, and rapid decisionmaking. They also ensure that they have procedures to execute the operations process within the headquarters to enhance how they exercise mission command. Commanders use the battle rhythm, SOPs, and meetings to assist them with effective CP operations.

A. Standard Operating Procedures

SOPs that assist with effective mission command serve two purposes. Internal SOPs standardize each CP's internal operations and administration. External SOPs developed for the entire force standardize interactions among CPs and between subordinate units and CPs. Effective SOPs require all Soldiers to know their provisions and train to their standards. (Refer to FM 7-15 for more information on the tasks of command post operations.) Each CP should have SOPs that address the following:

- Organization and setup
- Staffing and shifts plans, including eating and sleeping plans
- Physical security and defense
- Priorities of work
- Equipment and vehicle maintenance, including journals and a maintenance log
- Load plans and equipment checklists
- Orders production and dissemination procedures
- Plans for handling, storing, and cleaning up hazardous materials
- Battle rhythm.
- Use of Army Battle Command Systems, such as Command Post of the Future, Advanced Field Artillery Tactical Data System, and Blue Force Tracker

In addition to these SOPS, each CP requires:

- CP battle drills
- Shift-change briefings
- Reports and returns
- Operations update and assessment briefings
- Operations synchronization meeting
- Procedures for transferring control between CPs.

III. Command Post (CP) Organization Considerations

Ref: FM 6-0 (C1), Commander and Staff Organization and Operations (May '15), pp. 1-3 to 1-4.

When organizing the CP, commanders must consider effectiveness and survivability. However, effectiveness considerations may compete with survivability considerations, making it difficult to optimize either. Commanders balance survivability and effectiveness considerations when organizing CPs.

A. Effectiveness Factors

CP staff and equipment are arranged to facilitate coordination, information exchange, and rapid decision making. CPs must effectively communicate with all subordinate units. Their organization enables them to quickly deploy throughout the unit's area of operations (AO). Five factors contribute to CP effectiveness: design, standardization, continuity, deployability, and capacity and range.

1. Design and Layout

Many design considerations affect CP effectiveness. At a minimum, commanders position CP cells and staff elements to facilitate communication and coordination. Other design considerations include, but are not limited to:

- Efficient facilitation of information flow
- User interface with communications systems
- Positioning information displays for ease of use
- Integrating complementary information on maps and displays
- Adequate workspace for the staff and commander
- Ease of displacement (setup, teardown, and mobility)
- Effective and efficient power generation and distribution.

Well-designed CPs integrate command and staff efforts. Meeting this requirement requires matching the CP's manning, equipment, information systems, and procedures against its internal layout and utilities. Organizing the CP into functional and integrating cells promotes efficiency and coordination.

2. Standardization

Standardization increases efficiency and eases CP personnel training. Commanders develop detailed SOPs for all aspects of CP operations during all operations. Standard CP layouts, battle drills, and reporting procedures increase efficiency. Units follow and revise SOPs throughout training. Units constantly reinforce using SOPs to make many processes routine. Staffs then effectively execute them in demanding, stressful times.

3. Continuity

Commanders staff, equip, and organize CPs to control and support 24-hour operations without interruptions by enemies, environmental conditions, or actions. However, duplicating every staff member within a CP is unnecessary. Commanders carefully consider the primary role and functions assigned to each CP and resource it accordingly. Internal CP SOPs address shifts, rest plans, and other CP activities important to operating continuously. Leaders enforce these provisions.

Maintaining continuity during displacement or catastrophic loss requires designating alternate CPs and procedures for passing control between them. SOPs address providing continuity when units lose communications with the commander, subordinates, and or a particular CP. Commanders designate seconds in command and inform them of all critical decisions. Primary staff officers also designate alternates.

4. Deployability

CPs deploy efficiently and move within the AO as required. Determining the capabilities, size, and sequence of CPs in the deployment flow requires careful consideration. Commanders can configure modular CP elements as an early-entry command post if needed. They also add or subtract elements to the early-entry command post as needed. CP size directly affects deployment and employment.

5. Capacity, Connectivity and Range

Efficient and effective CP organization allows the commander to maintain the capacity to plan, prepare, execute, and continuously assess operations. CPs require uninterrupted connectivity to effectively communicate with higher and subordinate headquarters. Commanders and staffs must consider various factors that can adversely affect the efficiency of communications systems, such as built-up areas, mountains, and atmospheric conditions.

B. Survivability Factors

CP survivability is vital to mission success. CPs often gain survivability at the price of effectiveness. CPs need to remain small and highly mobile. When concentrated, the enemy can easily acquire and target most CPs. However, when elements of a CP disperse, they often have difficulty maintaining a coordinated staff effort. When developing command post SOPs and organizing headquarters into CPs for operations, commanders use dispersion, size, redundancy, and mobility to increase survivability.

1. Dispersion

Dispersing CPs enhances survivability. Commanders place minimum resources forward and keep more elaborate facilities back. This makes it harder for enemies to find and attack them. It also decreases support and security requirements forward. Most of the staff resides in the main CP; the tactical CP contains only the staff and equipment essential to controlling current operations.

2. Size

A CP's size affects its survivability. Larger CPs ease face-to-face coordination; however, they are vulnerable to multiple acquisitions and means of attack. Units can hide and protect smaller CPs more easily but may not control all force elements. Striking the right balance provides a responsive yet agile organization. For example, commanders require information for decisions; they do not need every subject matter expert located with them.

3. Redundancy

Some personnel and equipment redundancy is required for continuous operations. Redundancy allows CPs to continue operating when mission command systems are lost, damaged, or fail under stress.

4. Mobility

CP mobility improves CP survivability, especially at lower echelons. Successful lower-echelon CPs and those employed forward in the combat zone move quickly and often. A smaller size and careful transportation planning allow CPs to displace rapidly to avoid the enemy.

Command Post Battle Drills

Each CP requires procedures to react to a variety of situations. Specific actions taken by a CP should be defined in its SOPs and rehearsed during training and operations. Typical CP battle drills include, but are not limited to:

- React to an air, ground, or chemical attack
- React to indirect fire
- React to jamming or suspected communications compromise
- Execute time-sensitive targets
- Execute a close air support or joint fires mission
- React to a mass casualty incident
- React to a civil riot or incident
- React to significant collateral damage
- React to incorrect information affecting an operational environment.
- React to a degraded network.
- React to a duty status and whereabouts unknown incident.

Shift-Change Briefings

During continuous operations, CPs operate in shifts. To ensure uninterrupted operations, staffs execute a briefing when shifts change. Depending on the situation, it may be formal or informal and include the entire staff or selected staff members. Normally key CP leaders meet face-to-face. The COS (XO) oversees the briefing, with participants briefing their areas of expertise. The briefing's purpose is to inform the incoming shift of:

- Current unit status
- Significant activities that occurred during the previous shift
- Significant decisions and events anticipated during the next shift

The commander may attend and possibly change the focus of the briefing. If the commander issues guidance or makes a decision, issuing a fragmentary order may be necessary. The shift-change briefing format and emphasis change based on the situation. For example, the format for a force supporting civil authorities in a disaster area differs from a force conducting offensive operations abroad. To facilitate a quick but effective shift-change briefing, unit SOPs should contain tailored formats.

The shift-change briefing provides a mechanism to formally exchange information periodically among CP staff members. CP staff members coordinate activities and inform each other continuously. They give information that answers a commander's critical information requirement and exceptional information to the commander immediately. They disseminate information that potentially affects the entire force to the commander, higher headquarters, and subordinate units as the situation dictates. Situational understanding for CP staff members includes knowing who needs what relevant information and why they need it.

See facing page (p. 5-21) for a sample shift-change briefing.

Reports and Returns

A unit's reporting system facilitates timely and effective information exchange among CPs and higher, lower, and adjacent headquarters. An established SOP for reports and returns drives effective information management. These SOPs state the writer, the frequency and time, and recipient of each report. List nonstandard reports in Annex R (Reports) of the operation plan and operation order.

Operation Update and Assessment Briefing

An operation update and assessment briefing may occur daily or anytime the commander calls for one. Its content is similar to the shift-change briefing but has a different audience. The staff presents it to the commander and subordinate commanders. It provides all key personnel with common situational awareness. Often

Sample Shift-Change Briefing

Ref: FM 6-0 (C1), Commander and Staff Organization and Operations (May '15), table 1-1, p. 1-1.

Current mission and commander's intent (COS [XO])

Enemy situation (G-2 [S-2])
- Significant threat or local populace attitudes and actions during the last shift.
- Current enemy situation and changes in the most likely enemy courses of action
- Anticipated significant threat or undesired local populace activity in the next 12/24/48 hours
- Changes in priority intelligence requirements (PIRs)
- Weather update and weather effects on operations in the next 12/24/48 hours.
- Changes to information collection priorities.
- Status of information collection units and capabilities.

Civil Situation (G-9 [S-9])
- Significant actions by the population during the last shift
- Current civil situation
- Disposition and status of civil affairs units and capabilities
- Significant activities involving the population anticipated during the next shift

Friendly situation (G-3 [S-3])
- Significant friendly actions during the last shift
- Subordinate units' disposition and status
- Higher and adjacent units' disposition and status
- Major changes to the task organization and tasks to subordinate units that occurred during the last shift
- Answers to CCIRs and changes in CCIRs
- Changes to reconnaissance and surveillance
- Disposition and status of selected reconnaissance and surveillance units and capabilities
- Answers to FFIRs and changes in FFIRs
- Significant activities/decisions scheduled for next shift (decision support matrix)
- Anticipated planning requirements

Running estimate summaries by warfighting function and staff section —

- Fires
- Air liaison officer
- Aviation officer
- Air and missile defense officer
- G-7 (S-7)
- Engineer officer
- Chemical officer
- Provost marshal
- G-1 (S-1)
- G-4 (S-4)
- G-6 (S-6)

Briefings include—
- Any significant activities that occurred during the last shift
- The disposition and status of units within their area of expertise
- Any changes that have staff wide implications (for example, "higher headquarters changed the controlled supply rate for 120 mm HE, so that means...").
- Upcoming activities and anticipated changes during the next shift

CP operations and administration (headquarters commandant or senior operations NCO).

- CP logistic issues
- CP security
- CP displacement plan and proposed new locations
- Priority of work

COS or XO guidance to the next shift, including staff priorities and changes to the battle rhythm.

IV. Command Post Cells and Staff Sections

Ref: FM 6-0 (C1), Commander and Staff Organization and Operations (May '15), pp. 1-5 to 1-8.

Within CPs, commanders cross-functionally organize their staffs into CP cells and staff sections to assist them in the exercise of mission command. A command post cell is a grouping of personnel and equipment organized by warfighting function or by planning horizon to facilitate the exercise of mission command.

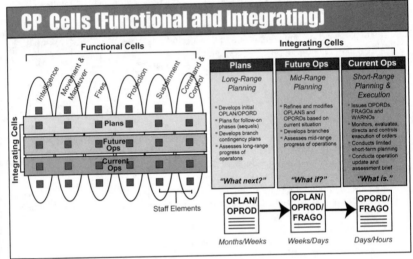

A. Functional Cells

Functional cells coordinate and synchronize forces and activities by warfighting function. The functional cells within a CP are intelligence, movement and maneuver, fires, protection, and sustainment. Echelons above brigade are resourced for all five functional cells.

- **Intelligence Cell.** The intelligence cell coordinates activities and systems that help commanders understand the enemy, terrain and weather, and civil considerations. The intelligence cell requests, receives, and analyzes information from all sources to produce and distribute intelligence products. This includes tasks associated with intelligence preparation of the battlefield and intelligence, surveillance, and reconnaissance. Most of the intelligence staff section resides in this cell. The unit's intelligence officer leads this cell.

- **Movement and Maneuver Cell.** The movement and maneuver cell coordinates activities and systems that move forces to achieve a position of advantage in relation to the enemy. This includes tasks associated with combining forces with direct fire or fire potential (maneuver) and force projection (movement) related to gaining a positional advantage over an enemy. Elements of the operations, airspace command and control, aviation, engineer, geospatial information and service, and space staff sections form this cell. The operations officer leads this cell. Staff elements in this cell also form the core of the current operations cell.

- **Fires Cell.** The fires cell coordinates activities and systems that provide collective and coordinated use of Army indirect fires, joint fires, and C2 warfare through the targeting process. The fires cell is comprised of elements of fire support, Air Force (or air component), and electronic warfare staff section. The chief of fires (or fire support officer brigade and below) leads this cell.

- **Protection Cell.** The protection cell coordinates the activities and systems that preserve the force through composite risk management. This includes tasks associated with protecting personnel, physical assets, and information. Elements of the following staff sections form this cell: air and missile defense; chemical, biological, radiological, and nuclear;

engineer; operations security; personnel recovery; and provost marshal. Additionally, safety exists in theater army. The protection cell coordinates with the signal staff section in the C2 cell to further facilitate the information protection task. The chief of protection leads this cell.

- **Sustainment Cell.** The sustainment cell coordinates activities and systems that provide support and services to ensure freedom of action, extend operational reach, and prolong endurance. It includes those tasks associated with logistics, personnel services, and Army health service support. The following staff sections form this cell: personnel, logistics, financial management, and surgeon. The chief of sustainment (or logistics officer brigade and below) leads this cell.

B. Integrating Cells

Whereas functional cells are organized by warfighting functions, integrating cells are organized by planning horizons. They coordinate and synchronize forces and warfighting functions within a specified planning horizon and include the plans cell, future operations cell, and current operations integration cell. A planning horizon is a point in time commanders use to focus the organization's planning efforts to shape future events (ADRP 5-0). The three planning horizons are long, mid, and short (generally associated with the plans cell, future operations cell, and current operations integration cell, respectively).

Planning horizons are situation-dependent and are influenced by events and decisions. For example, the plans cell normally focuses its planning effort on the development of sequels—the subsequent next operation or phase of the operation based on possible outcomes (success, stalemate, or defeat) of the current operation or phase. The future operations cell normally focuses its efforts on branch plans—options built into the base plan that changes the concept of operations based on anticipated events, opportunities, or threats. Planning guidance and decisions by the commander or that of the higher headquarters influence the planning horizons.

Not all echelons and types of units are resourced for all three integrating cells. Battalions, for example, combine their planning and operations responsibilities in one integrating cell. The brigade combat team has a small, dedicated plans cell but it is not resourced for a future operations cell.

- **Plans Cell.** The plans cell is responsible for planning operations for the long-range planning horizons. It prepares for operations beyond the scope of the current order by developing plans, orders, branch plans, and sequels. The plans cell also oversees military deception planning. After completing the initial operation order, the plans cell normally develops plans for the next operation or the next phase of the current operation. The plans cell consists of a core group of planners and analysts led by the plans officer (or the operations officer at brigade and battalion levels). All staff sections assist as required.

- **Future Operations Cell.** The future operations cell is responsible for planning operations in the mid-range planning horizon. It focuses on adjustments to the current operation—including the positioning or maneuvering of forces in depth—that facilitates continuation of the current operation. The cell consists of a core group of planners led by an assistant operations officer (the chief of future operations). All staff sections assist as required. Divisions and above headquarters have a future operations cell. Battalion and brigade headquarters do not. In many respects, the future operations cell serves as a fusion cell between the plans and current operations cells. The future operations cell monitors current operations and determines implications for operations within the mid-range planning horizon. In coordination with the current operations cell, the future operations cell assesses whether the ongoing operation must be modified to achieve the current phase's objectives.

- **Current Operations Cell.** The current operations cell is the focal point for the execution of the operations. This involves assessing the current situation while regulating forces and war fighting functions in accordance with the mission, commander's intent, and concept of operations. The current operations cell displays the common operational picture and conducts shift changes, assessments, and other briefings as required. It provides information on the status of operations to all staff members and to higher, subordinate, and adjacent units. All staff sections are represented, either permanently or on call. See also p. 1-44.

commanders require this briefing shortly before an operation begins to summarize changes made during preparation, including changes resulting from reconnaissance and surveillance efforts.

During the briefing, staff sections present their running estimates. Subordinate commanders brief their current situation and planned activities. Rarely do all members conduct this briefing face-to-face. All CPs and subordinate commanders participate using available communications, including radio, conference calls, and video teleconference. The briefing follows a sequence and format specified by SOPs. That keeps transmissions short, ensures completeness, and eases note taking. This briefing normally has a format similar to a shift-change briefing. However, it omits CP administrative information and includes presentations by subordinate commanders in an established sequence.

Operations Synchronization Meeting

The operations synchronization meeting is the key event in the battle rhythm in support of the current operation. Its primary purpose is to synchronize all war fighting functions and other activities in the short-term planning horizon. It is designed to ensure that all staff members have a common understanding of current operations, including upcoming and projected actions at decision points.

The operations synchronization meeting does not replace the shift-change briefing or operation update and assessment briefing. Chaired by the G-3 (S-3), representatives of each CP cell and separate staff section attend the meeting. The operations synchronization meeting includes a fragmentary order addressing any required changes to maintain synchronization of current operations, and any updated planning guidance for upcoming working groups and boards. All war fighting functions are synchronized and appropriate fragmentary orders are issued to subordinates based on the commander's intent for current operations.

Transferring Control of Operations Between CPs

The employment and use of CPs are important decisions reflected in the operation order. Often, a particular CP may control part or all of the operation for a specific time. Effectively transferring control between CPs requires a well-understood SOP and clear instructions in the operation order. While all CPs have some ability to exercise control on the move, they lose many capabilities they have when stationary. Therefore, CPs normally control operations from a static location. During moves, they transfer control responsibilities to another CP. Transfer of control requires notifying subordinates since many network operations change to route information to the new controlling CP. SOPs establish these requirements to minimize interruptions when transferring control.

B. Battle Rhythm

A headquarters' battle rhythm consists of a series of meetings, briefings, and other activities synchronized by time and purpose. Battle rhythm is a deliberate daily cycle of command, staff, and unit activities intended to synchronize current and future operations. The COS (XO) oversees the battle rhythm. Staffs should logically sequence each meeting, to include working groups and boards, so they have one meeting's outputs available as another meeting's inputs (to include higher headquarters meetings). The COS (XO) balances other staff duties and responsibilities with the time required to plan, prepare for, and hold meetings and conduct briefings. The COS (XO) also critically examines attendance requirements. Some staff sections and CP cells may lack the personnel to attend all events. The COS (XO) and staff members constantly look for ways to combine meetings and eliminate unproductive ones. The battle rhythm enables:

- Establishing a routine for staff interaction and coordination
- Facilitating interaction between the commander and staff

- Synchronizing activities of the staff in time and purpose
- Facilitating planning by the staff and decision making by the commander

The battle rhythm changes during execution as operations progress. For example, early in the operation a commander may require a daily plans update briefing. As the situation changes, the commander may only require a plans update every three days. Some factors that help determine a unit's battle rhythm include the staff's proficiency, higher headquarters' battle rhythm, and current mission. In developing the unit's battle rhythm, the chief COS (XO) considers:

- Higher headquarters' battle rhythm and report requirements
- Subordinate headquarters' battle rhythm requirements
- The duration and intensity of the operation
- Integrating cells' planning requirements

C. Meetings

Meetings are gatherings to present and exchange information, solve problems, coordinate action, and make decisions. They may involve the staff; the commander and staff; or the commander, subordinate commanders, staff, and other partners. Who attends depends on the issue. Commanders establish meetings to integrate the staff and enhance planning and decision making within the headquarters. Commanders also identify staff members to participate in the higher commander's meeting, including working groups and boards. (JP 3-33 discusses the various working groups and boards used by joint force commanders.) The number of meetings and subjects they address depend on the situation and echelon. While numerous informal meetings occur daily within a headquarters, meetings commonly included in a unit's battle rhythm and the cells responsible for them include:

- A shift-change briefing (current operations integration cell)
- An operation update and assessment briefing (current operations integration cell)
- An operations synchronization meeting (current operations integration cell)
- Planning meetings and briefings (plans or future operations cells)
- Working groups and boards (various functional and integrating cells)

Often, the commander establishes and maintains only those meetings required by the situation. Commanders—assisted by the COS (XO)—establish, modify, and dissolve meetings as the situation evolves. The COS (XO) manages the timings of these events through the unit's battle rhythm. For each meeting, a unit's SOPs address:

- Purpose
- Frequency
- Composition (chair and participants)
- Inputs and expected outputs
- Agenda

Working Groups and Boards

Boards and working groups are types of meetings and are included in the unit's battle rhythm. A board is a grouping of predetermined staff representatives with delegated decision authority for a particular purpose or function. Boards are similar to working groups. However, commanders appoint boards to make decisions. When the process or activity being synchronized requires command approval, a board is the appropriate forum.

A working group is a grouping of predetermined staff representatives who meet to provide analysis, coordinate, and provide recommendations for a particular purpose or function. Their crossfunctional design enables working groups to synchronize contributions from multiple CP cells and staff sections. For example, the targeting working group brings together representatives of all staff elements concerned with targeting. It synchronizes the contributions of all staff elements with the work of the fires cell. It also synchronizes fires with future operations and current operations integration cells.

Working groups address various subjects depending on the situation and echelon. Battalion and brigade headquarters normally have fewer working groups than higher echelons have. Working groups may convene daily, weekly, monthly, or intermittently depending on the subject, situation, and echelon. Typical working groups and the lead cell or staff section at division and corps headquarters include the following:

- Assessment working group (plans or future operations cell)
- Operations and intelligence working group (intelligence cell)
- Targeting working group (fires cell)
- Protection working group (protection cell)
- Civil affairs operations working group (civil affairs operations staff section)
- Information operations working group (movement and maneuver cell)
- Cyber electromagnetic activities working group (electronic warfare element)

Sample Working Group SOP

Sample SOP for a division civil-military operations working group.

Purpose/Frequency	Purpose: • Establish policies, procedures, priorities, and overall direction for all civil-military operations projects • Provide update on ongoing civil-military operations projects • Identify needs within the area of operations • Present suggested future projects Frequency: Weekly
Composition	Chair: G-9 Attendees: • Civil affairs battalion representative • Public Affairs BCT and Marine Corps liaison officer • G-2 planner • Military information support element representative • G-3 operations representative • Provost marshal or force protection representative • G-5 planner • G-7 representative • Special operations forces liaison officer • Staff Judge Advocate representative • Surgeon • Military information support planner • Chaplain • Host-nation liaison officers • Project manager and contractor representatives • Engineer planner
Inputs/Outputs	Inputs: • Project management status • Information Operations working group (last week's) • Targeting board • Higher headquarters operation order Outputs: • Updated project status matrix • Proposed project matrix • Long-range civil-military operations plan adjustment
Agenda	• G-2 update or assessment • Operations update • Public perception update • Civil affairs project update • Engineer project update • Staff Judge Advocate concerns • Discussion or issues • Approval of information operations working group inputs

Ref: FM 6-0 (C1), Commander and Staff Organization and Operations, table 1-2, p. 1-14.

IV. Liaison

Ref: FM 6-0 (C1), Commander and Staff Organization and Operations (May '15), chap. 13.

This section discusses liaison fundamentals and responsibilities of liaison officers and teams. It addresses requirements distinct to contingency operations and unified action. It includes liaison checklists and an example outline for a liaison officer handbook.

I. Liaison Fundamentals

Liaison is that contact or intercommunication maintained between elements of military forces or other agencies to ensure mutual understanding and unity of purpose and action (JP 3-08). Liaison helps reduce uncertainty. Most commonly used for establishing and maintaining close communications, liaison continuously enables direct, physical communications between commands. Commanders use liaison during operations and normal daily activities to help facilitate communications between organizations, preserve freedom of action, and maintain flexibility. Effective liaison ensures commanders that subordinates understand implicit coordination. Liaison provides commanders with relevant information and answers to operational questions, thus enhancing the commander's confidence.

Liaison activities augment the commander's ability to synchronize and focus combat power. They include establishing and maintaining physical contact and communications between elements of military forces and nonmilitary agencies during unified action. Liaison activities ensure:

- Cooperation and understanding among commanders and staffs of different headquarters
- Coordination on tactical matters to achieve unity of effort
- Synchronization of lethal and non-lethal operations
- Understanding of implied or inferred coordination measures to achieve synchronized results

A. Liaison Officer

A liaison officer (LNO) represents a commander or staff officer. Laos transmit information directly, bypassing headquarters and staff layers. A trained, competent, trusted, and informed LNO (either a commissioned or a noncommissioned officer) is the key to effective liaison. LNOs must have the commander's full confidence and experience for the mission.

Senior liaison officer rank by echelon	Recommended rank
Multinational or joint force commander[1]	Colonel
Corps	Lieutenant Colonel
Division	Major
Brigade, regiment, or group	Captain
Battalion	Lieutenant
[1]These include joint force commanders and functional component commanders and may also include major interagency and international organizations.	

Ref: FM 6-0 (C1), table 13-1, p. 13-1. Senior liaison officer rank by echelon.

The LNO's parent unit or unit of assignment is the sending unit. The unit or activity that the LNO is sent to is the receiving unit, which may be a host nation. An LNO normally remains at the receiving unit until recalled. LNOs represent the commander and they:

- Understand how the commander thinks and interpret the commander's messages
- Convey the commander's intent, guidance, mission, and concept of operations
- Represent the commander's position

As a representative, the LNO has access to the commander consistent with the duties involved. However, for routine matters, LNOs work for and receive direction from the chief of staff (COS) or the executive officer (XO). Using one officer to perform a liaison mission conserves manpower while guaranteeing a consistent, accurate flow of information. However, continuous operations require a liaison team.

The professional capabilities and personal characteristics of an effective LNO encourage confidence and cooperation with the commander and staff of the receiving unit. In addition to the above discussion, effective LNOs:

- Know the sending unit's mission; current and future operations; logistics status; organization; disposition; capabilities; and tactics, techniques, and procedures
- Appreciate and understand the receiving unit's TTP, organization, capabilities, mission, doctrine, staff procedures, and customs
- Are familiar with:
  - Requirements for and purpose of liaison
  - The liaison system and its reports, documents, and records
  - Liaison team training
  - Observe the established channels of command and staff functions
  - Are tactful
  - Possess familiarity with local culture and language, and have advanced regional expertise if possible

B. Liaison Elements

Commanders organize liaison elements based on the mission variables (known as METT-TC) and echelon of command. Common ways to organize liaison elements include, but are not limited to:

- A single LNO
- A liaison team consisting of one or two LNOs, or an LNO and a liaison NCO in charge, clerical personnel, and communications personnel along with their equipment
- Couriers (messengers) responsible for the secure physical transmission and delivery of documents and other materials
- A digital liaison detachment comprised of several teams with expertise and equipment in specialized areas, such as intelligence, operations, fire support, air defense, and sustainment

Digital Liaison Detachments

Digital liaison detachments provide Army commanders units to conduct liaison with major subordinate or parallel headquarters. Digital liaison detachments consist of staff officers with a broad range of expertise who are capable of analyzing the situation, facilitating coordination between multinational forces, and assisting in cross-boundary information flow and operational support. These 30-Soldier teams are essential not only for routine liaison, but also for advising and assisting multinational partners in conducting planning and operations at intermediate tactical levels. These detachments can operate as a single entity for liaison with a major multinational headquarters, or provide two smaller teams for digital connectivity and liaison with smaller multinational headquarters.

II. Liaison Duties

Ref: FM 6-0 (C1), Commander and Staff Organization and Operations (May '15), pp. 13-7 to 13-8.

LNOs also inform the receiving unit's commander or staff of the sending unit's needs or requirements. The LNO's ability to rapidly clarify questions about the sending unit can keep the receiving unit from wasting planning time. During the liaison tour, LNOs:

- Arrive at the designated location on time
- Promote cooperation between the sending and receiving unit
- Follow the receiving unit's communication procedures
- Actively obtain information without interfering with receiving unit operations
- Facilitate understanding of the sending unit's commander's intent
- Help the sending unit's commander assess current and future operations
- Remain informed of the sending unit's current situation and provide that information to the receiving unit's commander and staff
- Expeditiously inform the sending unit of the receiving unit's upcoming missions, tasks, and orders
- Ensure the sending unit has a copy of the receiving unit's SOP
- Inform the receiving unit's commander or COS (XO) of the content of reports transmitted to the sending unit
- Keep a record of their reports, listing everyone met (including each person's name, rank, duty position, and telephone number)
- Attempt to resolve issues within receiving unit before involving the sending unit
- Notify the sending unit promptly if unable to accomplish the liaison mission
- Report their departure to the receiving unit's commander at the end of their mission
- Arrive at least two hours before any scheduled briefings
- Check in with security and complete any required documentation
- Present your credentials to the COS (XO)
- Arrange for an "office call" with the commander
- Meet the coordinating and special staff officers
- Notify the sending unit of arrival
- Visit staff elements, brief them on the sending unit's situation, and collect information from them
- Deliver all correspondence designated for the receiving unit
- Annotate on all overlays the security classification, title, map scale, grid intersection points, effective date-time group, and date-time group received
- Pick up all correspondence for the sending unit when departing
- Inform the receiving unit of your departure time, return route, and expected arrival time at the sending unit

After the Tour

After returning to the sending unit, LNOs promptly transmit the receiving unit's requests to the sending unit's commander or staff, as appropriate. They also brief the COS (XO) on mission-related liaison activities and prepare written reports, as appropriate.

Accuracy is paramount. Effective LNOs provide clear, concise, complete information. If the accuracy of information is not certain, they quote the source and include the source in the report. LNOs limit their remarks to mission-related observations.

- Deliver all correspondence
- Brief the COS (XO) and the appropriate staff elements
- Prepare the necessary reports
- Clearly state what you did and did not learn from the mission

Mission Command

III. Liaison Responsibilities

Ref: FM 6-0 (C1), Commander and Staff Organization and Operations (May '15), pp. 13-3 to 13-7.

Both the sending and receiving units have liaison responsibilities before, during, and after operations.

Sending Unit

The sending unit's most important tasks include selecting and training the soldiers best qualified for liaison duties.

Sample Questions

LNOs should be able to answer the following questions:

- Does the sending unit have a copy of the receiving unit's latest OPLAN, OPORD, and FRAGOs?
- Does the receiving unit's plan support the plan of the higher headquarters? This includes logistics as well as the tactical concept. Are MSRs and RSRs known? Can the CSR support the receiving unit's plan?
- What are the receiving unit's CCIR?
- Which sending commander decisions are critical to executing the receiving unit operation? What are the "no-later-than" times for those decisions?
- What assets does the unit need to acquire to accomplish its mission? How would they be used? How do they support attaining the more senior commander's intent? Where can the unit obtain them? from higher headquarters? other Services? multi-national partners?
- How are aviation assets (rotary and fixed-wing) being used?
- How can the LNO communicate with the sending unit? Secure comms?
- What terrain has been designated as key? decisive?
- What weather conditions would have a major impact on the operation?
- What effect would a chemical environment have on the operation?
- What effect would large numbers of refugees or EPWs have?
- What is the worse thing that could happen during the current operation?
- How would you handle a passage of lines by other units?
- What HN support is available to the sending unit? IRs?
- Required reports (from higher and sending units' SOPs)

Packing list

- Credentials
- Forms: DA Form 1594 and other blank forms as required
- Computers and other INFOSYS required for information and data exchange
- Signal operating instructions extract and security code encryption device
- Communications equipment, including remote FM radio equipment
- Sending unit telephone book
- List of commanders and staff officers
- Telephone calling (credit) card
- Movement table
- Admin equipment (for example, pens, paper, scissors, tape, and hole punch)
- Map and chart equipment
- Tent (camouflage net, cots, stove, as appropriate)
- Foreign phrase book and dictionary and local currency as required
- References: Excerpts of higher and sending headquarters' orders and plans, sending unit SOP, sending unit's command diagrams, mission briefings, etc.

The sending unit provides a description of the liaison party (number and type of vehicles and personnel, call signs, and radio frequencies) to the receiving unit:

- Identification and appropriate credentials for the receiving unit
- Appropriate security clearance, courier orders, transportation, and communications equipment
- The SOP outlining the missions, functions, procedures, and duties of the sending unit's liaison section
- Individual weapons and ammunition
- Rations for the movement to the receiving unit

Liaison Checklist-Before Departing the Sending Unit

- Understand what the sending commander wants the receiving commander to know
- Receive a briefing from operations, intelligence, and other staff elements on current and future operations
- Receive and understand the tasks from the sending unit staff
- Obtain the correct maps, traces, and overlays
- Arrange for transport, communications and cryptographic equipment, codes, signal instructions, and the challenge and password-including their protection and security. Arrange for replacement of these items, as necessary.
- Complete route-reconnaissance and time-management plans so the LNO party arrives at the designated location on time
- Verify that the receiving unit received the liaison team's security clearances and will grant access to the level of information the mission requires
- Verify courier orders
- Know how to destroy classified information in case of an emergency during transit or at the receiving unit
- Inform the sending unit of the LNO's departure time, route, arrival time, and, when known, the estimated time and route of return
- Pick up all correspondence designated for the receiving unit
- Conduct a radio check
- Know the impending moves of the sending unit and the receiving unit
- Bring INFOSYS needed to support LNO operations
- Pack adequate supplies of classes I and III for use in transit

Receiving Unit

The receiving unit is responsible for:

- Providing the sending unit with the LNO's reporting time, place, point of contact, recognition signal, and password
- Providing details of any tactical movement and logistic information relevant to the LNO's mission, especially while the LNO is in transit
- Ensuring that the LNO has access to the commander, the COS (XO), and other officers for important matters
- Giving the LNO an initial briefing and allowing the LNO access necessary to remain informed of current operations
- Protecting the LNO while at the receiving unit
- Publishing a standing operating procedure (SOP) outlining the missions, functions, procedures, and duties of the LNO or team at the receiving unit
- Providing access to communications equipment (and operating instructions, as needed) when the LNO needs to communicate with the receiving unit's equipment
- Providing administrative and logistic support

IV. Liaison Considerations

Joint, interagency, and multinational operations require greater liaison efforts than most other operations.

Joint Operations

Current joint information systems do not meet all operational requirements. Few U.S. military information systems are interoperable. Army liaison teams require information systems that can rapidly exchange information between commands to ensure Army force operations are synchronized with operations of the joint force and its Service components.

Interagency Operations

Army forces may participate in interagency operations across the range of military operations, especially when conducting stability or defense support of civil authorities tasks. Frequently, Army forces conduct operations in cooperation with or in support of civilian government agencies. Relations in these operations are rarely based on standard military command and support relationships; rather, national laws or specific agreements for each situation govern the specific relationships in interagency operations. Defense support of civil authorities provides an excellent example. Federal military forces that respond to a domestic disaster will support the Federal Emergency Management Agency, while National Guard forces working in state active duty status (Title 32 United States Code) or conducting National Guard defense support of civil authorities will support that state's emergency management agency. National Guard forces federalized under Title 10 United States Code will support the Federal Emergency Management Agency. The goal is always unity of effort between military forces and civilian agencies, although unity of command may not be possible. Effective liaison and continuous coordination become keys to mission accomplishment.

Some missions require coordination with nongovernmental organizations. While no overarching interagency doctrine delineates or dictates the relationships and procedures governing all agencies, departments, and organizations in interagency operations, the National Response Framework provides some guidance. Effective liaison elements work toward establishing mutual trust and confidence, continuously coordinating actions to achieve cooperation and unity of effort. In these situations, LNOs and their teams require a broader understanding of the interagency environment, responsibilities, motivations, and limitations of nongovernmental organizations, and the relationships these organizations have with the U.S. military.

Multinational Operations

Army units often operate as part of a multinational force. Interoperability is an essential requirement for multinational operations. The North Atlantic Treaty Organization (NATO) defines interoperability as the ability to operate in synergy in the execution of assigned tasks. Interoperability is also the condition achieved among communications-electronics systems or items of satisfactory communication between them and their users. The degree of interoperability should be defined when referring to specific cases. Examples of interoperability include the deployment of a computer network (such as the Combined Enterprise Network Theater Information Exchange System) to facilitate inter-staff communication. Nations whose forces are interoperable can operate together effectively in numerous ways. Less interoperable forces have correspondingly fewer ways to work together. Although frequently identified with technology, important areas of interoperability include doctrine, procedures, communications, and training. Factors that enhance interoperability include planning for interoperability, conducting multinational training exercises, staff visits to assess multinational capabilities, a command atmosphere that rewards sharing information, and command emphasis on a constant effort to eliminate the sources of confusion and misunderstanding.

V. Military Deception

Ref: FM 6-0 (C1), Commander and Staff Organization and Operations (May '15), chap. 11.

This section provides information on military deception. Initially this chapter addresses the principles of military deception. It then discusses how commanders use military deception to shape the area of operations in support of decisive action. The chapter concludes with a discussion of how to plan, prepare, execute, and assess military deception.

I. Military Deception Process and Capability

Modern military deception is both a process and a capability. As a process, military deception is a methodical, information-based strategy that systematically, deliberately, and cognitively targets individual decisionmakers. The objective is the purposeful manipulation of decisionmaking. As a capability, military deception is useful to a commander when integrated early in the planning process as a component of the operation focused on causing an enemy to act or react in a desired manner.

Refer to JP 3-13 for a discussion in information operations and JP 3-13.4 for a more detailed discussion on military deception.

II. Principles of Military Deception

Military deception is applicable during any phase of military operations in order to create conditions to accomplish the commander's intent. The Army echelon that plans a military deception often determines its type. The levels of war define and clarify the relationship between strategic and tactical actions. The levels have no finite limits or boundaries. They correlate to specific levels of responsibility and military deception planning. They help organize thought and approaches to a problem. Decisions at one level always affect other levels. Common to all levels of military deception is a set of guiding principles:

- Focus on the target
- Motivating the target to act
- Centralized planning and control
- Security
- Conforming to the time available
- Integration

Focus On The Target

Leaders determine which targeted decisionmaker has the authority to make the desired decision and then can act or fail to act upon that decision. Many times it is one, key individual, or it could be a network of decisionmakers who rely on each other for different aspects of their mission or operation.

Motivating The Target To Act

Leaders determine what motivates the targeted decisionmaker and which information-related capabilities are capable of inducing the targeted decisionmaker to think a certain way. The desired result is that the targeted decisionmaker acts or fails to act as intended. This result is favorable to friendly forces. Often, the military objective is

III. Military Deception in Support of Operations

Ref: FM 6-0 (C1), Commander and Staff Organization and Operations (May '15), pp. 11-2 to 11-4.

Military deception often relies on the basic understanding that the complexities and uncertainties of combat make decisionmakers susceptible to deception. The basic mechanism for any deception is either to increase or decrease the level of uncertainty, or ambiguity, in the mind of the deception target (or targeted decisionmaker). Military deception and deception in support of operations security present false or misleading information to the targeted decisionmaker with the deliberate intent to manipulate uncertainty. The aim of deception is to either increase or decrease the targeted decisionmaker's ambiguity in order to manipulate the target to perceive friendly motives, intentions, capabilities, and vulnerabilities erroneously and thereby alter the target's perception of reality.

Ambiguity-Decreasing Deception

Ambiguity-decreasing deception reduces uncertainty and normally confirms the enemy decisionmaker's preconceived beliefs, so the decisionmaker becomes very certain about the selected course of action (COA). This type of deception presents false information that shapes the enemy decisionmaker's thinking, so the enemy makes and executes a specific decision that can be exploited by friendly forces. By making the wrong decision, which is the deception objective, the enemy could misemploy forces and provide friendly forces an operational advantage. For example, ambiguity-decreasing deceptions can present supporting elements of information concerning a specific enemy's COA. These deceptions are complex to plan and execute, but the potential rewards are often worth the increased effort and resources.

Ambiguity-Increasing Deception

Ambiguity-increasing deception presents false information aimed to confuse the enemy decisionmaker, thereby increasing the decisionmaker's uncertainty. This confusion can produce different results. Ambiguity-increasing deceptions can challenge the enemy's preconceived beliefs. These deceptions draw enemy attention from one set of activities to another, create the illusion of strength where weakness exists, create the illusion of weakness where strength exists, and accustom the enemy to particular patterns of activity that are exploitable at a later time. For example, ambiguity-increasing deceptions can cause the target to delay a decision until it is too late to prevent friendly mission success. They can place the target in a dilemma for which there is no acceptable solution. They may even prevent the target from taking any action at all. Deceptions in support of operations security (OPSEC) are typically executed as this type of deception.

Tactical Deception

Most often, Army commanders will be faced with deciding when and where to employ military deception in support of tactical operations. The intent of tactical deception is to induce the enemy decisionmakers to act in a manner prejudicial to their interests. This is accomplished by either increasing or decreasing the ambiguity of the enemy decisionmaker through the manipulation, distortion, or falsification of evidence. Military deception undertaken at the tactical level supports engagements, battles, and stability tasks. This focus is what differentiates tactical deception from other forms of military deception.

Refer to JP 3-13.4 for more information on military deception.

Strategic and Operational Military Deception

Less frequently, Army commanders will employ strategic and operational military deception to influence enemy strategic decisionmakers' abilities to successfully oppose U.S. national interests and goals or to influence enemy decisionmakers' abilities to conduct operations. These deceptions are joint or multinational efforts. In these cases, Army commanders usually opt to form a military deception cell to plan, coordinate, integrate, assess, and terminate the deception.

On occasion, Army commanders will employ deception in support of OPSEC. This is a military deception that protects friendly operations, personal, programs, equipment, and other assets against foreign intelligence security services collection. The intent of deception in support of OPSEC is to create multiple false indicators to confuse or make friendly intentions harder to interpret by foreign intelligence security services and other enemy intelligence gathering apparatus. This deception limits the ability of foreign intelligence security services to collect accurate intelligence on friendly forces. Deceptions in support of OPSEC are general in nature, and are not specifically targeted against particular enemy decisionmakers. Deceptions in support of OPSEC are instead used to protect friendly operations and forces by obscuring friendly capabilities, intentions, or vulnerabilities.

Military Deception Tactics

The selection of military deception tactics and their use depends on an understanding of the current situation as well as the desired military deception goal and objective. (See appendix A for a discussion of operational and mission variables.) As a rule, Army commanders should be familiar with planning and conducting feints, ruses, demonstrations, and displays.

Feint

A feint, in military deception, is an offensive action involving contact with the adversary conducted for the purpose of deceiving the adversary as to the location and/or time of the actual main offensive action (JP 3-13.4).

Ruse

A ruse, in military deception, is a trick of war designed to deceive the adversary, usually involving the deliberate exposure of false information to the adversary's intelligence collection system (JP 3-13.4).

Demonstration

A demonstration, in military deception, is a show of force in an area where a decision is not sought that is made to deceive an adversary. It is similar to a feint but no actual contact with the adversary is intended (JP 3-13.4).

Display

A display, in military deception, is a static portrayal of an activity, force, or equipment intended to deceive the adversary's visual observation (JP 3-13.4).

Common Military Deception Means

Army commanders should also be familiar with some of the more commonly available military deception means that can be employed to support a given military deception. They cover the full scope of units, forces, personnel, capabilities, and resources available to the commander for the conduct of decisive action. In most cases, Army commanders have at their disposal the use of the following six information-related capabilities and other activities to support a planned military deception:

- Military information support operations (MISO)
- OPSEC
- Camouflage, concealment and decoys
- Cyber electromagnetic activities
- Physical attack and destruction capabilities
- Presence, posture, and profile

to manipulate the targeted decisionmaker's thinking and subsequent actions. This can be accomplished in a variety of ways. Leaders—

- **Exploit target biases.** Leaders provide the targeted decisionmakers with information that fulfills their expectations. This reinforces the target's preexisting perceptions and can be exceptionally powerful.

- **Employ variety.** The target should receive information, true and false, through multiple means and methods, from many angles, throughout the information and operational environment.

- **Avoid windfalls.** Important military information that is too easy to obtain is usually suspect. Information that "falls" into the enemy's hands must appear to be the result of legitimate collection activities.

- **Leverage the truth.** Any deception must conform to the target's perception of reality. It is much simpler to have the deception adhere to the target's belief than to make the target accept an unexpected reality as truth.

Centralized Planning And Control

Centralized planning and control ensures continuity. The assistant chief of staff, plans (G-5 [S-5]) usually leads the planning. However, there may be times when the commander designates a military deception officer to assist the G-5 (S-5) throughout the planning, hand-off, and termination of the deception operation. Centralizing the planning and control is imperative. It keeps the deception operation on track and limits unintended leaks and compromises.

Security

Successful military deception requires strict security and protection measures to prevent compromise of both the deception and the actual operation. This includes counterintelligence, computer network defense, operations security, camouflage, and concealment.

Refer to AR 530-1 for more detailed information and regulations on operations security.

Conforming To The Time Available

Planning, preparing, executing, and assessing military deception must conform to the time available for both sides to "play their parts" in the deception. The targeted decisionmaker requires time to see, interpret, decide, and act upon the deception. Equally important, friendly forces require time to detect and assess the targeted decisionmaker's reaction to the deception.

Integration

A military deception is an integral part of the concept of an operation. It is not an afterthought or a stand-alone operation. The military deception officer assists the staff in integrating the deception operation throughout all phases of the operation. This begins with planning, the hand-off to current operations, and eventually the termination of the deception. Integration involves the use of information-related capabilities and activities. Military information support operations can contribute to the deception plan by providing a means to disseminate both accurate and deceptive information to the targeted decisionmakers by discreetly conveying approved tailored deception messages to selected target audiences. Therefore, the individual assigned as the military deception officer is often well versed in the use and integration information-related capabilities and activities.

IV. Military Deception Planning Steps

Ref: FM 6-0 (C1), Commander and Staff Organization and Operations (May '15), pp. 11-6 to 11-7.

The basic steps of military deception planning come together during COA analysis, comparison, and approval and are overseen by the military deception officer. (These are MDMP steps 2, 3, and 4. See chapter 9 for a detailed discussion of the MDMP.) The G-5 (S-5)-developed COAs provide the basis for military deception COAs. The military deception officer develops military deception COAs in conjunction with the G-5 (S-5). Basing the military deception COAs on the operational COAs ensures deception COAs are feasible, practical, and nested and effectively support the operational COAs.

The military deception officer and G-5(S-5) planners consider the military deception COAs as the staff war-games the COAs. They analyze the strengths and weaknesses of each military deception COA and compare it against the criteria established by the military deception officer for evaluating the military deception COAs.

The military deception officer, working with the G-5 (S-5) planners, prepares the military deception plan after the commander approves the military deception COA. Once the G-5 (S-5) planner completes, coordinates, and reviews the military deception for consistency, it is presented to the commander for tentative approval. To ensure synchronization of military deception at all levels, approval authority for military deception resides two echelons above the originating command. After the approving authority has approved the military deception plan, it becomes a part of the operation plan (OPLAN) or operation order (OPORD). It is important that military deception plans are not widely distributed. In order to ensure every opportunity to succeed and to protect the military deception from compromise, access to the military deception operation is strictly limited to those with a need to know.

The military deception officer ensures that each military deception plan is properly constructed. There are ten steps in military deception planning:

- Step 1—Determine the military deception goal
- Step 2—Determine the deception objective
- Step 3—Identify the military deception target
- Step 4—Identify required perceptions of the military deception target
- Step 5—Develop the military deception story
- Step 6—Identify the military deception means
- Step 7—Develop military deception events
- Step 8—Develop OPSEC and other protection measures
- Step 9—Develop assessment criteria
- Step 10—Develop a termination plan

V. Military Deception in the Operations Process

Military deception is considered in all activities of the operations process. Planning, preparing, executing, and continually assessing military deception does not take place in isolation. It occurs simultaneously with the operations process. If it does not, then the risk increases exponentially for the military deception to be under resourced and not integrated into the larger operation as the military deception evolves. It is unlikely that an under resourced and nonintegrated military deception will succeed. Because military deception supports a range of missions, and to prevent one unit's military deception from compromising another unit's operations, leaders coordinate military deceptions both laterally and vertically. Deception operations are approved by the headquarters two operational echelons higher than the originating command. Only two authorities can direct a military deception: a higher headquarters and the originating unit commander.

Planning

Planning develops the information needed to prepare, execute, and assess a military deception. The output of the military deception mission analysis is the running estimate, prepared by the military deception officer. The running estimate identifies military deception opportunities, information and capability requirements, and recommends feasible deception goals and objectives. The military deception officer presents this estimate during the mission analysis briefing. The estimate considers current capabilities based on enemy susceptibilities, preconceptions, and biases; available time; and available military deception means. A key outcome of the running estimate is the determination of whether or not there is a viable military deception opportunity. (See chapter 8 for more information on running estimates.) Military deception may be a feasible option, if it is appropriate to the mission, and if there is a possibility of success. Issues to consider when determining if military deception is a viable course of action include:

Availability of Assets
The commander determines if sufficient assets exist to support both the operation and the military deception. There are few assets specifically designed and designated for military deception. This means the commander must shift assets from the operation to support the military deception. Commanders must be certain that shifting assets to support a military deception does not adversely affect the operation or prevent mission success.

Understanding the Military Deception Target
The commander determines if sufficient information exists on how the military deception target acquires information and makes decisions, what knowledge the target has of the situation, and how the target views the friendly force. The commander also determines if sufficient information exists to reveal the targeted decisionmaker's biases, beliefs, and fears. If necessary, the staff can make assumptions about the military deception target, but it must avoid mirror imaging its preconceptions onto the military deception's targeted decisionmaker.

Suitability
Some missions are better suited to military deception than others. When a unit has the initiative and has some control over the area of operations, then military deception is more suitable.

Time
The commander determines if sufficient time exists to execute a military deception. Execution of the military deception must provide sufficient time for the military deception target to observe the military deception activities, form the desired perceptions, and act in a manner consistent with the deception objective.

I. Rehearsals

Ref: FM 6-0 (C1), Commander and Staff Organization and Operations (May '15), chap. 12.

Rehearsals allow leaders and their Soldiers to practice executing key aspects of the concept of operations. These actions help Soldiers orient themselves to their environment and other units before executing the operation. Rehearsals help Soldiers to build a lasting mental picture of the sequence of key actions within the operation. Rehearsals are the commander's tool to ensure staffs and subordinates understand the commander's intent and the concept of operations. They allow commanders and staffs to identify shortcomings (errors or omissions) in the plan not previously recognized. Rehearsals also contribute to external and internal coordination as the staff identifies additional coordinating requirements.

Rehearsal Techniques

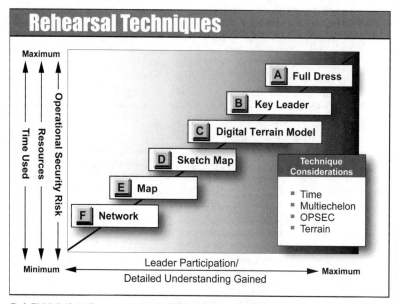

Ref: FM 6-0 (C1), Commander & Staff Organization and Operations, fig. 12-1, p. 12-3.

Effective and efficient units habitually rehearse during training. Commanders at every level routinely train and practice various rehearsal types and techniques. Local standard operating procedures (SOPs) identify appropriate rehearsal types, techniques, and standards for their execution. All leaders conduct periodic after action reviews to ensure their units conduct rehearsals to standard and correct substandard performances. After action reviews also enable leaders to incorporate lessons learned into existing plans and orders, or into subsequent rehearsals.

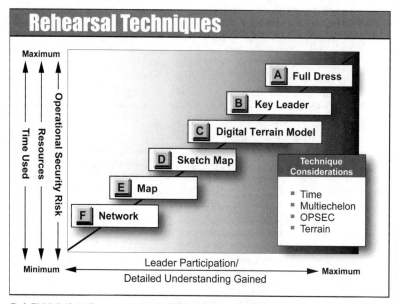

I. Methods of Rehearsals

Ref: FM 6-0 (C1), Commander and Staff Organization and Operations (May '15), pp. 12-2 to 12-6.

Techniques for conducting rehearsals are limited only by the commander's imagination and available resources. Generally, six techniques are used for executing rehearsals.

A. Full-dress Rehearsal

A full-dress rehearsal produces the most detailed understanding of the operation. It involves every participating soldier and system. If possible, organizations execute full-dress rehearsals under the same conditions-weather, time of day, terrain, and use of live ammunition-that the force expects to encounter during the actual operation.

- **Time**. Full-dress rehearsals are the most time consuming of all rehearsal types. For companies and smaller units, the full-dress rehearsal is the most effective technique for ensuring all involved in the operation understand their parts. However, brigade and task force commanders consider the time their subordinates need to plan and prepare when deciding whether to conduct a full-dress rehearsal.
- **Echelons involved**. A subordinate unit can perform a full-dress rehearsal as part of a larger organization's reduced-force rehearsal.
- **OPSEC**. Moving a large part of the force may attract enemy attention. Commanders develop a plan to protect the rehearsal from enemy surveillance and reconnaissance. One method is to develop a plan, including graphics and radio frequencies, that rehearses selected actions but does not compromise the actual OPORD. Commanders take care to not confuse subordinates when doing this.
- **Terrain**. Terrain management for a full-dress rehearsal can be difficult if it is not considered during the initial array of forces. The rehearsal area must be identified, secured, cleared, and maintained throughout the rehearsal.

B. Key Leader Rehearsal

Circumstances may prohibit a rehearsal with all members of the unit. A key leader rehearsal involves only key leaders of the organization and its subordinate units. Often commanders use this technique to rehearse fire control measures for an engagement area during defensive operations. Commanders often use a reduced-force rehearsal to prepare key leaders for a full-dress rehearsal.

- **Time**. A reduced-force rehearsal normally requires less time than a full-dress rehearsal. Commanders consider the time their subordinates need to plan and prepare when deciding whether to conduct a reduced-force rehearsal.
- **Echelons involved**. A small unit can perform a full-dress rehearsal as part of a larger organization's reduced-force rehearsal.
- **OPSEC**. A reduced-force rehearsal is less likely to present an OPSEC vulnerability than a full-dress rehearsal because the number of participants is smaller. However, the number of radio transmissions required is the same as for a full-dress rehearsal and remains a consideration.
- **Terrain**. Terrain management for the reduced-force rehearsal can be just as difficult as for the full-dress rehearsal. The rehearsal area must be identified, secured, cleared, and maintained throughout the rehearsal.

C. Terrain-model Rehearsal (or "Digital" Terrain-model)

The terrain-model rehearsal is the most popular rehearsal technique. It takes less time and fewer resources than a full-dress or reduced-force rehearsal. When possible, commanders place the terrain model where it overlooks the actual terrain of the AO. (reverse slope for OPSEC, though).The model's orientation coincides with that of the terrain. The size of the terrain model can vary from small (using markers to represent units) to large (on which the participants can walk).

- **Time**. Often, the most time-consuming part of this technique is constructing the terrain model.
- **Echelons involved**. Because a terrain model is geared to the echelon conducting the rehearsal, multiechelon rehearsals using this technique are difficult.
- **OPSEC**. This rehearsal can present an OPSEC vulnerability if the area around the site is not secured. The collection of cdrs & vehicles can draw enemy attention.
- **Terrain**. Terrain management is less difficult than with the previous techniques. An optimal location overlooks the terrain where the operation will be executed. With today's digital capabilities, users can construct terrain models in virtual space.

D. Sketch-map Rehearsal

Commanders can use the sketch-map technique almost anywhere, day or night. The procedures are the same as for a terrain-model rehearsal, except the commander uses a sketch map in place of a terrain model. Effective sketches are large enough for all participants to see as each participant walks through execution of the operation. Participants move markers on the sketch to represent unit locations and maneuvers.

- **Time**. Sketch-map rehearsals take less time than terrain-model rehearsals and more time than map rehearsals.
- **Echelons involved**. Because a sketch map is geared to the echelon conducting the rehearsal, multiechelon rehearsals using this technique are difficult.
- **OPSEC**. This rehearsal can present an OPSEC vulnerability if the area around the site is not secured. The collection of cdrs & vehicles can draw enemy attention.
- **Terrain**. This technique requires less space than a terrain model rehearsal. A good site is easy for participants to find, yet concealed from the enemy. An optimal location overlooks the terrain where the unit will execute the operation.

E. Map Rehearsal

A map rehearsal is similar to a sketch-map rehearsal, except the commander uses a map and operation overlay of the same scale used to plan the operation.

- **Time**. The most time-consuming part is the rehearsal itself. A map rehearsal is normally the easiest technique to set up, since it requires only maps and current operational graphics.
- **Echelons involved**. Because a map is geared to the echelon conducting the rehearsal, multiechelon rehearsals using this technique are difficult.
- **OPSEC**. This rehearsal can present an OPSEC vulnerability if the area around the site is not secured. The collection of cdrs & vehicles can draw enemy attention.
- **Terrain**. This technique requires the least space. An optimal location overlooks the terrain where the ops will be executed, but is concealed from the enemy.

F. Network Rehearsal

Units conduct network rehearsals over wide-area networks or local area networks. Commanders and staffs practice these rehearsals by talking through critical portions of the operation over communications networks in a sequence the commander establishes. The organization rehearses only the critical parts of the operation. CPs can also rehearse battle tracking.

- **Time**. If the organization does not have a clear SOP and if all units are not up on the net, this technique can be very time consuming.
- **Echelons involved**. This technique lends itself to multiechelon rehearsals. Participation is limited only by cdr's desires and the availability of INFOSYSs.
- **OPSEC**. If a network rehearsal is executed from current unit locations, the volume of the communications transmissions and potential compromise of information through enemy monitoring can present an OPSEC vulnerability.
- **Terrain**. If a network rehearsal is executed from unit locations, terrain considerations are minimal.

II. Rehearsal Responsibilities

Ref: FM 6-0 (C1), Commander and Staff Organization and Operations (May '15), pp. 12-6 to 12-9.

This discussion addresses responsibilities for conducting rehearsals. It is based on the combined arms rehearsal. Responsibilities are the same for support rehearsals.

Rehearsal Planning

Commanders and chiefs of staff (COSs) plan rehearsals.

Commander

Commanders provide the following information as part of the cdr's guidance during the initial mission analysis. They re-evaluate it when they select a COA:

• Type of rehearsal
• Rehearsal technique
• Place
• Attendees
• Enemy COA to be portrayed

Chief of Staff (XO)

The COS (XO) ensures that all rehearsals are included in the organization's time-management SOP. COS (XO) responsibilities include:

• Publishing the rehearsal time and location in the OPORD or in a warning order
• Completing any staff rehearsals
• Determining rehearsal products, based on type, technique, and METT-TC
• Coordinating liaison officer (LNO) attendance from adjacent units

Rehearsal Preparation

Commander

Cdrs prepare to rehearse operations with events phased in proper order, from start to finish, when time allows:

• Identify and prioritize key events to rehearse
• Allocate time for each event
• Perform personal preparation, including reviews of: task organization, personnel and materiel readiness, and organizational level of preparation

Chief of Staff (XO)

The COS (XO), through war-gaming and coordinating with the commander:

• Prepares to serve as the rehearsal director
• Coordinates and allocates time for key events requiring rehearsal
• Establishes rehearsal time limits per the commander's guidance and METT-TC
• Verifies rehearsal site preparation. A separate rehearsal site may be required for some events, such as a possible obstacle site. A good rehearsal site includes: appropriate markings and associated training aids, parking areas, local security
- Determines the method for controlling the rehearsal and ensuring its logical flow, for example, a script

Subordinate Leaders

Subordinate leaders are responsible for:

• Completing unit OPORDs
• Identifying issues derived from the parent organization's OPORD
• Providing a copy of their unit OPORD, with graphics, to the parent org
• Performing personal preparation similar to that of the commander
• Ensuring they and their subordinates bring necessary equip (maps, etc).

Conducting HQ's Staff

• Develop an OPORD and necessary overlays
• Deconflict all subordinate unit graphics. Composite overlays are the first step for leaders to visualize the organization's overall plan
• Publish composite overlays at the rehearsal including, at a minimum: maneuver, fire support, mobility and survivability, and CSS

Rehearsal Execution

Commander

Commanders command the rehearsal, just as they will command the fight. They maintain the focus and level of intensity, allowing no potential for subordinate confusion. Although the staff refines the OPORD, it belongs to the commander, who uses it to fight. An effective rehearsal is not a commander's brief to subordinates. Its purpose is to validate synchronization - the what, when, and where-of tasks subordinate units will perform to execute the operation and achieve the commander's intent.

Chief of Staff (XO)

Normally, the COS (XO) serves as the rehearsal director. This officer ensures each unit will accomplish its tasks at the right time and cues the commander to upcoming decisions. The chief of staff's (executive officer's) script is the execution matrix and the decision support template. The COS (XO) as the rehearsal director—:

- Starts the rehearsal on time
- Conducts a formal roll call
- Ensures everyone brings the necessary equipment. This equipment includes organizational graphics and previously issued orders.
- Validates the task organization. Linkups must be complete or on schedule, and required materiel and personnel on hand. The importance of this simple check cannot be overemphasized.
- Ensures sustaining operations are synchronized with shaping operations and the decisive operation
- Rehearses the synchronization of combat power from flank and higher organizations, which are often beyond communication range of the commander and G-3 (S-3) when they are away from the CP
- Synchronizes the timing and contribution of each BOS by ensuring the rehearsal of operations against the decisive points, by time or event that connect to a decision.
- For each decisive point, defines the conditions required to: 1) commit the reserve or striking force, 2) move a unit, 3) close or emplace an obstacle, 4) fire planned targets, 5) move a medical station, change a supply route, alert specific observation posts

- Disciplines leader movements, enforces brevity, and ensures completeness. The OPORD, decision support template (DST), and execution matrix are the COS's tools.
- Keeps within time constraints
- Ensures that the most important events receive the most attention
- Ensures that absentees and flank units receive changes to the OPORD. Transmits changes to them by courier or radio immediately.

Asst Chief of Staff, G-3 (S-3)
- Portrays friendly scheme of maneuver
- Ensures compliance with the plan
- Normally provides the recorder

Asst Chief of Staff, G-2 (S-2)
The G-2 (S-2) plays the enemy commander during rehearsals. He bases his actions on the enemy COA the commander selects during the MDMP. The G-2/S-2:

- Provides participants with current intelligence
- Portrays the best possible assessment of the enemy COA
- Communicates the enemy commander's presumed concept of operations, desired effects, and intended end state

Subordinate Leaders
- Effectively articulate their units' actions and responsibilities
- Record changes on their copies of the graphics or OPORD

Recorder
During the rehearsal, the recorder:

- Captures all coordination made during execution
- Captures unresolved problems

At the end of the rehearsal, the recorder:

- Presents any unresolved problems to the commander for resolution
- Restates any changes, coordination, or clarifications directed by the commander
- Estimates when a written FRAGO codifying the changes will follow

Conducting HQ's Staff
The staff updates the OPORD, DST, and execution matrix.

III. Rehearsal Types

Ref: FM 6-0 (C1), Commander and Staff Organization and Operations (May '15), pp. 12-1 to 12-2.

Each rehearsal type achieves a different result and has a specific place in the preparation timeline.

A. Backbrief

A back brief is a briefing by subordinates to the commander to review how subordinates intend to accomplish their mission. Normally, subordinates perform back briefs throughout preparation. These briefs allow commanders to clarify the commander's intent early in subordinate planning. Commanders use the back brief to identify any problems in the concept of operations.

The back brief differs from the confirmation brief (a briefing subordinates give their higher commander immediately following receipt of an order) in that subordinate leaders are given time to complete their plan. Back briefs require the fewest resources and are often the only option under time-constrained conditions. Subordinate leaders explain their actions from start to finish of the mission. Back briefs are performed sequentially, with all leaders reviewing their tasks. When time is available, back briefs can be combined with other types of rehearsals. Doing this lets all subordinate leaders coordinate their plans before performing more elaborate drills.

B. Combined Arms Rehearsal

A combined arms rehearsal is a rehearsal in which subordinate units synchronize their plans with each other. A maneuver unit headquarters normally executes a combined arms rehearsal after subordinate units issue their operation order. This rehearsal type helps ensure that subordinate commanders' plans achieve the higher commander's intent.

C. Support Rehearsal

The support rehearsal helps synchronize each war fighting function with the overall operation. This rehearsal supports the operation so units can accomplish their missions. Throughout preparation, units conduct support rehearsals within the framework of a single or limited number of war fighting functions. These rehearsals typically involve coordination and procedure drills for aviation, fires, engineer support, or casualty evacuation. Support rehearsals and combined arms rehearsals complement preparations for the operation. Units may conduct rehearsals separately and then combine them into full-dress rehearsals. Although these rehearsals differ slightly by warfighting function, they achieve the same result.

D. Battle Drill or SOP Rehearsal

A battle drill is a collective action rapidly executed without applying a deliberate decision making process. A battle drill or SOP rehearsal ensures that all participants understand a technique or a specific set of procedures. Throughout preparation, units and staffs rehearse battle drills and SOPs. These rehearsals do not need a completed order from higher headquarters. Leaders place priority on those drills or actions they anticipate occurring during the operation. For example, a transportation platoon may rehearse a battle drill on reacting to an ambush while waiting to begin movement.

All echelons use these rehearsal types; however, they are most common for platoons, squads, and sections. They are conducted throughout preparation and are not limited to published battle drills. All echelons can rehearse such actions as a command post shift change, an obstacle breach lane-marking SOP, or a refuel-on-the-move site operation.

Adequate time is essential when conducting rehearsals. The time required varies with the complexity of the mission, the type and technique of rehearsal, and the level of participation. Units conduct rehearsals at the lowest possible level, using the most thorough technique possible, given the time available. Under time-constrained conditions, leaders conduct abbreviated rehearsals, focusing on critical events determined by reverse planning. Each unit will have different critical events based on the mission, unit readiness, and the commander's assessment.

The rehearsal is a coordination event, not an analysis. It does not replace war-gaming. Commanders war-game during the military decisionmaking process (MDMP) to analyze different courses of action to determine the optimal one. Rehearsals practice that selected course of action. Commanders avoid making major changes to operation orders (OPORDs) during rehearsals. They make only those changes essential to mission success and risk mitigation.

IV. Conducting the Rehearsal

All participants have responsibilities before, during, and after a rehearsal. Before a rehearsal, the rehearsal director states the commander's expectations and orients the other participants on details of the rehearsal as necessary. During a rehearsal, all participants rehearse their roles in the operation. They make sure they understand how their actions support the overall operation and note any additional coordination required. After a rehearsal, participants ensure they understand any changes to the operation order and coordination requirements, and they receive all updated staff products.

Commanders do not normally address small problems that arise during rehearsals. Instead, these are recorded. This ensures the rehearsal's flow is not interrupted. If the problem remains at the end of the rehearsal, the commander resolves it then. However, if the problem can wait until the end of the rehearsal, it may not have been a real problem. If the problem jeopardizes mission accomplishment, the staff accomplishes the coordination necessary to resolve it before the participants disperse. Identifying and solving such problems is a major reason for conducting rehearsals. If corrections are not made while participants are assembled, the opportunity to do so may be lost. Coordinating among dispersed participants and disseminating changes to them is more difficult than accomplishing these actions in person.

A. Before the Rehearsal

Before the rehearsal, the rehearsal director calls the roll and briefs participants on information needed for execution. The briefing begins with an introduction, overview, and orientation. It includes a discussion of the rehearsal script and ground rules. The detail of this discussion is based on participants' familiarity with the rehearsal SOP.

Before the rehearsal, the staff develops an operation order with at least the basic five paragraphs and necessary overlays. Annexes may not be published; however, the responsible staff officers should know their content.

1. Introduction and Overview

Before the rehearsal, the rehearsal director introduces all participants as needed. Then, the director gives an overview of the briefing topics, rehearsal subjects and sequence, and timeline, specifying the no-later-than ending time. The rehearsal director explains after action reviews, describes how and when they occur, and discusses how to incorporate changes into the operation order. The director explains any restraints, such as pyrotechnics use, light discipline, weapons firing, or radio silence. For safety, the rehearsal director ensures that all participants understand safety precautions and enforces their use. Last, the director emphasizes results and states the commander's standard for a successful rehearsal. Subordinate leaders state any results of planning or preparation (including rehearsals) they have already conducted. If a subordinate recommends a change to the operation order, the rehearsal director acts on the recommendation before the rehearsal begins, if possible. If not, the commander resolves the recommendation with a decision before the rehearsal ends.

2. Orientation

The rehearsal director orients the participants to the terrain or rehearsal medium. Orientation is identified using magnetic north on the rehearsal medium and symbols representing actual terrain features. The director explains any graphic control measures, obstacles, and targets and then issues supplemental materials, if needed.

3. Rehearsal Script

An effective technique for controlling rehearsals is to use a script. It keeps the rehearsal on track. The script provides a checklist so the organization addresses all warfighting functions and outstanding issues. It has two major parts: the agenda and the response sequence.

See facing page (p. 6-9) for discussion of the agenda and response sequence.

Special staff officers should brief by exception when a friendly or enemy event occurs within their area of expertise. Summarizing these actions at the end of the rehearsal can reinforce the coordination requirements identified during the rehearsal. The staff updates the decision support template and gives a copy to each participant. Under time-constrained conditions, the conducting headquarters staff may provide copies before the rehearsal and rely on participants to update them with pen-and-ink changes.

4. Ground Rules

After discussing the rehearsal script, the rehearsal director:

- States the standard (what the commander will accept) for a successful rehearsal
- Ensures everyone understands the parts of the operation order to rehearse. If the entire operation will not be rehearsed, the rehearsal director states the events to be rehearsed.
- Quickly reviews the rehearsal SOP if all participants are not familiar with it. An effective rehearsal SOP states:
  - Who controls the rehearsal
  - Who approves the rehearsal venue and its construction
  - When special staff officers brief the commander
  - The relationship between how the execution matrix portrays events and how units rehearse events
- Establishes the timeline; it designates the rehearsal starting time in relation to H-hour. For example, have the rehearsal begin by depicting the anticipated situation one hour before H-hour. One event executed before rehearsing the first event is deployment of forces.
- Establishes the time interval to begin and track the rehearsal. For example, specify a ten-minute interval equates to one hour of actual time.
- Updates friendly and adversary activities as necessary, for example, any ongoing reconnaissance

The rehearsal director concludes the orientation with a call for questions.

The Rehearsal Script

Ref: FM 6-0 (C1), Commander and Staff Organization and Operations (May '15), pp. 12-10 to 12-11.

An effective rehearsal follows a prescribed agenda that everyone knows and understands.

Agenda

An effective rehearsal includes, but is not limited to:

- Roll call
- Participant orientation to the terrain
- Location of local civilians
- Enemy situation brief
- Friendly situation brief
- Description of expected adversary actions
- Discussion of friendly unit actions
- Review of notes made by the recorder

The execution matrix, decision support template, and operation order outline the rehearsal agenda. These tools, especially the execution matrix, both drive and focus the rehearsal. The commander and staff use them to control the operation's execution. Any templates, matrices, or tools developed within each of the warfighting functions (for example an intelligence synchronization matrix or fires execution matrix) should tie directly to the supported unit's execution matrix and decision support template.

An effective rehearsal requires the enemy force and other operational environmental factors to be portrayed realistically and quickly without distracting from the rehearsal. One technique for doing this has the G-2 (S-2) preparing an actions checklist. It lists a sequence of events much like the one for friendly units but from the enemy or civilian perspective.

Response Sequence

Participants respond in a logical sequence: either by war fighting function or by unit as the organization is deployed, from front to rear. The commander determines the sequence before the rehearsal. It is posted at the rehearsal site, and the rehearsal director may restate it.

Effective rehearsals allow participants to visualize and synchronize the concept of operations. As the rehearsal proceeds, participants talk through the concept of operations. They focus on key events and the synchronization required to achieve the desired effects. The commander commands the rehearsal. The commander gives orders during the operation. Subordinate commanders enter and leave the discussion at the time they expect to begin and end their tasks or activities during the operation. This practice helps the commander assess the adequacy of synchronization. They do not "re-war-game" unless absolutely necessary to ensure subordinate unit commanders understand the plan.

The rehearsal director emphasizes integrating fires, events that trigger different branch actions, and actions on contact. The chief of fires (fire support officer) or fires unit commander states when fires are initiated, who is firing, from where the firing comes, the ammunition available, and the desired target effect. Subordinate commanders state when they initiate fires per their fire support plans. The rehearsal director speaks for any absent staff section and ensures all actions on the synchronization matrix and decision support template are addressed at the proper time or event.

The rehearsal director ensures that key sustainment and protection actions are included in the rehearsal at the times they are executed. Failure to do this reduces the value of the rehearsal as a coordination tool.

B. During the Rehearsal (Rehearsal Steps)

Ref: FM 6-0 (C1), Commander and Staff Organization and Operations (May '15), pp. 12-12 to 12-13.

Once the rehearsal director finishes discussing the ground rules and answering questions, the G-3 (S-3) reads the mission statement, the commander reads the commander's intent, and the G-3 (S-3) establishes the current friendly situation. The rehearsal then begins, following the rehearsal script.

The outline below is based on a generic set of rehearsal steps developed for combined arms rehearsals. However, with a few modifications, these steps support any rehearsal technique. The products depend on the rehearsal type.

1. Step 1 – Enemy Forces Deployed

The G-2 (S-2) briefs the current enemy situation and operational environment and places markers on the map or terrain board (as applicable) indicating where enemy forces and other operationally significant groups or activities would be before the first rehearsal event. The G-2 (S-2) then briefs the most likely enemy course of action and operational context. The G-2 (S-2) also briefs the status of reconnaissance and surveillance operations (for example, citing any patrols still out or any observation post positions).

2. Step 2 – Friendly Forces Deployed

The G-3 (S-3) briefs friendly maneuver unit dispositions, including security forces, as they are arrayed at the start of the operation. Subordinate commanders and other staff officers brief their unit positions at the starting time and any particular points of emphasis. For example, the chemical, biological, radiological, and nuclear officer states the mission-oriented protective posture level, and the chief of fires (fire support officer) or fires unit commander states the range of friendly and enemy artillery. Other participants place markers for friendly forces, including adjacent units, at the positions they will occupy at the start of the operation. As participants place markers, they state their task and purpose, task organization, and strength. Sustainment and protection units brief positions, plans, and actions at the starting time and at points of emphasis the rehearsal director designates. Subordinate units may include forward arming and refueling points, refuel-on-the-move points, communications checkpoints, security points, or operations security procedures that differ for any period during the operation. The rehearsal director restates the commander's intent, if necessary.

3. Step 3 – Initiate Action

The rehearsal director states the first event on the execution matrix. Normally this involves the G-2 (S-2) moving enemy markers according to the most likely course of action. The depiction must tie enemy actions to specific terrain or to friendly unit actions. The G-2 (S-2) portrays enemy actions based on the situational template developed for staff war-gaming.

As the rehearsal proceeds, the G-2 (S-2) portrays the enemy and other operational factors and walks through the most likely enemy course of action (per the situational template). The G-2 (S-2) stresses reconnaissance routes, objectives, security force composition and locations, initial contact, initial fires (artillery, air, and attack helicopters) probable main force objectives or engagement areas, and likely commitment of reserve forces.

4. Step 4 – Decision Point

When the rehearsal director determines that a particular enemy movement or reaction is complete, the commander assesses the situation to determine if a decision point has been reached. Decision points are taken directly from the decision support template.

If the commander determines the unit is not at a decision point and not at the end state, the commander directs the rehearsal director to continue to the next event on the execution matrix. Participants use the response sequence and continue to act out and describe their units' actions.

When the rehearsal reaches conditions that establish a decision point, the commander decides whether to continue with the current course of action or by selecting a branch. If electing the current course of action, the commander directs the rehearsal director to move to the next event in the execution matrix. If selecting a branch, the commander states why that branch, states the first event of that branch, and continues the rehearsal until the organization has rehearsed all events of that branch. As the unit reaches decisive points, the rehearsal director states the conditions required for success.

When it becomes obvious that the operation requires additional coordination to ensure success, participants immediately begin coordinating. This is one of the key reasons for rehearsals. The rehearsal director ensures that the recorder captures the coordination and any changes and all participants understand the coordination.

5. Step 5 – End State Reached

Achieving the desired end state completes that phase of the rehearsal. In an attack, this will usually be when the unit is on the objective and has finished consolidation and casualty evacuation. In the defense, this will usually be after the decisive action (such as committing the reserve or striking force), the final destruction or withdrawal of the enemy, and casualty evacuation is complete. In a stability operation, this usually occurs when a unit achieves the targeted progress within a designated line of effort.

6. Step 6 – Reset

At this point, the commander states the next branch to rehearse. The rehearsal director resets the situation to the decision point where that branch begins and states the criteria for a decision to execute that branch. Participants assume those criteria have been met and then refight the operation along that branch until they attain the desired end state. They complete any coordination needed to ensure all participants understand and can meet any requirements. The recorder records any changes to the branch.

The commander then states the next branch to rehearse. The rehearsal director again resets the situation to the decision point where that branch begins, and participants repeat the process. This continues until the rehearsal has addressed all decision points and branches that the commander wants to rehearse.

If the standard is not met and time permits, the commander directs participants to repeat the rehearsal. The rehearsal continues until participants are prepared or until the time available expires. (Commanders may allocate more time for a rehearsal but must assess the effects on subordinate commanders' preparation time.) Successive rehearsals, if conducted, should be more complex and realistic.

At the end of the rehearsal, the recorder restates any changes, coordination, or clarifications that the commander directed and estimates how long it will take to codify changes in a written FRAGORD.

Rehearsals
& AARs

C. After the Rehearsal

After the rehearsal, the commander leads an after action review. The commander reviews lessons learned and makes the minimum required modifications to the existing plan. (Normally, a FRAGORD effects these changes.) Changes should be refinements to the operation order; they should not be radical or significant. Changes not critical to the operation's execution may confuse subordinates and hinder the synchronization of the plan. The commander issues any last minute instructions or reminders and reiterates the commander's intent.

Based on the commander's instructions, the staff makes any necessary changes to the operation order, decision support template, and execution matrix based on the rehearsal results. Subordinate commanders incorporate these changes into their units' operation orders. The chief of staff (executive officer) ensures the changes are briefed to all leaders or liaison officers who did not participate in the rehearsal.

A rehearsal provides the final opportunity for subordinates to identify and fix unresolved problems. The staff ensures that all participants understand any changes to the operation order and that the recorder captures all coordination done at the rehearsal. All changes to the published operation order are, in effect, verbal fragmentary orders. As soon as possible, the staff publishes these verbal fragmentary orders as a written fragmentary order that changes the operation order.

Rehearsal Assessment

The commander establishes the standard for a successful rehearsal. A properly executed rehearsal validates each leader's role and how each unit contributes to the overall operation—what each unit does, when each unit does it relative to times and events, and where each unit does it to achieve desired effects. An effective rehearsal ensures commanders have a common vision of the enemy, their own forces, the terrain, and the relationships among them. It identifies specific actions requiring immediate staff resolution and informs the higher commander of critical issues or locations that the commander, COS (XO), or G-3 (S-3) must personally oversee.

The commander (or rehearsal director in the commander's absence) assesses and critiques all parts of the rehearsal. Critiques center on how well the operation achieves the commander's intent and on the coordination necessary to accomplish that end. Usually, commanders leave the internal execution of tasks within the rehearsal to the subordinate unit commander's judgment and discretion.

II. The After Action Review (AAR)

Ref: FM 6-0 (C1), Commander and Staff Organization and Operations (May '15), chap. 16 and A Leader's Guide to After Action Reviews (Aug '12).

An after action review (AAR) is a guided analysis of an organization's performance, conducted at appropriate times during and at the conclusion of a training event or operation with the objective of improving future performance. It includes a facilitator, event participants, and other observers (ADRP 7-0, Training Units and Developing Leaders, Aug '12). The AAR provides valuable feedback essential to correcting training deficiencies. Feedback must be direct, on-the-spot and standards-based.

After Action Review Steps

1 **Plan the AAR**

2 **Prepare the AAR**

3 **Conduct the AAR**

4 **Follow-up (using AAR results)**

Ref: FM 6-0 (C1), Commander and Staff Organization and Operations, p. 16-3.

AARs are a professional discussion of an event that enables Soldiers/units to discover for themselves what happened and develop a strategy (e.g., retraining) for improving performance. They provide candid insights into strengths and weaknesses from various perspectives and feedback, and focus directly on the commander's intent, training objectives and standards. Leaders know and enforce standards for collective and individual tasks. Task standards are performance measures found in the respective training and evaluation outlines (T&EO) found on the Army Training Network (ATN) and the Digital Training Management System (DTMS).

Leaders must avoid creating the environment of a critique during AARs. Because Soldiers and leaders participating in an AAR actively self-discover what happened and why, they learn and remember more than they would from a critique alone. A critique only gives one viewpoint and frequently provides little opportunity for discussion of events by participants. The climate of the critique, focusing only on what is wrong, prevents candid and open discussion of training events and stifles learning and team building.

Leaders make on-the-spot corrections and take responsibility for training Soldiers and units. This occurs when leaders understand the commander's intent and the tasks to be trained, and then exercise the principles of Mission Command to improve Soldier, leader, and unit performance. Units that conduct AARs and empower subordinates to make on-the-spot corrections are more effective.

Types Of After Action Reviews

Two types of after action reviews exist: formal and informal. Commanders generally conduct formal action reviews after completing a mission. Normally, only informal after action reviews are possible during the conduct of operations.

Types of After-Action Reviews

Formal Reviews	Informal Reviews
■ Conducted by either internal or external leaders and external observer and controllers (OC)	■ Conducted by internal chain of command
■ Takes more time to prepare	■ Takes less time to prepare
■ Uses complex training aids	■ Uses simple training aids
■ Scheduled - events and / or tasks are identified beforehand	■ Conducted as needed. Primarily based on leaders assessment
■ Conducted where best supported	■ Held at the training site

Ref: A Leader's Guide to After Action Reviews, p. 5.

A. Formal

Leaders plan formal after action reviews when they complete an operation or otherwise realize they have the need, time, and resources available. Formal after action reviews require more planning and preparation than informal after action reviews. Formal after action reviews require site reconnaissance and selection; coordination for aids (such as terrain models and large-scale maps); and selection, setup, maintenance, and security of the after action review site. During formal after action reviews, the after action review facilitator (unit leader or other facilitator) provides an overview of the operation and focuses the discussion on topics the after action review plan identifies. At the conclusion, the facilitator reviews identified and discussed key points and issues, and summarizes strengths and weaknesses.

B. Informal

Leaders use informal after action reviews as on-the-spot coaching tools while reviewing Soldier and unit performance during or immediately after execution. Informal after action reviews involve all Soldiers. These after action reviews provide immediate feedback to Soldiers, leaders, and units after execution. Ideas and solutions leaders gathered during informal after action reviews can be applied immediately as the unit continues operations. Successful solutions can be identified and transferred as lessons learned.

The After Action Review (AAR)

Ref: FM 6-0 (C1), Commander and Staff Organization and Operations (May '15), pp. 16-3 to 16-4.

Formal and informal after action reviews generally follow the same format:

1. Review what was supposed to happen

The facilitator and participants review what was supposed to happen. This review is based on the commander's intent for the operation, unit operation or fragmentary orders (FRAGORDs), the mission, and the concept of operations.

2. Establish what happened

The facilitator and participants determine to the extent possible what actually happened during execution. Unit records and reports form the basis of this determination. An account describing actual events as closely as possible is vital to an effective discussion. The assistant chief of staff, intelligence (G-2 [S-2]) provides input about the operation from the enemy's perspective.

3. Determine what was right or wrong with what happened

Determine what was right or wrong with what happened. Participants establish the strong and weak points of their performance. The facilitator guides discussions so that the conclusions the participants reach are operationally sound, consistent with Army standards, and relevant to the operational environment.

4. Determine how the task should be done differently the next time

The facilitator helps the chain of command lead the group in determining how participants might perform the task more effectively. The intended result is organizational and individual learning that can be applied to future operations. If successful, this learning can be disseminated as lessons learned.

Leaders understand that not all tasks will be performed to standard. In their initial planning, they allocate time and other resources for retraining after execution or before the next operation. Retraining allows participants to apply the lessons learned from after action reviews and implement corrective actions. Retraining should be conducted at the earliest opportunity to translate observations and evaluations from after action reviews into performance in operations. Commanders ensure Soldiers understand that training is incomplete until the identified corrections in performance have been achieved.

After action reviews are often tiered as multi-echelon leader development tools. Following a session involving all participants, senior commanders may continue after action reviews with selected leaders as extended professional discussions. These discussions usually include a more specific review of leader contributions to the operation's results. Commanders use this opportunity to help subordinate leaders master current skills and prepare them for future responsibilities. After action reviews are opportunities for knowledge transfer through teaching, coaching, and mentoring.

Commanders conduct a final after action review during recovery after an operation. This after action review may include a facilitator. Unit leaders review and discuss the operation. Weaknesses or shortcomings identified during earlier after action reviews are identified again and discussed. If time permits, the unit conducts training to correct these weaknesses or shortcomings in preparation for future operations.

Lessons learned can be disseminated in at least three ways. First, participants may make notes to use in retraining themselves and their sections or units. Second, facilitators may gather their own and participants' notes for collation and analysis before dissemination and storage for others to use. Dissemination includes forwarding lessons to other units conducting similar operations as well as to the Center for Army Lessons Learned, doctrinal proponents, and generating force agencies. Third, units should publicize future successful applications of lessons as lessons learned.

Step 1. Planning the After Action Review
Ref: FM 6-0 (C1), Commander and Staff Organization and Operations (May '15), pp. 16-3 to 16-4.

To maximize the effectiveness of AARs, formal or informal, leaders must plan and prepare to execute AARs. AAR planning is part of each training event. All leaders must understand the unit's mission and the commander's intent for the operation (event).

The amount and level of detail needed during the planning and preparation process depends on the type of AAR to be conducted and available resources. The AAR process has four steps: planning, preparing, conducting, and follow up (using AAR results).

I. Planning the AAR

1. **Selecting and training observer controllers (OCs)**
2. **Reviewing the training and evaluation outline (T&EO)**
3. **Scheduling stopping points**
4. **Determining attendance**
5. **Choosing training aids**
6. **Reviewing the AAR plan**

Commanders are responsible for training their units. They hold subordinate leaders responsible for training their respective organizations. Commanders instill mission command by using orders for events to enable disciplined initiative within the commander's intent to empower agile and adaptive leaders. The AAR helps Soldiers develop a mutual understanding of the unit's strengths and weaknesses. Commanders issue guidance and specify their intent for an upcoming event's AAR.

The AAR plan provides the foundation for successful AARs. Commanders provide their intent and guidance to develop an AAR plan for each training event. Subordinates then determine how to achieve the commander's intent. The guidance applies for formal and informal AARs and should contain—

- Which tasks are trained and are the focus of the AAR
- Which events / phases of the operation are AARs conducted
- Who observes the training and who conducts the AAR
- Who attends
- When and where the AAR occurs
- What training aids are required

Leaders or OCs use the AAR plan to identify critical places and events they must observe to provide the unit a timely and valid assessment; examples include unit maintenance collection points, passage points, and unit aid stations. The AAR plan also includes who (either internal or external to the unit) facilitates the AAR for a particular event. The leader or OC is the individual tasked to observe training, provide control for the training, and lead the AAR.

1. Selecting and Training Observer Controllers (OC)
When planning an AAR, commanders select leaders/OCs who—

- Demonstrate proficiency in the tasks to be trained
- Are knowledgeable of the duties they are to observe
- Are knowledgeable of current doctrine and TTPs

When using external OCs, commanders strive to have OCs that are at least equal in rank to the leader of the unit they will assess. If commanders must choose between experience and an understanding of current TTPs or rank, they should go with experience. A staff sergeant with experience as a tank platoon sergeant is a better platoon OC than a sergeant first class who has no platoon sergeant experience.

Commanders are responsible for training and certifying OCs, to include providing training on how to conduct an AAR. Ideally, inexperienced OCs should observe properly conducted AARs beforehand.

2. Reviewing the Training & Evaluation Outline (T&EO)

The commander must specify their intent for the event along with the objectives and tasks to be trained. The commander also states the operational environment that is to be replicated during the event and the focus of the tasks trained. The leaders then review the T&EO which provides the conditions and standards for the respective collective or individual tasks. Leaders use the T&EOs to measure unit and soldier performance.

T&EOs are located on the Digital Training Management System (DTMS) and via the Army Training Network (ATN). Leaders and OCs must review the tasks to be trained as specified in the commander's guidance and intent for an upcoming event. The respective T&EOs are not only provided to remaining OC team members, but also to the Soldiers in the unit. The T&EO states the performance measures and the order specifies the commander's intent. All members of the unit must review these documents to gain a complete and mutual understanding of the critical places and phases to assess task performance.

3. Scheduling Stopping Points

Commanders schedule the time and place to conduct AARs as an integral part of training events. Commanders plan for an AAR at the end of each critical phase or major training event. For example, a leader may plan a stopping point after issuing an OPORD, when the unit arrives at a new position, or after consolidation on an objective, etc.

Commanders plan to allow approximately 30-45 minutes for platoon-level AARs, 1 hour for company-level AARs, and about 2 hours for battalion-level and above. Soldiers receive better feedback on their performance and remember the lessons longer as result of a quality AAR.

4. Determining Attendance

The AAR plan specifies who attends each AAR. At each echelon, an AAR has a primary set of participants. At squad and platoon levels, everyone attends and participates. At company or higher levels, it may not be practical to have everyone attend because of continuing operations or training. In this case, unit and OPFOR commanders, unit leaders, and other key players may be the only participants. Leaders or OCs may recommend additional participants based on specific observations.

5. Choosing Training Aids

Training aids add to AAR effectiveness. Training aids should directly support discussion of the training and promote learning. Local training support center (TSC) catalogs list training aids available to each unit. Dry-erase boards, video equipment, digital maps, terrain models, and enlarged maps are all worthwhile under the right conditions. For example, if reconnaissance reveals there are no sites which provided a view of the exercise area, the AAR facilitator may want to use a terrain table, or digital map if available.

6. Reviewing the AAR Plan

The AAR plan is only a guide. Commanders issue their intent and subordinates determine how to achieve that intent. Commanders, leaders and OCs should review the AAR plan regularly (e.g., training meeting) to make sure it is on track and meets the training needs of the units. The plan may be adjusted as necessary, but changes take preparation and planning time away from subordinate leaders or OCs. The purpose of the AAR plan is to allow OCs and leaders as much time as possible to prepare for the AAR.

Step 2. Preparing the After Action Review

Ref: FM 6-0 (C1), Commander and Staff Organization and Operations (May '15), pp. 16-3 to 16-6.

Preparation is the key to the effective execution of any plan. Preparation for an AAR begins before the training and continues until the actual event.

II. Preparing for the AAR

1. Reviewing training objectives, T&EOs, orders and doctrine
2. Identify key events
3. Observing the training and taking notes
4. Selecting AAR sites
5. Collecting observations
6. Organize the AAR

1. Reviewing Objectives, Orders, Plans, and Doctrine

Facilitators review the unit's mission before the after action review. The mission's objectives form the after action review's focus and the basis for observations. Facilitators review current doctrine, technical information, and applicable unit standard operating procedures to ensure they have the tools needed to properly guide discussion of unit and individual performance. Facilitators read and understand all warning orders (WARNORDs), OPORDs, and FRAGORDs issued before and during execution to understand what the commander wanted to happen. The detailed knowledge that facilitators display as a result of these reviews gives added credibility to their comments.

2. Identifying Key Events

Facilitators identify critical events and ensure they collect data on those events or identify personnel who observed them. Examples of critical events include, but are not limited to:

- Issue of OPORDs and FRAGOs
- Selected planning steps.
- Contact with opposing forces.
- Civil security attacks while conducting stability tasks.
- Passages of lines and reliefs in place.

3. Collecting Observations

AAR Facilitators are either internal (participating in the training) leaders or external (OCs) to the organization. Both have the requirement to make and consolidate observations to facilitate the discussion of what happened. The OCs keep accurate records of what they see and hear, and record events, actions, and observations by time sequence to prevent loss of valuable information and feedback. OCs can use any recording system (notebook, mobile device, prepared forms, 3x5 cards, etc) as long as it is reliable, sufficiently detailed (identifying times, places, and names), and consistent. They include the date-time group (DTG) of each observation so it can be easily integrated with observations of other OCs. This provides a comprehensive and detailed overview of what happened. When the OC has more time, they review the notes and fill in any details not written down earlier.

At times this may be challenging for leaders that are actively participating in the event and also facilitating the AAR. But this can be mitigated through professional discussions, feedback and involvement of all participants in the AAR to develop a clear understanding of the event.

4. Organizing the AAR

Once facilitators have gathered all available information, they organize their notes chronologically to understand the flow of events. They select and sequence key events in terms of their relevance to the unit's mission and objectives. This helps them identify key discussion and teaching points.

An effective after action review leads participants to discover strengths and weaknesses, propose solutions, and adopt a course of action to improve future operations. Facilitators organize an after action review using one of three methods: chronological order of events, warfighting functions, or key events, themes, or issues:

- Chronological Order of Events
- Warfighting Functions
- Key Events/Themes/Issues

5. Selecting After Action Review Sites

After action reviews should occur at or near where the operation occurred. Leaders should identify and inspect the after action review site and prepare a diagram showing placement of aids and other equipment. A good site minimizes wasted time by allowing rapid assembly of key personnel and positioning of aids. For larger units, this might not be possible for the whole operation. However, higher echelon after action reviews may include visits to selected actual sites to provide learning opportunities.

The after action review site should let Soldiers see the terrain where the operation occurred or accurate representations of it. If this is not possible, facilitators find a location that allows Soldiers to see where the critical or most significant actions happened. Facilitators should have a map or other representation of the area of operations detailed enough to help everyone relate key events to the actual terrain. The representation may be a terrain model, enlarged map, or sketch. Facilitators also require a copy of the unit's graphics or recovered displays of the situation from the information systems databases.

Facilitators provide a comfortable setting for participants by encouraging Soldiers to remove helmets, providing shelter, and serving refreshments. These actions create an environment where participants can focus on the after action review without distractions. Participants should not face into the sun. Key leaders should have seats up front. Vehicle parking and equipment security areas should be far enough away from the after action review site to prevent distractions.

6. Rehearse

After thorough preparation, the facilitator reviews the agenda and prepares to conduct the after action review. Facilitators may opt to conduct a walkthrough of the after action review site as well as review the sequence of events planned for the after action review.

Formal AARs - After thorough preparation, the OC reviews the AAR format and gets ready to conduct the AAR. The OC then announces to unit leaders the AAR starting time and location. This allows enough time for the OCs to prepare and rehearse at the AAR site while unit leaders account for personnel and equipment, perform actions which their unit SOP requires, and move to the AAR site.

Informal AARs – Often leaders have minimal time to prepare for AARs and as time permits they identify and prioritize key observations. They then mentally review the training event in light of the observations gathered personally and from subordinates based on one of the three techniques discussed previously. This allows the leader to mentally step through the AAR.

Step 3. Executing After Action Reviews

Ref: FM 6-0 (C1), Commander and Staff Organization and Operations (May '15), pp. 16-6 to 16-7.

Facilitators start an after action review by reviewing its purpose and sequence: the ground rules, the objectives, and a summary of the operation that emphasizes the functions or events to be covered. This ensures that everyone present understands what the commander expects the after action review to accomplish.

III. Conducting the AAR

1. **Introduction and rules**
2. **AAR agenda: commander's mission, intent and concept of the operation (what was supposed to happen).**
3. **Summary of events (what happened)**
   - Identify what was right or wrong
   - Determine how the task should be done differently
4. **Closing comments (summary)**

1. Introduction and Rules

The following rules apply to all after action reviews. Facilitators emphasize them in their introduction.

- An after action review is a dynamic, candid, professional discussion that focuses on unit performance. Everyone with an insight, observation, or question participates. Total participation is necessary to maintain unit strengths and to identify and correct deficiencies.

- An after action review is not a critique. No one—regardless of rank, position, or strength of personality—has all the information or answers. After action reviews maximize learning benefits by allowing Soldiers to learn from each other.

- An after action review assesses weaknesses to improve and strengths to sustain.

Soldier participation is directly related to the atmosphere created during the introduction. Effective facilitators draw in Soldiers who seem reluctant to participate. The following ideas can help create an atmosphere conducive to maximum participation:

- Reinforce the fact that it is permissible to disagree
- Focus on learning and encourage Soldiers to give honest opinions
- Use open-ended and leading questions to guide the discussion
- Facilitators enter the discussion only when necessary

2. Review of Objectives and Intent

After the introduction, facilitators review the after action review's objectives. This review includes the following:

- A restatement of the events, themes, or issues being reviewed
- The mission and commander's intent (what was supposed to happen)
- The enemy's mission and intent (how the enemy tried to defeat the force)

The commander or a facilitator restates the mission and commander's intent. Facilitators may guide the discussion to ensure that everyone present understands the plan and intent. Another method is to have subordinate leaders restate the mission and discuss the commander's intent. Automated information systems, maps, operational graphics, terrain boards, and other aids can help portray this information.

Intelligence personnel then explain as much of the enemy plan and actions as they know. The same aids the friendly force commander used can help participants understand how the plans related to each other.

3. Summary of Events (What Happened)

The facilitator guides the review, using one of the methods to describe and discuss what actually happened. Facilitators avoid asking yes-or-no questions. They encourage participation and guide the discussion by using open-ended and leading questions. Open-ended questions allow those answering to reply based on what they think is significant. These questions are less likely to put Soldiers on the defensive. Open-ended questions work more effectively in finding out what happened.

As the discussion expands and more Soldiers add their perspectives, what really happened becomes clearer. Facilitators do not tell Soldiers and leaders what was good or bad. Instead, they ensure that the discussion reveals the important issues, both positive and negative. Facilitators may want to expand this discussion and ask, "What could have been done differently?" Skillful guiding of the discussion ensures that participants do not gloss over mistakes or weaknesses.

4. Closing Comments (Summary)

During the summary, facilitators review and summarize key points identified during the discussion. The after action review should end on a positive note, linking conclusions to learning and possible training. Facilitators then depart to allow unit leaders and Soldiers time to discuss the learning in private.

The After Action Report

One of the most important collection techniques used in the Army and many other organizations is the after action report. The concept of the after action report can be easily adapted to fit any unit's lessons learned program.

The after action report provides observations and insights from the lessons learned that allow the unit to reflect on the successes and shortcomings of the operation, and share these lessons with the Army.

The reporting unit organizes the after action report in a logical order, usually by operational phase or warfighting function. It should be arranged chronologically when doing so facilitates the understanding and flow of the information reported. Documenting what worked well should receive as much attention as what did not.

FM 6-0, Table 16-1 on pages 16-8 and 16-9 is an example of what a commander and staff may elect to cover in their unit's written after action report. This approved brigade after action report template can apply across all echelons.

Rehearsals
& AARs

Step 4. Follow-up (Benefits of the AAR)

Ref: A Leader's Guide to After Action Reviews (Aug '12), pp. 14 to 15.

AARs are the dynamic link between task performance and execution to standard. They provide commanders a critical assessment tool to plan Soldier, leader and unit training. Through the professional and candid discussion of events, Soldiers can compare their performance against the standard and identify specific ways to improve proficiency

IV. Follow-Up

1. **Identify tasks requiring retraining**
2. **Fix the problem**
   - **Retrain immediately (same training event)**
   - **Revise Standing Operating Procedure (SOP)**
   - **Integrate into future training plans**
3. **Use to assist in making commander's assessment**

Leaders should not delay retraining except when absolutely necessary. If the leader delays retraining, the Soldiers and unit must understand they did not perform the task to standard and that retraining will occur later.

The true benefits of AARs come from applying results in developing future training. Leaders can use the information to assess performance and to plan future training to correct deficiencies and sustain demonstrated task proficiency.

Retraining
Time or complexity of the mission may prevent retraining on some tasks during the same exercise. When this happens, leaders must reschedule the mission or training. As part of this process, leaders must ensure that deficient supporting tasks found during the AAR are also scheduled and retrained.

Revised Standing Operating Procedures
AARs may reveal problems with unit SOPs. If so, unit leaders must revise the SOP and ensure units implement the changes during future training.

AAR Fundamentals:
- Conducted during or immediately after each event
- Focus is on commander's intent, training objectives and standards
- Focus is also on Soldier, leader, and unit performance
- Involves all participants in the discussion
- Uses open-ended questions
- Encourages initiative and innovation in finding more effective ways to achieve standards and meet training objectives and commander's intent
- Determines strengths and weaknesses
- Links performance to subsequent training

I. Operational Terms & Acronyms

Ref: ADRP 1-02, Operational Terms and Military Symbols (Feb '15).

ADRP 1-02, Operational Terms and Military Symbols

Army Doctrine Reference Publication (ADRP) 1-02 constitutes approved Army doctrinal terminology and symbology for general use. It builds on the foundational doctrine established in Army Doctrine Publication (ADP) 1-02.

The Feb 2015 revision of Army Doctrine Reference Publication (ADRP) 1-02 compiles definitions of all Army terms approved for use in Army doctrinal publications, including Army doctrine publications (ADPs), Army Doctrine Reference Publications (ADRPs), field manuals (FMs), and Army techniques publications (ATPs). It also includes joint terms appearing in the glossaries of Army doctrinal publications as of January 2014. ADRP 1-02 also lists shortened forms (whether considered acronyms or abbreviations) approved for use in Army doctrinal publications. In addition, unlike the 2013 edition of ADRP 1-02, this revision incorporates North Atlantic Treaty Organization (NATO) terms appearing in the glossaries of Army doctrinal publications as of January 2014.

The principal audience for ADRP 1-02 is all members of the profession of Arms. Commanders and staffs of Army headquarters serving as joint task force or multinational headquarters should also refer to applicable joint or multinational doctrine concerning the range of military operations and joint or multinational forces. Trainers and educators throughout the Army will also use this publication.

Commanders, staffs, and subordinates ensure their decisions and actions comply with applicable U.S., international, and, in some cases, host nation laws and regulations. Commanders at all echelons ensure their Soldiers operate in accordance with the law of war and the rules of engagement. (See Field Manual [FM] 27-10.)

ADRP 1-02 uses joint terms where applicable. ADRP 1-02 applies to the Active Army, Army ADRP 1-02 applies to the Active Army, Army National Guard/Army National Guard of the United States, andUnited States Army Reserve unless otherwise stated.

ADP 5-0 and ADRP 5-0 (New & Modified Terms)

ADRP 5-0, Introductory Table-1. New Army terms

Term	Remarks
Army design methodology	Replaces design.

ADRP 5-0, Introductory Table-2. Modified Army terms

Term	Remarks
assessment	Adopts the joint definition.
design	Formal definition replaced by Army design methodology.
direct support	Modifies the definition.
general support-reinforcing	Modifies the definition.
military decisionmaking process	Modifies the definition.
operational approach	Adopts the joint definition.
planning	Modifies the definition modified.

Glossary (ADRP 5-0/6-0)

This glossary -- compiled from both ADRP 5-0 The Operations Process (Aug '12) and ADRP 6-0 Mission Command (May '12)-- lists operational planning and mission command-related acronyms and terms with Army or joint definitions. Where Army and Joint definitions differ, (Army) precedes the definition. Terms for which ADRP 5-0 or ADRP 6-0 is the proponent are marked with an asterisk (*) as appropriate. The proponent publication for other terms is listed in parentheses after the definition.

administrative control - Direction or exercise of authority over subordinate or other organizations in respect to administration and support, including organization of Service forces, control of resources and equipment, personnel management, unit logistics, individual and unit training, readiness, mobilization, demobilization, discipline, and other matters not included in the operational missions of the subordinate or other organizations. (JP 1)

airspace control - A process used to increase operational effectiveness by promoting the safe, efficient, and flexible use of airspace. (JP 3-52)

Army design methodology - A methodology for applying critical and creative thinking to understand, visualize, and describe problems and approaches to solving them. (ADP 5-0)

art of command - The creative and skillful exercise of authority through timely decision making and leadership. (ADP 6-0)

assessment - Determination of the progress toward accomplishing a task, creating a condition, or achieving an objective. (JP 3-0)

assign - (Joint) To place units or personnel in an organization where such placement is relatively permanent, and/or where such organization controls and administers the units-or personnel for the primary function, or greater portion of the functions, of the unit or personnel. (JP 3-0)

attach - (Joint) The placement of units or personnel in an organization where such placement is relatively temporary. (JP 3-0)

Authority - The delegated power to judge, act, or command. (ADP 6-0)

battle rhythm - (Joint) A deliberate daily cycle of command, staff, and unit activities intended to synchronize current and future operations. (JP 3-33)

*civil considerations - The influence of manmade infrastructure, civilian institutions, and activities of the civilian leaders, populations, and organizations within an area of operations on the conduct of military operations.

*collaborative planning - Commanders, subordinate commanders, staffs, and other partners sharing information, knowledge, perceptions, ideas, and concepts regardless of physical location throughout the planning process.

command - The authority that a commander in the armed forces lawfully exercises over subordinates by virtue of rank or assignment. Command includes the authority and responsibility for effectively using available resources and for planning the employment of, organizing, directing, coordinating, and controlling military forces for the accomplishment of assigned missions. It also includes responsibility for health, welfare, morale, and discipline of assigned personnel. (JP 1)

commander's critical information requirement - An information requirement identified by the commander as being critical to facilitating timely decisionmaking. (JP 3-0)

Acronyms & Abbreviations

Ref: FM 6-0 (C1), Commander and Staff Organization and Operations (May '15), glossary.

ABCT	armored brigade combat team	JP	joint publication
ACOS	assistant chief of staff	KMO	knowledge management officer
ADCON	administrative control	LNO	liaison officer
ADP	Army doctrine publication	MDMP	military decisionmaking process
ADRP	Army doctrine reference publication	METT-TC	mission, enemy, terrain and weather, troops and support available, timeavailable, and civil considerations
AO	area of operations		
AR	Army regulation		
ASCC	Army Service component commander	MISO	military information support operations
ASCOPE	areas, structures, capabilities, organizations, people, and events	MOE	measure of effectiveness
		MOP	measure of performance
		NCO	noncommissioned officer
ATTP	Army tactics, techniques, and procedures	OAKOC	observation and fields of fire, avenues of approach, key terrain, obstacles, and cover and concealment
BCT	brigade combat team		
CBRN	chemical, biological, radiological, and nuclear		
		OPCON	operational control
CCIR	commander's critical information requirement	OPLAN	operation plan
		OPORD	operation order
CJCSM	Chairman of the Joint Chiefs of Staff manual	OPSEC	operations security
		PIR	priority intelligence requirement
CMOC	civil-military operations center	PMESII-PT	political, military, economic, social, information, infrastructure, physical environment, and time
COA	course of action		
COP	common operational picture		
COS	chief of staff	RSOI	reception, staging, onward movement, and integration
CP	command post		
DA	Department of the Army	SBU	Sensitive But Unclassified
EEFI	essential element of friendly information	SOP	standard operating procedure
		TACON	tactical control
FFIR	friendly force information requirement	TF	task force
		TLP	troop leading procedures
FM	field manual	TOE	table of organization and equipment
FOUO	for official use only		
FRAGORD	fragmentary order	TTP	tactics, techniques, and procedures
GSR	general support-reinforcing		
IPB	intelligence preparation of the battlefield	U.S.	United States
		WARNORD	warning order

Ops Terms & Graphics

commander's intent - A clear and concise expression of the purpose of the operation and the desired military end state that supports mission command, provides focus to the staff, and helps subordinate and supporting commanders act to achieve the commander's desired results without further orders, even when the operation does not unfold as planned. (JP 3-0)

commander's visualization - The mental process of developing situational understanding, determining a desired end state, and envisioning an operational approach by which the force will achieve that end state. (ADP 5-0)

Common operational picture - (Army) A single display of relevant information within a commander's area of interest tailored to the user's requirements and based on common data and information shared by more than one command.

*concept of operations - (Army) A statement that directs the manner in which subordinate units cooperate to accomplish the mission and establishes the sequence of actions the force will use to achieve the end state.

*confirmation brief - A briefing subordinate leaders give to the higher commander immediately after the operation order is given. It is the leaders' understanding of the commander's intent, their specific tasks, and the relationship between their mission and the other units in the operation.

control - (Army) The regulation of forces and war fighting functions to accomplish the mission in accordance with the commander's intent. (ADP 6-0)

control measure - A means of regulating forces or warfighting functions. (ADRP 6-0)

decision point - (Joint) A point in space and time when the commander or staff anticipates making a key decision concerning a specific course of action. (JP 5-0)

*decision support matrix - A written record of a war-gamed course of action that describes decision points and associated actions at those decision points.

decision support template - A combined intelligence and operations graphic based on the results of wargaming. The decision support template depicts decision points, timelines associated with movement of forces and the flow of the operation, and other key items of information required to execute a specific friendly course of action. (JP 2-01.3)

decisive point - A geographic place, specific key event, critical factor, or function that, when acted upon, allows commanders to gain a marked advantage over an adversary or contribute materially to achieving success. (JP 3-0)

*direct support - (Army) A support relationship requiring a force to support another specific force and authorizing it to answer directly to the supported force's request for assistance.

*essential element of friendly information - (Army) A critical aspect of a friendly operation that, if known by the enemy, would subsequently compromise, lead to failure, or limit success of the operation and therefore should be protected from enemy detection.

*evaluating - Using criteria to judge progress toward desired conditions and determining why the current degree of progress exists.

execution - Putting a plan into action by applying combat power to accomplish the mission. (ADP 5-0)

*execution matrix - visual and sequential representation of the critical tasks and responsible organizations by time.

friendly force information requirement - (Joint) Information the commander and staff need to understand the status of friendly force and supporting capabilities. (JP 3-0)

general support - That support which is given to the supported force as a whole and not to any particular subdivision thereof. (JP 3-09.3)

*general support-reinforcing - (Army) A support relationship assigned to a unit to support the force as a whole and to reinforce another similar-type unit.

graphic control measure - A symbol used on maps and displays to regulate forces and warfighting functions. (ADRP 6-0)

*indicator - (Army) In the context of assessment, an item of information that provides insight into a measure of effectiveness or measure of performance.

information collection - An activity that synchronizes and integrates the planning and employment of sensors and assets as well as the processing, exploitation, and dissemination of systems in direct support of current and future operations. (FM 3-55)

information management - The science of using procedures and information systems to collect, process, store, display, disseminate, and protect data, information, and knowledge products. (ADRP 6-0)

information protection - Active or passive measures used to safeguard and defend friendly information and information systems. (ADRP 6-0)

information requirement - Any information element the commander and staff require to successfully conduct operations. (ADRP 6-0)

intelligence synchronization – The "art" of integrating information collection and intelligence analysis with

operations to effectively and efficiently support decisionmaking. (ADRP 2-0)

information system - (Army) Equipment that collects, processes, stores, displays, and disseminates information. This includes computers—hardware and software—and communications, as well as policies and procedures for their use. (ADP 6-0)

liaison - That contact or intercommunication maintained between elements of military forces or other agencies to ensure mutual understanding and unity of purpose and action. (JP 3-08)

*key tasks - Those activities the force must perform as a whole to achieve the desired end state.

knowledge management - The process of enabling knowledge flow to enhance shared understanding, learning, and decision making. (ADRP 6-0)

line of effort - (Army) A line that links multiple tasks using the logic of purpose rather than geographical reference to focus efforts toward establishing operational and strategic conditions. (ADRP 3-0)

line of operations - (Army) A line that defines the directional orientation of a force in time and space in relation to the enemy and that links the force with its base of operations and objectives. (ADRP 3-0)

main effort - A designated subordinate unit whose mission at a given point in time is most critical to overall mission success. (ADRP 3-0)

measure of effectiveness - A criterion used to assess changes in system behavior, capability, or operational environment that is tied to measuring the attainment of an end state, achievement of an objective, or creation of an effect. (JP 3-0)

Ops Terms & Graphics

measure of performance - A criterion used to assess friendly actions that is tied to measuring task accomplishment. (JP 3-0)

military decisionmaking process - An iterative planning methodology to understand the situation and mission, develop a course of action, and produce an operation plan or order. (ADP 5-0)

mission - The task, together with the purpose, that clearly indicates the action to be taken and the reason therefore. (JP 3-0)

mission command - (Army) The exercise of authority and direction by the commander using mission orders to enable disciplined initiative within the commander's intent to empower agile and adaptive leaders in the conduct of unified land operations. (ADP 6-0)

mission command warfighting function - The related tasks and systems that develop and integrate those activities enabling a commander to balance the art of command and the science of control in order to integrate the other warfighting functions. (ADRP 3-0)

mission orders - Directives that emphasize to subordinates the results to be attained, not how they are to achieve them. (ADP 6-0)

*monitoring - Continuous observation of those conditions relevant to the current operation.

*nested concepts - A planning technique to achieve unity of purpose whereby each succeeding echelon's concept of operations is aligned by purpose with the higher echelons' concept of operations.

objective - 1. (Joint) The clearly defined, decisive, and attainable goal toward which every operation is directed. (JP 5-0) 2. (Army) a location on the ground used to orient operations, phase operations, facilitate changes of direction, and provide for unity of effort. (FM 3-90)

operational approach - A description of the broad actions the force must take to transform current conditions into those desired at end state. (JP 5-0)

operational art - The cognitive approach by commanders and staffs — supported by their skill, knowledge, experience, creativity, and judgment — to develop strategies, campaigns, and operations to organize and employ military forces by integrating ends, ways, and means. (JP 3-0)

operational control - A command authority that may be exercised by commanders at any echelon at or below the level of combatant command. Operational control is inherent in combatant command (command authority) and may be delegated within the command. Operational control is the authority to perform those functions of command over subordinate forces involving organizing and employing commands and forces, assigning tasks, designating objectives, and giving authoritative direction necessary to accomplish the mission. Operational control includes authoritative direction over all aspects of military operations and joint training necessary to accomplish missions assigned to the command. Operational control should be exercised through the commanders of subordinate organizations. Normally this authority is exercised through subordinate joint force commanders and Service and/or functional component commanders. Operational control normally provides full authority to organize commands and forces and to employ those forces as the commander in operational control considers necessary to accomplish assigned missions; it does not, in and of itself, include authoritative direction for logistics or matters of administration, discipline, internal organization, or unit training. (JP 3-0)

operational environment - A composite of the conditions, circumstances, and influences that affect the employment of capabilities and bear on the decisions of the commander. (JP 3-0)

operations process - The major mission command activities performed during operations: planning, preparing, executing, and continuously assessing the operation. (ADP 5-0)

organic - Assigned to and forming an essential part of a military organization. Organic parts of a unit are those listed in its table of organization for the Army, Air Force, and Marine Corps, and are assigned to the administrative organizations of the operating forces for the Navy. (JP 1-02)

*parallel planning - Is two or more echelons planning for the same operation sharing information sequentially through warning orders from the higher headqarters prior to the headquarters publishing their operation plan or operation order.

phase - (Army) A planning and execution tool used to divide an operation in duration or activity. (ADRP 3-0)

planning - The art and science of understanding a situation, envisioning a desired future, and laying out effective ways of bringing that future about. (ADP 5-0)

*planning horizon - A point in time commanders use to focus the organization's planning efforts to shape future events.

preparation - Those activities performed by units and Soldiers to improve their ability to execute an operation. (ADP 5-0)

priority intelligence requirement - (Joint) An intelligence requirement, stated as a priority for intelligence support, that the commander and staff need to understand the adversary or the operational environment. (JP 2-0)

protection - The preservation of the effectiveness and survivability of mission-related military and nonmilitary personnel, equipment, facilities, information, and infrastructure deployed or located within or outside the boundaries of a given operational area. (JP 3-0)

*priority of support - A priority set by the commander to ensure a subordinate unit has support in accordance with its relative importance to accomplish the mission.

prudent risk - A deliberate exposure to potential injury or loss when the commander judges the outcome in terms of mission accomplishment as worth the cost. (ADP 6-0)

*rehearsal - A session in which a staff or unit practices expected actions to improve performance during execution.

*reinforcing - A support relationship requiring a force to support another supporting unit.

responsibility - The obligation to carry forward an assigned task to a successful conclusion. With responsibility goes authority to direct and take the necessary action to ensure success. (JP 1-02)

risk management - The process of identifying, assessing, and controlling risks arising from operational factors and making decisions that balance risk cost with mission benefits. (JP 3-0)

running estimate - The continuous assessment of the current situation used to determine if the current operation is proceeding according to the commander's intent and if planned future operations are supportable. (ADP 5-0)

Ops Terms
& Graphics

science of control - Systems and procedures used to improve the commander's understanding and support accomplishing missions. (ADP 6-0)

security operations - Security operations are those operations undertaken by a commander to provide early and accurate warning of enemy operations, to provide the force being protected with time and maneuver space within which to react to the enemy, and to develop the situation to allow the commander to effectively use the protected force. (FM 3-90)

situational understanding - The product of applying analysis and judgment to relevant information to determine the relationships among the operational and mission variables to facilitate decisionmaking. (ADP 5-0)

tactical control - Command authority over assigned or attached forces or commands, or military capability or forces made available for tasking, that is limited to the detailed direction and control of movements or maneuvers within the operational area necessary to accomplish missions or tasks assigned. Tactical control is inherent in operational control. Tactical control may be delegated to, and exercised at any level at or below the level of combatant command. Tactical control provides sufficient authority for controlling and directing the application of force or tactical use of combat support assets within the assigned mission or task. (JP 3-0)

targeting - The process of selecting and prioritizing targets and matching the appropriate response to them, considering operational requirements and capabilities. (JP 3-0)

*task organization - (Army) A temporary grouping of forces designed to accomplish a particular mission.

task-organizing - The act of designing an operating force, support staff, or sustainment package of specific size and composition to meet a unique task or mission. (ADRP 3-0)

*terrain management - The process of allocating terrain by establishing areas of operation, designating assembly areas, and specifying locations for units and activities to deconflict activities that might interfere with each other.

troop leading procedures - A dynamic process used by small-unit leaders to analyze a mission, develop a plan, and prepare for an operation. (ADP 5-0)

unified action - The synchronization, coordination, and/or integration of the activities of governmental and nongovernmental entities with military operations to achieve unity of effort. (JP 1)

unified action partners - Those military forces, governmental and nongovernmental organizations, and elements of the private sector with whom Army forces plan, coordinate, synchronize, and integrate during the conduct of operations. (ADRP 3-0)

unified land operations - How the Army seizes, retains, and exploits the initiative to gain and maintain a position of relative advantage in sustained land operations through simultaneous offensive, defensive, and stability operations in order to prevent or deter conflict, prevail in war, and create the conditions for favorable conflict resolution. (ADP 3-0)

unity of effort - The coordination and cooperation toward common objectives, even if the participants are not necessarily part of the same command or organization—the product of successful unified action. (JP 1)

warfighting function - A group of tasks and systems (people, organizations, information, and processes) united by a common purpose that commanders use to accomplish missions and training objectives. (ADRP 3-0)

II. Military Symbology Basics

Ref: ADRP 1-02, Operational Terms and Military Symbols (Feb '15), chap. 3

This section discusses framed symbols, locations of amplifiers, the bounding octagon, and the locations of icons and modifiers. It also discusses the building process for framed symbols and unframed symbols.

A military symbol is a graphic representation of a unit, equipment, installation, activity, control measure, or tactical task relevant to military operations that is used for planning or to represent the common operational picture on a map, display, or overlay. Military symbols are governed by the rules in Military Standard (MIL-STD) 2525D.

Military symbols fall into two categories: framed, which includes unit, equipment, installation, and activity symbols; and unframed, which includes control measure and tactical symbols:

A. Framed

A framed symbol is composed of a frame, color (fill), icon, modifiers, and amplifiers. Framed symbols include:

- Unit, individuals, and organization symbols *(see pp. 7-17 to 7-20)*
- Equipment symbols *(see pp. 7-22 to 7-23)*
- Installation symbols *(see p. 7-21)*
- Activity symbols *(see p. 7-24)*

B. Unframed

Control measure symbols and mission task verb symbols are unframed symbols. They conform to special rules for their own elements. Unframed symbols include:

- Control measure symbols *(see pp. 7-25 to 7-30)*
- Tactical symbols *(see pp. 7-31 to 7-34)*

Tactical Mission Task Symbols

The tactical mission task symbols are graphical representations of many of the tactical tasks. However, not all tactical tasks have an associated symbol. Tactical task symbols are for use in course of action sketches, synchronization matrixes, and maneuver sketches. They do not replace any part of the operation order. The tactical task symbols should be scaled to fit the map scale and the size of unit represented.

See pp. 7-31 to 7-34.

A. Framed Symbols

Ref: ADRP 1-02, Operational Terms and Military Symbols (Aug '12), pp. 3-1 to 3-3.

The frame is the border of a symbol. It does not include associated information inside or outside of the border. The frame serves as the base to which other symbol components are added. The frame indicates the standard identity, physical domain, and status of the object being represented.

Standard Identity

Standard identity reflects the relationship between the viewer and the operational object being monitored. The standard identity categories are unknown, assumed friend, friend, neutral, suspect, and hostile.

Standard identity	Friendly	Hostile	Neutral	Unknown
	Assumed friend	Suspect		Pending
Unit				
Equipment				
Installation				
Activity				

Table 3-1. Frame shapes for standard identities.

In the realm of surface operation symbols, a circle or rectangle frame is to denote friend or assumed friend standard identity, a diamond frame to denote hostile or suspect standard identity, a square frame to denote neutral standard identity, and a quatrefoil frame to denote unknown and pending standard identity. Table 3-1 shows frame shapes for standard identities for land symbols.

Physical Domain

The physical domain defines the primary mission area for the object within the operational environment. An object can have a mission area above the earth's surface (in the air domain or space domain), on the earth's surface, or below the earth's surface (that is, in the land domain or maritime domain). The land domain includes those mission areas on the land surface or close to the surface (such as caves, mines, and underground shelters). Maritime surface units are depicted in the sea surface dimension.

Aircraft, regardless of Service ownership, are depicted in the air dimension while air facilities are depicted as land installations. Land equipment is depicted in the land dimension. Likewise, a landing craft whose primary mission is ferrying personnel or equipment to and from shore are represented in the sea surface dimension. However, a landing craft whose primary mission is to fight on land is a ground asset and is represented in the land dimension.

Status

Status indicates whether an operational object exists at the location identified (status is "present" or "confirmed"), will in the future reside at that location (status is "planned" or "anticipated"), or is thought to reside at that location (suspected). The symbol frame is a solid line when indicating a present status and a dashed line when indicating anticipated, planned, or suspected status. When the standard identity of the frame is uncertain, as is the case for assumed friend, suspect, or pending, the status cannot be displayed. Additionally, the status cannot be shown when the symbol is unframed (equipment only) or is displayed as a dot.

	Present	Planned
Friendly		
	Present	Suspect
Hostile		

Table 3-2. Examples of status.

Color (Fill)

In framed symbols, color provides a redundant clue with regard to standard identity. The fill is the interior area within a symbol. If color is not used, the fill is transparent. In unframed symbols (equipment), color is the sole indicator of standard identity, excluding text amplifiers. Blue for friendly or assumed friend, red for hostile or suspect, green for neutral, and yellow for unknown or pending are the default colors used to designate standard identity. Affiliation color without the fill may also be used for the frame, main icon, and modifiers.

Icons for Framed Symbols

The icon is the innermost part of a symbol. The icon provides an abstract pictorial or alphanumeric representation of units, equipment, installations, or activities. This publication distinguishes between icons that must be framed and icons for which framing is optional.

Modifiers for Framed Symbols

A modifier provides an abstract pictorial or alphanumeric representation, displayed in conjunction with an icon. The modifier provides additional information about the icon (unit, equipment, installation, or activity) being displayed. Modifiers conform to the bounding octagon and are placed either above or below the icon. ADRP 1-02 defines various types of modifiers and indicates where each is to be placed in relation to the icon within the symbol.

Amplifiers for Framed Symbols

Ref: ADRP 1-02, Operational Terms and Military Symbols (Aug '12), pp. 3-3 to 3-10.

An amplifier provides additional information about the symbol being portrayed and is displayed outside the frame. Figure 3-1 shows the essential amplifier fields around a friendly land unit symbol frame. To avoid cluttering the display, only essential amplifiers should be used. Arabic numerals are used to show the unique designation of units, except for corps, which use Roman numerals.

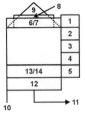

The amplifier locations in figure 3-1 are changed from previous editions of this manual. The amplifier locations also vary from MIL-STD-2525D. The new amplifier locations are designed to reduce the amount of space used by a framed symbol and provide only critical information around the symbol.

Figure 3-1. New amplifier locations.

The purpose of amplifier placement is to standardize the location of information. Figure 3-1 also illustrates the placement of amplifiers around a frame. The placement of amplifier information is the same regardless of frame shape. Table 3-3 provides a description of those amplifiers for framed symbols.

Field	Description
1	Indicates whether the unit is **reinforced, detached, or both**.
2	An accepted code that shows the **country indicator**.
3	A **unique alphanumeric designation** that identifies the unit being displayed. *Note:* When showing unique alphanumeric designations for combat arms regimental units (air defense artillery, armor, aviation, cavalry, field artillery, infantry, and special forces) the following rules apply: **No regimental headquarters:** A dash (-) will be used between the battalion and the regimental designation where there is no regimental headquarters. (Example: A/6-37 for A Battery, 6th Battalion, 37th Field Artillery) **Regimental headquarters:** A slash (/) will be used between the battalion and the regimental designation where there is a regimental headquarters of an active operational unit to show continuity of the units. (Example: F/2/11 for F Troop, 2d Squadron/11th Armored Cavalry Regiment)
4	Number or title of the next **higher formation** of the unit being displayed.
5	Free text **staff comments** for information required by the commander. Can also be used for unit location if required.
6	**Echelon** indicator of the symbol. (See table 4-5 on page 4-27.)
7	**Quantity** that identifies the number of items present.
8	**Task force** amplifier placed over the echelon. (See table 4-6 on page 4-30.)
9	**Feint or dummy indicator** shows that the element is being used for deception purposes. *Note*: The dummy indicator appears as shown in figure 3-1 on page 3-4 and can be used for all framed symbol sets. For control measures, it is a control measure symbol used in conjunction with other control measures. (See table 8-6 on page 8-71 for feint or dummy symbols.)
10	**Headquarters staff indicator** identifies symbol as a headquarters. (See figure 4-3 on page 4-11.)
	Offset location indicator is used to denote precise location of headquarters or to declutter multiple unit locations and headquarters. (See figure 4-3 on page 4-11.)
11	The **direction of movement arrow** indicates the direction the symbol is moving or will move.
	The **offset location indicator** without the arrow is used to denote precise location of units or to declutter multiple unit locations, except for headquarters. (See figure 4-2 on page 4-34.)
12	**Combat effectiveness** of unit or equipment displayed. (See Table 4-9 on page 4-36.)
13	**Mobility indicator** of the equipment being displayed. (See figure 5-1 on page 5-15 and table 5-3 on page 5-13.)
14	Indicates what type of **headquarters element** is being displayed. (See table 4-8 on page 4-35.)

Table 3-3. Description of amplifier fields.

Ops Terms & Graphics

The Bounding Octagon and the Location of Icons and Modifiers for Framed Symbols

The bounding octagon serves as the spatial reference for placement of icons and modifiers within the frame of a symbol. It is divided into three sectors. The three sectors specify where icons and modifiers are positioned and how much space is available for sizing of icons and modifiers. Table 3-4 provides examples showing the horizontal and vertical bounding octagons and all examples for all frame shapes.

In general, icons should not be so large as to exceed the dimensions of the main sector of the bounding octagon or touch the interior border of the frame. However, there are exceptions to this size rule. In those cases the icons will occupy the entire frame and must, therefore, exceed the dimensions of the main sector of the bounding octagon and touch the interior border of the frame. These are called full-frame icons and occur only in the land domain.

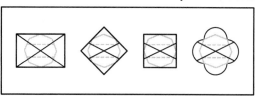

Figure 3-2. Example of full-frame icon.

The Building Process for Framed Symbols

ADRP 1-02 chapters 4 through 7 provide an extensive number of icons and modifiers for building a wide variety of framed symbols. No attempt has been made to depict all possible combinations. Instead, a standard method for constructing symbols is presented. Soldiers should avoid using any icon or modifiers or combinations and modifications that differ from those in this publication. If, after searching doctrinal icons and modifiers, it is necessary to create a new symbol, users should explain the symbol in an accompanying legend. Computer-generated systems will have difficulty in passing nonstandard symbols.

Step	Description	Example
1	Choose appropriate frame shape from table 3-1 on page 3-2.	
2	Choose appropriate main icon from chapters 2 through 5 and combine it with frame.	
3	Choose appropriate sector 1 modifier from chapters 2 through 5.	
4	Choose appropriate sector 2 modifier from chapters 2 through 5.	
5	Choose minimum essential amplifiers from those listed in table 3-3 on page 3-6.	

Table 3-5. Building process for framed symbols.

Ops Terms & Graphics

B. Unframed Symbols

Ref: ADRP 1-02, Operational Terms and Military Symbols (Feb '15), pp. 3-10 to 3-11.

This section discusses unframed symbols. Control measure symbols and mission task verb symbols are unframed symbols. They conform to rules within their own elements.

Control Measure Symbols

A control measure is a means of regulating forces or warfighting functions. Control measures may be boundaries, special area designations, or other unique markings related to an operational environment's geometry and necessary for planning and managing operations. Control measure symbols represent control measures that can be portrayed graphically and provide operational information. They can be displayed as points, lines, and areas. Control measure symbols can be combined with other military symbols, icons and amplifiers to display operational information. Control measure symbols follow the same basic building rules as framed symbols but are built in accordance with their template. Control measure symbols can be black or white, depending on display background: blue (friendly), red (hostile), green (obstacles), or yellow (chemical, biological, radiological, and nuclear [CBRN] contaminated area fill).

See pp 7-25 to 7-30 for more information about control measure symbols.

Step	Description	Example
1	Choose the appropriate control measure symbol.	
2	Choose the appropriate control measure template that will show the possible amplifiers.	
3	Choose the appropriate amplifier information by field.	3 / GOLD
4	Choose the next appropriate amplifier information by field.	16 / 140600MAR2010 / 16-1 / Not required
5	Choose the appropriate framed icon.	

Table 3-7. Building process for control measure symbols.

Icons for Control Measures

The icon provides an abstract pictorial representation of the control measure. Icons can be depicted as points, lines, or areas.

Modifiers for Control Measures

Only chemical, biological, radiological, and nuclear events and contaminated areas have modifiers. The remaining control measures use amplifiers.

Amplifiers for Control Measures

As with the framed symbols, the amplifier in a control measure provides additional information about the icon being displayed. However, the location of the amplifiers for control measures varies and is dependent on the control measure symbol being displayed. Because the location of amplifiers varies, there is no standardized amplifier placement location for all types of control measures. ADRP 1-02, chapter 8 provides numerous figures and tables that identify the location of amplifiers for each of the different types of control measures. For multiple entries of the same type or similar information, the field number will be followed by a dash and a number designating the second or more uses. For example, a from-to date-time group may use 16 for the start time and 16-1 for the end time, or an airspace coordination area may use 3 to name an operational name or designation for the airspace coordination area and use 3-1 for the unique alphanumeric designation that identifies the unit establishing the airspace control area. Arabic numerals are normally used when showing the unique designation of units. However, corps echelon units are identified with Roman numerals.

Field	Description
2	An accepted code that shows the **country indicator**.
3/3-1	A **unique alphanumeric designation** that identifies the unit being displayed. *Note:* When showing unique alphanumeric designations for combat arms regimental units (air defense artillery, armor, aviation, cavalry, field artillery, infantry, and special forces) the following rules apply: **No regimental headquarters:** A dash (-) will be used between the battalion and the regimental designation where there is no regimental headquarters. (Example: A/6-37 for A Battery, 6th Battalion, 37th Field Artillery) **Regimental headquarters:** A slash (/) will be used between the battalion and the regimental designation where there is a regimental headquarters of an active operational unit to show continuity of the units. (Example: F/2/11 for F Troop, 2d Squadron/11th Armored Cavalry Regiment)
	An **operational name/designation** given to a control measure to clearly identify it.
	For targets, this is a **target number** as described in Appendix H of FM 3-60. The target number is comprised of six alphanumeric characters of two letters followed by four numbers (for example, AB1234).
5	Free text **staff comments** for information required by the commander.
6	**Echelon** indicator of the symbol.
7	**Quantity** that identifies the number of items present. For a nuclear event, identifies the actual or estimated **size of the nuclear weapon** used in kilotons (KT) or megatons (MT).
11	The **direction of movement arrow** indicates the direction the symbol is moving or will move. For chemical, biological, radiological or nuclear events, the direction of movement arrow indicates **downwind direction**.
	The **offset location indicator** without the arrow is used to denote precise location of units or to declutter multiple unit locations, except for headquarters.
15	Denotes **enemy** symbol. The letters "ENY" are used when the color red is not an option.
16	An alphanumeric designator for displaying a **date-time group** (for example, DDHHMMSSZMONYYYY) or "O/O" for on order.
16-1	Used with 16 for displaying a **date-time group** for a from-to specified time period.
17	Identifies unique designation for **type of equipment**.
18	Denotes the **location** in latitude and longitude or grid coordinates.
19	Denotes the **altitude**
20/20-1	Denotes the **range**
21/21-1	Denotes the **azimuth**
22	Denotes the width

Table 3-6. Description of control measure symbol amplifier fields.

Ops Terms & Graphics

C. Echelon Amplifiers (Field 6)

Ref: ADRP 1-02, Operational Terms and Military Symbols (Feb '15), table 4-7, p. 4-33.

An echelon is a separate level of command (JP 1-02). In addition, there is also a separate echelon known as a command. A command is a unit or units, an organization, or an area under the command of one individual. It does not correspond to any of the other echelons. Figure 4-1 shows the template for an echelon amplifier. The height of the echelon amplifier is one-fourth of the size of the height of the frame. Table 4-7 shows the field 6 amplifiers for Army echelons and commands.

Echelon	Amplifier	Example of amplifier with friendly unit frame
Team or crew *Note: This is the smallest echelon and should not be confused with company team and brigade combat team in the next paragraph.*	Ø	
Squad	●	
Section	● ●	
Platoon or detachment	● ● ●	
Company, battery, or troop	I	
Battalion or squadron	II	
Regiment or group	III	
Brigade	x	
Division	x x	
Corps	x x x	
Army	x x x x	
Army group	x x x x x	
Theater	x x x x x x	
Nonechelon	Amplifier	Example of amplifier with friendly unit frame
Command	+ +	

Table 4-7. Echelon amplifiers.

Chap 7

III. Units, Individuals, and Organizations

Ref: ADRP 1-02, Operational Terms and Military Symbols (Feb '15), chap. 4.

A unit is a military element whose structure is prescribed by a competent authority, such as a table of organization and equipment; specifically, part of an organization (JP 1-02). Icons in the main sector of the bounding octagon reflect the main function of the symbol (see p. 7-13).

Main Icons for Units

Icons in the main sector of the bounding octagon reflect the main function.

Function (historical derivation of icon shown in italics)	Icon
Armored (tank track)	⬭
Army aviation or rotary wing aviation	▸◂
Chemical, biological, radiological, and nuclear (Crossed retorts)	☓
Civil affairs	CA
Chaplain (religious support)	REL
Combined arms (modified cross straps and tank track)	⊗
Electronic warfare	EW
Engineer (bridge)	⊓
Explosive ordnance disposal	EOD
Field artillery (cannonball)	●
Military intelligence (abbreviation)	MI
Military police (abbreviation)	MP
Missile (missile)	⋔
Mortar	⚲
Ordnance (bursting Bomb)	♉
Special forces (abbreviation)	SF
Surveillance	▲
Sustainment (abbreviation)	SUST
Transportation (wheel)	✳
Water	⌐

Table 4-1. Main icons for units (pp. 4-1 to 4-24).

Ops Terms & Graphics

(Operational Terms & Graphics) III. Units, Individuals, & Organizations 7-17

Main Icons for Units

Ref: ADRP 1-02, Operational Terms and Military Symbols (Feb '15), pp. 4-1 to 4-8.

Full-Frame Icons for Units

Full-frame icons may reflect the main function of the symbol or may reflect modifying information.

Function (Hstorical derivation in italics)	Icon	Example
Air defense (radar dome)		
Antitank or antiarmor (upside down V)		
Armored cavalry		
Armored infantry (mechanized infantry)		
Corps support		
Headquarters or headquarters element		
Infantry (crossed straps)		
Medical (Geneva cross)		
Reconnaissance (cavalry) (cavalry bandoleer)		
Signal (lightning flash)		
Supply		
Theater or echelons above corps support		

Sector 1 Modifiers for Units

Sector 1 modifiers reflect a unit's specific capability.

Description	Modifier
Attack	A
Armored	⬭
Biological	B
Bridging	⤛
Chemical	C
Command and control	C2
Detention	DET
Maintenance	⤜⤛
Meteorological	MET
Multiple rocket launcher	⩘
Nuclear	N
Radar	℘
Radiological	R
Search and rescue	SAR
Sensor	◆
Smoke	S
Sniper	̄I̅
Unmanned systems	⌄
Utility	U
Video imagery	⌷

Sector 2 Modifiers for Units

Sector 2 modifiers reflect the mobility of the unit size, range, or altitude of unit equipment.

Description	Icon
Air assault	V
Airborne	⌒⌒
Amphibious	~~~~
Arctic (sled)	⊔
Bicycle-equipped	O
Decontamination	D
Heavy	H
High altitude	HA
Light	L
Long range	LR
Low altitude	LA
Medium	M
Medium altitude	MA
Medium range	MR
Mountain	▲
Pack animal	⋀⋀
Railroad	∞–∞
Recovery	⤜⤛
Riverine	⌣
Short range	SR
Ski	⤬
Towed	o–o
Tracked/SP	⬭
Wheeled	ooo

Echelon Amplifiers (Field 6)

An echelon is a separate level of command (JP 1-02). In addition, there is also a separate echelon known as a command. A command is a unit or units, an organization, or an area under the command of one individual. It does not correspond to any of the other echelons. Table 4-7 shows the field 6 amplifiers for Army echelons and commands.

Echelon	Amplifier
Team/crew	Ø
Squad	●
Section	●●
Platoon/detachment	●●●
Company/battery/troop	I
Battalion/squadron	II
Regiment/group	III
Brigade	✕
Division	✕✕
Corps	✕✕✕
Army	✕✕✕✕
Army group	✕✕✕✕✕
Theater	✕✕✕✕✕✕
Nonechelon	Amplifier
Command	✚✚

Task Force Amplifiers (Field 8)

A task force is a temporary grouping of units under one commander formed to carry out a specific operation or mission, or a semi-permanent organization of units under one commander formed to carry out a continuing specified task.

Task force amplifier	Example	Example with echelon
⌐¬	(symbol)	(symbol)

Table 4-8. Task force amplifier.

Reinforced, Detached or Both Amplifiers (Field 1)

This amplifier is used at division level and below. The reinforced amplifier + (plus) indicates that the capability of one unit has been augmented by the capability of another unit. The detached amplifier – (minus) indicates that the capability of a unit has been reduced by the detachment of one or more of its units. If a unit has been both reinforced and detached, then the + amplifier is used.

Description	Amplifier
Reinforced	**+**
Reduced	**–**
Both (reinforced and reduced)	**±**

Table 4-9. Reinforced, reduced, or both amplifiers.

Command Posts and Command Group Amplifiers (Field 14)

A command post is a unit headquarters where the commander and staff perform their activities. A command group is the commander and selected staff members who accompany commanders and enable them to exercise mission command away from a command post. The headquarters staff indicator (field 10) is always used in conjunction with the command post and command group amplifiers.

Description	Amplifier
Combat trains command post	CTCP
Command group	CMD
Early entry command post	EECP
Emergency operations center	EOC
Forward trains command post	FTCP
Main command post	MAIN
Tactical command post	TAC

Table 4-10. Command post and command group amplifiers.

Combat Effectiveness Amplifiers (Field 12)

Combat effectiveness is the ability of a unit to perform its mission. Factors such as ammunition, personnel, fuel status, and weapon systems are evaluated and rated. The ratings are—

- Fully operational (green)
- Substantially operational (amber)
- Marginally operational (red)
- Not operational (black)

Field 12 is used to display the level of combat effectiveness of the unit or equipment symbol.

Offset Locator Indicator Amplifier (Field 11) and HQs Staff Offset Locator Indicator Amplifier (Field 10)

The center of mass of the unit symbol indicates the general vicinity of the center of mass of the unit. To indicate precise location or reduce clutter in an area with multiple units, a line (without an arrow) extends from the center of the bottom of the frame to the unit location displayed as field 11. The line may be extended or bent as needed.

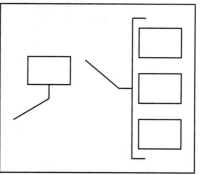

To indicate precise location or reduce clutter of headquarters unit symbols, a staff extends from the bottom left hand corner to the headquarters location displayed as field 10.

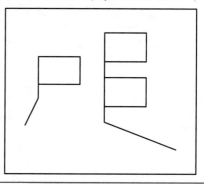

Main Icons for Individuals (Civilian) and Organizations

Ref: ADRP 1-02, Operational Terms and Military Symbols (Feb '15), pp. 4-42 to 4-50.

Symbols for individuals and organizations represent civilians and normally do not have prescribed structures. Organization symbols can reflect civic, ethnic, religious, social, or other groupings. Icons in the main sector reflect the main function of the icon.

Function	Icon
Fire department	
Governmental	GO
Nongovernmental	NGO
Pirates	
Police department	
Unspecified individual or organization	
Unspecified individual Note: Only this icon uses the vertical bounding octagon. All other icons in this table use the horizontal bounding octagon.	
Unspecified organization	
Criminal activities victim	
Criminal activities victims	
Attempted criminal activities victim	
Attempted criminal activities victims	

Table 4-11. Main icons for civilian individuals and organizations.

Sector 1 Modifiers

Sector 1 modifiers reflect the function of civilian individuals or organizations.

	Characteristic	Modifier
Types of killing victims	Assassinated	AS
	Executed	EX
	Murdered	MU
Types of criminal activities victims	Hijacked	H
	Kidnapped	K
	Piracy	PI
	Rape	RA
Types of civilian individuals and organizations	Displaced persons, refugees, and evacuees	DPRE
	Foreign fighters	FF
	Gang	GANG
	Leader	LDR
	Religious	REL
	Terrorist	TER

Table 4-14. Sector 1 modifiers for civilian individuals and organizations.

Sector 2 Modifiers

Sector 2 modifiers reflect the nature of the relationship of civilian individuals or organizations.

Characteristic	Modifier	Example of modifier with friendly unit frame: Note: This does not imply that individuals and organizations are friendly, but only servers as a single frame reference for the symbol. Example of most common usage
Horizontal bounding octagon		
Vertical bounding octagon		
Types of recruitment		
Coerced	CR	
Willing	WR	
Leader	L D R	

Table 4-15. Sector 2 modifiers for civilian individuals and organizations

IV. Equipment, Installations, Activities

Ref: ADRP 1-02, Operational Terms and Military Symbols (Feb '15), chaps. 5, 6 & 7.

Main Icons for Installations

Ref: ADRP 1-02, Operational Terms and Military Symbols (Aug '12), chap. 6.
Installations are sites that incorporate permanent, semipermanent, and temporary structures. Icons in the main sector reflect the main function of the symbol.

Function	Icon
Airport	
Electric power plant	
Mass grave	
Mine	
Sea port	
Telecommunications	

Table 6-1. Main icons for installations.

Sector 1 Modifiers for Installations

Sector 1 modifiers reflect the specific capability of the installation.

	Description	Modifier
Electric power plant fuel source	Coal	CO
	Geothermal	GT
	Hydroelectric	HY
	Natural gas	NG
	Petroleum	
	Description	Modifier
Telecommunications	Radio	R
	Telephone	T
	Television	TV

Table 6-2. Sector 1 modifiers for installations.

Sector 2 Modifiers for Installations

Sector 2 modifiers reflect the specific type of installation.

Description	Modifier
Production	PROD
Repair	RPR
Research	RSH
Service	SVC
Storage	STOR
Test	TEST

Table 6-3. Sector 2 modifiers for installations

Ops Terms & Graphics

Main Icons for Equipment

Ref: ADRP 1-02, Operational Terms and Military Symbols (Feb '15), chap. 5.

Equipment is all nonexpendable items needed to outfit or equip an individual or organization. Equipment symbols can be used with or without frames. When frames are not used,
then standard identity color must be used. Icons in the main sector reflect the main function of the symbol. Equipment can use either the horizontal or vertical bounding octagon
depending on the icon. (samples)

Description	Icon
Weapon systems	
Note. Weapon systems, missile launchers, and nonlethal weapons use the horizontal bounding octagon and a unique system for indicating size, altitude, or range. Weapons size is indicated by a horizontal line(s) perpendicular to the weapon icon. If an equipment symbol has no lines, it is a basic equipment symbol. Adding one line designates it as light, low altitude, or short-range. Adding two lines designates it as medium, medium altitude, or medium-range. Finally, adding three lines designates it as heavy, high altitude, or long-range. If a weapon system is designated as greater than heavy, high altitude, or long-range, then a heavy, high-altitude, or long-range indicator is used.	
Unspecified weapon	
Flame thrower	
Grenade launcher	

Description	Icon
Guns	
Air defense gun	
Antitank gun	
Direct fire gun	
Recoilless gun	
Howitzer	
Machine gun	

Description	Icon
Missile launchers	
Missile launcher	
Air defense missile launcher surface-to-air missile launcher	
Antitank missile launcher	
Surface-to-surface missile launcher	
Mortar	
Rifle	

Description	Icon
Rockets	
Single rocket launcher	
Multiple rocket launcher	
Antitank rocket launcher	

Description	Icon
Nonlethal weapons	
Nonlethal weapon	
Taser	
Water cannon	

Description	Icon
Vehicles	
Note: Vehicle systems use a unique system for indicating size or range. Vehicle size is indicated by either horizontal or vertical line(s) within the icon depending on the orientation of the symbol. If an equipment symbol has no lines, it is a basic equipment symbol. Adding one line designates it as light or short-range. Adding two lines designates it as medium or medium-range. Finally, adding three lines designates it as heavy or long-range. Note: Armored fighting vehicles, armoured personnel carriers, earthmovers, and tanks use the horizontal bounding octagon. All remainin equipment icons use the vertical bounding octagon.	
Armored fighting vehicle	
Armored personnel carrier	
Armored protected vehicle	
Earthmover	
Tank	
Train locomotive	
Utility vehicle	
Description	Icon
Other equipment	
Bridge	
Chemical, biological, radiological, or nuclear (CBRN) equipment	
Improvised explosive device	IED
Description	Icon
Mines	
Antipersonnel mine	
Antitank mine	
Unspecified mine	
Radar	
Sensor	

Table 5-1. Main icons for equipment.

Sector 1 Modifiers for Equipment (samples)

This is a change to the previous system.

Description	Modifier	Example of modifier with friendly equipment frame / Example of most common usage / Icon or symbol without frame
Horizontal bounding octagon		
Vertical bounding octagon		
Attack	A	Attack helicopter

Sector 2 Modifiers for Equipment (samples)

Description	Modifier
Light	L
Medium	M
Heavy	H

Mobility Indicator Amplifier (Field 13)

Description	Amplifier
Amphibious	
Barge	
Over snow (prime mover)	
Pack animal	M
Railway	
Sled	
Towed	
Tracked	
Wheeled (cross-country)	
Wheeled (limited mobility)	
Wheeled and tracked	

Activities

Ref: ADRP 1-02, Operational Terms and Military Symbols (Feb '15), chap. 7.

Activities symbols are applicable across the range of military operations, but they normally focus on stability activities and defense support of civil authorities activities. Activities can affect military operations. Activities represented by icons can include acts of terrorism, sabotage, organized crime, disrupting the flow of vital resources, and the uncontrolled movement of large numbers of people. Icons in the main sector reflect the main function of the symbol.

Function	Icon
Arrest	(icon)
Attempted against an individual	(icon)
Attempted against multiple individuals or an organization	(icon)
Demonstration	MASS
Drug related	DRUG
Explosion	(icon)
Extortion	$
Graffiti	(icon)
Killing—individual	(icon)
Killing—multiple individuals or an organization	(icon)
Killing—poisoning	(icon)
Killing—riot	RIOT

Table 7-1. Main icons for activities.

Sector 1 Modifiers for Activities

Sector 1 modifiers reflect the function of civilian individuals or organizations.

	Characteristic	Modifier
Types of killing victims	Assassinated	AS
	Executed	EX
	Murdered	MU
Types of criminal activities victims	Hijacked	H
	Kidnapped	K
	Piracy	PI
	Rape	RA
Types of civilian individuals and organizations	Displaced persons, refugees, and evacuees	DPRE
	Foreign fighters	FF
	Gang	GANG
	Leader	LDR
	Religious	REL
	Terrorist	TER

Table 4-12. Sector 1 modifiers for civilian individuals and organizations.

V. Control Measure Symbols

Ref: ADRP 1-02, Operational Terms and Military Symbols (Feb '15), chap. 8.

A control measure symbol is a graphic used on maps and displays to regulate forces and warfighting functions. Definitions of terms related to control measure symbols are provided in ADRP 1-02, chapter 1. The control measure symbols in this chapter are organized by the six warfighting functions: mission command, movement and maneuver, fires, protection, sustainment, and intelligence. Also included are airspace control measures, which are a combination of movement and maneuver, fires, and protection. Control measure symbols generally fall into one of three categories: points, lines, or areas. The coloring and labeling of control measure symbols is almost identical to framed symbols.

See pp. 7-14 to 7-15 for discussion and overview of the building process for control measure symbols (unframed).

Color of Control Measure Symbols

Friendly graphic control measures are shown in black or blue. Hostile graphic control measures are shown in red. If red is not available, they are shown in black with the abbreviation "ENY" placed on the graphic in amplifier field 15. If a special requirement arises to show neutral or unknown graphic control measures, they are shown in black, and the abbreviations of "NEU" for neutral or "UNK" for unknown are used in amplifier field 15. All obstacles, regardless of standard identity, are shown in green. If green is not available, obstacles should be shown using black. Yellow is used for the cross-hatching of areas with chemical, biological, radiological, or nuclear (CBRN) contamination. The use of green and yellow for obstacles and CBRN contamination is in contradiction to the standard identities.

Lettering for Control Measure Symbols

All lettering for control measure symbols must be in upper case (all capital letters). All lettering should be oriented horizontally, from left to right, so readers can see it easily without having to tilt their heads. All lettering should be sized as large as possible, so a reader can easily understand it. However, the lettering should not be so large that it interferes with other symbols or icons.

Abbreviations for Control Measure Symbols

Acronyms and abbreviations for use with control measure symbols are shown in this section and must be used for Army control measure symbols. No abbreviations other than those provided in ADRP 1-02 may be used.

Amplifier Fields for Control Measure Symbols

See table 3-6 for descriptions of all the amplifier fields for control measure symbols. For control measures, field 3 can represent either a unique alphanumeric designation that identifies the establishing unit, serviced unit, or a name, letter, or number. There is no requirement for all amplifier fields to be filled in for control measure symbols. Only required amplifier fields must be filled in.

See Table 3-6, Amplifier Fields for Control Measure Symbols, on p. 7-15.

Point, Line, Boundary, and Area Symbols

Ref: ADRP 1-02, Operational Terms and Military Symbols (Feb '15), pp. 8-1 to 8-4.

Point Symbols

A point is a control measure symbol that has only one set of coordinates. Most Army point symbols follow a standard format. Figure 8-1 shows the composition and placement of an icon, its modifiers, and its amplifiers for a standard point and a supply point. The external amplifier field 3 is used to designate the unit being service or other unique designation, while the internal amplifier field 3 is used to designate the unit providing the service. Point symbols cannot be rotated; therefore, text must be written horizontally only (not on an angle or diagonal).

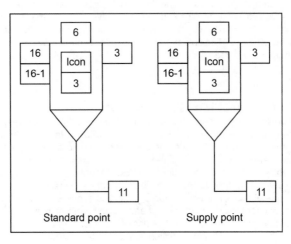

Figure 8-1. Standard point and supply point templates.

Line Symbols

A line is a control measure symbol with multiple sets of coordinates. Figure 8-2 shows the composition and placement of an icon, its modifiers, and its amplifiers for a standard line. Most lines are also labelled as phase lines for easy reference in orders and during transmissions. A phase line is marked as PL, with the line's name in field 3. When lines representing other purposes are marked as phase lines, they should show their primary purpose in the icon field (such as NFL for no fire line). The purpose of the line is labelled on top of the line at both ends inside the lateral boundaries or as often as necessary for clarity. Field 3 is used for fire support coordination measures, to show the designation of the controlling headquarters. The use of phase lines to mark line control measure symbols is not mandatory.

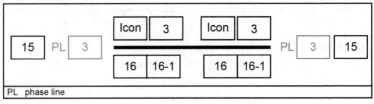

Figure 8-2. Standard line template.

Boundary Symbols

A boundary is a line that delineates surface areas for the purpose of facilitating coordination and deconfliction of operations between adjacent units, formations, or areas (JP 3-0). There are three types of boundary lines: lateral, rear, and forward. Amplifiers are displayed perpendicular to the boundary line. Figure 8-3 shows standard horizontal (east-west) and vertical (north-south) boundary lines and the orientation of their amplifiers. The graphic for the highest echelon (field 6) unit on lateral boundaries is used for the boundary line. The graphic for the lower echelon (field 6) unit on a rear or forward boundary is used for the boundary line. When units of the same echelon are adjacent to each other, the abbreviated echelon designator (field 3, such as CO, BN, or BDE) can be omitted from the alphanumeric designator. When the boundary is between units of different countries, the three-letter country code (field 2) is shown in parentheses behind or below the unit designation.

See p. 7-30 for a list of abbreviations and acronyms used in field 3.

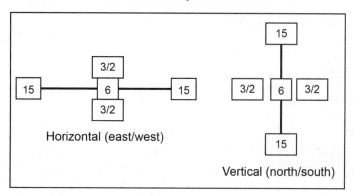

Figure 8-3. Horizontal and vertical boundary templates.

Area Symbols

An area is a control measure symbol with multiple sets of coordinates that start and finish at the same point. Figure 8-4 shows the composition and placement of an icon, its modifiers, and its amplifiers for a standard area. Areas normally are marked with the abbreviation for the type of area in the icon field, followed by a name in field 3. This labeling should be in the center of the area unless the area is too small or the labeling would interfere with locating units. The type of area determines the number of fields being used. Not all fields are required for each area. Some areas may use only one field, while other will use several.

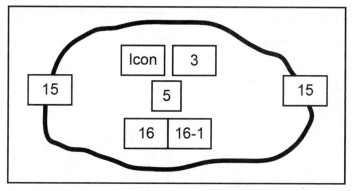

Figure 8-4. Standard area template.

Control Measure Symbols

Ref: ADRP 1-02, Operational Terms and Military Symbols (Feb '15), tables 8-1 to 8-7.

Mission Command (C2)

Type	Icon
Points	
Coordination point	(⊗)
Decision point	☆ (3)
Checkpoint	CKP
Linkup point	LU
Passage point	PP
Rally point	RLY
Release point	RP
Start point	SP
Type	**Icon**
Lines	
Light line	LL
Type	**Icon**
Areas	
Area of operations	AO
Named area of interest	NAI
Targeted area of interest	TAI

Movement and Maneuver

Type	Icon
General	
Points	
Point of interest	⬇ (3)
Lines	
Forward line of troops	∿∿∿
Handover line	HL
Phase line	PL
Areas	
Assembly area	AA
Drop zone	DZ
Extraction zone	EZ
Landing zone	LZ
Pickup zone	PZ
Defensive	
Points	
Combat outpost	△
Observation post	△
Lines	
Final protective line	FPL
Areas	
Battle position	⬭ (3) (6) Note:The side opposite (field 6) always faces toward the hostile force.

Movement and Maneuver (cont)

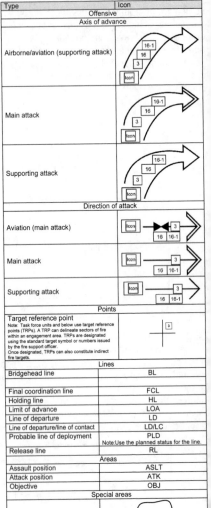

Type	Icon
Offensive	
Axis of advance	
Airborne/aviation (supporting attack)	
Main attack	
Supporting attack	
Direction of attack	
Aviation (main attack)	
Main attack	
Supporting attack	
Points	
Target reference point Note: Task force units and below use target reference points (TRPs). A TRP can delineate sectors of fire within an engagement area. TRPs are designated using the standard target symbol or numbers issued by the fire support officer. Once designated, TRPs can also constitute indirect fire targets.	
Lines	
Bridgehead line	BL
Final coordination line	FCL
Holding line	HL
Limit of advance	LOA
Line of departure	LD
Line of departure/line of contact	LD/LC
Probable line of deployment	PLD Note:Use the planned status for the line.
Release line	RL
Areas	
Assault position	ASLT
Attack position	ATK
Objective	OBJ
Special areas	
Airhead/airhead line	AL Note: An airhead/airhead line can be an area or a line.

Intelligence

Point, line, or area	
Type	**Icon**
Decoy/dummy/ feint/phoney	Note: The icon refers to another control measure icon, such as axis of advance, direction of attack, or minefield.

Fires

Type	Icon
Fire support coordination measures	
Points	
Fire support station	✕ FSS 3
Lines	
Coordinated fire line	CFL
Fire support coord line	FSCL
Restrictive fire line	RFL
Areas	
Airspace coordination area	ACA 3 / MIN ALT MAX ALT / 3 / 16 16-1
Free fire area	FFA
No-fire area	NFA 3 / 16 16-1 / Note No fire area has black cross-hatching.
Restrictive fire area	RFA

Protection

Type	Icon
Points	
Chemical, biological, radiological, or nuclear (CBRN) events	

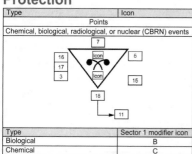

Type	Sector 1 modifier icon
Biological	B
Chemical	C
Nuclear	N
Radiological	R
Type	Sector 2 modifier icon
Toxic industrial material	T
Displaced Persons, Refugees, and Evacuees	
Type	Icon
Civilian collection point	CIV
Detainee collection point	DET
Enemy prisoner of war collection point	EPW
Areas	
Chemical, biological, radiological, or nuclear (CBRN) contaminated	

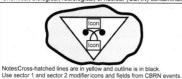

Notes Cross-hatched lines are in yellow and outline is in black.
Use sector 1 and sector 2 modifier icons and fields from CBRN events.

Displaced Persons, Refugees, and Evacuees	
Type	Icon
Detainee holding area	DET
Enemy prisoner of war holding area	EPW
Refugee holding	REF

Sustainment

Type	Icon
Points	
Ammunition supply point	ASP
Ammunition transfer point	ATP
Rearm, refuel, and resupply	R3P
Refuel on the move	ROM
Class I	☾
Class II	II
Class III	▽
Class IV	⊓
Class V	⌂
Class VI	♀
Class VII	☏
Class VIII	+
Class IX	☼
Class X	CA
Lines	
Icon 3 / Icon	
Alternate supply route	ASR
Main supply route	MSR
Areas	
Brigade support area	BSA
Fwd arming & refuel point	FARP

Airspace Control Measures

Type	Icons
Air control point	ACP 3
Communications checkpoint	CCP 3
Air corridor	ACP 1 / 3 HEADING IN / HEADING OUT / CCP 1
Low-level transit route	ACP 1 / LLTR / 16 16-1 / ACP 2
Minimum risk route	ACP 1 / MMR / 16 16-1 / ACP 2
Standard Army aircraft flight route	NAME WIDTH MIN ALT MAX ALT / ACP 1 / 3 / ACP 2
Unmanned aerial vehicle/ unmanned aircraft route	ACP 1 / UAV / 16 16-1 / ACP 2
	Icon / UNIT ID MIN ALT MAX ALT TIME FROM TIME TO
High-altitude missile engagement zone	HIMEZ
High-density airspace control zone	HIDACZ

Abbreviations and Acronyms for use with Control Measure Symbols

Ref: ADRP 1-02, Operational Terms and Military Symbols (Feb '15), pp. 8-83 to 8-84.

Boundaries

Echelon	Abbreviation or acronym
Army group	AG
Army	A
Corps	CORPS
Division	DIV
Air assault division	AAD
Airborne division	ABD
Armoured division	AD
Cavalry division	CD
Infantry division	ID
Mechanized division	MD
Mountain division	MTND
Multinational division	MND
Brigade	BDE
Air assault brigade	AAB
Airborne brigade	ABB
Brigade combat team	BCT
Fires brigade	FB
Multinational brigade	MNB
Naval infantry brigade	NIB
Separate armor brigade	SAB
Separate infantry brigade	SIB
Regiment	REGT
Airborne regiment	ABR
Group	GP
Battle group	BG
Battalion	BN
Company	CO[1]
Platoon	PLT
Team	TM

[1] North Atlantic Treaty Organization (NATO) uses COY

Table 8-8. Abbreviations and acronyms for use with boundaries.

Unit Functions

Function	Abbreviation or acronym
Air defense	ADA Note: ADA used to prevent confusion with AD for armored division.
Armor	AR
Antitank/anti-armor	AT
Aviation	AVN
Cavalry	CAV
Chemical, biological, radiological, and nuclear (CBRN)	CB Note: CB used in lieu of CBRN.
Civil affairs	CA
Combined arms	CAR
Counterintelligence	CI
Electronic warfare	EW
Engineer	EN
Explosive ordnance disposal	EOD
Field artillery	FA
Infantry	IN
Logistics	LOG
Maintenance	MNT Note: MNT used in lieu of MAINT.
Medical	MED
Military intelligence	MI
Military police	MP
Naval	NAV
Ordnance	ORD
Quartermaster	QM
Reconnaissance	REC Note: REC used in lieu of RECON.
Signal	SIG
Special forces	SF

Table 8-9. Abbreviation and acronyms used in control measure symbols for unit functions.

VI. Tactical Mission Tasks (and Symbols)

Ref: ADRP 1-02, Operational Terms and Military Symbols (Feb '15), chap. 1 and 9.

A tactical mission task is a specific activity performed by a unit while executing a form of tactical operation or form of maneuver. A tactical mission task may be expressed as either an action by a friendly force or effects on an enemy force. The tactical mission tasks describe the results or effects the commander wants to achieve.

Not all tactical mission tasks have symbols. Some tactical mission task symbols will include unit symbols, and the tactical mission task "delay until a specified time" will use an amplifier. However, no modifiers are used with tactical mission task symbols. Tactical mission task symbols are used in course of action sketches, synchronization matrixes, and maneuver sketches. They do not replace any part of the operation order.

A. Mission Symbols

Counterattack (dashed axis)	CATK	A form of attack by part or all of a defending force against an enemy attacking force, with the general objective of denying the enemy his goal in attacking (FM 3-0).
Cover	c ☐ c	A form of security operation whose primary task is to protect the main body by fighting to gain time while also observing and reporting information and preventing enemy ground observation of and direct fire against the main body.
Delay	D	A form of retrograde in which a force under pressure trades space for time by slowing down the enemy's momentum and inflicting maximum damage on the enemy without, in principle, becoming decisively engaged (JP 1-02, see delaying operation).
Guard	G ☐ G	A form of security operations whose primary task is to protect the main body by fighting to gain time while also observing and reporting information and preventing enemy ground observation of and direct fire against the main body. Units conducting a guard mission cannot operate independently because they rely upon fires and combat support assets of the main body.
Penetrate		A form of maneuver in which an attacking force seeks to rupture enemy defenses on a narrow front to disrupt the defensive system (FM 3-0).
Relief in Place	RIP	A tactical enabling operation in which, by the direction of higher authority, all or part of a unit is replaced in an area by the incoming unit.
Retirement	R	A form of retrograde [JP 1-02 uses operation] in which a force out of contact with the enemy moves away from the enemy (JP 1-02).
Screen	S ☐ S	A form of security operations that primarily provides early warning to the protected force.
Withdraw	W	A planned operation in which a force in contact disengages from an enemy force (JP 1-02) [The Army considers it a form of retrograde.]

B. Effects on Enemy Forces

Block		*Block* is a tactical mission task that denies the enemy access to an area or prevents his advance in a direction or along an avenue of approach.
		Block is also an engineer obstacle effect that integrates fire planning and obstacle effort to stop an attacker along a specific avenue of approach or prevent him from passing through an engagement area.
Canalize		*Canalize* is a tactical mission task in which the commander restricts enemy movement to a narrow zone by exploiting terrain coupled with the use of obstacles, fires, or friendly maneuver.
Contain		*Contain* is a tactical mission task that requires the commander to stop, hold, or surround enemy forces or to cause them to center their activity on a given front and prevent them from withdrawing any part of their forces for use elsewhere.
Defeat	*No graphic*	*Defeat* occurs when an enemy has temporarily or permanently lost the physical means or the will to fight. The defeated force is unwilling or unable to pursue his COA, and can no longer interfere to a significant degree. Results from the use of force or the threat of its use.
Destroy		*Destroy* is a tactical mission task that physically renders an enemy force combat-ineffective until it is reconstituted. Alternatively, to destroy a combat system is to damage it so badly that it cannot perform any function or be restored to a usable condition without being entirely rebuilt.
Disrupt		*Disrupt* is a tactical mission task in which a commander integrates direct and indirect fires, terrain, and obstacles to upset an enemy's formation or tempo, interrupt his timetable, or cause his forces to commit prematurely or attack in a piecemeal fashion.
		Disrupt is also an engineer obstacle effect that focuses fire planning and obstacle effort to cause the enemy to break up his formation and tempo, interrupt his timetable, commit breaching assets prematurely, and attack in a piecemeal effort.
Fix		*Fix* is a tactical mission task where a commander prevents the enemy from moving any part of his force from a specific location for a specific period. Fixing an enemy force does not mean destroying it. The friendly force has to prevent the enemy from moving in any direction.
		Fix is also an engineer obstacle effect that focuses fire planning and obstacle effort to slow an attacker's movement within a specified area, normally an engagement area.
Interdict		*Interdict* is a tactical mission task where the commander prevents, disrupts, or delays the enemy's use of an area or route. Interdiction is a shaping operation conducted to complement and reinforce other ongoing offensive or defensive
Isolate		*Isolate* is a tactical mission task that requires a unit to seal off-both physically and psychologically-an enemy from his sources of support, deny him freedom of movement, and prevent him from having contact with other enemy forces.
Neutralize		*Neutralize* is a tactical mission task that results in rendering enemy personnel or materiel incapable of interfering with a particular operation.
Turn		*Turn* is a tactical mission task that involves forcing an enemy element from one avenue of approach or movement corridor to another.
		Turn is also a tactical obstacle effect that integrates fire planning and obstacle effort to divert an enemy formation from one avenue of approach to an adjacent avenue of approach or into an engagement area.

C. Actions by Friendly Forces

Term	Graphic	Description
Attack by Fire		*Attack-by-fire* is a tactical mission task in which a commander uses direct fires, supported by indirect fires, to engage an enemy without closing with him to destroy, suppress, fix, or deceive him.
Breach		*Breach* is a tactical mission task in which the unit employs all available means to break through or secure a passage through an enemy defense, obstacle, minefield, or fortification.
Bypass		Bypass is a tactical mission task in which the commander directs his unit to maneuver around an obstacle, position, or enemy force to maintain the momentum of the operation while deliberately avoiding combat with an enemy force.
Clear		*Clear* is a tactical mission task that requires the commander to remove all enemy forces and eliminate organized resistance within an assigned area.
Control	*No graphic*	*Control* is a tactical mission task that requires the commander to maintain physical influence over a specified area to prevent its use by an enemy or to create conditions for successful friendly operations.
Counterrecon	*No graphic*	*Counterreconnaissance* is a tactical mission task that encompasses all measures taken by a commander to counter enemy reconnaissance and surveillance efforts.
Disengage	*No graphic*	*Disengage* is a tactical mission task where a commander has his unit break contact with the enemy to allow the conduct of another mission or to avoid decisive engagement.
Exfiltrate	*No graphic*	*Exfiltrate* is a tactical mission task where a commander removes soldiers or units from areas under enemy control by stealth, deception, surprise, or clandestine means.
Follow and Assume		*Follow and assume* is a tactical mission task in which a second committed force follows a force conducting an offensive operation and is prepared to continue the mission if the lead force is fixed, attritted, or unable to continue. The follow-and-assume force is not a reserve but is committed to accomplish specific tasks.
Follow and Support		*Follow and support* is a tactical mission task in which a committed force follows and supports a lead force conducting an offensive operation. The follow-and-support force is not a reserve but is a force committed to specific tasks.
Occupy		*Occupy* is a tactical mission task that involves moving a friendly force into an area so that it can control that area. Both the force's movement to and occupation of the area occur without enemy opposition.
Reduce	*No graphic*	*Reduce* is a tactical mission task that involves the destruction of an encircled or bypassed enemy force.
Retain		*Retain* is a tactical mission task in which the cdr ensures that a terrain feature controlled by a friendly force remains free of enemy occupation or use. The commander assigning this task must specify the area to retain and the duration of the retention, which is time- or event-driven.
Secure		*Secure* is a tactical mission task that involves preventing a unit, facility, or geographical location from being damaged or destroyed as a result of enemy action. This task normally involves conducting area security operations.
Seize		*Seize* is a tactical mission task that involves taking possession of a designated area by using overwhelming force. An enemy force can no longer place direct fire on an objective that has been seized.
Support by Fire		*Support-by-fire* is a tactical mission task in which a maneuver force moves to a position where it can engage the enemy by direct fire in support of another maneuvering force. The primary objective of the support force is normally to fix and suppress the enemy so he cannot effectively fire on the maneuvering force.

Tactical Doctrinal Taxonomy

Ref: ADRP 3-90, Offense and Defense (Aug '12), fig. 2-1, p. 2-3.

The following shows the Army's tactical doctrinal taxonomy for the four elements of decisive action (in accordance with ADRP 3-0) and their subordinate tasks. The commander conducts tactical enabling tasks to assist the planning, preparation, and execution of any of the four elements of decisive action. Tactical enabling tasks are never decisive operations in the context of the conduct of offensive and defensive tasks. (They are also never decisive during the conduct of stability tasks.) The commander uses tactical shaping tasks to assist in conducting combat operations with reduced risk.

Elements of Decisive Action (and subordinate tasks)

Offensive Tasks
Movement to Contact
Search and attack
Cordon and search
Attack
Ambush*
Counterattack*
Demonstration*
Spoiling attack*
Feint*
Raid*
Also known as special purpose attacks
Exploitation
Pursuit

Forms of Maneuver
Envelopment
Frontal attack
Infiltration
Penetration
Turning Movement

Defensive Tasks
Area defense
Mobile defense
Retrograde operations
Delay
Withdrawal
Retirement
Forms of the Defense
Defense of linear obstacle
Perimeter defense
Reverse slope defense

Stability Tasks
Civil security
Civil control
Restore essential services
Support to governance
Support to economic and infrastructure development

Defense Support to Civil Authorities
Provide support for domestic disasters
Provide support for domestic CBRN incidents
Provide support for domestic law enforcement agencies
Provide other designated support

Tactical Enabling Tasks

Reconnaissance Operations
Zone
Area
Route
Recon in force
Security Operations
Screen
Guard
Cover
Area (also route & convoy)
Local

Troop Movement
Administrative movement
Approach march
Road march
Encirclement Operations
Passage of Lines
Relief in Place

Mobility Operations
Breaching operations
Clearing operations (area and route)
Gap-crossing operations
Combat roads and trails
Forward airfields and landing zones
Traffic operations

Tactical Mission Tasks

Actions by Friendly Forces
Attack-by-Fire
Breach
Bypass
Clear
Control
Counterreconnaissance
Disengage
Exfiltrate
Follow and Assume
Follow and Support

Occupy
Reduce
Retain
Secure
Seize
Support-by-Fire

Effects on Enemy Force
Block
Canalize
Contain
Defeat
Destroy
Disrupt
Fix
Interdict
Isolate
Neutralize
Suppress
Turn

[BSS5]
Index

Index